SATYAGRAHAS IN BENGAL : 1921-39

# SATYAGRAHAS
# IN BENGAL
## 1921-39

**BUDDHADEVA BHATTACHARYYA**

*in collaboration with*

**Tarun Kumar Banerjee**          **Dipak Kumar Das**

South Asia Books

SOUTH ASIA BOOKS
Box—502 : Columbia, Mo. 65201, U.S.A.
By arrangement with
Minerva Associates (Publications) Pvt. Ltd.
7-B, Lake Place : Calcutta-700 029
INDIA

Printed in India by Narendra Chandra Roy at Anulipi,
180, B. B. Ganguly Street, Calcutta-700 012 and
Published by T. K. Mukherjee on behalf of South
Asia Books, Box 502, Columbia, Mo. 65201, U.S.A.

IN MEMORY OF MY TEACHER
NIRMAL KUMAR BOSE

# Acknowledgements

I AM GRATEFUL to the Khadi and Village Industries Commission for an honorarium which made it possible to write this report. I owe a great deal of debt to Sri Soumen Datta, Sri Prabhat Kumar Datta, Lecturer, Syamaprasad College, Calcutta, Sri Amartya Mukhopadhyay, Lecturer, Katwa College, and Sri Sambhu Nath Chatterjee who took it as a labour of love to collect material from the dusty heaps of old newspaper files. Professor Sukumar Chakrabarti of Uluberia College was kind enough to go through the entire manuscript and offer suggestions which have largely helped me in editing the report. To him my gratitude is too deep for words. I wish to take this opportunity to express my thanks to the Librarians and the staff of the National Library, Calcutta University Library, Asiatic Society and Mahajati Sadan for having made available to us many of the books and old files of contemporary dailies. I gratefully remember the kind services of the late Nakul Chattopadhyay of *Ananda Bazar Patrika* who cheerfully supplied us old newspaper files. The authorities of *Amrita Bazar Patrika*, *Jugantar* and *Nihar* were good enough to make available to us old files of their dailies. It was through the kind courtesy of Sri Dasarathi Tah, himself a participant in the Damodar Canal Tax movement, that we could collect much of the material published in *Vardhaman Varta*. Sri Kiran Chandra Datta and Sri Srikumar Mitra were kind enough to hand over to us some rare material and documents relating to the Canal Tax movement. To them I owe much.

I am specially indebted to the veterans of the satyagraha movements who were kind enough to take the trouble of recollecting their experiences and narrating them to us. I gratefully acknowledge the kind encouragement and help I received from Professor Sugata Das Gupta, former Director, Gandhian Institute of Studies, Varanasi and now of the Department of Political Science, University of Queensland, Australia, and Sri Sailes

Kumar Bandyopadhyay, Director, Khadi and Village Industries Commission, Bihar.

The Indian Council of Social Science Research deserves grateful thanks for partly subsidizing the publication of the report. The responsibility for the facts stated, opinions expressed or conclusions reached in this book is entirely that of the author and the ICSSR has no responsibility for them.

I am thankful to Sri Bijay Kumar Bhattacharyya, Sri Satish Kumar Samanta, Sri Basanta Kumar Das, Sri Rabin Sarkar, Sri Pijush Maitra, Sri Pradip Biswas, Dr Bangendu Ganguly, Reader, Department of Political Science, Calcutta University, Sri Saila Kumar Ghosh, Research Fellow, Indian Institute of Management, Calcutta, Sri Sudhakanta Dey, ex-Principal, Rammohun College, Radhanagar, Sri Bikash Chakravarty, Lecturer, Nabadwip Vidyasagar College, Sri Satyendra Nath Maity, Sri Dibyesh Lahiry, Sri Aparna Mitra, Sri Hari Mohan Saha, Sri Asok Krishna Datta M.P. and Sri Adhir Chandra Banerjee for their help in various ways. I warmly thank Sri Prosanta Kumar Mukherjee for typing the script.

I thank Sri Sushil Mukherjea of Minerva Associates ( Publications) Pvt. Ltd. for the kind interest he took in getting the book through the press. The Index I owe to the kindness of Sri Bijoy Pada Mookerjee, Assistant Librarian, IIT, Kharagpur. To Smriti I owe much for her forbearance.

BUDDHADEVA BHATTACHARYYA

Department of Political Science
University of Calcutta
9 August 1977

# CONTENTS

## ON NOTES AND REFERENCES

A. References to newspapers and weeklies have been given in the following order : Name of the newspaper/weekly, date of publication, page number and column number. Figures in the brackets indicate column number/s. For example, *Ananda Bazar Patrika*, 24.7.29, 9(5) ; *Amrita Bazar Patrika*, 29.10.29, 4 (3-4). It has not been possible to mention the page and column numbers in all cases, because of the brittle condition of old newspapers/weeklies.

B. The details of the publication of the books consulted have been mentioned in the Bibliography. Only in those cases where more editions than one of a book have been referred to, the year of publication of the editions consulted have been given in Notes and References.

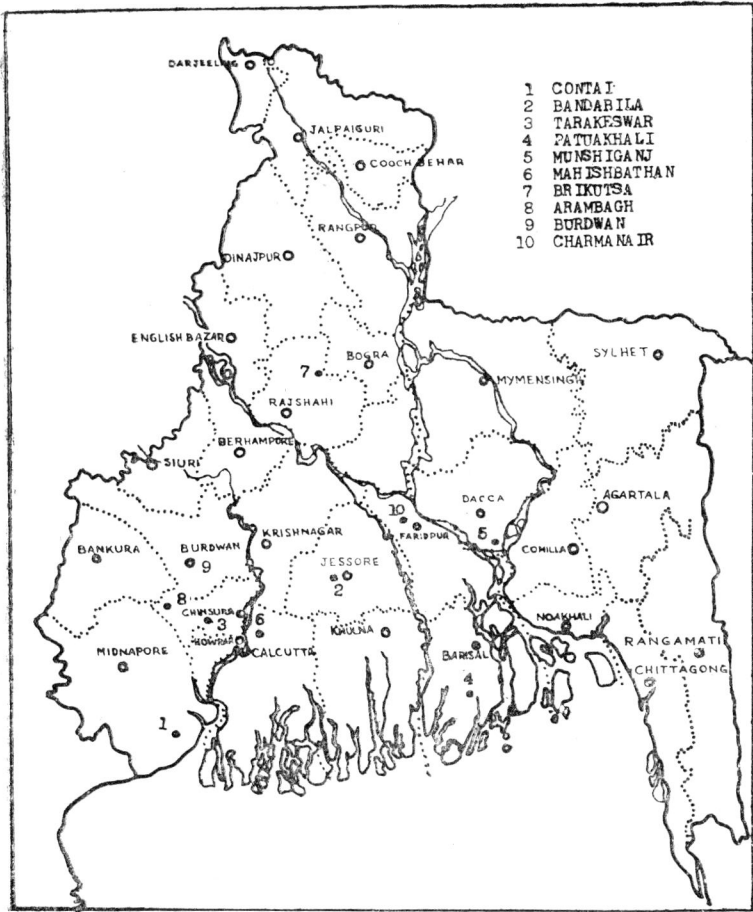

1  CONTAI
2  BANDARILA
3  TARAKESWAR
4  PATUAKHALI
5  MUNSHIGANJ
6  MAHISHBATHAN
7  BRIKUTSA
8  ARAMBAGH
9  BURDWAN
10 CHARMANAIR

## Chapter I

## INTRODUCTION

GANDHI'S SUPEME INVENTION, discovery or creation was satya-graha.[1]  To a man in the street or to an unsophisticated vil-lager in any part of India, satyagraha stood for Gandhi's way of fighing the British Raj.  It was in a sense another name for war with an alien government.  But satyagraha may better be understood as a technique for solving conflict and a method for fighting evil.  It is, so to say, a synonym for non-violent direct action'.[2]  As Bondurant says : "Satyagraha be-came something more than a method of resistance to particular legal norms ; it became an an instrument lof struggle for positive objectives and for fundamental change..."[3]

Satyagraha, according to Gandhi, is not a method limited merely to a conflict-situation that subsisted between an alien ruler and a subject people.  The scope of satyagraha is wider than that.  Krishnalal Sridharani classified conflicts, according to the nature of the unit of action pitted on each side, as follows :

(1) An individual versus another individual, or an indi-vidual pitted against a group ; (2) A group pitted against another group ; or (3) A community versus the state.

The second and third types of conflict-situation are more important from the standpoint of group-behaviour and action. A group pitted against another group, according to the above classification, runs one entire gamut of conflicts.  There is mass action on either side in this type of struggle.  When one such party employs the non-violent method with a view to achieving its objectives, it naturally has to work out satyagraha on a mass scale.  In this form, satyagraha can take place either (a) bet-ween a minority and a majority, or (b) between two economic classes such as the zamindars and the peasants or the employ-ers and the employees, or (c) between a section of the commu-nity and the Government.[4]

In India, ever since Gandhi's entry into public life and till his death in 1948, there were numerous applications of satyagraha in this country. Some of these were for the realization of the national political goal of independence, while others were of local origin limited to specific demands of various nature—economic, civic, social and political. One finds a number of studies on large-scale, nation-wide, major satyagraha campaigns in India. Competent analyses have also been made of well-known non-violent group actions like those at Champaran, Kheda, Ahmedabad, Bardoli and Vaikom which took place under the direct leadership or indirect influence of Gandhi.[5] But no systematic study has yet been made of the local or minor satyagraha campaigns which were launched in different parts of the country for the redress of specific wrongs. The numerous local or minor satyagrahas may be looked upon as exercises in the practice of non-violence.[6]

This is a modest attempt to make a study of local satyagrahas in Bengal. This also incorporates a case study of Mahishbathan Salt Satyagraha. We have chosen this as a sample to examine the response of the masses of a particular area in Bengal to Gandhi's call of salt satyagraha. It is evident from the pages below that our enquiry is limited to the conflict-situation as enumerated in the second and third categories of the classification mentioned above. Only in one case we have made a study of the first category of classification. Secondly, this work does not include all the local satyagraha campaigns for obvious reasons. The present study covers the satyagraha campaigns noted below.

    I.   Contai Union Board Boycott Movement (District : Midnapore, West Bengal, 1921)

   II.  Bandabila Union Board Boycott Movement (District : Jessore, Bangladesh, 1929-30)

 III.  Tarakeswar Satyagraha (District : Hooghly, West Bengal, 1924-25)

 IV  Patuakhali Satyagraha (District : Buckergune [Barisal], Bangladesh, 1926-28)

  V.  Munshiganj Kali Temple Satyagraha (District : Dacca, Bangladesh, 1929-30)

VI. Mahisbathan Salt Satyagraha (District : 24 Parganas, West Bengal, 1930-31)

VII. Brikutsa Tenants' Satyagraha (District : Rajsahi, Bangladesh, 1931-32)

VIII. Arambagh Settlement Boycott (District : Hoogly, West Bengal, 1931-32)

IX. Damodar Canal Satyagraha (District : Burdwan, West Bengal, 1936-39)

X. Charmanair Satyagraha (District : Faridpur, Bangladesh, 1923-25)

In our investigation we made a study of

(a) the aim of the movement and the issues involved therein : social or religious, or economic or political and how the movement corresponded to the nature of issues involved ;

(b) the organization of the movement and the steps taken for launching satyagraha : negotiation and arbitration, preparation of groups of direct action, agitation, issuing of an ultimatum, economic and social boycott, and forms of strike, non-co-operation, and civil disobedience ;

(c) the relationship between constructive programme like Khadi and Village Industries work and satyagraha campaigns ;

(d) the magnitude of response and the extent of participation by the people in the movement, and the character of participants ;

(e) response of the direct opponents, if any, in each case ;

(f) the reaction of the Government ;

(g) the relation between the leadership and the common masses of the people in the action-process of the movement ;

(h) difference of opinion, if any, among the leaders as regards the method to be followed or the end to be achieved and if so, how it affected the over-all progress of the movement ;

(i) the results.

We have advisedly included (c) in our investigation. For in

the Gandhian scheme militant, non-violent direct action is not the only part of satyagraha. As is well known, constructive programme is a concomitant of civil resistance. It is, to put it briefly, the *modus operandi* of non-violent revolution as envis-aged by Gandhi. The connexion between civil disobedience and constructive programme has been explained elaborately by Nirmal Kumar Bose.[7] One may profitably refer to his study on the subject for a clear exposition of the relationship between the two aspects of Gandhi's technique. To put it briefly : Gandhi proposed to (i) build up the economic strength or staying power of the masses in a long-drawn struggle, (ii) he felt that continuous constructive work brought the 'classes' and the 'masses' together and progressively dissolved the differences between them, and (iii) it made the masses familiar with the kind of equalitarian life which they would be able to build up when they had access to political power.

The methods followed in our enquiry are as follows :

(i) Field investigations (excepting the areas which are now in Bangladesh) ;

(ii) Interviews—both structured and unstructured—with direct participants in these movements and the people who have intimate knowledge of the course of the movements under study ;

(iii) Collection of data : (a) Books and pamphlets, (b) News reports from contemporary dailies and weeklies, local newspapers, bulletins, leaflets, etc. published by differ-ent satyagraha campaign committees ; (c) Memoranda by individuals and organizations ; (d) resolutions of meetings and conferences ; (e) Proceedings of the Bengal Legislative Assembly and Council ; and (f) Administration Reports of the Government of Bengal, Government of India Publications and archival mate-rials.

Since no detailed investigation has yet been made of local satyagrahas in Bengal, or for that matter of India, we have thought it proper to give a descriptive account of the cases we have examined in detail. This will, we believe, represent a total and connected story of non-violent mass actions as they developed in this part of the country in a given historical period. In our account we have tried to arrange, as far as practicable, the course of these satyagrahas in chronological order, the purpose being to make an analysis of the phasewise development of each campaign.

We have made free and copious use of all such material as we could collect, for we feel that hard and solid facts make analysis easier. The documents appended in this volume will, we are sure, be considered as source material for an authentic history of the freedom movement in India. These case studies will serve as supplementary reference material for understanding the theoretical bases of satyagraha as well.

## NOTES AND REFERENCES

1. Vincent Sheean, *Lead, Kindly Light*, 244.

2. Krishnalal Sridharani, *War Without Violence*, 16.

3. Joan V. Bondurant, *Conquest of Violence*, 3-4.

4. Sridharani, op. cit., 61 and 79.

5. See Nirmal Kumar Bose, *Studies in Gandhism* (1972), 87-90 and 132-40 ; *Lectures on Gandhism*, 30-43 ; Judith M. Brown, *Gandhi's Rise to Power*, 52-122 : Joan V. Bondurant, op. cit., 45-73 ; Krishnalal Sridharani, op. cit., 87-100 ; R. R. Diwakar, *Saga of Satyagraha* 122-35 ; *Satyagraha : Its Technique and History ; Satyagraha in Action* ; Richard B. Gregg. *The Power of Non-violence*. For Champaran Satyagraha, see B. B. Misra (ed.), *Select Documents on Mahatma Gandhi's Movement in Champaran 1917-18* ; K. K. Datta (ed.), *Writings And Speeches of Mahatma Gandhi Relating to Bihar 1917-1947*, 71-142 ; Gene Sharp, *Gandhi Wields the Weapon of Moral Power*, 10 37 ; Rajendra Prasad, *Satyagraha in Champaran* ; P. C. Ray Chaudhury, *Gandhiji's First Struggle in India* ; D. G. Tendulkar, *Gandhi in Champaran* ; D. N. Dhanagre, *Agrarian Movements and Gandhian Politics*, Lecture II.

6. Nirmal Kumar Bose, *Studies in Gandhism*, op. cit., 163.

7. Nirmal Kumar Bose, *Studies in Gandhism* (1947), 177-95. See also Buddhadeva Bhattacharyya, *Evolution of the Political Philosophy of Gandhi*, 326-8.

## CHAPTER II

# CONTAI UNION BOARD BOYCOTT MOVEMENT

## I

THE RAPID TRANSFORMATION of the world situation in the years following the First World War and the great Russian Revolution accelerated the pace of political movement in India. As the general crisis of capitalism intensified and was about to engulf the whole structure of imperialism and the world revolutionary wave began to awaken the millions of subject people and nationalities, the freedom struggle in India, so long confined to a small section of the upper class, started reaching out to the masses of the people. The period 1919-1922 witnessed an unprecedented tide of mass revolutionary unrest all over the country. In view of the changing scene, in 1920 Gandhi and the main body of the Congress leadership executed a decisive change of front, shunned co-operation with the Reforms, resolved to lead the rising mass movement and for this purpose evolved the plan of non-violent non-co-operation. The resolution on non-violent non-co-operation was carried at the Calcutta Special Congress in September 1920 and at the Nagpur Session in December the new plan was finally adopted. The mass movement of the period was marked not only by the development of non-co-operation but also by other forms of struggle in all parts of the country. [1] It is in this context that the nature of the Contai Union Board Boycott Movement is to be understood.

## II

Contai, a subdivisional town of the district of Midnapore, became a focal point of attention in the middle of 1920 when the Government began to issue orders regarding the establishment of union boards in the villages within the jurisdiction of Contai and Ramnagar thanas in accordance with section 5 of the Bengal Village Self-Government Act, 1919 (Bengal Act No. V of 1919) and on the recommendation of the District Board of Midnapore and the Local Board of Contai. The initial efforts of the Government under the supervision of the Circle Officer, Jitendriya Mukherjee, set aflame the fire of enthusiasm for non-co-operation already kindled by Gandhi.[2]

The Government authorities at the local level prepared a voters' list, fixed 30 November 1920 as the last date for submission of nomination papers for the election of members to the Union Board and announced that the election would commence on January 15, 1921 and continue up to the 29th instant.[3] Since the Government and its agencies there did not take the least trouble to acquaint the people with the contents of the Bengal Village Self-Government Act, the advantages expected to result from it, the mode of its implementation, the basis of the voters' list and the dates and places of election, the people showed little or no enthusiasm in the election.[4]

On 11 March 1921 the newly elected and nominated members of the Contai Union Board assembled at the local board building at the invitation from the Subdivisional Officer, J. De, to elect the office-bearers of the Union Board.[5]

While these attempts were being made by the local authorities to establish union boards in the rural area, an intense resentment prevailed among the people. They took it for granted that union boards were but an excuse for imposing a fresh burden of taxation on their shoulders. They had already been thrown into a pool of misery. Half-starved, half-naked, they could not pay the *chaukidari* rate in time, and the Government very often resorted to attachment of the movable goods of the defaulters. Hence any addition to the existing taxes would be the last straw for the overburdened people. The local newspapers like *Nihar* and *Medinibandhava* started ventilating the grievances and anti-Union-Board feeling of the people. They went on appealing to the Government to repeal the Act. But, curiously enough, with the connivance of the Government authorities some members of the union boards were threatening the people with dire consequences if they did not consent to the plundering acts of the union boards.[6] Nevertheless, side by side with the spontaneous expression of people's resentment against the Act, organizational activities started.[7]

## III

Birendranath Sasmal, the accredited leader of the Contai Union Board Boycott Movement, knew it very well that the Bengal Village Self-Government Act could not benefit the people in any way whatsoever and, consequently, they would certainly try to resist its introduction, even without any proper leadership and necessary organization. He also realized that he could utilize the people's anti-union-board sentiment to give a positive content to the campaign for non-co-operation. Apart from the political motive which seems to have actuated Sasmal to organize the Union Board Boycott Movement as part of a greater mass movement and to secure a wider basis of his leadership, the Act carried much combustible material within itself. On several occasions Sasmal virulently attacked the Act on various grounds.[8]

Sasmal put forth the following arguments in support of his statement that the Bengal Village Self-Government Act, 1919[9] had not given any important powers to the people which should have been given them if it had been the intention of the Act to 'develop self-government' in the true sense of the term. First, the union boards had been given no share of the huge amount of money that the local people used to pay to the Government. Sir Surendranath Banerjea had once observed from the Congress platform that "the Indian tax-payers pay a tax of 8 per cent. upon his income of Rs. 27."* Now, the people were not allowed under his ministry to touch a single pice of this 8 per cent for the improvement of their villages. This meant, according to Sasmal, that the people would continue to send their taxes as before to the fat-salaried members of the top-heavy administration regardless of their bearing of all that on the interests at the bottom. Secondly, the union boards had not been given any discretion to refuse to tax themselves on any account or to tax according to their ideas of local needs. The mandate had been issued to the effect that the rural people

---

* According to *Speeches of Surendranath Banerjea*, I (106), the tax that the Indian taxpayers had to pay was "5 p.c. upon his income of Rs. 27". Banerjea said in his speech referred to above that five per cent. upon an income of Rs. 27 was a much more serious matter and it involved "a much heavier sacrifice than 7 per cent. upon an income of £ 33."

should improve their villages and for that purpose their taxes under this Act might go up to Rs. 84. Even Sir Surendranath as the President of the Indian National Congress said in 1895 that in India the farthest limits of taxation had already been reached. Though Banerjea had once as the President of the Indian National Congress admitted that the people of India were the poorest on earth and their taxes the highest on record, now as minister-in-charge of self-government he could ask the people to change themselves and consent to pay more and more taxes, since he had himself changed with time. If the people did not consent, the District Magistrate or his nominee could call for assessment papers and pass such orders as they deemed necessary. Hence the union boards were to tax according to the dictates from above and could not raise a voice of protest against the high-handedness of government officials. Thirdly, even if the people, adversely affected by the present economic crisis, consented to bear the burden of fresh taxation, the *chaukidars* and *dafadars* were to remain, as before, under the control of the District Magistrate or his delegates. Fourthly, a perpetual system of tutelage had been prescribed for the union boards not only in matters relating to appointment and dismissal of their own servants and staff officers but also in matters of law and even informal management. Hence the union boards were destined to be perpetual minors.

Birendranath also adduced arguments to show how the Act affected the interests of the people. In the first place, the taxes to be imposed under the Act might be seven times the prevailing *chaukidari* rate. Persons, too poor to pay half an anna a month, would only be exempted from payment of any rate under the Act. Curiously enough, said Sasmal, the rich who constituted the union boards had been called upon to govern the poor by imposing fresh taxes upon themselves. In practice, he observed, they would realize the whole amount of new taxes from the poor as usual by increasing the rates of interests of money and paddy or by lowering the rates of wages to the labourers. And they would do all these things with impunity. In the second place, Sasmal argued that the Bengal Village Self-Government Act, 1919 had put no limit to an individual tax-

payer's capacity to pay. He would not be saved even if he had
agreed to pay Rs. 84/- annually, in place of his present Rs. 11/-
a year, if he happened to have circumstances and hold property
in more than one union. Thirdly, Sasmal said that the Act had
specified multifarious duties of the union boards, of course,
without indicating the sources of funds, and, where so indicating, without saying anything as regards their availability and
adequacy.

Further, Sasmal criticised the Act for a reason altogether
different from those stated above. He said that the declared
object of the Act was to modernize the village life of Bengal
through mild doses of Western civilization. He was not opposed
to the municipal, sanitary and other arrangements of the West
as such nor was he eager to erect a Chinese Wall between the
East and the West. He stood for a proper assimilation of the
noblest of our ideals with what is best in Western civilization. But in actuality he saw the failure of the British rulers to
keep up the characteristics of Indian civilization and pave the
way for people's spontaneous acceptance of those ideals of the
West that might be beneficial to them. The Act in question
made no provision to enable the union boards to chalk out
their educational policies and impart moral, spiritual and political training necessary for salvation of their 'racial soul'. The
Act would bring to the remotest village of Bengal a 'Godless
materialistic atmosphere', the result of which would be deplorable and disastrous. The 'outer artificialities and even com-
forts' would lead to the complete cultural conquest of the
people. Hence Sasmal said : "I therefore enter my emphatic
protest against this open and widespread attempt to modernize
our village social life which is already in a process of disinteg-
ration and which some of us are striving hard to build anew,
and declare that in the present circumstances it is a question of
principle with me to have anything to do with the Bengal
Village Self-Government Act."[10] Sasmal's opposition to materialistic civilization reminds us of Gandhi's indictment against
modern civilization in *Hind Swaraj*.[11]

IV

In the foregoing paragraphs we have discussed the arguments put forward by Birendranath Sasmal against the Bengal Village Self-Government Act. Now to focus our attention on the different phases of development of the Union Board Boycott Movement : We would first refer to the meetings organized by the local leaders which played a very important role in the initial stage of the movement.

Probably the first meeting was organized by the local businessmen of Kantanala Bazar on 9 June 1921.[12] Since then a series of meetings had been held at different places of the town, which were addressed by the local leaders like Birendranath Sasmal, Pramatha Nath Bandyopadhyay, Satish Chandra Jana and Surendranath Das.[13] In the first few meetings they tried to ascertain people's opinion about the newly established union boards. Even the supporters of the union board type of self-government were usually invited to address the meetings and bring home to the people the benefits to be derived from these self-governing institutions. But whatever be their reason, members of the union boards or their supporters did not accept such invitations. The leaders of the movement, however, successfully gauged the anti-union-board feelings of the people and utilized it for the next higher stage. The speakers elaborately discussed from time to time the demerits of union boards and showed how indiscriminately and inconsistently taxes had been assessed.[14] The people assembled at different meetings, adopted resolutions against the union boards and sent copies of the same to the Subdivisional Officer, the District Magistrate, the Chairman of the District Board, the Chief Secretary, Government of Bengal, the Minister-in-charge of Local Self-Government and also to the members of the Bengal Legislative Council. They appealed to the Government to revoke the notification regarding the extension of union boards to the Contai subdivision. They also urged the members of the union boards to resign, because the latter, as members of union boards, could not do any good to the people. It is interesting to note that in response to the appeal of the people, Kedar Nath Das, Ganendra Maity, Upendra Nath Das, Brajendra Nath Das, Amar Nandi and Tarak Nath Pal resigned from the union boards.[15]

Besides, several meetings were reported to have been held at different places in rural areas like Manibagan, Meergoda, Balisai, Deuli, Islampur, Namal, Basantia, Phuleswar, etc. The meetings were attended by people belonging to both the Hindu and Muslim communities.[16] In order to win the support of the Muslims the organizers of the movement invited the Muslim leaders of East Bengal to attend some meetings. It was reported that Maulavi Rayhan Uddin Ahmed came from East Bengal and discussed the union board issue at several meetings in *mofussil* areas.[17]

On 14 August 1921 Sasmal declared at a meeting that he himself had decided not to pay the union board taxes and was ready to bear any punishment the Government would inflict on him for non-payment of taxes.[18] Since then the people of Contai and Ramnagar thanas began to express their unwillingness to pay the union board taxes. This attitude was evident from the incident that took place in the village of Fatehpur. Seven people of Fatehpur refused to pay union board taxes, though they were ready to pay the *chaukidari* rate. The president of the union board alleged that since he had not resigned as president of the union board some people maliciously pulled down some pillars of one of his farm-houses and committed nuisance there. Some Government officials came down to Fatehpur village to inquire into the allegations of the President against those people. Fifteen days after the date of inquiry those people were summoned and their trial took place at the Ramnagar P.S. and they were jailed for a few days.[19]

The organizers of the no-tax campaign appealed to the people through their speeches at different meetings to remain peaceful and non-violent during the movement. Their pronounced stand on the no-tax campaign was that they were ready to pay *chaukidari* rate against *chaukidari* receipt. They were decidedly opposed to any acceptance of union board receipt against their payment of *chaukidari* rate, since that would mean an indirect recognition of the legitimacy of the authority of the newly established union boards which they had so long refused to recognize.[20]

## V

The movement entered a new phase when Government officers accompanied by armed forces started attaching the movables of the tax-payers who refused to pay the *chaukidari* rate against union board receipts. On 23 September 1921 the Circle Officer, Norman Basu, the Sub-Deputy, Alexander Mitter, the Nazir, Biharilal Bhattacharyya and his son, Sati Kumar Bhattacharyya (newly appointed *Tahsildar*), divided into three groups, went on an attachment operation. At first, the movables of the Bhuinya family of Darua were attached. Then, wherever they went the villagers blew conch-shell and raised *haridhvani* and peacefully submitted to attachment of their properties. Even the poorest man allowed his most essential utensils to be attached.[21]

From the last week of September onwards the attachment continued unabated. Movable goods worth many times the taxes due under the new Act were seized. But one thing which worried the officers on duty was the want of carts and the refusal by the cartmen to carry the attached goods to places of auction.

Regarding the situation at Contai at this stage of development of the movement, B. N. Sasmal wrote to the Editor, *Amrita Bazar Patrika*, dated 21 October 1921, as follows : "The situation in Contai is the same as before. They are attaching movables of the villagers for about a month, and the villagers are delivering them all this time without the least touch of violence anywhere. They are to attach movables of about 35 thousand tax-payers in all, but during the last four weeks they have attached movables of 4 thousand people only. There has absolutely been no sign of break or leakage anywhere among the six lacs of people. The same old story of want of labourers and carts and cartmen for carrying the attached movables are (*sic*) still being repeated in the whole subdivision. Recently the Government had to send up to the District Headquarters a few lacs of rupees. This they always did in bullock carts, but this time they had to improvise two motor cars for the purpose. The present S.D.O. of Contai has been gazetted (*sic*) to Hooghly, but whether this transfer is of any importance to Contai, it remains to be seen. In the meantime, the idea is spreading to other subdivisions of Midnapur..."[22]

*Nihar*, dated 8.11.21, reported that Government officers, on their failure to collect *chaukidari* rate through the receipt form under the new Act, had tried, during the last few weeks, to attach the movable properties of the defaulters, under J. De's orders, and the various offensive measures resorted to by them during the attachment operations bore no fruit. First, they could not persuade any labourer or cartman to carry the attached goods to the place of auction, and next, they failed to secure any bidder for the goods put on auction. The tax-payers were of unanimous opinion that they did not want union boards, and hence would not pay any taxes assessed or imposed by these institutions in exchange of receipts to be issued under the new Act.

Meanwhile, the District Magistrate, A. W. Cook, and the Joint Magistrate, Satyendra Nath Roy, came to this subdivision to investigate the causes behind the tense situation there. On their arrival attachment operations came to a stop. Satyendra Nath Roy undertook a painstaking visit to different villages and listened to the allegations levelled by the villagers against the officers in charge of attachment proceedings. During his extensive tour and thorough inquiry, the newly posted Sub-divisional Officer, Mr Younie, accompained him. They observed in their reports that it would not be wise to continue union boards in Contai.[23]

On 22 November 1921 in the fifth session of the Bengal Legislative Council Dr A. Suhrawardy, the then Chairman of the Midnapore District Board, moved a resolution recommending to the Government that operation of the Bengal Village Self-Government Act be suspended in such areas where local conditions were not favourable to the growth of self-governing institutions. In that connexion he referred to the subdivision of Contai. He mentioned B. N. Sasmal's articles (to which we have already referred) published in the *Amrita Bazar Patrika*. He told the House that the people of Contai were condemning the Act, the operation of which, they said, was neither beneficial to them nor designed to cure the evils which they suffered from. Hundreds and thousands of villagers in Contai subdivision had refused to pay their dues under the Act, whilst they cheerfully submitted to the attachment of their property which was ten times more valuable. Dr Suhrawardy observed in fine that he was opposed to the idea of any measures, however beneficial, being thrust upon an unwilling people. In reply, Sir Surendranath Banerjea, the Minister for Local Self-Government, said that "if in any particular locality circumstances are unfavourable and public sentiment demands the discontinuance of union boards then in accordance with the spirit of local self-government, we must give the utmost consideration to the circumstances and take note of them, and deal with them in accordance with the principles of local self-government, however, reluctant we may be to do so." He also added that "...if we feel that circumstances are so unpropitious to the continuance of these institutions, we shall have to take note of the fact and, if necessary, with great reluctance, suspend them." In view of this assurance, Dr Suhrawardy withdrew the motion.[24]

In December the Secretary to the Government of Bengal, Mr Wood, declared in the *Calcutta Gazette* that in accordance with Section I (3) of the Act V of 1919 the Government revoked the notification of the extension of the Act from all places of Midnapore except Gopalnagar Union within the jurisdiction of Panskura thana. Later, on the basis of the reports of the District Magistrate of Midnapore and the Sub-Divisional Officer, Tamluk, the Government even decided to withdraw the Act from the area under the jurisdiction of the Gopalnagar Union Board. Accordingly, notices were issued to the people concerned to get back the attached goods. As a result 227 union boards were dissolved in the district of Midnapore.[25]

## VII

Here in this section we would trace the attitude of the Government towards the movement and the steps taken against the people who defied the law and also briefly touch upon the leadership problem.

As regards the policy of the Government we find some hints in Narendranath Das's *History of Midnapur*, Vol. II. He says that the policy of the Government towards the movement was to secure liberty for the law-abiding people so that they could pursue their lawful business, to declare the volunteer corps to be an unlawful association under the Bengal Criminal Law Amendment Act of 1908, to exercise control over the holding of meetings and processions in certain areas and finally to take steps against anyone deliberately defying the law. In accordance with the policy, says Narendranath Das, the Government prohibited public meetings and processions in the Sadar, Contai and Tamluk subdivisions under Bengal Police Acts and enforced the Prevention of Seditious Meetings Act of 1911 and Criminal Law Amendment Act of 1908. But all these measures, he observes, failed and 'the forces of lawlessness and disorder' continued to muster strength in increasing measure among the masses. A widespread contempt for foreign rule resulted in boycott and 'intimidation of the loyal supporters of the Government,' 'active molestation of Government servants,' persistent conflict with the police, dissuading *chaukidars* from doing their normal duties and growing refusal to pay the *chaukidari* tax. The participation of ladies in large number in the movement and organized attempts on their part to defy the law-enforcing authorities added to the difficulties of the situation. An additional police force was posted at the expense of the inhabitants of Midnapore. The author also says that the leaders including Birendranath Sasmal were arrested and imprisoned, and one among them, Gunadhar Hazra, the Headmaster of the National School at Mahishadal, died in Midnapore Central Jail on 28 April 1922 at 8-15 p.m. and became a martyr. Twenty-five persons were committed to rigorous imprisonment and nine to simple imprisonment under section 17 (1) and (2) of the Criminal Law Amendment Act of 1908.[26]

The information which we have gathered from contemporary newspapers including the local ones, official documents and the interviews with the participants in the movement do not fully corroborate the views of Narendranath Das with regard

to the Government attitude in particular. Our inquiry leads
to certain conclusions which are noted below.

In September 1919 the Subdivisional Officer first sent some
leaflets to police officers for distribution in the panchayats
narrating the aims and objects of the Village Self-Government Act and called meetings at Contai to explain the advantages of union boards and the necessity of increased taxation for the improvement of villages. Encouraged by the
'success' of these meetings and of the initial efforts for the
election to union boards, the supporters of the Government
including a few local pleaders and muktears and 'outsider'
*bhadraloks* started publishing *Hijli Hitaishi* in May 1921 to
advocate the case of self-government. In the middle of
August the Government withheld certificate notices and sale
notices from *Nihar* which played an important role in the
movement. Official patronage in the form of giving adver-
tisement to *Hijli Hitaishi* further strengthened people's suspicion about its pro-Government bias. When the movement
gathered momentum the Subdivisional Officer and the Circle
Officer made certain attempts to counter the anti-union-board
propaganda but without any success. Failing in all its efforts
the Government brought huge armed forces to collect *chaukidari*
taxes against receipts to be issued under the new Act. But
even in the face of all kinds of provocation, for example,
the breaking open of doors and molestation of inmates during
attachment, the people remained absolutely peaceful and submitted to the attachment proceedings. The Government,
denied all sorts of rural transport facilities, adopted the methods
of torture and intimidation of the *garwans* and cartmen.
Only two or three instances of the Government's going to
the extreme may be cited. As has been noted above only
seven persons of Fatehpur village were arrested and imprisoned.
The volunteers who closely followed the officers in charge
of attachment operations were not punished in any way. In
the course of the movement Pramatha Nath Bandyopadhyay,
Satish Chandra Jana and Birendranath Sasmal were arrested
and jailed. The Government became very much cautious and
hesitant to adopt any repressive measure of extreme nature

2

when it completly failed to disrupt the movement and disin-
tegrate the leadership. Moreover, Government officers who
made on-the-spot enquiry feared that unless the Local Self-
Government Act was revoked without delay, the people might
be incited by the 'non-co-operators' to refuse to pay even
the *chaukidari* tax. Accordingly, the Government hurriedly
withdrew the Act from the district of Midnapore by the beginning of 1921.[27]

## VIII

In fine we would like to point out that the unique leadership provided by Birendranath Sasmal was unparalleled in
the contemporary history of mass movement in Bengal. He, in
collaboration with a few others, organized the movement
through propaganda, mass meetings, extensive tour of the
villages and personal contacts in the National School established in his own house and other volunteer organizations.
His strong personality and deep-seated sympathy for people's
misery enabled him to enlist the active support of the rural
masses and command respect from the public in general. For
all these reasons he was hailed by Acharya Prafulla Chandra
Ray as the 'Uncrowned King' ('Mukutheen Raja') of Midnapore.

But the leadership problem centred round the conflict
between Birendranath Sasmal and the dominant Congress
leadership regarding the launching of the movement. Though
Sasmal had not an iota of doubt as regards the futility of
the union boards, he could not decide whether an anti-union-
board movement should be organized on behalf of the Congress.[28] "At the Nagpur Congress in 1920 he tried to move
a resolution that the Union Board provisions in the village
self-government acts in different provinces should be fought
against, but he was not successful."[29] Birendranath tried to
secure permission from Gandhi to launch a no-tax campaign
in his native district. "But the permission was refused as
an all-India policy by the Mahatma."[30] "At the Bengal
Provincial Congress Conference in 1921, however, he moved
a resolution to fight the Union Boards in which the villagers
were asked not to pay union and village taxes. But after

the resolution was passed at Barisal, the Executive Council of the Bengal Provincial Congress did a wonderful thing."[31] Birendranath could not be present at the meeting of the executive council,[32] which "in defiance of the earlier Barisal resolution passed a resolution to the effect that the Village Self-Government Act should not be fought against and no movement should be organized against the payment of union or *chaukidari* taxes. It is amazing how a Provincial Committee's Executive Council could go against the resolution of the general session of the Congress Committee which was the provincial conference."[33] Thus circumscribed, Birendranath was at first in a quandary to resolve the contradiction between the Congress decision and the pursuit of people's cause. Very soon he chose a course of action for upholding people's interests without directly flouting the Congress mandate. Even though he was not fortunate enough to have "the blessing of the Mahatma and active financial, moral and organizational support of the Congress", he started organizing the movement in his personal capacity and as a step independent of the Congress.[34]

Thus we have seen that the Congress was reluctant to support Birendranath in launching and organizing the anti-Union-Board movement and the latter, from the start, conducted the movement in his personal capacity and always disclaimed any connexion of the anti-union-board agitation with the non-co-operation movement of the Congress. According to Bimalananda Sasmal, the Congress was opposed to the anti-union-board movement in the form of no-tax campaign.[35] But the 'curious thing', says Bimalananda Sasmal, is that the Congress claimed the credit for the success of the movement while the name of his father was not mentioned. To substantiate his opinion he quotes Hugh Tinker as follows : "In Bengal also the political fervour of 1921 had its echoes in local government—at first indirectly, in the withdrawal of thousands of pupils from board schools...and then directly in the Swarajist campaign against the new Village Self-Government Act. The new Union Boards were represented as an excuse to impose fresh taxation, and so much was public feeling aroused, that Government was forced to dissolve the

227 Union Boards established in Midnapore District, whilst elsewhere the campaign prevented the formation of new boards for a considerable time."[36]   Here Bimalananda Sasmal comments that this statement is an absolute negation of facts and a clear distortion of history. For, as he has already pointed out, the Congress executive refused to fight union boards and passively supported the Village Self-Government Act. He also observes that he could not agree to the claim that it was a Swarajist movement since the Swarajist party was not even formed at that time.[37]

We, however, cannot agree with Bimalananda Sasmal when he says that the Contai Union Boycott Movement was a 'great agrarian movement' and it took the shape of a 'no-rent campaign' and that his father championed 'the cause of famished peasantry indirectly flouting the anti-peasant resolution of the Congress', since he gives no substantial argument to establish his thesis. On a scrutiny of the material at our disposal we could not arrive at the conclusion that Birendranath ever tried to organize or lead any movement of the local peasantry against their overlords. On the contrary, we find him voicing his protest against the B.V.S.G. Act for the mild doze of tax to be imposed under the Act on the landed gentry. Birendranath himself commented in his article entitled 'Beware of Union Boards'[39] that "...by introducing lands in place of houses and cutcheries, the permanent settlement of this Province...has at last been indirectly attacked by this self-governing measure...One thing absolutely clear now is that a new taxation is being imposed under this Act upon our permanently settled lands, which must for ever remain immune from fresh taxation of any kind according to the provisions of Regulation I of 1793. It does not matter by what means they are taking the money from us now, for their demand is based upon income from the permanently settled lands. And therefore they are not only directly taxing our agricultural income, but also indirectly putting a fresh tax upon our lands permanently settled, in direct violation of the existing provisions of law on the subject." Birendranath's argument that the B.V. S.G. Act, while redefining the taxable capacity of the assessees, indirectly attacked the Permanent Settlement of this province under the provisions of Regulation I of 1793, was untenable. He said that both the resident and the absentee landlords, having 'circumstances' and 'properties' in several districts, extending over several unions in each district, and already involved, would have to pay under this Act a lot of money. While we agree with him in his criticisms of the Act on other reasonable grounds, we fail to accept his view that this Act should be 'unmade' since it encroached upon the interests of the landed gentry. When we compare this argument of Birendranath Sasmal (see his letter to J. De, S.D.O.) with the rather sweeping comments of his son, Bimalananda Sasmal, that the members of the Executive Council of the Bengal Provincial Congress Committee which defied the Barisal resolution were 'mostly representatives of the landed aristocracy', 'stooges of the vested interests', 'the bond slaves of the propertied class and opposed to the interests of the poor peasantry' and only his father truly represented the interests of the millions of peasants and organized an 'agrarian movement' for their liberation,[39] we are driven to the conclusion that his son's statement betrays an emotional feeling. But emotion is not reason.

Further, we can furnish one more fact that Birendranath had always held the British Government responsible for provoking the otherwise peaceful and non-violent people by forcibly imposing on them unwanted union boards. In this context, it may be mentioned, in one public meeting he compared the efforts of the Government to extend the Western municipal system to the remote villages with 'the spreading tentacle of formidable Bolshevism,' and called it a menace to India.[40] This seems to indicate his attitude towards the toiling people's philosophy of emancipation.

Nonetheless, it is true that the credit for this movement has not been duly apportioned and the anti-union-Board agitation suffered a 'complete blackout'[41] in the columns of the nationalist press. The historians also displayed an attitude of cynical indifferrence to this unique movement. In spite of so many extravagant claims from different quarters, we would like to conclude that the anti-Union-Board Movement in

Midnapore forced the Government to revoke the notifications regarding the extension of the provisions of the Bengal Village Self-Government Act, 1919 to this district. And this was made possible by the united opposition of the common people under the leadership of Birendranath Sasmal.

## NOTES AND REFERENCES

1. R. Palme Dutt, *India Today*, 310-21.

For an in-depth analysis of the Rowlatt Satyagraha, see R. Kumar (ed.), *Essays on Gandhian Politics*.

For details about the Non-Co-operation Movement, see R. C. Majumdar, *History of the Freedom Movement in India*, III, ch. 3 ; Judith M. Brown, *Gandhi's Rise to Power*, 250-304 and Sukhbir Choudhary, *Indian People Fight for National Liberation*, chs. 2 and 3.

For the official analysis, see P. C. Bamford, *Histories of the Non-Co-operation and Khilafat Movements*, chs. I-III.

2. *Nihar* (a local Bengali weekly), Contai, 29.6.20. See also Appendix II.

3. *Nihar*, 29.6.20 ; 23.11.20 ; 11.1.21. See also Appendix II.

4. *Nihar*, dates mentioned above and 1.2.21. See also Appendix II.

5. *Nihar*, 15.3.21.

6. ibid., 3, 24 and 31 May, 1921.

7. ibid., 7.6.21.

8. Our discussion of the arguments put forward by Birendranath Sasmal against the Bengal Village Self-Government Act is based on Sasmal's article, 'Beware of Union Boards', published in two parts in *Amrita Bazar Patrika*, 21.10.21, 4(4-5) and 22.10.21, 4(5-6) [later published under the title, 'Sabdhan, Oi Union Board Aschhe', with an introduction by Kumar Jana, in *Ananda Bazar Patrika*, 12.10.35, 12(3-5) ; 13.10.35, 16(3-5) ; 15.10.35, 12(2-3) and 16.10.35, 11(3-5)] and his letter dated 7.8.21 to the Subdivisional Officer, published in *La Verite*, 1968 Puja Special, 21.9.68, 9-13, and also in Pramatha Nath Pal, *Deshapran Sasmal*, 43-52. Reports of the meetings where Sasmal and others elaborately discussed these arguments can be found in *Nihar*, 7.6.21, 12.7.21, 19.7.21, 23.8.21, 30.8.21, 6.9.21.

9. Bengal Act No. V of 1919, The Bengal Village Self-Government Act, 1919, *West Bengal Code*, III (Bengal Acts 1890 to 1919).

10. *La Verite*, op.cit., 10-1 ; Pramatha Nath Pal, op.cit., 46.

11. For an analysis of Gandhi's *Hind Swaraj*, see Buddhadeva Bhattacharyya, *Evolution of the Political Philosophy of Gandhi*, 151-72.

12. *Nihar*, 7.6.21, 2. We have been told by Sudhir Chandra Das

(4.10.71) that the first meeting was held at the Lagar-hat maidan of Darua.

13.  Reports of these meetings can be found in *Nihar*, 12.7.21, 19.7.21, 26.7.21, 16.8.21, 23.8.21, 30.8.21, 6.9.21.  See also Appendix II.

14.  *Nihar*, 19.7.21, 2-3.  See also Appendices II and III.

The allegation made by the speakers can be substantiated from the list given below :

| Names of the Assessees | Amount of Average Income within the Union (in Rupees) | Amount of Quarterly Taxes | | |
|---|---|---|---|---|
| Kalipada Maitra | 1680 | Rs. | 2—4 | annas |
| Jnanada Charan Basu | 1352 | Rs. | 2—4 | ,, |
| Gopinath Maity | 1300 | Rs. | 2—4 | ,, |
| Naresh Chandra Banerjee | 960 | Rs. | 2—4 | ,, |
| Anandaram Nanda | 800 | Rs. | 2—4 | ,, |
| Abanti Kumar Maity | 700 | Rs. | 2—4 | ,, |
| Uma Charan Mitra | 200 | Rs. | 2—4 | ,, |
| Sridhar Manna and Arjun Bera | 150 | Rs. | 2—4 | ,, |
| Surendranath Jana | 150 | Rs. | 2—4 | ,, |
| Naba Kumar Bera | 1000 | Rs. | 2—4 | ,, |
| Bhupendranath Das | 1000 | Rs. | 4—8 | ,, |
| Basanta Kumar Das Mahapatra | 1000 | Rs. | 5—4 | ,, |
| Haripada Pahari | 1000 | Rs. | 4—12 | ,, |
| Ramrup Pare | 1000 | Rs. | 1—14 | ,, |
| Baranasi Bandyopadhyay and Gopal Chandra Bandyopadhyay | 1000 | Rs. | 4—2 | ,, |
| Debendranarayan Hazra | 500 | Rs. | 4—8 | ,, |
| Satyendranath Batabyal | 7200 | Rs. | 9—0 | ,, |
| Radhakrishna Maity | 600 | Rs. | 6—0 | ,, |
| Trailokyanath Maity | 1200 | Rs. | 3—0 | ,, |
| Hiralal Lala | 100 | Rs. | 3—12 | ,, |
| Dwarikanath Singha | 2000 | Rs. | 3—12 | ,, |
| Padmalochan Sahu | 50 | Rs. | 1—2 | ,, |
| Nandalal Senapati | 130 | Rs. | 0—3 | ,, |
| Chandramohan Pradhan | 40 | Rs. | 0—12 | ,, |
| Surendranath Barik | 100 | Rs. | 3—0 | ,, |
| Bhudev Mazumdar | 1400 | Rs. | 3—6 | ,, |
| Srinath Chandra Pairah | 200 | Rs. | 1—2 | ,, |
| Gopal Chandra Maity | 350 | Rs. | 2—10 | ,, |
| Pitambar Panda | 400 | Rs. | 0—9 | ,, |
| Kunjabehari Das | 200 | Rs. | 0—9 | ,, |
| Trailokyanath Bera | 100 | Rs. | 1—2 | ,, |
| Nagendra Chandra Bakshi | 3000 | Rs. | 9—0 | ,, |

| Names of the Assessees | Amount of Average Income within the Union (in Rupees) | Amount of Quarterly Taxes |
|---|---|---|
| Naba Kanta Panda | 360 | Rs. 0—9 ,, |
| Bipinbehari Sasmal | 500 | Rs 6—4 ,, |
| Upendranarayan Mazumder, Bhupendranarayan Mazumder and Debendranarayan Mazumder | 500 | Rs. 15—0 ,, |
| Jiban Krishna Maity | 900 | Rs. 1—14 ,, |
| Abinash Chandra Mitra | 4225 | Rs. 9—12 ,, |

It was reported in *Nihar* that although the union board authority tried to explain away the discrimination on the pretext of 'circumstances', the basis of assessment was not made known to the public.— 26.7.21, 3.

15. ibid., 26.7.21.

16. ibid., 30.8.21, 2.

17. Interview with Surendranath Das, 2.10.71. *Nihar*, 30.8.21, 2, corroborates his statement.

18. ibid., 23.8.21, 2-3. See also *The Statesman*, 21.8.21, 17 and 6.9.21, 12.

19. From Sasmal's speech in a meeting held at Contai on 23 August as reported in *Nihar*, 30.8.21, 2. See also Birendranath Sasmal, *Sroter Trina*, 13 ff ; Prahlad Pramanik, *Deshapran Birendranath*, 13. Narendranath Maity narrated this story in his interview (4.10.71).

20. *Nihar*, 20.9.21, 2-3 ; 8.11.21, 2. See also Appendix II.

21. *Nihar*, 27.9.21, 3 ; Appendix I. Also interviews with Narendranath Maity and Sudhir Chandra Das.

22. 'Village Self-Government Situation in Midnapur', *Amrita Bazar Patrika*, 21.10.21.

Discrepancies as to the number of persons whose properties were attached and the estimate of the total number of attachment proceedings to be executed exist between Sasmal's letter (as referred to above) and S. N. Roy's report (as appended below).

23. *Nihar*, 8.11.21, 2-3 ; 15.11.21, 2. See also Appendices I, II and III.

24. *Bengal Legislative Council Proceedings* (Official Report), Fifth Session 1921, V (November 21st to December 2nd, 1921), 137-8, 149-50. See also *Nihar*, 29.11.21, 2.

25. *Nihar*, 27.12.21, 2 ; 17.1.22, 2. See also *Report on the Administration of Bengal 1920-21*, XVIII ; L.F. Rushbrook Williams, *India in 1921-22*, 261 and Appendix IV.

26. Narendranath Das, *History of Midnapur*, II, 89.

Gunadhar Hazra was arrested in connexion with the non-co-operation movement.

27. See Appendix II and *Nihar*, 31.5.21, 3 ; 30.8.21, 2 ; 27.9.21, 3 ; 4.10.21, 2-3 ; 8.11.21, 2 and 3 ; 15.11.21, 2 ; 27.12.21, 2 ; 17.1.22, 2 ; 31.1.22, 2. Also interviews with Sudhir Chandra Das and Narendranath Maity.

*Hijli Hitaishi* (12.5.21) described the Bengal Village Self-Government Act as a "blessing of God". The pro-Government attitude of this paper is to be found in all its issues. See especially the numbers dated 12.5.21, 16.6.21, 23.6.21, 21.7.21, 18.8.21, 22.9.21, 6.10.21, 1.12.21, 15.12.21, 14.2.22, 2.3.22.

28. Birendranath Sasmal, *Sroter Trina*, 9.

29. Interview with Bimalananda Sasmal (son of Birendranath Sasmal), 5.8.71.

30. Narendranath Das, op.cit., 87. Also interview with Sudhir Chandra Das.

31. See note no. 29.

32. Birendranath Sasmal, op.cit., 10.

33. See note no. 29. See also note no. 32 and Jogesh Chandra Basu, *Medinipurer Pradhan Janhara*, 67-8.

34. See note no. 29. Also interviews with Sudhir Chandra Das (4.10.71) and Kangal Chandra Giri (25.10.71). See *The Statesman*, 21.8.21, 17.

35. See note no. 29.

36. Hugh Tinker, *The Foundations of Local Self-Governments in India, Pakistan and Burma*, 147.

37. But this observation is off the mark, because Tinker, it may reasonably be assumed, did not use the term 'Swarajist' to denote the Swarajya Party. Here he means by 'Swarajist campaign' non-co-operation movement in general. But he should have been clear and specific about that.

38. Birendranath Sasmal, 'Beware of Union Boards', II, *Amrita Bazar Patrika*, 22.10.21, 4(5-6).

39. See note no. 29.

40. *Nihar*, 19.7.21, 2-3.

41. See note no. 29.

One should not take the phrase 'complete blackout', in its literal sense. Though the movement received rare mention and occupied scant space in the newspapers, it was duly taken note of by eminent leaders. See Subhas Chandra Bose, *The Indian Struggle 1920-1934*, 84-5. See also Surendranath Banerjea, *A Nation in Making*, 332 and Jadu Gopal Mukhopadhyay, *Biplabi Jibaner Smriti*, 491.

Broomfield mentions the Contai movement in his *Elite Conflict in Plural Society : Twentieth Century Bengal*, 210-2.

No. 997 C., dated Midnapore, the 3rd November, 1921.

From—A. W. Cook, Esq., C.I.E., I.C.S., District Magistrate of Midnapore.

To—The Commissioner of Burdwan Division.

I have the honour to address you on the subject of the Union Board in this district and to forward herewith copies of a note prepared by Mr. S. N. Ray, I.C.S. (See Appendix II—B. B.) dealing immediately with the Union Board in Contai subdivision, together with a note by Mr. Birley in which he explains why he is forced to take up an attitude with regard to their retention, opposed to that he had adopted when he discussed the matter with you in Darjeeling.

2. Mr. Ray was deputed by me to make this enquiry in view of the fact that the Subdivisional Officers of Tamluk and Ghatal had already reported that the people in their subdivisions were watching what was being done in Contai. You are aware that in Contai the Union Board members had, in most Unions, refused to work and Tahsildars had to be appointed to collect the chaukidar's pay. It was found that very few people paid the tax preferring to hand over, of their own accord, utensils, etc., to the distraining officer. Mr. Ray's note shows how this state of affairs had arisen from a variety of causes. The principal cause was undoubtedly the unscrupulous propaganda carried on by the non-co-operation party headed by Mr. B. N. Sasmal.

3. Copies of reports from Subdivisional Officers, Tamluk, Ghatal and Sadar have been forwarded to you with my demi-official No. 989C., dated the 31st October 1921. I forward with a supplementary report from the Subdivisional Officer, Sadar, which shows that the Contai poison has spread to many Unions in the Sadar also and has effectively stopped the working of the Union Boards. The President and Vice-President of the Pingla Union, who had striven to carry on, have at length been overpowered by the social boycott that has been brought to bear on them and the loyalists in their Union. This is not the only place where loyalty has been made to suffer and

we are powerless to help. This report was received after Mr. Birley had written his note. After perusing it he was more than ever convinced that our position was untenable.

4. From all their reports, it is abundantly clear that it is impossible to work the Act in Contai. I have discussed the question with Mr. Birley, Additional District Magistrate, and Mr. Ray, and I see no way of avoiding the withdrawal of the Act. We are agreed that if it is withdrawn in Contai, it will be impossible to work it in any other Subdivision. A piecemeal withdrawal would be of no advantage. Mr. Birley in his note has embodied our proposals, on which I would ask that Government order may be obtained at as early a date as possible. To emphasize the necessity for early orders I submit copy of a confidential report received from Subdivisional Officer this morning. The reasons for this will appear from Mr. Ray's note. They are principally that it is all important to collect as much of the chaukidari tax under Act VI as we can before the end of the year stated briefly. Our proposal is that to each member of the Union Boards as they existed after being constituted a copy of draft notice to be approved by Government be sent, asking them if they wish to retain the Village Self-Government Act in their Union. Unless they reply within a certain date that they wish to retain the Act, silence will be taken to mean that they do not desire to retain it. The notice, a draft of which is included in Mr. Birley's note, gives a reasoned account of the Government position with regard to Union Boards and leaves the responsibility with the members and ultimately with the villagers who will, no doubt, be consulted of depriving themselves of an Act which undoubtedly would have made possible much improvement in their villages.

5. I regret that we should have had to come to this conclusion, but I think there is no help for it. We shall be in a much better position to meet civil disobedience if we withdraw now and let the villagers pay up their chaukidars' pay under Act VI than if we persist and stiffen the present opposition. I have no doubt whatsoever that but for the non-co-operation propaganda we should have succeeded in

getting the Boards to work. I admit that possibly we should
have been in a better position to meet this insidious attack,
if we had the groundwork more thoroughly done by Circle
Officers, as was the case in other districts. The local officers
are not to blame for the absence of this groundwork
as Contai was not supplied with a Circle Officer till July
1920 and then an officer was sent who had no experience
and was otherwise unfitted for the work. It is to be regretted
that one of the initial causes of failure should have arisen
from over-enthusiasm. I honestly believed that not only were
the people willing to have the Act, but were also willing to
pay something extra for the improvement of their villages, and
I am still of this belief.

I doubt whether the Act would have been successfully introduced in any district, whatever the preparation, had the same
venomous non-co-operation propaganda been rampant at the
time of introduction.

6. I would draw special attention to the end of Mr. Birley's
note and would ask that Government will arrange to have
printed 2,000 copies of the Bengali version of the draft notice
if Government accepts the prososal now put forward. These
should be sent to me as early a date as possible, so that
the notices can be sent out in time to get an answer by
30th November from any Union which wishes to retain the
Act.

7. One other point. I venture to draw your attention
to and that is the necessity for Government Orders as to
how to deal promptly with anyone who goes round preaching
civil disobedience in the form of non-payment of taxes, chaukidari or any other kind. Would it be fair to leave it to the
District Officer to decide that section 108, Criminal Procedure
Code, or 124A, Indian Penal Code, applied ? In such circums-
tance something must be done and at once.

[GB, Local Self-Government Department,
Local Self-Government (Local Boards)
Branch L. 2-U—5(1).]

## APPENDIX II

*Report by S. N. Ray, Esq., Joint Magistrate, dated the 1st November, 1921.*

DISTRICT MAGISTRATE—

I reached Contai on the afternoon of the 22nd October. The 23rd and 24th I spent at Contai looking up office papers and interviewing local gentlemen and officials. I have fairly full notes of my conversations with them and with members of Union Board, of which I can submit copies if required. On the 25th I left Contai with the Circle Officer, Mr. Norman Bose, for a tour in Ramnagar thana. On that date I visited Unions X, V and III (Kalindi, Islampur, Kantabani). I halted at Ramnagar for the night and on the 26th visited Union IX, VI and III (Ramnagar, Balishai, Depal) on my back to Contai. I met the Vice-President of Union No. VII at Kantabani, the President of Union II at the Ramnagar bungalow and the President and Secretary of Union I at Depal—Unions which I had intended to visit, but could not owing to inclement weather. At most of the places I went to, some villagers besides the President of the Union Board were present and I took the opportunity to explain the Act and combat misrepresentations. But all the members of the Boards which I visited did not turn up on the plausible pretext of bad weather. At Kalindi alone did all the members of the Board meet me. In Ramnagar thana therefore, I visited 6 out of 10 Unions and met the representatives of 3 of the 4 Unions I did not visit. In Contai where the people are most under the influence of the Congress party and where opposition has stiffened as a result of the attachment proceedings it was unnecessary to attempt to visit most of the Unions. It was more important to try to understand the attitude of mind of the educated people. On the 27th, therefore, I did not go out, but received some local gentlemen at the bungalow. On the 28th, I visited Unions I and II of Contai thana where I met the President of these Unions. I also visited Durmut hat where I met a member of Union No. I who has now resigned, viz., Babu Kali Charan

Maity, and the bazar people to whom I spoke about local
needs and Union Boards. In the afternoon of the same day
the members of the Contai Union Boards (all but two) came
to see me and Mr. Younie at the bungalow at our request.
On the 29th, I had a long talk with the editor of *Nihar*,
the more influential of the two local newspapers. The same
evening five members of the Namal Union Board (Union III,
Contai) came to discuss matters with us. On the 30th Mr.
Younie and I visited Union II where attachments had been
carried out and met the villagers who, we heard, had complaints
to make about the way in which they had been done. On
the 31st I returned to Midnapore.

2. When I went to Contai I had some hope of being
able to argue the villagers into a more reasonable frame of
mind. I soon found that hope to be illusory. The morning
after my arrival I went into the Contai bazar to find out
what the shop-keepers, who were used to a Union Committee
regime, thought about it. I soon had a crowd round me
vigorously showing their disapprobation of Union Boards.
They had not good crops for years, they could hardly afford
to pay for their food and clothing in the present state of
the market and now they were asked to pay more taxes.
It was all very well to say that it rested with them to decide
whether they should raise taxes or not, but the "Babus"
were going to raise it all the same—how else were they to
interpret the order of about a 50 per cent increase over previous
taxation ! The order might now have been revoked, but it
would be passed again as soon as opposition died down !
They were, therefore, not prepared to accept receipts under
the Village Self-Government Act, but they would gladly pay
up if the old system were restored and old receipts were given !

On people labouring under such fixed ideas argument is
thrown away. They have lost faith, they are panic-stricken
at the thought of fresh impositions. It was, therefore, useless
to attempt persuasion and I limited my enquiries to three
points and where possible tried to dispel mistaken impressions.
They were :—

(i) Had they understood the intention of the Act and the

benefits they would desire from it before it was introduced and had they consented to its introduction ?

(ii) What had they in their minds when they went to the plots to vote for the candidates ?

(iii) Have they understood the Act now and do they not want it ?

In Contai itself I spent some time trying to discover the cause of the gentry who obviously did either ask for the introduction of the Act or at any rate consent tacitly to its introduction.

3. To begin with, a brief statement is necessary of the steps taken to test local opinion before the Act was brought into force and the history of the growth of the opposition to it. In July 1919 (on 22nd July 1919 to be accurate) the Contai Local Board under the Chairmanship of Rai Bhupendra Nath Gupta Bahadur, the then Subdivisional Officer, recommended the introduction of the Act as an experimental measure in thana Contai only. A month later a requisition was received from 3 members, viz., Babus Ambica Charan Das, Biswanath Maity and Abanti Kumar Maity, for a special meeting to consider the extension of the Act throughout the subdivision. A special meeting was accordingly convened on the 31st August 1919 in which it was unanimously resolved to introduce the Act throughout the subdivision. It is not quite clear on what grounds the Local Board came to this momentous decision after their cautious recommendations of the previous month. The Subdivisional Officer (Mr. Dey) himself appears to have had some doubt about the wisdom of this recommendation, but was unable to make up his mind. In forwarding a copy of the resolution with his letter dated the 5th September 1919, he suggested in the first paragraph that as some of the Unions in Contai and Ramnagar were quite backward and might be slow to appreciate the benefits of the Act, it might be tried throughout the district (a somewhat inverted argument) and in the second that as Circle Officers were somewhat scarce and the District Board was likely to be parsimonious, it might be as well to apply the Act in selected areas. The original proposal of applying the Act to Contai and Ramnagar first

was, however, adhered to and on the 6th September 1919
the Subdivisional Officer in furtherance of the instruction of
Government that the views of villagers should be ascertained
and where this was not possible the conditions justifying the
extension of the Act stated, issued leaflets to thana officers
for distribution to panchayats describing the main provisions
of the Act and calling a meeting at Contai on the 14th
September. A meeting was duly held which was attended by
people variously estimated as between 1,000 and 2,000 people.
It appears that the advantages of having Union Boards were
carefully explained as was the necessity of increased taxation
if improvement were to be effected. But other subjects were
also discussed at the meeting, among them influenza, water-
hyacinth, cattle disease, co-operative credit, Bengalee regiment,
etc., and a second meeting was held immediately after to
consider the question of the establishment of a college. The
Subdivisional Officer was pleased with the meeting and drew
up his proposals which he sent to the District Officer. The
meeting or meetings were evidently a success, for soon after
two letters appeared in the *Nihar* enquiring whether the Act
was to be introduced in thanas Khedgree, Bahiri and Banideb-
pur and, if not, why not ? However that may be, between
this date, viz., the 14th September 1919 and January 1921,
when the elections were held, nothing more appears to have
been done by way of organized propaganda. There was no
Circle Officer till July or August 1920 and when he did come
his time was mainly taken up with flood relief. He must,
however, have done some amount of propaganda in the course
of his ordinary duties. The preparation of the voters' lists
was taken up in December 1920 when unfortunately elections
of the Legislative Council and Assembly were also taking place
and the result appears to have been that the villagers were
thoroughly mystified. Elections were literally showered upon
the villages and as one voter told me they thought that they
were electing their local officers who would take the place
of the "Hakims" and administer justice to them without the
intermediary of costly lawyers. The elections were held in
January 1921 and the Boards were constituted in April. Mean-

while in May 1920 the first Divisional Conference was held at the Howrah Town Hall under the presidency of Mr. J. N. Gupta at which a rough scale of self-taxation by Union Boards amounting to half the chaukidari tax in addition to that tax was resolved upon and a model budget adopted. In accordance with these resolutions, apparently, the Subdivisional Officer and the Circle Officer gave instructions to the Union Board members for the preparation of budgets under sections 37 (a) and (b), the amounts to be assessed under (b) to be half the sum assessed under (a). In accordance with a resolution of the same conference each Board allowed to appoint a Secretary on a salary varying from Rs. 10 to Rs. 15 per month and the Boards were asked to include the extra cost under sec. 37 (a). The villagers appear to have resented the extra imposition at once and the majority of the Boards were unable to make any headway with their budgets. When the present Circle Officer took over charge from his predecessor Babu Jitendriya Mukherjea some resignations had already taken place. He found that the proposal to raise the tax by 50 per cent. was being freely utilized by agitators and it was being given out that it was the intention of Government to raise the tax gradually to Rs. 84 in each case. The Circle Officer hastened to explain that his predecessor's suggestion was merely by way of advice and that they need not do more than provide for chaukidars and establishment under section 37 (a). It was, however, too late. B. N. Sasmal, who after standing as a candidate for the Bengal Legislative Council had turned non-co-operator and had unsuccessfully tried to form labour unions, was quick to seize the opportunity to appear in the role of a champion of the peoples' rights and their spokesman. Here was an admirable opportunity to form a combination to thwart Government and to strengthen his own influence. If he failed, it did not matter. If he succeeded, the possibilities were boundless. Once the mob had learnt to combine against Government, they might combine for civil disobedience also, while if he decided on resuming practice the lean months of non-co-operation would be more than amply compensated. A personal

antagonism to Mr. Dey lent additional zest to the undertaking
and Mr. Sasmal proceeded to misread carefully every section
of the Act and to misrepresent wilfully every intention of
Government.   Meetings were organized all over the two thanas,
with the help of Babus Pramatha Nath Banerjea and Satish
Chandra Jana, Mr. Sasmal himself paying special attention
to Contai where, with a splendid show of disinterestedness,
he invited the members of the Contai Union Board to prove
him wrong by public discussion—an invitation which the
members were foolish not to accept until too late.   This was
an act to which Lord Sinha stood sponsor.   Therefore it was
one of these insidious pills of the moderate party intended to
destroy the national peculiarities of the Indians, it was a
measure for turning the villages of Bengal into "Yorkshire
towns".   It was a measure not of Self-Government but of "self-
civilization" in the European sense.   Let not the people delude
themselves that they would have a free hand to settle their own
affairs.   Had not the higher powers dictated a 50 per cent.
increase ? The increase would go on and on untill it reached
the maximum of seven times the present figure.   It inevitably
must, for if they wanted to make improvements, if they wanted
to excavate tanks, be decided in what way buildings and huts
should be constructed, if they wanted to build privies, the money
must come from them.   If they say you need not tax yourself,
if you do not want to, even if this were *bonafide*, then as you
are too poor to pay more taxes for your own improvement the
Union Boards are useless.   They only saddle you with an extra
staff in the shape of a Secretary.   Therefore, beware, do not
pay any taxes except chaukidari taxes and that only under
a receipt under the Chaukidari Act.   The Village Self-Government Act is nothing but a fowlers' bait to inveigle the unsuspec-
ting cultivator into the meshes of ever-increasing taxation and
more in the same vein.   The subtlety of the whole campaign
lay in the fact the Sasmal as a lawyer was interpreting the
sections of the Act to them.   Those who had got vernacular
copies of the Act got them out, looked at section 29, at section
101 and were convinced that Sasmal was right and Sasmal
never failed to touch, like an endless refrain, on the fear of

taxation. By the middle of June the campaign had proved a great success, by the end of the month it had gained sufficient strength to resort to intimidation. On June 22nd the Circle Officer reported to the Subdivisional Officer that inflammatory posters threatening members with violence had been and were being displayed prominently in bazars and hats and even along public thoroughfares. Many of the Presidents had by then resigned. Several Vice-Presidents and a large number of members had also, through fear, resigned and the number was daily on the increase. The Subdivisional Officer and the Circle Officer then appear to have made some attempt at counter-propaganda, but without any success.

The result was that although it was possible with difficulty to rate up assessment lists from the Unions under section 37(a) it was not possible to get them signed by the members for many of them had by this time resigned. By August a complete dead-lock had ensued and Tahsildars had to be appointed under section 54(3) and appear to have adopted them under section 2. But no collection could be made. Attachment of the proper-ties of defaulters was, therefore, commenced from 22nd September and continued till 23rd October, during which period the properties of almost 400 defaulters in Contai thana were attached. There has been no attachment yet in Union Nos. VI and VII of Contai thana or in any of the Unions of Ramnagar thana. On a rough estimate the properties of 13,000 more men will have to be attached if this procedure is to continue. For the present under the verbal orders of the District Magistrate the attachment proceedings have been stayed.

4. I turn now to the points mentioned in paragraph 2 to which my enquires specifically related. I take them *seriatim* :—

(i) Wherever I went I was told that neither the members of the Union Board nor the villagers had understood what the introduction of the Act would, in actual practice, involve. I have reason to believe that some members of Union Boards in Contai thana have deliberately lied, because they have now either resigned or are not prepared to work, but I have no doubt that generally speaking this explanation is correct. The leaflets issued by the Subdivisional Officer in September 1919 through thana officers do not appear to have reached their destination in a very large number of cases and even where they did, the recipients either out of apathy or lack of understanding did not attempt either to discuss them with their co-villagers or to clear up their own doubts. The vernacular copies of the Act did not reach their hands till after the construction of Boards late in April or May this year. Some of the Union Board members complained that when they asked the late Circle Officer about the Act they were told to wait and find out from the vernacular copies. These were a long time coming. I cannot do better than quote from my note-book :—

"*26th October 1921*. Visited Kalindi (Union X, Ramnagar), all the members were present. Babu Mritunjoy Sasmal, the President, said emphatically that they knew nothing about the provisions of the Act before the Board was constituted. There was an idea that Union Boards meant settlement of their cases in their villages by village authorities and this the people were anxious to welcome. They had no idea whatever that Union Boards would involve the possibility of increased taxation. The people were poor and they were not prepared to have anything, however good, if they do not even understand the meaning of votes or election contests (the President incidentally did not himself understand what a contest meant). They were perfectly happy under the old Chaukidari Act. Let that be restored. The members had themselves only come to understand the Act after the Board was constituted. They realized that the intention of Government was good, but they could not make the people understand. The fact of the matter was that they themselves were not unselfish men, at least not all of them, and in some quarters there is the feeling that having got the power they would use them for their own ends. Attitude of all very respectful ; much impressed."

Or again, under same date.

"Union VIII (Alankarpur), police-station Ramnagar. Only the President and some villagers present. The President went to the Contai meeting of 1919, except that meeting nothing was done by way of propaganda. At the meeting the advantages of the Village Self-Government Act were explained, e.g., that the scarcity of water would be removed, civil and criminal jurisdiction would be given to the Boards, etc., but nothing was said as to how the cost would be met. They thought the District Board and Government would pay. Hence they agreed. Later when the people realized that they would have to pay increased taxes they made a dead set against it. The voters did not know what they were voting for. They were asked to vote and so they did. The only thing they now think is that the tax will be increased. The President himself is in favour of the Act, but the people do not understand. They have been told that their tax will be increased 12 times and they believe that even if no extra tax is imposed this year it will be imposed next year, either by the Board itself or by Government. If anything is said to contradict it, they say we are deceiving them.

These two quotations are typical of the rest which are practically variations on the same theme. To my mind there is little doubt that so far as the thanas are concerned, the majority had very vague ideas about Union Boards and those that came to the Contai meeting went away with their head full of village arbitration courts, water-supply, influenza cure and medical relief without a thought of how these were going to be effected. Nor is this to be wondered at in an area which is educationally backward and has never known either the President system or Union Committee system. The *bhadralogs* who comprised the local Board indeed unanimously asked for it, but they were probably an unsafe guide. But some even comparatively educated people apparently did not have any clear notion as will appear from the note of the statement of Nazimuddin Miah, a retired Nazir and Treasurer of the Contai subdivisional office and a member of the Namal Union Board (Union No. VII, Contai) :—

"Does not remember having seen any printed leaflet before the meeting of September 1919. At that meeting the question of Village Self-Government was first discussed and then the College. About 500 to 1,000 people were present. People came from all parts of the subdivision and not merely from thanas Contai and Ramnagar. They went back under the impression

that Self-Government meant that they would try their own
cases, and would be saved court-fee stamps and pleaders' costs.
Nothing was mentioned about taxation (the President, Saiyed
Inayat Buksh, interrupts and says that it was stated by the Sub-
Deputy Collector, Suresh Gupta, that the tax would be increas-
ed seven times)."

(ii)  This has already been answered in part. There was no
lack of candidates.  In a very large number of wards there
were contested elections, but the voters had no clear idea of
what they were voting for.  Two elections had already taken
place and this was another.  If there was any clear idea at all,
it was that they were electing men who could settle their village
disputes.  I may quote the statement of the President of Union
V, Ramnagar : 'The villagers now say that they were told that
they would get their disputes settled locally and these Boards
would be replicas of Legislative Councils. They were then
assessed heavily and on their protesing the extra assessment
was withdrawn—what guarantee is there that the tax will not
be increased later again ? They say how can we trust you ?'

(iii)  The result is that now all that they understand is that
Union Boards mean extra taxation and they will have none
of it.  Moreover, they have, during the last few months, heard
repeatedly of deficit and suspect that Government is out to
make good the deficit.  They are, therefore, not prepared to
accept the views of Government officer without question.  Mr.
Sasmal, on the other hand, is like the majority of them a
Mahishya, their own casteman who has renounced a lucrative
practice to serve them.  He has worked with them during the
last two floods, he does not appear to have any axe to grind.
They are, therefore, prepared to accept his interpretation of
what the Act really means than ours.'

5.  One might have reasonably expected that the educated
people of Contai would, at any rate, attempt to counteract the
poisonous propaganda started by Mr. Sasmal. They must have
formed the majority of those who wanted Union Boards. They
have had an Union Committee working at Contai for years.
They know the advantages of self-taxation.  It is not easy to
discover why this expectation has not been fulfilled.  I am

inclined to ascribe it mainly to the rivalry of two sections of the educated community, one consisting of the local residents and the other of people from other districts who have established a practice in the Contai courts or have flourished in other spheres. The *Nihar*, which is edited by Madhusudan Jana, a local man, is the organ of the first party. The paper has been in existence for over 20 years and commands a large circulation. In 1919 it saw in favour of Union Boards and published the proceedings of the September meeting of that year. During 1920 only two articles on Union Boards appeared in the paper which goes to show that the subject was not exciting much public interest. In January this year it voiced the fear of excessive taxation and complained that sufficient attention had not been paid to preparing the ground. Again in February, in commenting on the elections, it declared that the men who had been elected were not of the right type and if the Government nominees were equally bad, the Village Self-Government Act would be a dead failure. There is only one article in March, but from the middle of May there is hardly an issue which does not contain something about Union Boards. The paper was content, however, to publish reports of the meetings and letters of correspondents both for and against Union Boards though the latter were the larger in number, without giving a definite lead. The Council elections of December have introduced complications. A gentleman by the name of Asoke Dutt stood as a candidate from Contai. He was regarded as an outsider and interloper and a rumour was spread to the effect that he had said that the Mahishyas understood nothing and were, therefore, gullible and he would have no difficulty in persuading them of his fitness to represent them. This gave umbrage to the Mahishya community who at once proceeded to denounce him, but his cause was espoused by Babu Nagendra Chandra Bakshi who himself, I understand, is a Contai man but is a *persona grata* amongst the foreign settlers. The *Nihar* opposed Mr. Dutt's candidature. It was rumoured, however, that Mr. Dey, the Subdivisional Officer, was interested in Mr. Dutt owing to the fact that he was a relation by marriage and the *Nihar* imagined that it had incurred his displeasure on that account. I have already mentioned the personal antagonism between Mr. Sasmal and Mr. Dey into the reasons of which it is not necessary to enter here. It required very little therefore to bring Mr. Sasmal and the *Nihar* together. They were probably already in sympathy, but the action of the authorities about the middle of August in withholding their certificate notices and sale notices from this paper accomplished this effectively. Mr. Sasmal at once held this up as an instance of Government tyranny and of its attempt to suppress free discussion and appealed to the people to support the paper by increasing its circulation. The situation was rendered worse by the advertisements being given to the *Hijli Hitaishi*, a newspaper started in May last and the organ of the foreigners headed by Babu Nagendra Nath Bakshi, the Chairman of the Contai Union Board. The split was thus complete. The *Nihar* had now a grudge not only against the party of Babu Nagendra Nath Bakshi but against Government. The editor of the *Nihar* offered to show that he had never written any article against Government. He had published letters opposing Union Boards, but as a journalist it was his business to allow his paper to be made use of for free discussion. He had never refused articles in favour of Union Boards. I have gone through the articles in the paper and am inclined to think that the matter was one for tactful handling and not for drastic action.

6. However that may be, the question now is whether in the circumstances described above it is either possible or politic to enforce Union Boards in Contai subdivision. I think there can only be an answer, viz., that it is neither possible without an enormous staff nor politic. I would go further and say that even if it were possible, it would not be politic. The attitude of the people throughout was very respectful. They were anxious and lay their grievances before me. Even Babu Tarak Nath Pal of Darua, who has now assumed the role of a village Hampden (he was a member of the Union Board) and presided at the monster meeting of the 28th October in Khaddar turned out with all the villagers to lay their grievances before me. But there is beneath it all a stubbornness which is unusual and which springs from the

belief, however it might have been inspired, that these Boards mean extra taxation which they are not prepared to pay. I believe as do all the local officers that the experience of the Unions in which distraint has already been carried out will be repeated in the remaining Unions, viz., that taxes will not be paid, goods will have to be taken, sometimes under painful circumstances, but there will be no one to buy them and the alleged harsh treatment which cannot altogether be avoided will be made immense capital out of. It is already being widely asked why, if the Village Self-Government Act is a measure of Self-Government to be granted only if the people want it, is Government so anxious to enforce it in the face of the unmistakable determination of the majority of the people not to have it ? The people, though they are now under Sasmal's influence, are not non-co-operators. They ask why it is that their representations to the District Magistrate, the Commissioner, His Excellency the Governor have not borne fruit, but they have not lost faith yet that the higher authorities will enquire and remove what they feel to be a grievance. Wherever I have been they have promised to pay chaukidari taxes if the old receipts are granted. I think to delay longer would be to throw these people into the arms of the non-co-operators altogether. There are people who are eagerly waiting for a chance to begin civil disobedience. If we delay in withdrawing the Act it will give them the chance. The mob has been quick to realize that distraint has not been as easy as Government expected it to be. It will be easy in the present state of their mind to raise successfully the cry of "No chaukidari taxes". Moreover, even legally I think our position is weak. Initially it was a mistake to ask them to prepare a budget under sections 37 (a) and (b). Under the assessment rules the budget has to be prepared $2\frac{1}{2}$ months before the new year. Before the mistake was noticed and the Boards asked to assess only under section 37(a) many of the members had resigned and even that assessment has not been signed by all the members. The Tahsildars were appointed under section 54 and they have adopted under section 2 the rate which was in force "in such area".

The boundaries of the existing Union Boards, however, are not coterminous with the boundaries of the Chaukidari Unions which have been superseded. There were in the two thanas 29 Chaukidari Unions. These have been formed into 22 Union Board areas. Does section 2 apply in such cases? I doubt it. The difficulty might probably be got over by having one Tahsildar for each thana. Even so, we should, I think, be going against the spirit of the Act in proceeding in this manner. This would normally be a clear case for a withdrawal of the notifications under section 1(3).

The difficulty is that withdrawal now does mean a loss of prestige to Government, for the Sasmal party would make it out to be a victory of their agitation and what is worse it means an enormous gain in prestige to Sasmal and his party. It might mean also a set-back to village Self-Government not only in other parts of this district, but in other districts also. Babu Bishnupada Chatterjea, a pleader at Contai, who is a resident of Howrah district, told me that in Howrah they are enquiring what is happenning in Contai. It is not unlikely that an agitation may be started in that and other districts. I believe the matter is under the consideration of the Provincial Congress Committee despite their resolution of February last in which they recommend co-operation in regard to local self-governing institution.

Nevertheless we must face it, for I firmly believe that there are stormy times ahead and it is of the utmost importance that we should choose our ground carefully before that time comes. The Congress have promised Swaraj by the 1st January. They must, therefore, either go in for civil disobedience or cease to exist. There is at any rate one party who are going to do their level best to carry that resolution. If they succeed, they will inevitably attack the chaukidari tax. Seeds have already been sown in Contai with which I am at the moment concerned, and it is not unlikely that Mr. Sasmal will attempt to utilize the influence he has gained to prevent chaukidari taxes being paid. It will take some time and Government must decide what they should do in such a contingency. If he is allowed a free hand he may achieve success.   If, however, the Act is withdrawn at once and the present willingness of the people to pay chaukidari taxes is utilized to secure realization fully or in part before the end of December, we shall have gained a march over Mr. Sasmal.

The only alternative to complete withdrawal is to withdraw it from part of the two thanas.   This is a cause which I would not willingly recommend in these times.   It is not at all unlikely that appeal will be made to the newly acquired feeling of solidarity and cohesion to secure withdrawal from such Unions, also by getting the people of neghbouring Unions to refuse payment until the Act is completely withdrawn.   This would be a situation which may mean piecemeal defeats and, therefore, greater loss of prestige.

I would add that if withdrawal is decided upon so far as Contai is concerned, this is the most opportune time.   A new Subdivisional Officer has taken charge, the District Magistrate has recently been there and during my tours I have tried to make it clear that if they do not really want the Board the loss will be theirs and not Government's and that Government would probably in such circumstances not want to force them on them.

[GB,  Local Self-Government Department. Local Self-Government (Local Boards) Branch. L. 2-U—5(1), A 36-43, July 1922. ]

APPENDIX III

*Extract from the report of J. Younie, Esq., Subdivisional Officer, Contai, dated the 2nd November, 1921.*

Anti-Union Board feeling has been intensified during the past week by the visit of Mr. Sasmal, accompanied by Babu Ramesh Chandra Sen Gupta, a relative of Jogendra Sen Gupta of Chittagong.  A meeting was held on Tuesday, the

29th October, but the attendance was small and the speakers confined themselves to semi-religious effusions
on the present deplorable state of the country. On Friday the Union Board question was discussed at length in an enormous meeting held on Darua Maidan. Estimates of the size of the crowd vary from 10,000 to 50,000. All the old arguments were reproduced and the crowd was asked whether they were willing to pay chaukidari taxes if the Village Self-Government Act were withdrawn. The answer was enthusiastically in the affirmative. A warning, however, was thrown out by Mr. Sasmal to the effect that there was a limit to their patience and that if Government did not speedily listen to the united voice of the people, the question of paying even chaukidari taxes would be seriously considered.

*Incidents of political importance and general political outlook and any other matter of importance (worth mentioning)*

This morning we heard at length Mr. S. N. Ray's account of his enquiry at Contai. I was impressed by the thoroughness of his enquiry and the soundness of his opinions. His conclusion that it is impracticable to keep the Village Self-Government Act in force in the 22 Unions of Contai subdivision in which it has been introduced is unanswerable and I fully accept it.

The next point is that if we withdraw the Act in Contai, we must do the same in all the 227 Unions in the district unless any of them will now give us a definite declaration that they want the Act and though some of them do want it, none of them will say so. We have recently had very unfavourable reports from Ghatal and Tamluk. The position in the Sadar subdivision is clearly much better than that in Ghatal or Tamluk, but in Midnapore and Keshpur thanas of the Sadar subdivision, the two thanas in which I have seen a good deal and in which the Unions are better than elsewhere, it is quite certain that after withdrawal in Contai we cannot succeed. Therefore though I have no first-hand knowledge about Ghatal and Tamluk, there is no use in my waiting until I can get it, because they are known to be worse than the Sadar subdivision. We all agree that withdrawal in Contai means withdrawal all round and it would be intolerable to wait until we are gradually defeated everywhere.

The next point is whether we shall, after withdrawing the Village Self-Government Act, find it any easier to collect the chaukidar's pay under the Chaukidari Act.   There is reason to believe that  sooner or later we  shall have opposition to that, but on the whole the  indications are that, provided that we begin to  collect  under  the  Chaukidari  Act  before civil disobedience  becomes the  declared policy of the  Congress, we shall probably be successful.  We shall have the advantage of  beginning  at  a  time  when  the  price  of  rice  is falling rapidly  and  an  excellent  harvest  is  being  reaped.   But  it  is essential  that  we  should  be  able  to  begin  not  later  than December 1st.

The next point is what  will be the  effect on other  districts. We  must  leave  this  for  Government  to  judge.   It  will  un-doubtedly  be  bad,  but  it will not  be  worse than that of failure here later on which  be certain.

The next point is  that this  defeat  should  be  acknowledged in the manner which will do  least harm.   The  following points are  essential :—

(1)   It must be made  clear that  Government are  acting on the advice of the District Officer.

(2)   It must be  made clear that  Government  are accepting the wishes of the people.

(3)   An  opportunity  must  be  offered  (though  it will not be taken)  to the  members of any Union Board to say that they wish to go on.

(4)   It must be announced  that the people have been misled by false statements of the non-co-operators.

If  it is done in this  way we shall,  as  far as  possible,  save ourselves  from  the  accusation  of  deserting  those  who  have supported us and we shall  gain a great advantage  in getting in the first word by declaring that the  non-co-operators  have lied to the people, before the  non-co-operators  begin  to  crow over their success.

With  these objects  in view  I attach a draft  which I suggest should  be  translated  into Bengali and  issued  in  print  to  every member of every  Union  Board  in  the  District  by  post after being approved by Government.

In October I expressed a very decided opinion at Darjeeling to His Excellency, to the Hon'ble Minister in charge of Local Self-Government and to the Commissioner, that we should not give in. I owe some explanation for this sudden change of opinion, which is based entirely on my acceptance of Mr. Ray's views about Contai.

Between September 3 and October 2, I visited 14 Unions, all in the Sadar subdivision, 7 in Midnapore thana, 4 in Keshpur thana, 2 in Dantan thana and 1 in Pingla thana. Some of them were in a very bad state, but I was confident then and I am confident now that they could be induced to work in Midnapore and Kespur thanas and from what I heard from the Circle Officers of Dantan and Pingla-Sabang Circle I think that the Boards in these Circles could be induced to work. But they could not stand the effects of successful opposition elsewhere. The bad Unions in Keshpur thana are those in the borders of the Ghatal subdivision and the bad Unions in Dantan thana are those on the borders of Contai subdivision. Successful opposition is very contagious. I had not realized that the opposition in Contai had gone as far as Mr. Ray reports, i.e., that the people refuse to listen to a true description of the meaning of the Act.

The causes of this failure are perfectly clear. They are :—

(1) In spite of the recommendations of the Local Boards, the Act should not have been so widely introduced until Circle Officers had been in the district long enough to get the chaukidari assessments fairly made, revise the personnel of the panchayats, get the confidence of the people and explain the principles of the Act.

(2) When it was introduced the Circle Officers, as the result of a conference held at Howrah in May 1920, began by giving orders to increase taxation by 50 per cent. This was contrary to the intention of the Act and was the first cause of trouble. The proceedings of this conference were communicated by the Commissioner direct to Circle Officers.

(3) The Subdivisional Officer of Contai aroused the personal animosity of Mr. Sasmal by tactless and mistaken

action. Personal animosity is generally at the bottom of movements like this.

(4) When the trouble arose the unmanageable size of the district made it impossible to give sufficient attention to it. As long as there are districts of the unmanageable size of Midnapore the administration will continue to break down when something unusual occurs, for the simple reason that a man who already has more to do than any man can do is unable to do still more.

Finally, I think it is essential to decide now that when the Chaukidari Act has been restored the first man who openly incites people not to pay the chaukidari tax should be prosecuted immediately under section 108, Criminal Procedure Code or Section 124A, Indian Penal Code. If this is done, the opposition will probably be short-lived. The continual public meetings at which false information about the Village Self-Government Act is disseminated have been the principal means of organizing opposition to the Union Boards and it is not possible to find people to attend these meetings and contradict the false statements.

## Mr. Birley's draft notice to members of Union Boards

The Bengal Village Self-Government Act was passed in April 1919 and since then it has been introduced in ... Unions in ... districts of Bengal. In Midnapore district it was introduced in 1921 in 227 Unions. The Act was passed in response to a demand widely expressed in Bengal for better facilities for the inhabitants of villages to manage their own affairs and to improve the condition of their villages. It makes taxation for payment of the chaukidars compulsory as before and it allows taxation for other purposes at the option of two-thirds majority of the members of the Union Board, a majority of whom are elected. Government declare that they have no intention directly or indirectly of compelling Union Boards to impose taxation for purposes of village improvement. Possibly many Union Boards will not at first impose such taxation. But it is hoped that some Union Boards will do so, and that others will gradually follow their example seeing the beneficial results.

The decision to impose such extra taxation or not will rest absolutely with the members of the Union Boards as is provided by law. Government have been informed that in most districts, in which the Act has been introduced, it has been welcomed by the people. In Midnapore district, though public opinion was consulted before introduction of the Act, and was favourable, there is now opposition.

Government have definite information that the opposition to the Act in Midnapore district is largely based on false and distorted statements about the contents and purpose of the Act which have been maliciously spread by ill-disposed persons. It has been stated that the maximum tax of Rs. 84 will be imposed on well-to-do persons, that the rate-payers will have to pay the salaries of Circle Officers, the Presidents will have their property attached if the taxes are not realized and that innocent members will be held liable for defalcations of Presidents or Secretaries. All these statements are false. People have also been misled into the belief that the provisions of the Act, which are intended for small towns, will be made use of indiscriminately in rural villages. For example in some villages people have been wrongly induced to believe that all householders will be compelled to build privies. Every device has been used for deterring the people from taking advantage of an Act which is only intended to give them the opportunity of improving the condition of their villages in a reasonable and practical manner.

Government greatly regret to learn of this mistaken opposition in Midnapore district, and they realize that the withdrawal of the Act from any Union in which it is now in force will mean the withdrawal from the people of the opportunity for more extensive management of their own affairs and the postponement of the improvement of their villages.

Nevertheless this Act is solely meant for the benefit of the villages to which it is extended and if the people of all classes oppose it even on mistaken grounds it is clear that the Act cannot be beneficial.

Government, therefore, acting on the advice of the District Magistrate, have decided to withdraw the Act from every

Union in Midnapore District except those in which a majority of the members of the Union Board expressly state their desire for the retention of the Act. This letter is being addressed to every member of a Union Board in Midnapore District with the intention that such members shall inform the District Magistrate in writing not later than November 30th whether they now wish that the Bengal Village Self-Government Act shall remain in force in their Unions. On receipt of these reports, Government will declare the Act to be no longer in force in those Unions in which a majority of the members do not desire it to remain in force. The effect of such declaration will be to re-enact the Chaukidari Act, and to renew the liability to pay the old Chaukidari tax, and as in many Unions the pay of the chaukidars is in arrears it will be essential that their pay shall be collected speedily. In Unions in which no new assessment has been made the Chaukidari assessment of the preceding year will be in force until it is revised. In Unions in which a new assessment has been made under section 37 of the Village Self-Government Act, that assessment will be in force until a new assessment has been made.

If no reply to this notice is received by the 30th November, the District Magistrate will assume that you wish the Village Self-Government Act to be withdrawn from your Union. If you wish that Act to be retained you should please inform the District Magistrate immediately to that effect.

> [GB, Local Self-Government Department,
> Local Self-Government (Local Boards)
> Branch, L. 2-U—5(1), A 36-43, July 1922.]

## Appendix IVA

No. 6489 J. M., dated Midnapore, the 13th December, 1921.
From—L. BIRLEY, ESQ., I.C.S., Additional District Magistrate of Midnapore.
To—The Secretary to the Government of Bengal, Local Self-Government Department.

I have the honour to report that in the manner approved by Government a letter was addressed to every member of the 227

Union Boards in Midnapore district inviting them to inform the District Magistrate by the 12th December whether they wished the Bengal Village Self-Government Act to remain in force in their Unions.

2. The replies received up to December 12th, though 16 of them express a desire to retain the Act and many others express favourable opinions of the Act, do not, in the case of any Union in the district, show a majority of members in favour of retention of the Act.

3. In these circumstances I request that orders may be issued as early as possible withdrawing the Act from every Union. It will be convenient if the order of Government be communicated to me by telegram, as it is important that no time should be lost in appointing members of the Panchayat under the Chaukidari Act.

4. I will submit hereafter some observations on the opinions expressed in the replies received.

[GB, Local Self-Government Department,
Local     Self-Government     (Local Boards)
Branch, L. 2-U—5(2), A  44, July 1922.]

### Appendix IVB

No. 6635 J. M., dated Midnapore, the 19th December 1921.
From—L. BIRLEY, ESQ., C.I.E., I.C.S., Additional District
Magistrate of Midnapore.
To—The Secretary to the Government of Bengal, Local
Self-Government Department.

I have the honour to refer to my letter No. 6489 J. M., dated the 13th December 1921 and subsequent correspondence on the subject of withdrawal of the Bengal Village Self-Government Act from Midnapore district.

2. The members of Union Boards were directed to inform the District Magistrate by December 12th if they wished the Act to remain in force.

3. The Gopalnagar Union Board in Panskura thana has 4 elected and 2 appointed members. Three of the elected members and the 2 appointed members (amongst whom was the

President, who is an elected member) addressed the District Magistrate in letters, dated the 11th December, in which they stated without any reservation their desire that the Act should be retained in their Union. The letters were all put in one envelope and were addressed to Mr. Cook by name. He was on tour and the letter was forwarded to him unopened and he received it on December 16th, when I sent a telegram to you.

4. It appears, therefore, that the Gopalnagar Union Board complies with the conditions laid down for the retention of the Act, and Mr. Cook is strongly in favour of retaining the Act in that Union. I request that no notification may be issued withdrawing the Act from that Union.

5. I have not yet received the order withdrawing the Act from the remainder of the district, but, in view of your last telegram, I am instructing Subdivisional Officers to appoint panchayats under the Chaukidari Act for all Unions other than Gopalnagar.

> [GB, Local Self-Government Department, Local Self-Government (Local Boards) Branch, L. 2-U—5(A), A 45, July 1922.]

## Appendix IVC

No. 5025 L.S.-G., dated Calcutta, the 17th December, 1921. Notification by—The Government of Bengal, Local Self-Government Department.

In exercise of the power conferred by sub-section (3) of section 1 of the Bengal Village Self-Government Act, 1919 (Bengal Act V of 1919), the Government of Bengal (Ministry of Local Self-Government) are pleased to withdraw the said Act from the district of Midnapore save and except from the area under the jurisdiction of the Gopalnagar Union Board in the Panskura thana of the district.

The Hon'ble Sir Surendranath Banerjea, Kt., Minister-in-charge

2. The following notifications, except so far as they relate to the area under the jurisdiction of the Gopalnagar Union Board, are hereby cancelled.

(1) Notification No. 1582 L. S.—G., dated the 17th

May 1920, extending the said Act to the district of Midnapore ;
and

(2) Notifications No. 1584-1587 L. S. – G., dated the
17th May 1920, and No. 2281 L. S.—G., dated the 5th August
1920, declaring certain local areas to be Union and constituting Union Boards for those areas.

No. 5026 L.S.—G., dated Calcutta, the 20th December 1921.
Memo. by G. C. SEN ESQ., Assistant Secretary to the
Government of Bengal, Local Self-Government Department.

Copy forwarded to the Commissioner of the Burdwan
Division for information, with the request that
the notification may be translated into the
vernacular and published as widely as possibe
within the district.

The Hon'ble
Sir Surendranath
Banerjea, Kt.,
Minister-in-
charge.

[GB, Local Self-Government Department,
Local Self-Government (Local Boards)
Branch, L. 2-U—5(3), A 44½, July 1922]


APPENDIX IVD

No. 7337 J. M., dated Midnapore, the 31st January 1922.
From—The District Magistrate of Midnapore
To—The Secretary to the Government of Bengal, Local
Self-Government Department.

With reference to Government order No. 5025 L.S.-G.,
dated the 17th December 1921, withdrawing the Village Self-
Government Act (Bengal Act V of 1919) from this district
save and except from the area under the jurisdiction of the
Gopalnagar Union Board in the Panskura thana of this district,
I have the honour to state as follows.

2. Since the order of withdrawal of the Union Boards
was known to the people of the Gopalnagar Union, they
have sent in representations to me, some asking for retention
of the Act, while others are for withdrawal of the Union
Board. I had the matter enquired into by the Subdivisional
Officer, Tamluk, whose report is enclosed herewith. In view
of the Subdivisional Officer's report, no useful purpose will

be served by retaining the Act in the Gopalnagar Union any longer.

3. In these circumstances, I request that orders may be issued as early as possible withdrawing the Act from the Gopalnagar Union and notification No. 1587 L.S.-G., dated the 17th May 1920.

No. 2733, dated Tamluk, the 23rd January 1925.
From—The Subdivisional Officer, Tamluk,
To—The District Magistrate of Midnapore.

With reference to your No. 1313 C., dated the 21st instant, endorsed on the petition of Satish Chandra Banerji and others of Gopalnagar in Union No. 37, in police-station Panskura, and in continuation of this office letter No. 2688, dated the 19th January 1922, I have the honour to report that the President of the Union Board of the said Union in his letter of yesterday informs this office that it will be impossible to carry on the Union Board there on account of increasing opposition to it by the public. I, therefore, request that Government may be pleased to withdraw the Union Board from Gopalnagar and reintroduce the Chaukidari Act there as early as possible. Your No. 6784 J. M., dated the 3rd January 1922, and No. 1313 C., dated the 21st January 1922, with copy of the letter of President, dated the 22nd January 1922, and enclosures, viz., three petitions, are returned herewith.

[GB, Local Self-Government Department, Local Self-Government (Local Boards) Branch, L.2-U 5(6), A 47-48, July 1922]

APPENDIX IVE

No. 1160 L.S.—G., dated Calcutta, the 1st March 1922.
Notification by—The Government of Bengal, Local Self-Government Department.
In exercise of the power conferred by sub-section (3) of

section 1 of the Bengal Village Self-Government Act, 1919 (Bengal Act V of 1919), the Government of

The Hon'ble Sir Surendra Nath Banerjea, Kt., Minister-in-charge

Bengal (Ministry of Local Self-Government) are pleased to withdraw the said Act from the area under the jurisdiction of the Gopalnagar Board in the Panskura thana of the Midnapore district.

2. The following notifications, so far as they relate to the area under the jurisdiction of the Gopalnagar Union Board, are hereby cancelled :

(i) Notification No. 1582 L.S.—G., dated the 17th May 1920 extending the said Act to the district of Midnapore ; and

(ii) Notification No. 1587 L.S.—G., dated the 17th May 1920 declaring certain areas in the Tamluk subdivision of the district of Midnapore to be Unions and constituting Union Board for those areas.

[GB, Local Self-Government Department, Local Self-Government (Local Boards) Branch, L. 2-U—5(7), A 49, July 1922]

CHAPTER III

# BANDABILA UNION BOARD BOYCOTT MOVEMENT

## I

AFTER THE CONGRESS decision to suspend the mass civil disobedience campaign in February 1922[1] there followed a temporary lull in the anti-imperialist movement in India which
continued till 1926. Nevertheless, it was a period of critical
assimilation of the experiences gathered during the first real
mass upsurge of the national liberation movement and of
preparing for the next stage. The changes that occurred in
the political situation of India during the period of lull made
themselves felt in 1927 when the masses of people started
moving again. A new awakening began in India in 1928-29
which was precipitated by the great revolutionary advance
made by the colonial and dependent countries of the East
in their struggle for emancipation, particularly by the revolutionary events in China and by increasing familiarity with
and growing interest in the Soviet Union. The despatch of
the Simon Commission angered the people of India and roused
anti-imperialist feeling among them. The National Congress,
particularly the left wing of it led by Jawaharlal Nehru and
Subhas Chandra Bose, began to favour active struggle against
imperialism and stood for complete independence. The new
leftward tendencies of a section of the Indian national bour-
geoisie and petty-bourgeoisie represented by Nehru and Bose
were clearly demonstrated in Madras Session in December
1927. The mass unrest during this period against the British
colonial rulers was not merely confined to the big cities and
industrial centres which organized huge demonstrations and
massive strikes against the Simon Commission. It also spilled
over to the remote villages of India. At Bardoli a no-tax
campaign, originating at the end of 1927 in the spontaneous
expression of peasants' grievances, took an organized form
in the beginning of 1928.[2] About the same time Bandabila,
a small village on the river Chitra about 10/12 miles from

the town of Jessore, staged a unique anti-union-board movement in the form of election boycott and no-tax campaign
with amazing skill and maturity and left its mark on the
history of national struggle for independence.[3]

## II

Before looking at the different phases of development of
the Bandabila Union Board Boycott Movement, it would be
worthwhile to discuss in brief the causes and issues involved
in the movement. Since we have made a detailed discussion
of the defects of the Bengal Village Self-Government Act 1919
in the chapter on Contai Union Board Boycott Movement
it would hardly be necessary to repeat them once again.
Broadly speaking, the causes and issues behind this movement were more or less similar to those of the earlier one,
since both were aimed against the same Act and the same
kind of institution.

The main cause of people's agitation was the fear of heavy
taxation at an enhanced rate under the B.V.S.G. Act. They
felt that when the Palli Samskar Samiti[4] had been carrying
on necessary municipal activities, the setting up of the union
boards was wholly unnecessary. Though on paper the para-
mount objective of the union board had been to train the
people in the art of self-government, it, in fact, contributed
much to promote party-strife in the villages and to educate
them in cliquism. In many places it had become the choicest
instrument in the hands of the British agents for causing
disaffection against national leaders and for creating dissension
among the people engaged in the struggle for national independence. Making the union board issue one of the planks for
a fresh movement against the foreign movement, the local
leaders thought it the opportune moment and right occasion
to cement the rift between Bose and Sen Gupta groups.[5] Further
they realized that the village reconstruction activities by the
Palli Samskar Samiti alone could not help the people to shake
off the imperialist stranglehold.[6] In order to awaken people's
consciousness and tone up their fighting morale, the leaders
plunged headlong into the union board boycott movement.

They seized the occasion to inspire the illiterate rural masses with confidence in their capacity to contribute to the impending struggle for independence.

## III

Perhaps, towards the close of 1927 or beginning of 1928,[7] the Government decided to establish a union board at Bandabila, and accordingly, issued a notice calling for the submission of nomination papers for the election of members to the union board.[8]

The organizers and leaders of the Bandabila Palli Samskar Samiti and of the Congress Committee reacted very sharply to the Government decision. They began to ascertain the opinion of the people in general of Bandabila about the imminent introduction of union board in place of *panchayats*. Soon they realized that the people were in a mood to oppose any move by the Government to establish a union board at Bandabila. Bijoy Chandra Roy went to Calcutta and discussed the matter with Subhas Chandra Bose and Jnananjan Niyogi. On his proposing to start a movement at Bandabila against the union board, both Subhas Chandra Bose and Jnananjan Niyogi inquired of him if the Hindus and the Muslims would unitedly join the movement. His answer was in the affirmative and he requested them to visit the place and satisfy themselves in regard to the possibility of starting the movement. On his return the local leaders, acting on the advice of Subhas Chandra Bose, began to intensify their organizational activities. They tried to dissuade the people from submitting any nomination paper. But the then *panchayat* president, Haridas Gangopadhyay, through his ceaseless efforts, got six nomination papers filed. As soon as the local leaders came to know of it, they also arranged six nominations to be filed, and started propaganda against the Government-sponsored candidates.[9]

It has been maintained that the conflict between the Government and the people of Bandabila began in the later part of 1928 on the issue of election of the union board.[10] During the first election the building of a minor school at Bandabila

was selected as the polling station. Near the school some
police camps were set up. The police officers accompanied by
several constables patrolled the villages within the Bandabila
union and began to intimidate the rural masses. They were
reported to have said that unwilling voters would be compelled to attend the polling centre and cast their votes. On
the other hand, the voters in a body decided to abstain from
casting votes. On the appointed day of election they assembled
at the local Congress Office, instead of going straight to the
polling station. At about 3 p.m. it was learnt that only 36
votes had been polled. 36 votes being less than 10 per cent
of the total number of votes, no candidate could be elected
that time. Then the people, assembled at the Congress office,
went out in a procession to the polling centre and there they
asked the Circle Officer about the result of the election. In
reply the latter said that since 10 per cent. votes had not been
polled, no candidate could be declared elected. Highly exasperated, the *panchayat* president, Haridas Gangopadhyay,
announced that a fresh election would be held within a month
and dared the leaders of the boycott movement to interfere
with it and stop it.[11]

The Government, having failed to get its candidates elected
in the first election, fixed the date for the next. This time
the polling centre was not set up at Bandabila ; the venue
selected was a school premises near Khajura bazar, three
miles away from Bandabila, where a very big *hat* used to sit.
The date for the second election was a *hat* day. The leaders
of the election boycott movement exhorted the people of Bandabila to rise to the occasion. They all decided to boycott
the election this time too. The Government deployed huge
armed forces in the surrounding areas. The *chaukidars* and
*dafadars* numbering approximately 200 were posted near the
polling booth. Some leading organizers of the movement were,
on the other hand, directed by the boycott committee to
remain present at the *hat* on the day of election and to see
to it that no violent incident occurred by reason of any provocation by the armed forces. The polling agents of the boycotters took their seats beside the polling officers to count

the number of votes being polled. In the afternoon it was made public that not a single vote had been cast.[12]

## IV

In the foregoing paragraphs we have discussed the initial stage of the movement which may be called the election boycott stage. As regards the next higher phase we shall arrange the principal facts of the movement chronologically and call it the union board boycott stage, though, in reality, it took various forms and different dimensions during its long course. Thereafter we would discuss the organizational and leadership aspects, narrate the various measures resorted to by the Government and, side by side, describe people's reaction to the same.

The Government, after its failure to hold elections for the Bandabila Union Board, formed a 'sham' union board with nine nominated members, four from the Muslim community and five from the Hindu. And Haridas Gangopadhyay was selected its president.[13]

Within a short time it was found that most of the nominated members had remained aloof from the union board. A large number of *dafadars* and *chaukidars* had refused to do their routine job and returned their uniform and equipment out of fear of social boycott by the local people. The tax-collector also had tendered his resignation. Of course, the Government authorities threatened them in many ways but in vain. Finding no other way, they appointed two members of Kazi family *dafadars* and another the tax-collector. They also posted some Hindu and Muslim Circle Officers at Bandabila and engaged them in a propaganda campaign in favour of the newly established union board. They tried to coerce the people to work for them. They also endeavoured to win their support for tax-collection through false propaganda. In all these activities they were aided by the members of the District Board and the President of the Union Board.[14]

The people, on the other hand, started expressing their grievances against the nominated members in the form of social boycott, ex-communication and peaceful non-co-operation. When the situation had turned that way in July 1919, the District Congress appointed, in accordance with the resolution of the last District Conference on the Bandabila Union Board issue, an enquiry committee[15] to investigate the matter and report after an extensive tour in the villages within the Bandabila Union on the feasibility of no-tax compaign against the Union Board. At the end of July 1929 the members of the Congress Enquiry Committee came to Bandabila, talked to the inhabitants of different villages and brought home to them the various problems which might arise during the no-tax campaign. They understood from their interviews with the villagers that they were ready to resist the unwanted union board even in the face of all sorts of repression.[16]

Throughout the month of July the local organizers of the movement were reported to have been busy with preparatory activities regarding the no-tax campaign. Demonstrations were taken out and meetings, sometimes with the help of magic lanterns, were held and important provincial leaders came to investigate the local situation and to supervise organizational preparations.[17]

The next two months also witnessed hectic activities on the parts of both the boycotters and the Government authorities. Prominent leaders from Calcutta and other places visited Bandabila and undertook an on-the-spot study. Even some Muslim leaders stayed at Bandabila for a few days to enlist the support of the Muslim tax-payers for the no-tax campaign. The Government officers, on the other hand, went out on propaganda tour to the villages and tried to win over the village headmen to their side and disssuade the people from the boycott movement.[18]

By October the union board boycott movement in the form of no-tax campaign had attained a good measure of success. The police officers accompanied by sub-inspectors, constables, *dafadars* and *chaukidars* worked hard to frustrate the no-tax campaign. They started attaching movables of the tax-payers on the latter's refusal to pay arrears of taxes under the B.V.S.G. Act. They began to seize movable articles like fishing nets, utensils, etc. and plough-cattle under distress warrants. The villagers peacefully surrendered everything at the demand of the police.[19]

The movement took a serious turn when on 29 October 1929 eleven persons, namely, Benode Lal Bandyopadhyay, Akshoy Kumar Roy, Jnanendra Karmakar, Kalipada Mandal, Bholanath Karmakar, Satish Chandra Tantubai, Golak Hari Nandi, Pulin Behari Tantubai and Panchanan Bhattacharyya were arrested under the alleged offence of obstructing police officers in the discharge of their duties. In fact, these men were just following the officers on attachment duty and taking notes about the articles being attached.[20]

Meanwhile the Government authorities at the local level had tried to sell the attached properties and animals on auction at Bandabila, but failed on account of non-availability of bidders there. Then they arranged to send the attached goods and cattle to the Jessore Headquarters for auction sale and at the same time intensified, from the beginning of the first week of November, the attachment proceedings and extended it to the neighbouring villages.[21]

On 6 November a fresh attempt was made for auction sale of some of the cattle and articles already attached. It was learnt beforehand that the sale would be held at 8 a.m. Before the appointed time several leaders and workers of the movement including Chandra Kumar Bandyopadhyay, Bhudhar Halder, Ananda Mohan Choudhuri and Krishna Bindode Roy had arrived at the auction place to watch the situation and to see to it that the atmosphere remained peaceful. The local people also began to pour in to witness the sale. They knew it for certain that no bidder would be available. At about 4 p.m. it was announced that the sale was postponed and it would be held on the 9th. When the people protested, the members of the union board frankly confessed that the sale could not be held because of the non-availability of bidders.[22]

On the next occasion the Circle Officer, finding no bidder, brought out money from his pocket and offered the same to a relation of a member of the union board who was asked to bid in the auction. When objections were raised by the people that it was illegal for the Circle Officer to supply money to a bidder, the man was ordered to say that the money belonged to him.   At last on the insistence of the people the man refused to bid and thus the authorities were forced to stop the sale.[23]

Once again, another attempt to sell the attached cattle on auction at Jhikergacha failed ; for nobody wanted to purchase them, when they came to know that those had been seized for the realization of union board taxes at Bandabila.   Later, the cattle were taken to the Banapole *hat* for sale.[24]

Meanwhile the attachement operations, kept in abeyance for the last few days on account of the preoccupation of the Government officers with auction sale, again commenced on 25 November.   Thenceforward attachment and seizure of animals including plough-cattle, cows and utensils for paltry arrears of taxes continued unabated till the end of February 1930.   Several attempts to sell the attached goods and cattle on auction were made at Khajura *hat*.   Side by side, the Government authorities tried to persuade the people to pay the union board taxes voluntarily.   But much to their embarrassment they found the people impervious to all persuasions.[25]

By the middle of February 1930 the movement had taken a new turn.   The union board boycott movement had spread to the neighbouring villages.   The people of those villages decided not to pay any tax until the union boards were withdrawn. They remained resolute and firm in their determination even in the face of all sorts of repression.[26]

According to the Associated Press of India, the volunteers who had once boycotted the auction sale began by the end of February to purchase the attached goods and return the same to the owners.   The executive authorities, it was also reported, had nearly completed the realization of arrears of taxes.[27]   But other reports do not corroborate this and, on the contrary, suggest that the movement was going on full steam.[28]   However, from a scrutiny of the material as published in the contemporary press it seems that the movement came almost to a halt round the second week of March. The reasons behind this movement's drawing to a close all on a sudden were many but the chief amongst those was the call by Gandhi to join the impending Salt Satyagraha and the Civil Disobedience movement. Even in Bandabila preparations to the effect had started from the middle of March. As a result the union board boycott movement came to a stop and gradually merged in the greater mass movement.[29]

V

A brief account of the immediate background of the movement would enable us to make an objective analysis of its organizational and leadership aspects.

With the money collected by C. R. Das, Palli Samskar Samiti was established in different districts of Bengal. Such a committee was also formed in the district of Jessore. Its sole object was to carry on constructive work in the villages. A branch of this committee was opened in the village of Bandabila and it started functioning in 1925. Bijoy Chandra Roy was the principal organizer of this committee in Bandabila union. Jnananjan Niyogi was entrusted with the supervision of all Union branches on behalf of the Central Committee. Niyogi and his associates used to visit different centres to address meetings, deliver lantern lectures and organize constructive activities. The workers at the lower branches were brought to Calcutta for necessary training in village re-construction work. Like their counterparts in other villages the Bandabila Palli Samskar Samiti sent from time to time its workers to Calcutta for the same purpose. The functions of the Palli Samskar Samiti were as follows : to establish and run primary schools, night schools and physical training centres, to look after different municipal activities like public health and sanitation, construction of roads and ways, their cleaning and sweeping and to serve the poor and distressed people. In the villages the people were also trained in spinning wheels, handlooms and other cottage industries. Even some women joined these constructive activities. In this connexion it may be mentioned that Bina Bhowmik and others encouraged them in various ways. The workers engaged in village re-construction activities used to receive aid and advice from Jnananjan Niyogi, Satkaripati Roy, Ramanath Roy Choudhuri,

Bhupendra Kumar Dutta and Surendranath Niyogi and others.[30]

About the same time or earlier a Congress office had been opened at Bandabila. All this created buoyant enthusiasm among the local people and helped much in developing a harmonious relationship between the Hindus and the Muslims. The people of both the communities came to realize that they would be able to fight back any onslaught, however terrible it might be, of the Government, if they remained united. The Government authorities, on the other hand, became apprehensive of the communal harmony, which they feared, would frustrate their policy of 'divide and rule'.[31]

When the Government decided to establish the union board at Bandabila the local leaders approached Subhas Chandra Bose and other Congress leaders for permission to launch an anti-union-board movement. The latter advised them to strengthen their organization, raise volunteer corps and choose their leaders.[32]

During the election boycott stage the Provincial Congress sent two Muslim leaders, Ismail Hozea Seraji and Giasuddin Ahmed, on its behalf to fight the false propaganda then being carried on by the Government-backed candidates. Several members of the Palli Samskar Samiti joined them. But after the Government had failed twice to hold elections for the union board and decided to thrust a union board composed of nominated members only with a view to dissuading the people from joining village re-construction activities, to cutting them off from the mainstream of freedom struggle and to turning them, at least some of them, into its paid agents, the question that stirred the minds of the local leaders was whether to launch a no-tax campaign against the newly established union board. When Subhas Chandra Bose came down to Jessore to attend the District Conference of the Congress the Bandabila issue was raised. Later, in July 1929 in accordance with the resolution of the District Conference, the District Congress constituted an enquiry committee to investigate the issue.[33]

While the Provincial leadership of the Congress was still

hesitating to actively organize and lead the movement, the local organizers called upon the people through meetings and demonstrations to refuse to pay the union board taxes. The people who had so long boycotted the *panchayat* president and the other members of the union board and the collecting agents at once responded to their call. They peacefully submitted to attachment proceedings and refused to bid for the attached goods and cattle put on auction sale.

After six months of procrastination since July 1929 the B.P.C.C. at last decided to take over the charge of the movement at Bandabila, for the Enquiry Committee appointed by the B.P.C.C. had reported in favour of its taking up the issue.[34] A representative satyagraha committee[35] was formed to guide and supervise the movement. Subhas Chandra Bose visited Bandabila, addressed group meetings and issued appeals to the public and to all parties to sink all differences and contribute to the success of the no-tax campaign.[36]

Leaders from different corners of Bengal came to the place and tried to send men and money for the cause of the movement. Newspapers published day-to-day reports about the progress of the movement and wrote editorials condemning the Government policy of repression. To this the only exception was the Associated Press which published false reports that the movement had been fizzling out.[37]

Even the women-folk of the locality did not lag behind. Mothers of the arrested leaders like Manomohan Bhattacharyya and Bijoy Chandra Roy addressed meetings attended by village women and stressed the need for their participation in the movement. The active participation of these Brahmin ladies created great enthusiasm among *Namasudra* and *Kapalik* classes. Ashokelata Devi and Shanti Das of Deepali Sangha[38] visited the place, delivered lectures and participated in the movement.[39]

Bijoy Chandra Roy was in supreme command of the movement. It was only after his arrest that Ramanath Roy Choudhury took over its charge. There was no lack of zeal, efficiency and maturity on the part of the local organizers. But the organizational help and active guidance which they so badly needed and eagerly expected from the leaders and their organization at the top were not adequate, easily forthcoming or available.

## VI

As regards the reaction of the Government we would analyse the steps it undertook right from the election boycott stage.

During the election the Government, with the help of its agents, including Haridas Gangopadhyay, managed to get six nomination papers filed. Then the District Board engaged some *maulavis* to work in favour of the Government-sponsored candidates during the election campaign. The Government also set up several police camps near the polling station and tried to coerce the people to attend the polling centre and cast their votes in favour of the pro-Government candidates.[40]

When the Government failed to hold elections for the union board and, in consequence, established a nominated body, the people spontaneously boycotted its officials and collecting agents. The union board authorities offered advance salaries to their collecting agents, *dafadars and chaukidars* just to dissuade them from tendering resignation out of fear of social boycott by the people. They selected and appointed *dafadars* and collecting agents from some Muslim families and began to spread the rumour of coercion by the boycotters in order to estrange the respectable people from the boycott movement.[41]

With the beginning of the no-tax campaign the Government authorities chalked out newer plans of repression to strike terror into the minds of the rural masses. They started arresting innocent people on charge of dacoity and began to raid the houses of leaders and sympathizers of the movement.[42] For example, the house of Bijoy Chandra Roy was raided by the police and the Officer-in-charge during the raid used abusive language. Side by side, the Circle Officer organized several meetings in the villages to secure the support of the village headmen.[43]

When meetings and demonstrations became a regular phenomenon at Bandabila, the District Magistrate, in consultation with the Chairman of the District Board, promulgated section 144 Cr. P.C. in order to curb the influence of the boycotters. The notice under section 144 prohibited meetings, demonstrations, with or without objectionable flags, cries, sounds, etc. in four thanas, namely, Kotwali, Bagerpara, Kaligunj and Salkia of Jessore. The notice said that whereas a report submitted by the S.P. of Jessore to the District Magistrate stated that meetings were being held in certain parts of this district with a view to starting propaganda for boycotting union boards, etc. and whereas such meetings were likely to cause disaffection against the Government and class hatred among the different sections of His Majesty's subjects, etc., meetings, and demonstrations, with or without objectionable banners, cries, sounds, etc. were prohibited to be held and attended in the aforesaid four thanas. The motive behind the promulgation of the notice under section 144 Cr. P.C. was to terrorize the innocent villagers and to thwart the progress of the movement. The Government resorted to this measure on several occasions and served notices uuder the aforesaid section of Cr. P.C. for several reasons. For it realized that the union board boycott movement in the form of no-tax campaign had struck deep roots into the people's minds and attained a high degree of popularity. It was suspected by the local people that Nauser Ali had been pulling wires from behind.[44]

At the next stage of the movement the Inspector of Schools, Presidency Division, issued an order suspending the imperial grant of Rs. 25 per month to the Nimta Bandabila Minor School on the ground of alleged unsatisfactory conduct of the Headmaster, Bijoy Chandra Roy. Further, the D.B. grant of Rs. 18 per month to the said school was ordered to be cancelled. It was also feared that the branch post office of Bandabila would be closed. All this clearly points to the vindictive attitude of the Government.[45]

Even in the face of all these provocative measures the people remained non-violent but firm in their determination. They refused to pay their taxes under the new arrangement. In consequence, distress warrants were issued and indiscriminate attachments made. Though the Union Board Manual laid down that in execution of distress warrants plough-cattle should not be attached, the police officers and the collecting agents paid no heed to the provision of law. The people bore this with exemplary patience. When the executive authorities failed to attract any bidder on the appointed days of auction, they began to sell the attached animals and goods at a ludicrously low price stealthily without giving prior intimation to the people concerned. The auction very frequently took the character of private sale among the members of the union board and the executive staff.[46] Simultaneously, the Government officers strenuously tried to persuade the local people to receive the tax receipts on payment of whatever sum they could afford and to get back the properties attached for non-payment of taxes, but, unfortunately, all their efforts proved futile.[47]

Later, being exasperated at the situation that developed, the executive authorities directed their attacks against the leaders of the movement and their sympathizers. They arrested more than 500 persons and condemned them to various terms of imprisonment and fine in order to force the general masses to knuckle under their pressure. They hoped that, dejected and disspirited, the people would realize their mistake of fighting an unequal battle. The police often conducted sudden raids on meetings and dispersed the people assembled there. Refusal on the part of the people to obey orders of the police brought severe repression upon them. The meetings were broken up and arrests followed. The arrested leaders or volunteers were then tied with ropes and were abused as they were dragged on by the police and kept in dark damp lock-up and given no food or clothing. Arrested persons instead of being depressed very frequently resorted to hunger strike or any other form of protest against the ill-treatment meted out to them in the jail or *hajat*.[48]

Further, the police also arrested Bijoy Chandra Roy, his brother, Basanta Kumar Roy, Girindranath Bandyopadhyay, Jnanendra nath Chattopadhyay, Bijoy Chattopadhyay, Phani Bhusan Ghosh and Binode Lal Bandyopadhyay and put them to *hajat* on the charge of attempt to murder Abdur Rahman of Mirjapur, P.S. Bagerpara, a collecting agent of the union board. The facts of the case, according to the report dated 12.2.30, as alleged in the First Information Report, were briefly as follows. On 24.12.29 the aforesaid Abdur Rahman reported to the Officer-in-charge of Jessore P.S. to the effect that the previous day he had attached one bicycle of Phani Bhusan Tantubai for non-payment of union board taxes. When, on the day of occurrence, Abdur Rahman was going home in the afternoon accompanied by *dafadars* Kazi Bazlur Rahman and Kazi Golam Rahaman, the aforesaid accused persons armed with lathis and *daos* were alleged to have appeared before them and attacked Abdur Rahman on the road near the house of Bijoy Chandra Roy, under whose orders, Binode Lal Bandyopadhyay struck him with a *dao* which he warded off with the *daftar* in his hand, and *dafadar* Bazlur Rahman parried with a lathi the blow that was struck by the above mentioned Bijoy Chattopadhyay. The S.D.O. framed charge and committed all the accused to the Court of Sessions. All the accused persons were later released on bail excepting Bijoy Chandra Roy and Binodelal Bandyopadhyay. After a few months of detention both of them were found not guilty by the Court of Sessions.[49]

For all these reasons the Bandabila situation came to be debated in the Bengal Legislative Council and even in the remote House of Commons. But that too failed to move Kumar Sibsekhareswar Roy, the then Minister-in-charge of Local Self-Government. Instead, his government increasingly indulged in provocative actions to counteract the boycotters. In consequence, the boycott movement spread in the villages around Bandabila. The people of these adjacent areas, being infected by the Bandabila 'evil', began to march on the same road of boycotting union boards by refusing to pay their dues.[50]

Subsequently, the Government tried to stifle the propagada organs of the boycotters and to strengthen its media which were directed towards sowing seeds of dissension and disunity among different sections of the people. To indicate properly the extent of the efforts of the Government to strengthen its propaganda campaign, we should mention here that the District Board of Jessore sanctioned a large amount of money to finance the anti-satyagraha offensive. To highlight the fact we may quote the following resolution of the District Board. "Considered the motion of Maulavi Mashil Azam regarding the sanction of Rs. 5000/- for the propaganda work to be carried on in favour of union boards throughout the district wherever necessary against the anti-union board propaganda which is being carried on at Bandabila and other places. Resolved that a sum of Rs. 3000/- be sanctioned for the purpose, and the Chairman be authorized to spend the money by appointing maulavis and in [such] other ways as may be necessary." Further the paid communal agents did their best to divide the different sections of the people from each other. Several meetings were organized and addressed by *maulavis* and *pirs* who urged the people to pay union board taxes and co-operate with its officials. Nauser Ali and Abdul Rauf, respectively Chairman and Vice-chairman of the District Board of Jessore, Haji Ahmed Ali, Enayet Puri, Kayejuddin Ahmed, Amulyadhan Roy, leader of the low caste Hindus, and their associates tried through their speeches and actions to wean away the Muslims and low caste Hindus from the satyagraha leaders.[51]

As regards Government action against the press and publishers working in favour of the Bandabila movement, we may observe that the Government exceeded the farthest limits of provocation. It issued search warrants against printing establishments which printed and published leaflets on behalf of the organizers of the movement. Newspapers and weeklies which published reports on the progress of the movement and carried editorials on the repressive policies of the Government also suffered the same fate. For example, the Calcutta Police, armed with a search warrant issued at the instance of the District Magistrate of Jessore, raided the Saraswati Press on 10.1.30 and conducted a search lasting for a few hours. They tried to unearth the leaflets printed at the press containing accounts of the Bandabila movement and general appeal to the public to come forward with men and money and carry the fight to a successful end. The police also searched on January 16 the office and the press of a local weekly, namely *Ananda Patrika*, and raided the houses of the editor, the printer and the publisher of the same on the strength of a warrant issued by the District Magistrate in connexion with the printed appeal on the Bandabila union board boycott movement.[52]

## VII

Regarding ultimate results of the movement we must admit that the union board boycott movement at Bandabila, unlike its counterpart in Midnapore, could not reach the final stage of success. Though the decision to hold a fresh election for the union board was deferred,[53] the movement could not force the authorities to revoke the notice regarding the extension of union board even after a protracted battle for over a couple of years. This failure may be attributed to many factors. First of all, the main cause behind the people's agitation was the fear of enhanced taxation. Practically, a nominal increase in the burden of taxation could not by itself constitute a sufficient cause of a big and sustained movement. For that reason the people, not seriously aggrieved, could not withstand the repressive measures. A considerable section of the people, particularly the Muslims and the low caste Hindus, ran away from the movement and got relief by paying their paltry arrears of taxes.

Secondly, the movement could not attain the fullest measure of success since its area of operation was extremely limited, at least, for a considerable period of its duration.[54] It did not effectively spread over the neighbouring areas of Bandabila and hardly any effort was made to that effect. Only when the attachment of movables of the defaulters at Bandabila was on the verge of completion, other adjacent unions like Talkupi extended their help and joined the movement.

In the third place, the zamindary, the wealth, the business and education of the place were confined to a few upper caste men, Brahmins, Kayasthas and Vaidyas. The Congress leadership was mainly in the grip of these zamindars, upper caste

Hindus and some middle class people. As a result, when the Government appointed Nauser Ali and Amulyadhan Roy to wean away the Muslims and the low caste Hindus like *Kapaliks* and *Namasudras* from the 'clutches' of the satyagrahis, these people constituting a large section of the society fell into the well-laid trap. This had no doubt an adverse effect upon the growth and progress of the movement. In other words, the movement lost its wider base among the people.[55]

Lastly, the B.P.C.C. had never taken up the matter in right earnest. In spite of the appeal by the President of the B.P.C.C. the response from the general public was extremely poor. When the local leaders had been fighting a battle against heavy odds the factional quarrel in the Provincial Congress did not cease. As a result, the Congress as a whole failed to concentrate their resources for the success of the movement. They could have well engaged themselves in the movement and turned it into the starting point of an extensive civil disobedience movement in Bengal. Since the Congress never declared the boycott of local self-governing institutions as an all-India policy, its half-hearted participation in the Bandabila movement objectively helped the high priests of communalism and agents of bureaucracy in sowing seeds of frustration and dissension among the ranks of the people.[56]

Thus we have seen that the Bandabila Union Board Boycott movement did not attain the success it had been expected to attain. Still it deserves a special mention in the history of freedom struggle in Bengal, and particularly in the annals of union board boycott movement. It could rightly be assigned a place next to Contai.

## NOTES AND REFERENCES

1. After the Chaurichaura incident the Congress Working Committee which met at Bardoli on 11 and 12 February 1922 decided to suspend the programme of mass civil disobedience. When the All-India Congress Committee met on February 24 and 25 at Delhi, Gandhi moved his resolution which was the Bardoli resolution modified in respect of the restoration of the right of individual civil disobedience and the right of picketing of the foreign cloth shops and liquor booths with the

permission of the provincial Congress Committee concerned. See
B. Pattabhi Sitaramyya, *The History of the Indian National Congress*, I, 235-6,
D. G. Tendulkar, *Mahatma*, II, 90 ; J. B. Kripalani, *Gandhi : His Life
and Thought*, 93-4 ; Nirmal Kumar Bose, *Studies in Gandhism* (1972), 152.

For texts of the Bardoli Resolutions (presumably drafted by
Gandhi), see *Young India 1919-1922*, 1018-24 ; *The Collected Works of Mahatma
Gandhi*, XXII, 377-81.

2. V. V. Balabushevich and A. M. Dyakov (eds.), *A Contemporary
History of India*, 120, 163, 166-9, 192, 199.

For Bardoli no-tax campaign, see Mahadev Desai, *The Story of Bardoli*,
Part I ; V. B. Kulkarni. *The Indian Triumvirate : a political biography of
Gandhi-Patel-Nehru*, 309-18 ; B. Pattabhi Sitaramayya, op. cit., 323-5 ;
D. G. Tendulkar, op. cit., 327-30.

For Gandhi's stand on Bardoli satyagraha, see *The Collected Works
of Mahatma Gandhi*, XXXVI, 22 f.n., 35-6, 79-81, 88-90, 115, 152, 169-70,
315, 319-22, 352-4, 360, 368-70, 384-6, 411-20, 477-9.

3. The whole of our discussion is based on our interviews with
the leading participants in the movement, a letter of Jibananda Bhattacharyya addressed to Arun Chandra Guha, dated 12.6.71, and reports
of the contemporary dailies. The names of the persons interviewed
(figures in brackets indicate dates of interview) and detailed references
drawn from the contemporary newspapers are given below :

Bijoy Chandra Roy (28.12.71), Manomohan Bhattacharyya (28.10.71),
Krishna Binode Roy (28.5.72), Sudhir Kumar Mukhopadhyay (19.10.72)
and Amulya Kumar Biswas (5.6.72).

*Ananda Bazar Patrika*, 24.7.29, 9(5) ; 27.7.29, 7(3) ; 31.7.29, 11(1) ; 3.8.29,
11(2) ; 13.8.29, 9(1) : 19.8.29, 10(1) ; 26.8.29, 6(4) ; 28.9.29, 11(2) ; 19.10.29,
13(1) ; 21.10.29, 14(5) ; 28.10.29 ; 29.10.29, 5(3) ; 31.10.29, 8(3), 11(1) ;
1.11.29, 6(4), 9(3) ; 2.11.29, 4(3), 9(1) ; 4.11.29, 5(3) ; 6.11.29, 8(5) ; 7.11.29,
5(4), 8(2) ; 8.11.29, 5(3) ; 11.11.29, 8(2) ; 12.11.29, 11(2) ; 13.11.29, 7(3) ;
14.11.29, 4(5) ; 16.11.29, 6(3) ; 19.11.29, 4(3-4), 5(5), 7(3) ; 20.11.29, 7(3) ;
21.11.29, 8(5) ; 22.11.29, 8(3) ; 23.11.29, 8(2) ; 25.11.29, 5(2) ; 26.11.29,
8(5) ; 27.11.29, 8(2) ; 28.11.29, 10(1) ; 29.11.29, 5(1) ; 30.11.29, 9(1) ;
3.12.29, 9(1) ; 4.12.29, 9(2) ; 5.12.29, 5(5) ; 10.2.29, 3(4) ; 11.12.29, 9(2) ;
13.12.29, 2(5) ; 14.12.29, 8(2) ; 16.12.29, 3(5) ; 18.12.29, 10(1) ; 19.12.29,
3(5) ; 21.12.29, 3(5) ; 23.12.29, 11(1) ; 24.12.29, 8(1) ; 26.12.29, 5(5) ;
27.12.29, 7(2) ; 31.12.29, 6(3) ; 1.1.30, 11(2) ; 3.1.30, 2(5), 5(1) ; 4.1.30,
4(3-4), 5(1) ; 6.1.30, 3(5) ; 7.1.30, 6(4), 8(1) ; 8.1.30, 5(1) ; 10.1.30, 9(1) ;
11.1.30, 7(2) ; 13.1.30, 6(1) ; 14.1.30, 11(1) ; 15.1.30, 6(2) ; 18.1.30, 5(3) ;
20.1.30, 5(3), 6(5) ; 21.1.30, 9(1) ; 22.1.30, 10(1-2) ; 23.1.30, 10(1-2) ;
25.1.30, 8(3) ; 27.1.30, 11(1) ; 28.1.30, 4(5) ; 29.1.30, 6(3) ; 30.1.30, 8(5) ;
31.1.30, 10(1) ; 1.2.30, 8(1) ; 4.2.30, 12(4) ; 5.2.30, 5(5) ; 9(1-2) ; 7.2.30,
8(1-3) ; 8.2.30, 8(3) ; 11.2.30, 5(5), 7(3) ; 12.2.30, 8(5) ; 14.2.30, 8(5) ;
15.2.30, 5(5) ; 17.2.30, 4(5), 5(4), 9(1) ; 18.2.30, 6(3), 8(3) ; 19.2.30,
6(2) ; 21.2.30 8(4) ; 22.8.30, 8(2) ; 25.2.30, 10(2) ; 26.2.30, 8(5) ; 28.2.30,

8(2) ; 4.3.30, 9(3) ; 5.3.30, 3(4), 7(2) ; 6.3.30, 6(5) ; 7.3.30, 8(1) ; 14.3.30, 8(2) ; 17.3.30, 10(1) ; 18.3.30, 7(4) ; 20.3.30, 8(4) ; 22.3.30, 9(2) ; 25.3.30, 8(3) ; 26.3.30, 4(5) ; 11.4.30, 11(1) ; 18.4.30, 5(5) ; 22.4.30, 9(2) ; 24.4.30, 7(3) ; 26.4.30, 10(2).

*Amrita Bazar Patrika*, 29.10.29, 4(3-4), 5(1) ; 31.10.29, 11(2) ; 1.11.29, 2(7) ; 2.11.29, 4(4), 9(4) ; 3.11.29, 3(4) ; 7.11.29, 8(2) ; 8.11.29, 3(7) ; 9.11.29, 5(7) ; 10.11.29, 3(5), 4(2-3) ; 14.11.29, 5(6) ; 20.11.29, 3(2) ; 22.11.29, 5(2) ; 24.11.29, 5(2) ; 29.11.29, 5(7) ; 5.12.29, 3(2) ; 13.12.29, 5(1) ; 14.12.29, 5(5) ; 21.12.99, 6(4) ; 22.12.29, 4(4) ; 31.12.29, 3(4) ; 1.1.30, 9(7) ; 5.1.30, 3(7) ; 7.1.30, 4(4) ; 9.1.30, 5(6) ; 10.1.30, 4(2), 5(7) ; 11.1.30, 6(6) ; 12.1.30, 8(5) ; 14.1.30, 5(1-2) ; 15.1.30, 4(1) ; 16.1.30, 5(7) ; 17.1.30, 5(3) ; 18.1.30, 5(5) ; 19.1.30, 5(4) ; 21.1.30, 5(7) ; 22.1.30, 4(3) ; 23.1.30, 5(4) ; 24.1.30, 5(7) ; 25.1.30, 5(7) ; 26.1.30, 12(6) ; 28.1.30, 3(7) ; 29.1.30, 7(3) ; 30.1.30, 5(4) ; 31.1.30, 5(5-6) ; 1.2.30, 4(1-2) ; 2.2.30, 5(4) ; 5.2.30, 5(5), 6.2.30, 5(3 & 5) ; 7.2.30, 5(5) ; 8.2.30, 5(3) ; 9.2.30, 4(1-2) ; 11.2.30, 5(3), 9(1) ; 13.2.30, 5(3) ; 14.2.30, 6(3) ; 15.2.30, 5(4), 6(3) ; 16.2.30, 4(2-3) ; 18.2.30, 3(6) ; 21.2.30, 5(4) ; 26.2.30, 6(5) : 28.2.30, 6(1) ; 1.3.30, 5(7) ; 4.3.30, 3(4) ; 8.3.30, 3(3), 9.3.30, 14(4) ; 13.3.30, 7(4) ; 26.3.30, 9(6) ; 27.3.30, 5(2) ; 30.3.30, 3(5).

*The Bengalee*, 31.12.29, 6(1) ; 3.1.30, 5(6) ; 5.1.30, 10(4) ; 11.1.30, 5(5) ; 12.1.30, 5(1) ; 14.1.30, 5(4-5) ; 19.1.30, 3(3) ; 23.1.30, 5(5) ; 1.2.30, 5(3) ; 14.2.30, 6(3) ; 15.2.30, 5(1) ; 28.2.30, 5(1).

*Nabasakti* (a Bengali weekly), 1.11.29, 2(3) ; 22.11,29, 2(3) ; 24.1.30, 1(1-2).

4.  For details regarding this organization, see pp 73-4.

5.  For Bose-Sen Gupta group rivalry, see Bhola Chatterjee, *Aspects of Bengal Politics in the Early Nineteen Thirties* ; Leonard A. Gordon, *Bengal* : *The Nationalist Movement 1876-1940*, 223-63 ; J. A. Gallagher, G. Johnson and Anil Seal (eds.), *Locality Province and Nation*, 269-325.

6.  Interview with Bijoy Chandra Roy.

7.  The exact date cannot be ascertained from the material at our disposal. Newspaper reports about the movement are available only from July 1929.

8.  Here also the exact date fixed for the submission of nomination papers cannot be ascertained owing to the difficulties as noted above.

9.  See note no. 6. Also interview with Manomohan Bhattacharyya.

10.  From our interview with Krishna Binode Roy we may assume that the later part of 1928 was the period during which attempts were made by the Government to hold elections for the union board to be established at Bandabila. But Jibananda Bhattacharyya wrote in his letter (See note no. 3) that the conflict centring the question of union board election had started in early 1928. We would, however, state in the following paragraphs the events which had begun to take place only from July 1929 during the no-tax campaign period.

11.  See note no. 9. Jibananda Bhattacharyya's letter (referred to

above) corroborates this statement. But Manomohan Bhattacharyya disagrees. In his opinion, only the Government-backed candidates cast their votes.

12 & 13. See note no. 9.

14. See note no. 9. Also interview with Sudhir Kumar Mukhopadhyay.

15. Bijoy Krishna Roy and Jogendra Nath Sen were the most important members of the District Congress Enquiry Committee. See *Ananda Bazar Patrika*, 31.7.29, 11(1).

16. ibid., 24.7.29, 9(5) ; 31.7.29, 11(1).

17. ibid., 27.7.29, 7(3) ; 31.7.29, 11(1).

18. ibid., 13.8.29, 9(1) ; 19.8.29, 10(1) ; 26.8.29, 6(4) ; 28.9.29, 11(2).

19. *Ananda Bazar Patrika*, 29.10.29, 5(3) ; *Amrita Bazar Patrika*, 31.10.29, 11(2).

20. *Ananda Bazar Patrika*, 31.10.29, 8(3) ; 1.11.29, 6(4) ; *Amrita Bazar Patrika*, 1.11.29, 2(7).

21. *Ananda Bazar Patrika*, 2.11.29, 9(1) ; 4.11.29, 5(3) ; 6.11.29, 8(5) ; *Amrita Bazar Patrika*, 2.11.29, 9(4) ; 8.11.29, 3(7).

22. *Ananda Bazar Patrika*, 8.11 29, 5(3) ; *Amrita Bazar Patrika*, 9.11.29, 5(7).

23. *Ananda Bazar Patrika*, 11.11.29, 8(2) ; *Amrita Bazar Patrika*, 14.11.29, 5(6).

24. *Ananda Bazar Patrika*, 25.11.29, 5(2) ; *Amrita Bazar Patrika*, 24.11.29, 5(2).

25. *Ananda Bazar Patrika*, 27.11.29, 8(2) ; 28.11.29, 10(1) ; 29.11.29, 5(1) ; 3.12.29, 9(1) ; 10.12.29, 3(4) ; 11.12 29, 9(2) ; 13.12.29, 2(5) ; 14.12.29, 8(2) ; 18.12.29, 10(1) ; 19.12.29, 3(5) ; 21.12.29, 3(5) ; 24.12.29, 8(1) ; 4.1.30, 5(1) ; 8.1.30, 5(1) ; 10.1.30, 9(1) ; 14.1.30, 11(1) ; 23.1.30, 10(1-2) ; 25.1.30, 8(3) ; 27.1.30, 11(1) ; 29.1.30, 6(3) ; 30.1.30, 8(5) ; 31.1.30, 10(1) ; 4.2.30, 12(4) ; 5.2 30, 9(1-2) ; 7.2.30, 8(1-3) ; 8.2.30, 8(3) ; 12.2.30, 8(5) ; 14.2.30, 8(5) ; 17.2.30, 9(1) ; 18.2.30, 6(3) ; 19.2.30, 6(2) ; 21.2.30, 8(4) ; 22.2.30, 8(2) ; *Amrita Bazar Patrika*, 29.11.29, 5(7) ; 13.12.29, 5(1) ; 5.1.30, 3(7) ; 10.1.30, 5(7) ; 11.1.30, 6(6) ; 12.1.30, 8(5) ; 28.1.30, 3(7) ; 30.1.30, 5(4) ; 31.1.30, 5(5-6) ; 2.2.30, 5(4) ; 5.2.30, 5(5) ; 6.2.30, 5(3), 8.2.30, 5(3) ; 11.2.30, 5(3) ; 14.2.30, 6(3) ; 15.2.30, 5(4) ; 21.2.30, 5(4) ; 26.2.30, 6(5) ; and *The Bengalee*, 12.1.30.

26. *Amrita Bazar Patrika*, 13.2.30, 5(3) ; 16.2.30, 4(2-3) ; 26.2.30, 6(5).

27. ibid., 28.2.30, 6(1).

28. ibid., 28.2.30, 6(1) ; 4.3.30, 3(4) ; 8.3.30, 3(3).

29. *Ananda Bazar Patrika*, 18.3.30, 7(4) ; 22.3.30, 9(2) ; 22.4.30, 9(2) ; Interview with Bijoy Chandra Roy. Also the letter of Jibananda Bhattacharyya.

30 & 31. See note no. 9.

32. See note no. 6.

33. See note no. 6. See also *Ananda Bazar Patrika*, 24.7.29, 9(5).

34. *Ananda Bazar Patrika*, 23.12.29, 11(1) ; *Amrita Bazar Patrika*, 14.12.29, 5(5) ; 21.12.29, 6(4) ; 22.12.29, 4(4) ;

Ambika Charan Chakravarty, Giasuddin Ahmed and Benode Chandra Chakravorty were some among the members of the B.P.C.C. Enquiry Committee who visited Bandabila.

35. The Committee consisted of the following persons :

Subhas Chandra Bose, Brajendra Nath Bhadra (Assistant Secretary), Bijoy Chandra Roy (Assistant Secretary), Chandra Kumar Bandyopadhyay, Surendra Mohan Ghosh, Aswini Kumar Ganguly (Secretary), Bimalananda Tarkatirtha, Bhupendra Kumar Dutta, Maulavi Giasuddin Ahmed, Satkaripati Roy, Jatindra Mohan Das Gupta, Swami Jnanananda, Amarendranath Ghosh (Tangail) Satyendra Nath Mitra, Kiran Sankar Roy, Dr. Prafulla Chandra Ghose, Bipin Behari Gangopadhyay, Krishna Binode Roy, Trikendrajit Mazumdar, Gopal Chandra Roy, Ramanath Roy and Jnananjan Niyogi. See *Ananda Bazar Patrika*, 23.12.29, 11(1) ; *Amrita Bazar Patrika*, 21.12.29, 6(4).

36. *Ananda Bazar Patrika*, 16.12.29, 3(5) ; 23.12.29, 11(1) ; *Amrita Bazar Patrika*, 21.12.29, 6(4) ; 9.1.30, 5(6).

37. *Ananda Bazar Patrika*, 12.11.29, 11(2) ; 4.12.29, 9(2) ; 16.12.29, 3(5) ; 18.1.30, 5(3) ; *Amrita Bazar Patrika*, 10.11.29, 3(5) ; 5.12.29, 3(2) ; 17.1.30, 5(3) and *The Bengalee*, 14.1. 30, 5(4-5).

38. "Deepali Sangha was founded in 1929 by Miss Leela Nag as one of the first women's organizations in the nationalist movement. Perhaps its most important activity was working to improve the social and economic position of women in Bengal, especially through education. Deepali Sangha, through its ten to twenty branches in Dacca, operated a number of free elementary schools and two high schools for Dacca girls. A third high school owed its initial inspiration to the Deepali movement. In addition, Deepali Sangha emphasized adult female education and arts and craft training. Midday and evening classes were held to prepare women to pass the high school matriculation examination and to prepare them to earn their own living. Activities of the Deepali Sangha gradually spread to Calcutta where the organization was very active among women students at Calcutta University and Bethune College. Miss Nag extended her feminist activities in 1930 by beginning the publication of a ladies' monthly journal, *Jayashree*. Except for two interruptions due to Government suppression, *Jayashree* has been published continuously to the present day. Deepali Sangha also emphasized physical education for women. Pulin Das, the well-known old Anushilan revolutionary, was engaged to give instruction in lathi and dagger play and judo."—David M. Laushey, *Bengal Terrorism and Marxist Left*, 43.

39. *Ananda Bazar Patrika*, 5.2.30, 5(5), 9(1-2) ; 7.2.30, 8(1-3) ; *Amrita Bazar Patrika*, 5.2.30, 5(5) ; 8.2.30, 5(3).

40. See note no. 9.

41. See note no. 9. See also *Ananda Bazar Patrika*, 27.7.29, 7(3) ;
13. 8.29, 9(1) ; 19.8.29, 10(1) ; *Amrita Baxar Patrika*, 3.11.29, 3(4).

42. *Ananda Bazar Patrika*, 28.9.29, 11(2).

43. ibid., 19.10.29, 13(1) ; 21.10.29, 14(5).

44. ibid., 28.10.29 ; *Amrita Bazar Patrika* 29.10.29, 4(3-4), 5(1).

45. *Ananda Bazar Patrika*, 2.11.29, 9(1) ; *Amrita Bazar Patrika*, 2.11.29, 9(4).

46. *Ananda Bazar Patrika*, 29.10.29, 5(3) ; 31.10.29, 8(3), 11(1) ; 1.11.29, 6(4) ; 6.11.29, 8(5) ; 8.11.29, 5(3) ; 11.11.29, 8(2) ; 22.11.29, 8(3) ; 23.11.29, 8(2) ; 25.11.29, 5(2) ; 26.11.29, 8(5) ; 27.11.29, 8(2) ; 28.11.29, 10(1) ; 3.12.29, 9(1) ; 10.12.29, 3(4) ; 18.12.29, 10(1) ; 24.12.29, 8(1) ; 10.1.30, 9(1) ; 14.1.30, 11(1) ; *Amrita Baazr Patrika*, 31.10.29, 11(2) ; 1.11.29, 2(7) ; 8.11.29, 3(7) ; 9.11.29, 5(7) ; 14.11.29, 5(6) ; 22.11.29, 5(2) ; 24.11.29, 5(2) ; 29.11.29, 5(7) ; 13.12.29, 5(1) ; 10.1.30, 4(2), 5(7) ; 11.1.30, 6(6) and *The Bengalee*, 12.1.30.

47. *Amrita Bazar Patrika*, 16.2.30, 7(3, 4, 5). See also Appendix II.

48. *Ananda Bazar Patrika*, 31.10.29, 8(3), 11(1) ; 1.11.29, 6(4) ; 3.12.29, 9(1) ; 21.12.29, 3(5) ; 24.12.29, 8(1) ; 27.12.29, 7(2) ; 3.1.30, 5(1) ; 4.1.30, 5(1) ; 6.1.30, 3(5) ; 8.1.30, 5(1) ; 10.1.30, 9(1) ; 15.1.30, 6(2) ; 20.1.30, 5(3), 6(5) ; 21.1.30, 9(1) ; 23.1.30, 10(1-2) ; 25.1.30, 8(3) ; 28.1.30, 4(5) ; 30.1.30, 8(5) ; 31.1.30, 10(1) ; 7.2.30, 8(1-3) ; 17.2.30, 4(5) ; 28.2.30, 8(2) ; *Amrita Bazar Patrika*, 1.11.29, 2(7) ; 5.12.29, 3(2) ; 31.12.29, 3(4) ; 1.1.30, 9(7) ; 5.1.30, 3(7) ; 10.1.30, 4(2) ; 14.1.30, 5(1-2) ; 19.1.30, 5(4) ; 21.1.30, 5(7) ; 23.1.30, 5(4) ; 25.1.30, 5(7) ; 26.1 30, 12(6) ; 30.1.30, 5(4) ; 31.1.30, 5(5-6) ; 8.2.30, 5(3) ; 15.2.30, 5(4) ; 28.2 30, 6(1) and *The Bengalee*, 31.12.29, 5.1.30, 10(4) ; 14.1.30, 5(4-5) ; 23.1.30, 5(5). Also interview with Krishna Binode Roy.

49. *Ananda Bavar Patrika*, 27.12.29, 7(2) ; 10.1.30, 9(1) ; 18.1.30, 5(3) ; 15.2.30, 5(5) ; 21.2.30, 8(4) ; *Amrita Bazar Patrika*, 10.1.30, 4(2) ; 15.2.30, 5(4), 6(3) and *The Bengalee* 15.2.30, 5(1). See also note no 6.

50. *Ananda Bavar Patrika*, 5.3.30, 3(4) ; *Amrita Bazar Patrika*, 1.2.30, 4(1-2) ; 13.2.30, 5(3) ; 16.2.30, 4(2-3) ; 26.2.30, 6(5). See also *Bengal Legislative Council Proceedings*, XXXIV, I, 10.2.30, 133.

51. *Ananda Bavar Patrika*, 3.1.30, 5(1) ; 7.1.30, 6(4) ; 23.1.30, 10(1-2) ; *Amrita Bazar Patrika*, 23.1.30, 5(4) ; 6.2.30, 5(5) and *The Bengalee*, 3.1.30, 5(6). Also interview with Krishna Binode Roy.

52. *Ananda Bazar Patrika*, 18.1.30, 5(3) ; *Amrita Bazar Patrika*, 12.1.30, 8(5) ; 18.1.30, 5(5).

53. Jibananda Bhattacharyya's letter.

54 & 55. Interview with Krishna Binode Roy.

56. *Ananda Bazar Patrika*, 19.11.29, 4(3-4) ; *Amrita Bazar Patrika*, 15.1.30, 4(1) ; 9.2.30, 4(1-2).

## List of Leaders and Workers Involved in the Movement

Giasuddin Ahmed, Benode Lal Bandyopadhyay, Chandra Kumar Bandyopadhyay, Girindra Nath Bandyopadhyay, Gopal Chandra Bandyopadhyay, Amulya Kumar Biswas, Bahadur Biswas, Gangaram Biswas, Gayaram Biswas, Jagabandhu Biswas, Juran Biswas, Meghnath Biswas, Panchoo Biswas, Rakhal Chandra Biswas, Manindra Nath Bose, Satya Ranjan Bose, Subhas Chandra Bose, Brajendra Bhadra, Jibananda Bhatta-charyya, Manomohan Bhattacharyya, Nrisinha Prasad Bhatta-charyya, Panchanan Bhattacharyya, Pramathanath Bhatta-charyya, Purna Chandra Bhowmick, Amulya Chakraborty, Ambika Chakrabory, Ashutosh Chakraborty, Balai Chandra Chakraborty, Benode Chandra Chakraborty, Charu Chandra Chakraborty, Jatindra Nath Chakraborty, Nagendra Nath Chakraborty, Biswanath Chattopadhyay, Bejoy Chandra Chatto-padhyay, Jnanendra Chattopadhyay, Kanailal Chattopadhyay, Ananda Mohan Choudhury, Jagabandhu Das, Krishna Chandra Das, Satish Chandra Das, Shanti Das, Sukumar Ranjan Das, Madan Gopal Dhar, Dr. Jatindra Mohan Das Gupta, Satya Charan Das Gupta, Ashokelata Devi, Bhupendra Kumar Dutta, Kiran Chandra Dutta, Bepin Behari Gangopadhyay, Manmatha Gangopadhyay, Nagendra Nath Gangopadhyay, Amarendra Nath Ghosh, Gourprasad Ghosh, Narendra Nath Ghosh, Phani Bhusan Ghosh, Rajendra Ghosh, Surendra Mohan Ghosh, Janab Golam Rahain Hakim, Bhudhar Haldar, Jalaluddin Hashemy, Swami Jnanananda, Panchoo Kar, Bholanath Karma-kar, Jnanendra Karmakar, Upendranath Karmakar, Thanda Khan, Ibrahim Laskar, Chaitanya Mallik, Debendra Nath Mallik, Trikendrajit Majumdar, Kalipada Mandal, Hari Man-dal, Arun Kumar Mitra, Nripendra Chandra Mitra, Sona Mia, Kalipada Mukherjee, Sailendra Nath Mukhopadhyay, Sudhir Kumar Mukhopadhyay, Bipin Chandra Nayak, Jnananjan Niyogi, Jaharchand Pandey, Pandit Dukharam Pandey, Brinda-ban Chandra Poret, Swami Mahadev Prakash, Bajlur Rahaman, Akshoy Roy, Basanta Kumar Roy, Bijoy Chandra Roy, Gour

Gobinda Roy, Gopal Chandra Roy, Krishna Binode Roy,
Makhan Lal Roy, Satkaripati Roy, Ramanath Roy Choudhury,
Bibhuti Bhusan Saha, Balaram Sarkar, Matilal Sarkar,
Jaladhar Sen, Jogendra Nath Sen, Nagendra Nath Sen, Promode
Ranjan Sen, Abdul Maulavi Saharam, Ismail Hozea Siraji,
Phani Bhusan Tantubai, Pulin Behari Tantubai, Ramdayal
Tantubai, Satish Caandra Tantubai, Amulya Tanti, Kalipada
Tanti, Kaviraj Bimalananda Tarkatirtha, Mothers of Bejoy
Chandra Roy & Manomohan Bhattacharyya.

[Source : *Amrita Bazar Patrika,
Ananda Bazar Patrika* and *The
Bengalee,* 1929-30.]

## APPENDIX II

*Amrita Bazar Patrika* (dated February 16, 1930, p.7 cols.
3-5) published two facsimile (in Bengali) and translations of
eight letters to show how the authorities tried to persuade the
people to accept Union Board receipts by paying a nominal
tax in cash or otherwise in order to legitimate the Union Board
tax. Because of obvious limitations we cannot reproduce here
the facsimile. Two letters are reproduced below.

[facsimile in *Amrita Bazar Patrika*]

To
The Secretary,

Sir,

I, Suchitra Sikdar, offered my goods to the Circle Officer
to be taken away for non-payment of taxes. He said that
I was not to give up my goods to him that were so valuable
and that if I would pay him two annas only, he would give
me receipt. Thereafter, I would not be required to give him
goods. And if I were unable to do that even, I being a
carpenter might go to his Sisakhali camp and repair one or
two nails of a bedstead. That would be enough and he was
prepared to give me a receipt in advance. I did not agree,

so he broke the door of my house and left. I beseech you for the remedy of this vandalism done to me.

( Thumb impression )<br>Sri Suchitra Sikdar<br>Gaighata.

To
The Secretary,

Sir,

I, Sree Lankeswar Mandal, of Gaighata beg to state that on 5.2.30. the Circle Officer attached my goods including a pitcherful of molasses (21 seers) and a pitcher for a paltry sum of Rs. 1-8-0. He is insisting for these three days to pay annas four or six so that I may get the receipt and get back also the goods. In return I have refused the offer with all the contempt it deserves.

Yours obediently,<br>Sd. Lankeswar Mandal<br>Gaighata.

CHAPTER IV

## TARAKESWAR SATYAGRAHA

GANDHI SAID, "when there is an occasion everyone has a right to practise non-co-operation or satyagraha. It is not that there can be non-co-operation only with the Government but not among ourselves."[1] During the freedom movement sometimes satyagraha was launched to reform certain religious institutions. Among them the movement at Tarakeswar in Bengal and the Akali movement in the Punjab resulting in Nankana tragedy[2] may be especially mentioned. Both these movements originate in an effort to remove the glaring abuses in the management of old religious institutions with rich endowments, and received their inspiration from the political movement launched by Gandhi.[3]

At that time religious institutions were alleged to be dens of many corrupt and immoral activities. In fact those were sinks of 'rottenness and oppression'. Tarakeswar temple was not an exception to this. As a contemporary daily observed, "Oppression to [ sic ] pilgrims, injustice and extortion, and the sports of Belial are old, old stories at Tarakeswar, and have often been brought to the notice of the wider world... The evil has become strong [ sic ] for resistance, as a large estate has [ sic ] attached to the temple by way of trust properties and the propertied ease of the *Mohunts* has often made them forget the purpose and obligations of the trust."[4] The *Mohunts*, victims to the 'enervating sway of irresponsible power and authority', used to lead a life quite contrary to the injunctions of *brahmacharya* ; hence they did not deserve people's respect.

## II

Tarakeswar is one of the most important places of pilgrimage in Bengal. It is in the district of Hooghly and 46 kilometres away from Calcutta. The place is famous for the temple of god Taraknath (Siva). Every year pilgrims from

6

different parts of the country visit the place. Particularly during the *gajan* festival (held in honour of god Siva in the middle of April) pilgrims in large numbers flock to the place.

During the period under review the pilgrims expressed certain grievances against the *Mohunt*. They had often complained of the forcible exactions by the agents of the *Mohunt*. Those who refused to pay these unauthorized exactions were chastised by the Birbhadra Dal, alleged to be composed of a pack of roughs employed by the *Mohunt*. Sometimes women also were insulted by them. All these malpractices indeed caused much repulsion among the public. In order to redress these grievances it was suggested that a committee of eminent persons who enjoyed 'universal confidence' should be formed. The committee would have complete power over the purse and authority to exercise close supervision over the management of the trust properties and on due performance of the rites as enjoined by the *Sastras*. The *Mohunt*, it was further suggested, should have nothing to do excepting to carry out the directives of the committee of which he also was to be a member and that all forcible and illegal exactions should be forthwith abolished.[5]

The grievances of the pilgrims can be classified under four heads :

1. Charges against the private character of the *Mohunt* (It was alleged that the *Mohunt* was a person of voluptuous character. Even violations of women[6] were alleged against him) ;

2. Treatment of his tenants as a zamindar ;

3. Treatment meted towards the pilgrims and exaction of different kinds of illegal payments inside and outside the temple ;

4. Utter callousness towards the convenience of women pilgrims in the matter of bathing and sanitary arrangements.

Thus it is clear from the above grievances that the problem regarding the temple at Tarakeswar was a two-fold one : in the first place, problem of abolishing all illegal and enforced payments, providing for the convenience of the pilgrims and ensuring the safety and honour of the lady pilgrims ; and

secondly, the problem of determining who was the real proprietor of the trust property and what was the real function
of the *Mohunt*.[7]

For the purpose of redressing these grievances, the Mahabir
Dal, an organization of *sannyasins* under the leadership of
Swami Viswananda and Swami Satchidananda, came forward.[8] They decided to launch a satyagraha movement on
the eve of Sivaratri festival in the year 1924.[9] With a view
to enrolling volunteers and collecting money Swami Satchidananda made an appeal to the people. In his appeal he
put certain proposals before the public and solicited their
opinion in this regard. Those proposals were as follows :

1. To set up a trust for all properties by dislodging the
then *Mohunt* from his *gaddi* ;

2. To set up a committee to be composed of persons
conversant with the Hindu scriptures and of good moral
character for the proper functioning of the temple and other
things pertaining thereto.

3. Income derived from the temple's property should be
spent in the following manner :

a) 75% of the total income should be spent for the
betterment of the temple. Provisions must be made, in the
first place, to eradicate malaria and to arrange for drinking
water, and secondly, to improve the condition of the tenants
in such manner as would be laid down by the Ryot Committee
to be composed of members taken from among the villagers.

b) The remaining 25% should be deposited as reserve
fund.

4. Income accruing from the temple should be spent in
the following manner :

a) 10% should be spent for the development and repairs
of the temple building.

b) 10% should be given to the *Mohunt* for his livelihood
till his death.

c) The remainder should be spent for the offerings and
other charitable activities.

5. It was reported that gems and jewels worth lakhs of
rupees had been lying with the *Mohunt*. These were to be

deposited with banks or invested somewhere else and the income out of it was to be spent according to the directives of the Temple Committee.

6. Persons not conversant with the scriptures and of bad moral character should not be allowed in future to be appointed as *Mohunt*.[10]

After such announcement Swami Satchidananda wrote a letter to the President, Bengal Provincial Congress Committee, seeking the latter's permission in regard to the proposed satyagraha movement. "We want to start a satyagraha at Tarakeswar on the Sivaratri day as part of our propaganda for reformation of Hindu temples. But after the letter of Mahatma Gandhi to the Akalis on the Jatha question[11] we hesitate to start Satyagraha without your approval. It is absolutely certain that Satyagraha jatha that will regularly go to Tarakeswar will always be non-violent in body and spirit but it cannot be expected that the *Mohunt* of Tarakeswar or his men or the Government representing law and order will remain non-violent. We beg your permission to start the Satyagraha as suggested by Mahatma Gandhi before starting it as we do not want to stop it later when we have once done it."[12]

Pending this permission, Swami Viswananda began organizing the volunteers for Mahabir Dal in order to prepare for the proposed satyagraha movement. Already an office was opened at 179 Harison Road, Calcutta, and another at Tarakeswar.[13] The intention of the Mahabir Dal, as we have noted above, was to reform all temples and monasteries of India. Swami Viswananda requested the tenantry of all the *Mohunts* and keepers of monasteries to organize themselves. "It will be absolutely necessary to start the movement of non-payment of rents to such *Mohunts* and managers of monastries when Satyagraha will be started," he suggested. The members of monasteries willing to participate in the movement were asked to be ready as their help might be required at any time.[14] The satyagrahis were asked to fulfil the following conditions : (i) they were to look after the pilgrims and also to see that the agents of the *Mohunt* might not harass them ;

(ii) secondly, to offer satyagraha forthwith if anything wrong happened : and (iii) finally, during such action, a satyagrahi must be non-violent.[15]

Meanwhile with a view to inquiring into the matter and chalking out 'a line of reforms' after conferring with the *Mohunt* and other local residents, Chitta Ranjan Das, President of the BPCC, Subhas Chandra Bose, Secretary, BPCC and Srish Chandra Chatterjee visited Tarakeswar on 8 April 1924.[16] On inquiry the leaders found 'a reign of terror' at the place. As Subhas Chandra Bose observed, "The people who live at and round about the place will hardly venture to speak out publicly against the *Mohunt-Maharaj* as they would thereby endanger their life and property. In fact many residents of the locality and lady pilgrims, belonging to respectable families of Calcutta and Howrah, in giving evidence before Deshabandhu Das in our presence, enquired whether we would be able to protect them against the agents of *Mohunt-Maharaj*." The leaders, however, assured them that the satyagrahis were there to protect them and render all possible service to them. In his statement Subhas Chandra Bose asked 'the progressive section' of the Hindu Sabha (Bengal Branch) to take up the matter. At the same time he made it clear that if the Hindu Sabha failed in its duty in this regard, the BPCC would be 'reluctantly' compelled to take such action as it might think necessary and advisable.[17]

Another enquiry committee consisting of seven persons was set up by the Hindu Sabha, Burrabazar. On their inquiry, the Committee found (i) that pilgrims, traders, shopkeepers and residents of Tarakeswar were subjected to illegal exactions by the agents of the *Mohunt* interfering with the rights of the Hindus to free worship at the shrine ; (ii) that there had been a mass of evidence to prove violation of the chastity of women visiting the shrine, and finally (iii) that women of ill fame numbering between 300 and 400 had been allowed and encouraged to live in Tarakeswar in violation of all principles of decency and morality.[18]

All these observations of the different committees focussed on the main problem of the transfer of management and control of the temple and the lands appertaining thereto into the hands of the people. The organizers of the movement urged the formation of a strong representative committee to take charge of the holy shrine and the properties attached thereto. In his submission before the Divisional Commissioner, Burdwan and the District Magistrate, Hooghly, Swami Viswananda stated categorically that unless the Government took initiative to settle the dispute immediately, satyagraha would have to be started to achieve the end. 'The only course left open is to resort to direct action' was his bold assertion before the Government officials, but he deemed it necessary to state his case to the authorities before he took such a grave and momentous step. For he held that in case anything happened in consequence of the inevitable 'direct action', the Hindu community might be blamed on the ground that the Government was not informed beforehand. Finally, he urged the authorities to make necessary steps to satisfy the demands of the people, i.e., to recognize the people's right to the possession of the holy shrine to which they were entitled.[19]

The situation at Tarakeswar was on the other hand gradually taking a complex turn. On 7 April 1924 a fracas took place when some of the volunteers of Mahabir Dal who went to Tarakeswar for the proposed movement were, it was alleged, assaulted by the agents of the *Mohunt*. A counter-allegation was made by the *Mohunt* that the local market was looted and a further breach of peace was apprehended at the place. But a press representative on inquiry found that some of the *Mohunt*'s agents interfered while Swami Satchidananda with his volunteers was distributing leaflets at the market and a fracas resulted. However, it ceased as soon as the SDO, Serampore and the ASP, Hooghly arrived there.[20] It was reported that one of the *Mohunt*'s agents was arrested for beating two volunteers of the Mahabir Dal.[21]

Everything passed smoothly on the eve of *gajan* festival organized enthusiastically by the volunteers of Mahabir Dal. All collection at the gates or *gaddi*, excepting the *pranami* offered to god Tarakeswar, was totally stopped. No charge was even paid by the pilgrims for giving hairs except the barber's charge.[22]    All these rites, for which the *Mohunt* used to exact payments from the pilgrims, were observed by them free of charge. Thus by preventing the *Mohunt's* extortions the volunteers achieved a temporary success.

But the ultimate object of the movement was to secure the Tarakeswar shrine for free worship by the Hindu public without let or hindrance, or in other words, to demolish once for all the pretensions of the *Mohunt* as the proprietor of the temple. Hence the movement was put off for the time being to gain further strength by carrying on intensive propaganda in the country and by mobilizing public opinion in favour of the cause. Moreover, the fair on the eve of *Chaitra Samkranti* festival (*gajan*), when there was always a rush of pilgrims, was over and there was no pressure of work. That was why the leaders deemed it necessary to maintain the present strength of volunteer force at Tarakeswar. Some of the leaders left the place while Swami Viswanath with his volunteers of Mahabir Dal stayed there[23] and within a few days they occupied the temple. The volunteers themselves thenceforth began to perform the religious rites of the shrine.[24] After the temple was occupied by the satyagrahis, the *Mohunt* with his agents left Tarakeswar at night on April 24.[25]

After some days a rumour was current that efforts were being made to reach a settlement. The people felt aggrieved at the news. Swami Viswananda warned everyone against any compromise and made it clear that the Mahabir Dal would not be responsible if any loss happened to anybody as a result of this compromise, and that it would work as usual for the temple.[26]    The rumour of a compromise effected by C. R. Das in exchange of two lakhs of rupees was flatly contradicted by the leaders.[27]    On the other hand Swami Satchidananda and two volunteers were arrested under sections 379 and 147 Cr. P. C. while the distribution of *bhog* was going on.[28]    Swami Viswananda reacted sharply to such high-handedness and announced that if the Government sided with the *Mohunt* five volunteers would offer satyagraha regularly.[29]    However, Swami Satchidananda and the volunteers were ordered to be released on bail of Rs. 500.    But the volunteers refused to take bail.[30]

Against all these activities of the Mahabir Dal, the *Mohunt* prayed for Government help and the Government readily intervened in the matter under the plea of maintaining law and order. So long the movement had been a religious one but with the interference of the Government 'the issue became a political one.'[31]    It was reported that the Government also set up a committee to inquire into the matter.[32]

On the other hand as the agents of the *Mohunt* left the temple, the volunteers took over charge.[33]    It was also decided that five satyagrahis would daily court arrest by distributing the *bhog* and May 20 was announced as the day when the satyagraha movement would be launched with the object of occupying the palace of the *Mohunt*.

Once again it was rumoured that on May 5 C. R. Das had sent a telegram to Swami Satchidananda and to the Manager of *Mohunt*'s estates : "My advice is neither party should be aggressive. I am trying to bring about an amicable settlement of the *Mohunt*'s affairs."[34] The volunteers were much confused at such a rumour. To give the lie to this rumour Chitta Ranjan published a statement : "I hear from Swami Viswananda that many persons who have given evidence against the Mohunt are likely to be oppressed if a settlement is arrived at. There is no cause of any such apprehension. I assure everybody that I shall be no party to any settlement which will not protect the people of Tarakeswar or those who stood by a true religious spirit against the Mohunt. The temple and the Debuttor property (property devoted to god) must also be protected."[35] This statement of Deshabandhu Das was enough to remove the confusion among the volunteers.

So long the leaders of Mahabir Dal had been requesting the BPCC to take charge of the movement. Finally, the BPCC came forward to shoulder the responsibility. In a meeting dated 14 May 1924 the Council of the BPCC resolved to recommend to the BPCC that immediate steps should be taken for starting a satyagraha campaign at Tarakeswar. It also resolved that a contingent of volunteers should immediately be sent to Tarakeswar for the relief of the local people and of the pilgrims.[36]

As stated earlier the satyagraha movement was to be launched on May 20. But before its commencement another serious incident took place on May 16. It was reported that on the said day some people brought vegetables and fruits on the back of their oxen to the market for sale. When the sale was over and they were ready to leave the place, the *ijaradar* of the market who happened to be a relation of the *Mohunt* demanded toll. The people refused to pay it as this type of exaction had been postponed for the past two weeks due to the effort of the volunteers of Mahabir Dal. Thereupon several men, alleged to be goondas hired by the *Mohunt,* began to assault them and forcibly seized their oxen. When this news reached Swami Satchidananda, he immediately reached the place with some volunteers. Before his arrival at the spot some Gurkhas who were reported to have been employed by the *Mohunt* appeared there and assaulted the people right and left with their *kukris.* When the Gurkhas and the up-country men saw Swamiji coming there, they surrounded the latter and mercilessly beat him. He was then bodily carried by a few Gurkhas to an unknown place. All these caused panic and the market and shops were immediately closed. Several persons got injured seriously. Learning about this incident, the Inspector of Police came with two constables but he had to leave the place as the Gurkhas with their *kukris* hotly pursued him for a distance of nearly 200 feet ; he suddenly fell down and rolled into the drain. However, later he informed the Deputy Magistrate, specially stationed at the place, of the incident. He also asked the help of military police but as he had no authority to give orders for shooting, he waited for the arrival of the Deputy Magistrate.

Meanwhile people had been searching anxiously for Swami Satchidananda. But no trace of Swamiji was found and rumours were afloat that he had been murdered. On the basis of this rumour, Swami Viswananda sent a telegram to Calcutta that Swami Satchidananda had been killed.[37] However after a long time the police found Swami Satchidananda groaning in a corner of a room on the ground floor of the *dharmasala.* Ten or twelve Gurkhas who assaulted Swamiji were detected and

immediately arrested by the police. Later Swamiji reported
that an attempt was made to kill him but due to the timely
interference of an up-country Brahmin it was frustrated. He
also stated that he received severe injuries on his back.[38]

All these incidents infuriated the people. They set up a
barricade over about 200 yards of the railway line in protest
against the event.   In Calcutta also there prevailed tremendous
excitement when the news spread.   Accordingly, Shyam Sundar
Chakraborty on behalf of the BPCC left for Tarakeswar to
inquire into the matter.   When he reached, he saw the place
almost deserted.   Thereafter a few persons took him to the
railway station where the barricade was placed.   He then
met the volunteers and Swami Satchidananda.   They told
him that as long as activities of this type by the *Mohunt*
and his agents were not stopped they would not allow
any train to run up and down the line.   They demanded the
arrest of the culprits and the *Mohunt*.   Then the SDO
informed them that the culprits were arrested but as there
was no evidence against the *Mohunt* himself he could not be
apprehended.   This pacified the people and the barricade was
lifted by the volunteers.[39]

A meeting was organized the following day where the
leaders emphasized the necessity of forbearance and non-
violence.   They requested the people to carry on the struggle
to a successful end.   In protest against the assaults on Swami
Satchidananda and others hartal was observed in the local
market for one day, i.e., the day after the incident occurred.[40]

On the other hand, a person named Subodh Krishna Basu
introducing himself as the Secretary of Hindu Temple Reform
League sent a telegram to the Governor, the Viceroy, and
Mahatma Gandhi as follows :

"After publication of Deshbandhu Das's message to adopt
Satyagraha, rioting and violence started this morning in
Tarakeswar temple.   Satyagrahi volunteers rushed Mohunt's
house resulting in bloodshed assault on police Sub-Inspector,
Swami Abhedananda of Sanatani Hindu Sabha and Swami
Satchidananda of Mahabir Dal.   There was looting, stone
throwing, shouting Mahatma's name notwithstanding police

remonstrance. Public apprehends repetition of Chaurichaura. Pray immediate intervention and investigation through reliable agency."[41] However later it was understood that the said Subodh Krishna Basu was an agent of the *Mohunt*. Makhan Lal Sen of *Ananda Bazar Patrika* contradicted this telegraphic statement and sent ano ther telegram to Mahatma Gandhi assuring him that everything reported by Subodh Basu was a lie and the volunteers and people had been peaceful and non-violent.[42]

### III

After its intervention in the matter the Government endeavoured to arrive at a settlement. The officials in charge of Tarakeswar affairs made one such effort. Meanwhile the District Court, Hooghly, gave its verdict in favour of the appointment of a Receiver for the temple of Siva and the vegetable market, granting the appeal made by one Ranjanlal Sinha Roy.[43] Now the Government officials argued that the main complaints against the *Mohunt* were the exaction of exorbitant charges from the pilgrims, oppression in the temple, etc. But since the Receiver had been appointed the *Mohunt* would have no hand in the management of the temple and there would be no cause for complaint. Hence they urged the leaders of the movement not to make any further demonstration. But Swami Viswananda asserted that if any Receiver was to be appointed it was to be done by the people. At this the officers rejoined that there were only two ways open to them in this matter : (i) proving in the Court that the estates belonged to the deity, i.e., it was a public *debottar* property and (ii) getting necessary laws enacted by the legislature. Swamiji argued that he was in favour of a legislation but it must be based on public opinion. At the same time he made it clear that they would not budge an inch from their decision of starting satyagraha. They were ready to face any suffering for vindicating their rights. Hence it became clear that there would be a confrontation between the public and the Government—the one eager to vindicate its inherent right and the other to maintain law and order.[44]

In accordance with the decree of the District Court on May 19 Shyama Charan Ukil Banerjee, the Receiver, came to take charge of the temple and the local market. On his way to the temple he was accompanied by police officers. On hearing the news the people rushed towards the temple. They fell flat on the road and blocked the Receiver's access to the temple. It was reported that when the proclamation appointing a Receiver was being read out, the people cried out, "We do not want a Receiver appointed by Court. We want a committee, formed of the public and by the public for the management of the *debottar* property." Realizing the hostile mood of the people the Receiver left the place.[45]   Later he sent a report to to the District Judge, Hooghly : "I have prepared an inventory of the properties belonging to the temple but the list is incomplete owing to the fact the temple is under the control of the Mahabir Dal and Congress party and my men have no access to it to be able to enter the properties of the temple in the said list. The Mohanta is away and his whereabouts are not known. I have not yet taken the charge of the things as I have got no place to keep them in safe custody 'the ornaments of the deity'. I suggest that these things may be left in the custody of Mohanta's chela Prabhat Chandra Giri."[46]   A telegram was sent to the District Judge, Hooghly, on behalf of the ryots of Tarakeswar : "Ryots of Tarakeswar estate do not want any Receiver. Pray for a Committee appointed by the public."[47]

Later in the afternoon the Divisional Commissioner, Burdwan Division, accompanied by the DM and the SDO, visited the place to inquire into the matter ; he also had the same experience. The upshot of people's action was that the Receiver could not take charge of the temple.[48]   This marked another victory for the satyagrahis. However at night the police arrested twenty volunteers.[49]

## IV

At last came the long-awaited May 20 when the organizers had decided to start satyagraha.[50]   The Government made a last attempt to avert the satyagraha. In the morning on the day scheduled for satyagraha, the District Magistrate called on Anil Baran Roy, Secretary of the BPCC, to discuss the terms of settlement. The District Magistrate offered the following terms for a compromise : (i) possession of the Temple should be delivered to the Receiver ; (ii) the District Magistrate would endeavour to get all the parties in the suit pending in the Court apply for an Arbitration Board on the points of dispute ; (iii) The suit relating to the temple was to be decided by a committee acceptable to the public and the representative of the *Mohunt*. As against these terms, Anil Baran Roy set forth the following : (i) the *Mohunt* must accept the Arbitration Board to be appointed by C. R. Das as the President of the BPCC ; (ii) in the meantime the satyagrahis would be in possession of the temple ; and (iii) all prisoners should be released. But none of the terms offered by either side was acceptable to the other.[51]

As the compromise talks failed, there was no alternative to satyagraha as already announced. Accordingly, on May 20 at 12 noon four volunteers offered satyagraha before the *Mohunt*'s house defying the prohibitory order.[52] The action-pattern of satyagraha was as follows : the volunteers proceeded to the *Mohunt*'s palace and demanded entrance claiming it to be a public property. The police cordoned the palace gate preventing the satyagrahis' access to it. But the satyagrahis broke their way through the cordon and were arrested. Thenceforth regularly 16 to 20 satyagrahis courted arrest. On May 21 the Government took a drastic step in arresting Swami Viswananda. Earlier he was served with an order directing him to leave Serampore subdivision within 12 hours (from the time when the notice was received by Swamiji) and not to visit or stay in Dhaniakhali P.S. on the ground that he was trying to cause disturbance.[53]

The whole situation took a serious turn on May 22 when the Railways authorities under instructions from the Government stopped all communications with Tarakeswar by cancelling up trains in that direction. This was preceded by a minor incident. About 200 workers of Liluah workshop reached Tarakeswar Station to join the movement there. Apprehending trouble, the police detained them within the platform enclosure of the station. Fearing that a further batch of railwaymen might arrive, messengers were sent to the District Traffic Superintendent, Liluah, asking him to take steps. Accordingly, measures were taken to prevent the workers from proceeding to Tarakeswar. When the train for Tarakeswar arrived at Liluah about 2000 men of the workshop came out for boarding the train. The station authorities and the Railway Police ordered them not to board the train but in utter disregard of the warning they rushed into the train. Seeing this the authority ordered cancellation of the train. In protest the workers set up a barricade on the line. However, after much pursuasion they left the line but the trains remained cancelled.[54] Gandhi on learning this disapproved the action of the railwaymen.[55]

The satyagraha movement once again found new vigour due to the presence of C. R. Das, President of the BPCC. Deshabandhu Das visited Tarakeswar on 30 May 1924. The police did not allow him to enter the temple. During his visit to Tarakeswar he had a long conference with Swami Satchidananda. It was decided there that Das would take charge of Tarakeswar affairs after his return from Serajgunge Conference. It was reported that Swami Satchidananda had slight difference with Mahabir Dal volunteers over the question of conducting the movement at Tarakeswar. Swamiji decided to give up his leadership and to offer himself for arrest as he was disgusted with the 'party feeling' manifest in all the activities of the Mahavir Dal. Some people intervened with a view to effecting a compromise and ultimately everything was settled. C. R. Das advised Satchidananda not to take up the attitude of resignation and asked the workers to maintain cordial relationship with each other and to work unitedly for the common cause. The Secretary of Mahabir Dal, on the other hand, stated that there was no doubt some misunderstanding as a result of which Swamiji was annoyed with them and intended to hand over the key of the temple to the Receiver. The Secretary stated that as a result of this intervention the matter was settled.[56]

After visiting Tarakeswar C. R. Das made a statement which demands our close attention. He stated : "From what

I have seen I am confirmed in my view that it is the duty of every Hindu in Bengal to support this Satyagraha movement. In my opinion, unless the Mohunt accepts a reasonable settlement the Provincial Conference at Serajgunj should take it up and invite the whole of Bengal to this struggle for the purification of one of the most important shrines in the province. The Government has taken up an utterly unwarrantable position. Inside what is claimed to be the house of *Mohunt* there is a public temple of which the Bigraha (the presiding deity) is Lakshmi Narayan, and also the Dharmasala for the convenience of the pilgrims. It it utterly preposterous to support the Mohunt's claims that this is his private property." Finally, he concluded, "After this nothing remains but the struggle of Satyagraha."[57]

Meanwhile an appeal over the signatures of about 2000 villagers was sent to the BPCC and also to the Provincial Conference at Serajgunj requesting the BPCC to take charge of the movement. And the conference resolved to support the movement and recommended to the BPCC to take charge of it.[58]

### V

In pursuance of the resolution at Serajgunj[59] the BPCC took charge of the satyagraha movement at Tarakeswar on June 6. Accordingly C. R. Das with his wife, Basanti Devi, and Dr Pratap Chandra Guha Roy came to Tarakeswar and after consulting Swami Satchidananda he asked Dr Guha Roy to conduct the movement. Swamiji also endorsed that arrangement.[60] Thenceforth the movement began to be directed by the BPCC and the volunteers courted arrest under its leadership. And still the Receiver stayed at the place.[61] He also lodged a complaint with the local police against the Mahabir Dal that they had illegally sunk a tubewell within his jurisdiction and had stolen his building materials.[62]

Yet another grave incident occurred at Tarakeswar on June 11. On that day 35 arrested women volunteers were discharged by the Magistrate but they refused to leave the Court compound untill Swami Satchidananda was released.

In the afternoon when Swami Satchidananda was ordered
to be remanded to police custody and accordingly when he
was being taken to the lock-up by the police, a large number
of men and women formed a ring round him in the court
compound. In the meantime a meeting was held and addressed by Swami Satchidananda and Santosh Kumari Gupta
who exhorted the people to join the movement. At this the
Inspector of Police came to disperse the meeting and asked
Swamiji to follow the police to the lock-up. The Inspector
then ordered the police to take Swamiji to the police station.
There followed a mele'e as a result of which a woman was
hurt and fell down unconscious. Yet the women did not
leave Swamiji. Ultimately, the police attempted forcibly to
break the cordon made around Swamiji by the women. At
this stage Swamiji fell down unconscious. Later a procession
was taken out with his unconscious body in a stretcher carried
by the women to the hospital where he regained his senses.[63]
Meanwhile Dr Pratap Chandra Guha Roy left Tarakeswar
on June 13 to attend the famous Charmanair Defamation
case* handing over the charge of the movement to Lalmohan
Ghosh.[64]

From July 24 the satyagrahis adopted new tactics. Instead
of approaching the *Mohunt*'s house through the eastern gate
the satyagrahis now began to do the same at the south gate
of the *Mohunt*'s palace. Eventually the whole movement
reached its climax on August 22 culminating in a serious
riot at the gate of the *Mohunt*'s palace. The situation
getting out of hand, the police had to open fire. On
that day the *Janmastami* (the birthday of Lord Krishna)
festival was being observed by the pilgrims. According
to a long-standing custom the deity of Lakshmi Narayan
was taken out of the temple which was situated inside the
*Mohunt*'s palace to the temple of Tarakeswar for worship.
The satyagrahis, it may be recalled, had been offering satyagraha with a view to asserting their right to enter the temple
of Lakshmi Narayan. However, it was decided after negotiations that a few Brahmins would take the deity out of the

* See Chapter XI.

temple and that the procession of satyagrahis would come up to the palace gate. Now while negotiations were going on in the presence of the Magistrate specially stationed at the place, about 500 volunteers led by Swami Satchidananda, some of whom were armed with lathis, rushed through the eastern gate disregarding the warning of the Magistrate. Finding no other way the Magistrate ordered the constables to fire. Consequently, eight or nine satyagrahis including Swami Satchidananda were wounded. According to the police, however, the Magistrate and a few other constables were injured by brickbats which continued to be hurled for some time.[65] This news was contradicted by others and thus there was a confusion among the different parties as to who threw the brickbats. According to Satish Chandra Chakravorty, the Superintendent of the Satyagraha Committee at Tarakeswar, "As soon as Swamiji went close to the gate one constable gave him push and he fell down. The constables began to drag him towards the palace showering lathi blows on him. People standing outside unarmed protested and a scuffle ensued. Missiles and brickbats were thrown at the innocent people and gun shots were also made. To make the situation worse all the lights at or near the palace gate were put out just before the firing began."[66] *The Statesman*, known for its pro-Government bias, observed in its editorial column : "The disturbance which took place at Tarakeswar on Friday evening was clearly no part of Congress agitation, and deserves to be considered in its proper light. It was caused by genuine pilgrims who had arrived in large numbers at the shrine for worship and who had the right to expect that the images of Lakshmi Narayan should be exposed in the Janmasthami day. The Mohunt's chela refused to allow the images to leave the place, because he feared that they would not be brought back after the ceremony and the loss would be fatal to his master's prestige. Whether the images would have been restored or not it is impossible to say, though it is easy to understand chela's fears. But if the guardian of sacred things has quarelled so hopelessly with those for whose worship they are intended that he is afraid to let them be seen, he

7

is on that ground alone unfit to be their guardian." Finally, the daily concluded that "it is clear that the chela and the chela alone is responsible for the whole affair, save in so far as the situation had been embittered by the long-drawn-out wrangling about Mr. C. R. Das' 'emissaries' urging the Government to deal sternly with the peccant chela."[67]

Now one thing is evident from the above observation that the allegations against the satyagrahis were not true and that the agents of the *Mohunt* were solely responsible for the untoward incident.

When satyagraha was going on in full swing a certain rift was seen among the leaders. The leaders engaged themselves in vilifying one other. This campaign of vilification hampered the progress of the movement to a great extent. C. R. Das, the accredited leader of the movement, was the main victim of such vilification. Certain serious allegations were made against him : (i) that he wanted to create a friction between landlords and tenants ; (ii) that he wanted the removal of permanent settlement ; (iii) that he was a Brahmo and wanted to do away with Hindu shrines ; (iv) that he wanted to take up these shrines to finance his party and make Tarakeswar the headquarters of the Swarajya Party ; (v) failing that he wanted to remove the *Mohunt* ; (vi) by doing so he wanted to give the *Mohuntship* to some Bengali against the usual tradition which always had been to select someone from Hindi-speaking community. In a rejoinder C. R. Das stated : "I do not desire any friction between landlords and tenants. I have opposed the idea of such class war from public platforms. The question of the repeal of Permanent Settlement is an undesirable question to raise and in my opinion whatever steps are taken must be taken after the attainment of Self-Government and even then only as a matter of agreement between landlords and tenants.

"I am not a Brahmo. I am a Hindu and I claim to be sincere. It is absolutely untrue that I want to take up Hindu shrines to finance my party. My point of view is the Hindu point of view. I want the shrines to be purified and reformed. I do not want to remove Mohuntship but to have a devout

Mohunt appointed so that the service in the temple may be properly supervised and income applied to the good of the pilgrims and the locality by establishing such educational and charitable institutions as may be required for the good of the people. In my opinion this is not politics. But if it is so regarded I am not ashamed of it.

"Nor is it true that I want the Mohuntship to go to some Bengali instead of Hindi-speaking gentleman. I do not wish to interfere in the slightest degree with the traditions of the particular sect to which the Mohunt belongs."[68]

This type of wrangling manifested itself once again over the settlement issue. At the outset it was rumoured that a settlement was arrived at between C. R. Das and the *Mohunt*. It was learnt that the *Mohunt* was ready to come to a settlement if he was allowed to keep the properties which were in his name as the *Mohunt* and the temple with its property worth a lakh of rupees would be vested in a committee.[69] At first the report was contradicted by C. R. Das but finally he published certain terms for settlement,[70] the main provisions of which were the following : (i) Satish Chandra Giri, the present *Mohunt*, would abdicate, (ii) Prabhat Chandra Giri would become the *Mohunt* and would be under the complete control of the committee even to the extent that the committee would have power to remove him from the *gaddi*, (iii) properties of which the net income might be over Rs. 30,000 and the temple offerings which every year amounted to at least double that amount would be placed in the hands of the committee for the purpose of *seva* and necessary charities, educational or otherwise, (iv) that other properties of which the net income might be between Rs. 25,000 and Rs. 32,000 would be managed by the *Mohunt*, that is to say, Prabhat Giri and his successors for the time being, but the said income should be devoted to the maintenance of whoever the *Mohunt* might be. The *Mohunt* would have no right to any further sum for his maintenance out of the properties and the temple offerings would be placed in the hands of the committee, (v) Prabhat Giri and his successors would be bound by the scheme of management which was to be drawn up by the committee, (vi) that if the said Prabhat Chandra Giri oppressed the tenants for maintaining properties the committee would at once take possession of them and manage directly, (vii) the temple and the palace along with other properties would be public properties and be managed by the committee, and (viii) the worship of Luxmi Narayan Jiu should be opened to the public.[71]

After the announcement of the terms of settlement C.R. Das held that all these terms fulfilled the object of satyagraha.[72] But Swami Satchidananda who in the beginning was in charge of the movement did not accept this settlement. His main objections against the settlement were the appointment of Prabhat Giri as the *Mohunt* and the constitution of the various committees on the ground that the members of the Swarajya Party formed a majority in them.[73] The same stand was taken earlier by Acharya Prafulla Chandra Roy who took keen interest in the movement. According to Acharya Roy, "The first indispensable condition for a settlement of the Tarakeswar affair is, as Swami Satchidananda insists, that neither Satish Giri nor his 'chela' Prabhat Giri should be allowed to defile the 'gadi' of Tarakeswar. ... It is, therefore, right and proper that the terms of settlement with the Mohunt should not be discussed and settled in camera only by a particular party or a section of the people behind the back of the entire Hindu community. A committee should at once be formed which must not contain the majority of the Swarajya Party as is said to be the case with the present Satyagraha Committee, but in which should be adequately represented every section of the Hindu community. This committee will settle terms of compromise with the Mohunt."[74]

Thus one thing is clear from the above that the dissentients were ready to accept the settlement but objected to the appointment of Prabhat Giri as the *Mohunt* in place of Satish Giri and to the composition of the committee. However, later on Swami Satchidananda asked the Government to appoint a Receiver to set matters right and to facilitate the realization of land revenues as well as the management of temple affairs.[75]

In accordance with the terms of settlement, on 22 September 1924, the *Mohunt*, Satish Chandra Giri, abdicated in favour of

his *chela* Prabhat Chandra Giri. The police were also withdrawn from the gate of the *Mohunt*'s palace. As usual twenty
volunteers were ready to offer satyagraha but nobody was
arrested as the palace was declared a public property. Later
in a meeting in the presence of C. R. Das and Swami
Viswananda and others, Satish Chandra Giri declared : "if
I have done any wrong either consciously or unconsciously,
the public will pardon me. I request the public present here to
signify their attitude to (*sic*) forgiveness by raising their
hands." (It was reported that all raised their hands).[76]
Earlier he announced, "Repeated illness has made me weak
both in body and brain, so I am going to abdicate in favour
of Prabhat Giri whom I am leaving entirely in the hands of the
committee. Prabhat Giri will strictly follow the instruction of
the committee."[77]  In the same meeting C. R. Das made
it clear that he would be responsible for anything done
in connexion with the management of the temple and the
estate.[78]

   To make the terms of settlement effective it was decided
that the satyagraha movement at Tarakeswar would be
terminated.[79] And the civil suit pending in the Hooghly
District Court was agreed to be withdrawn by Dharanidhar
Sinha Roy and seven others who filed it. But by this time
three other members of the Brahman Sabha had added themselves as plaintiffs objecting to the compromise arrived at
between the original plaintiffs (that is, Dharanidhar Sinha Roy
& seven others) and Satish Giri and his *chela* Prabhat Giri on
the following grounds : (1) the proposed compromise was an
attempt to stifle a judicial and authoritative inquiry into the
merits of various questions : (2) the question which arose in
the suit affected the orthodox Hindus and they could not be
disposed of merely in accordance with the wishes of any particular individual and it was not a fit matter for private adjustment ; (3) the proposed compromise did not effectively secure
the rights of the deity in question and the scheme proposed by
the terms of the settlement was unsatisfactory and not in
consonance with law and custom, throwing 'a cloud upon the
title of the deity ; and (4) the compromise proposed for the

management of properties and affairs of the shrine did not command the confidence of worshippers at the temple and powers vested in the committee were illusory ; the terms were conflicting and contradictory in some respects.[80] The new plaintiffs also appealed to the Court for the appointment of a Receiver. In its judgment the Court ordered the appoinment of a Receiver. Accordingly, the Receiver, Amulya Chandra Bhaduri, took charge of the temple on 7 July 1925.[81]

During that time Gandhi was touring through Bengal. He was asked to give his opinion on the duty of satyagrahis in view of the judgment of the District Court of Hooghly in favour of the appointment of a Receiver. He asserted that it was impossible for satyagrahis to resist the possession by the Receiver nor was there any meaning in resisting his possession. The satyagrahis' duty would, therefore, be "to hand (over), on demand, the possession to the Receiver." According to Gandhi, "It will be time to reconsider the position when and if abuses creep in. It does not matter who become trustees of the Temple so long as there is a public trust properly managed. If the plaintiffs collude with the Mohunt, it will be again a matter for consideration as to what the satyagrahis should do."[82]

The Secretary of Satyagraha Committee was at one with Gandhi's views and declared the movement withdrawn. In a statement he said, "To the best knowledge of the public the Committee did rid the Temple of all abuses and corruption and secure public entry to the Lakshmi Narayan Deity. Their management regarding Puja, Bhog, pilgrims, etc., has been till now in very pure and proper condition and satisfactory to all orthodox Hindus. Thus the object of Satyagraha is attained."[83]

## VI

It is interesting to note the *Mohunt*'s attitude towards the movement. When the allegations were made against him, he contradicted all these on the ground that some interested persons had maliciously circulated those grievances to dislodge him from the *Mohuntship*. With a view to mobilizing opinion against the activities of Mahabir Dal, meetings were organized

by the *Mohunt*. In one such meeting, the *Mohunt* consented
to act according to the direction of an Advisory Committee set
up for the proper functioning of pilgrimage.[84] On March 12,
however, at the *Mohunt*'s conference at Tarakeswar it was
resolved that under the initiative of the *Mohunt* two lakhs of
rupees would be collected for the reassertion of the *Mohunt*'s
rights.[85]

In order to thwart the activities of the Mahabir Dal,
the *Mohunt*, it was reported, brought many goondas from
different places. He at the same time continued oppressing
the tenants.[86] The *Mohunt* also coerced the students
and tenants to work in favour of him, on pain of seizure
of lands from the tenants and expulsion of students from
school.[87]

But when all his efforts failed, he appealed to the Government for help on the ground that the leaders of the Mahabir
Dal threatened to kill him.[88] In a letter to the District
Magistrate dated April 21, he complained against the activities
of the Mahabir Dal making Swami Satchidananda and Swami
Viswananda responsible for the disturbances at Tarakeswar.
At the same time he suggested to the Magistrate the holding
of a conference to arrive at a settlement. He also told
the Magistrate that the conference failing to achieve its
purpose the whole dispute should amicably be settled through
the arbitration of leading members of the public, some
of whom would be nominated by him, an equal number of
arbitrators would be nominated by Swami Viswananda and
the rest by the Government. However, he did not forget to
mention in this connexion that the temple was not a public
endowment and, therefore, the public should have no right
to interfere in any way with the management of the trust.[89]
The *Mohunt* also went to Sir Asutosh Mukherjee to seek his
advice in this regard but it was reported that Sir Asutosh did
not pay any heed to him.[90]

Later on the *Mohunt* prayed for an injunction order against
Swami Viswananda and his volunteers so that they might not
interfere with the management of the temple and the properties
of the deity. In this petition allegations were made regarding

'the contemplated action' of the Mahabir Dal to take forcibly the possession of the *Mohunt*'s house.[91]

Efforts were also made on his part to create communal disturbances.[92]

But everything was in vain. Allegations against the *Mohunt* were so well founded that the people wholeheartedly supported the activities of the Mahabir Dal and enthusiastically participated in the movement. And the developments during the the movement left the *Mohunt* no other choice but to consent to a compromise. That was why when the compromise was suggested he immediately became a party to it.

## VII

In response to the *Mohunt*'s appeal the Government meddled in the Tarakeswar affair under the plea of 'apprehension of breach of peace'. A Special Magistrate was posted at the temple for the maintenance of law and order. An armed police force in addition to the local police was also stationed there to guard against any eventualities.[93] Arrangement for patrolling the streets during night was made to prevent any disturbance.[94]

As stated earlier, the satyagraha movement was launched on May 20. Precautions were taken by the Government to suppress the movement. The police were reinforced by contingents from Serampore and other places.[95] The District Magistrate announced that violations of law would be firmly death with.[96] On May 27 the Government issued a communique' reaffirming its previous stand.[97] In practice the Government sided with the *Mohunt* and applied its machine of oppression against the satyagrahis. It arrested a large number of satyagrahis and maltreated them inside the jail. Once the Government even resorted to shooting.[98] The arrested satyagrahis were transferred to jails in different districts of Bengal. Reports of merciless oppression in different jails perpetrated by the authorities clearly indicate the Government attitude towards the satyagrahis. It was reported that 14 boy-satyagrahis were mercilessly beaten in Bankura jail.[99] In protest against this maltreatment, several times the satyagrahi

prisoners resorted to hunger strike.[100]   The condition of the
jail in which the satyagrahi prisoners were kept was also not
good.  In Serampore jail where a large number of satyagrahis
were imprisoned no beds were provided for them to sleep
in and they were huddled together in a small unswept room.
Just outside the prisoners' room there was an accumulated
heap of filth.[101]   In Berhampore jail the authorities committed
indecent assaults and other sorts of oppression upon the
satyagrahi prisoners.  When the satyagrahis reported to the
Superintendent of Jail about the maltreatment, the latter rewarded them with penal diet and the satyagrahi prisoners went
on hunger strike in protest.  The authorities did not provide
even medical aid to the ailing satyagrahi prisoners.[102]

All this barbarous and inhuman oppression done on the
satyagrahi prisoners shows nothing but the revengeful attitude
of the Government.  It is no wonder, therefore, that Lord
Lytton described the movement as a 'colossal hoax'.[103]

## VIII

We have already seen that the Brahman Sabha played
an important role in this movement.  And that is why its
stand in the movement deserves attention.  From the beginning
it pitted itself against the satyagraha movement.[104]   The
Brahman Sabha was a religious group composed of orthodox
Brahmins.  When the BPCC formed a committee for the
satyagraha movement some of the members of the Sabha
were included in it.  But in a meeting it resolved not to
join the committee as it wanted to dislodge the *Mohunt* by
legal means.[105]   In fine it was the demand of the Brahman
Sabha that there should be a proper inquiry into the conduct
of the *Mohunt* and that if he was found unworthy of the post
he should be removed but the removal must be effected by legal
procedure.  It wanted that in place of Satish Giri a successor
should be appointed according to orthodox Hindu scriptures
and traditions.[106]

The Brahman Sabha also did not support the terms of
settlement formulated by C. R. Das.  As against these terms
the Sabha opined that :

1. The public would have the right of *darsan* of Lakshmi Narayan. The right of *seva* and *puja* would be according to the *sastras*.

2. Opinion as to the division of the property into two kinds and their management would be given after examination of the lists of properties. But neither Satish Giri nor Prabhat Chandra Giri should be allowed to reside in the palace of the *Mohunt* of Tarakeswar which would be considered and used as *debottar*.

3. There was no objection to establish a permanent Arbitration Committee. But the members of this committee should not be the members of the Managing Committee. The proposed Arbitration Committee should be constituted as follows : (1) Mahamahopadhyay Pandit Laxman Sastri (representative of the Brahman Sabha), (2) Pandit Madan Mohan Malaviya, (3) Deshabandhu C. R. Das. If there was a vacancy in any way in the Arbitration Committee, the remaining members of that committee and the members of the Managing Committee and of the Deva Seva Committee would together elect an orthodox Hindu. The decision would be by the majority.

4. The first Managing Committee would be made up of the following persons : (1) Maharajadhiraj Sir Rameswar Singh Bahadur, (2) Babu Anil Baran Roy, (3) Babu Satkaripati Roy, (4) Babu Brajendra Kishore Roy Choudhury, (5) Babu Madan Mohan Barman, (6) Babu Manohar De, (7) Prabhat Chandra Giri, (8) Babu Jogendra Nath Mukherjee, (9) Kumar Sibsekhareswar Roy, (10) Rai Jatindra Nath Choudhury, (11) Babu Manomohan Bhattacharyya. If there was a vacancy in any way in the committee it would be filled by election of an orthodox and prominent member of the Hindu community by the remaining members of the committee.

5. The first Deva Seva Samiti would be composed of the following persons : (1) the newly selected *Mohunt*, (2) Pandit Panchanan Tarakasastri, (3) Pandit Sitanath Vedantasastri, (4) Babu Jnanendra Nath Mukherjee (local), (65) Babu Tarak Nath Mukherjee (Uttarpara) (6) Pandit Sarat

Sankhya-Vedanta-Tirtha* (Brahman Sabha), (7) Babu Batu-keswar Mukherjee. If there would be any vacancies in the future in the committee, they should not be filled except by persons who were orthodox Brahmins prominent in Hindu society.

6. The following subjects would be in the hands of the Deva Seva Samiti : (1) the daily *puja*, *seva* and festive ceremonies of the temple ; (2) the management of Tarakeswar *chatuspathi* ; (3) arrangement for the board and lodging of guests and *sannyasins* as occasion would arise ; (4) offerings made to the deities and the *Mohunt* and all internal income of the temple would be considered as *debottar* and they would be made over by the Deva Seva Committee to the Managing Committee with an account. All this income would have to be spent on Deva Seva ; (5) At least half of the income of other *debottar* properties would have to be spent on the work entrusted to the Deva Seva Committee ; (6) at the beginning of every year, the Deva Seva Committee would submit a budget estimate to the Managing Committee which would sanction it, and at the end of the year the accounts would be audited by the auditors appointed by the Managing Committee.

7. Satish Chandra Giri should not be allowed to remain the *Mohunt*. Prabhat Chandra Giri should not be allowed to be installed to the *Mohuntship*. He might become a member of the Managing Committee. Arrangements would have to be made to instal a young *Brahmachari* of good character according to the rules of the temple. The charge of his education should be entrusted to the Deva Seva Committee.

8. The rules that were in force about the appointment of the *Mohunt* of the temple would have to be clearly recorded in the deed of settlement.

9. Charges corresponding to the above provisions would have to be made in the other portions of the proposed terms of settlement.[107]

However pious the above mentioned propositions might have been, all these revealed nothing but the fanatic attitude of the Brahman Sabha. This attitude was betrayed even earlier when the Brahman Sabha objected to the removal of the restrictions between touchables and untouchables made possible by the Satyagraha Committee.[108]

So it is no wonder that the Brahman Sabha would create difficulty in preventing the settlement from being effected. As already stated, the Brahman Sabha prayed to the District Court for the cancellation of the terms of settlement and also for the appointment of a Receiver which was later granted.

## IX

It hardly requires any evidence to state that the success of a movement depends to a great extent on organization, which means building up, co-ordination and utilization of human and material resources. The leaders of the satyagraha movement at Tarakeswar were aware of this. For our purpose we would like to divide the whole organizational activities under two heads—one under the leadership of the Mahabir Dal and the other under the BPCC.

We have already seen that the Mahabir Dal was the first to take up the issue. They decided to launch a movement against the *Mohunt*. For the purpose of recruitment of volunteers offices were opened at Calcutta and Tarakeswar. It was laid down that persons and volunteers who wanted to go to Tarakeswar must be prepared to offer themselves for satyagraha ; they must be ready to face imprisonment. Volunteers were directed to proceed to Tarakeswar through their respective District Congress Committees or the Hindu Sabha. Persons in Calcutta who were not organizationally attached to any Congress Committee were to first register themselves at the office of the Mahabir Dal, 179 Harrison Road, or at Hindu Sabha office, 10/1/1, Syed Gally Lane or at the Temple of Baldeoji, 25 Grey Street or at the offices of different area Congress committees. They were requested to proceed direct to Tarakeswar at their own cost. Arrangements were made by the Akalis to open a *langarkhana*.[109]

Public meetings were also arranged for mobilizing public opinion. In these meetings people were urged to find out means to remedy matters by putting another *Mohunt* on the *gaddi* who would prove worthy of such an office and also to pass the Religious Endowment Bill.[110]   On May 16 an important meeting was organized at Harish Park, Calcutta 'to consider how to devise means to form wards in the city for the voters to see for themselves and instruct the members of the Council'.   But that object was postponed as on that very day a fracas took place arising out of the maltreatment meted out to Swami Satchidananda by the agents of the *Mohunt*.   However, the speakers realizing the gravity of the situation at Tarakeswar resolved to support Congress which launched satyagraha there 'to keep the fair name of the fair sex intact'.   The speakers urged people that they 'should adopt non-violent non-co-operation.   Men should be sent there to preserve the honour of their mothers, wives and sisters."[111]

Actually the satyagraha started on 20 May 1924.   In order to reinforce the movement the volunteers began to pour into the place.   Arrangements for their board and lodging were made.   What was more the local people showed keen enthusiasm to join the movement.[112]   Swami Satchidananda and Swami Viswananda issued a statement regarding the ends and means of the proposed satyagraha.   As regards the ends they emphasized that the *Mohunt* should be dismissed and all the *debottar* property must be under the management of a representative Hindu committee and the said property should be utilized for the service of the country.   The Congress would select the members of the committee.   And as regards the means it was urged that satyagrahis would have to resort to peaceful means to achieve these ends.   For the purpose of occupying the temple volunteers in as good numbers as possible should offer satyagraha.   The participant satyagrahis must elect a leader from among themselves and everyone should abide by his orders and advice. The orders of the leader must not be inconsistent with the proposed ends and means.   Satyagrahis are always to take help from and act according to the advice of the Congress.[113]

Appeals were also made to the countrymen to join the movement.   Young men who were ready to follow the code as suggested above were asked to enroll themselves as volunteers and people were requested to help financially according to their mite. For the purpose of recruitment of volunteers and of collecting funds for the movement certain centres were opened in Calcutta: (1) Bengal Provincial Congress Committee, 38/1 Sukea Street; (2) Bagbazar Darjipara Rastra Samiti, 62 Syampukur Street; (3) Simla Garpar Rastra Samiti, 69 Simla Street; (4) North Calcutta Rastra Samiti, 42 Bana- mali Sarkar Street; (5) Jorabagan Rastra Samiti, 2 Lakshmi Narayan Mukherjee Lane; (6) Central Calcutta Rastra Samiti, 1 Lalbehari Thakur Lane; (7) South Calcutta Rastra Samiti, Bhawanipore.[114]

The movement received inspiration from distinguished per- sonalities like Acharya Prafulla Chandra Roy, Sarala Devi and others. Some leaders, however, doubted whether it was proper to launch satyagraha on this issue. In a statement Sarala Devi said, "when India launched into ( sic ) Satyagraha for the first time in 1919 on account of the Rowlatt Bill Mahatmaji had declared, 'Satyagraha is your Kamadhenu. It will fulfil all wishes'. Quite true ! But one must remember, specially after the direct evidence of 1919 events, that when the Kamadhenu shakes her tail spiritual force gives force to brutal force. It is from the tail of Vasistha's wishing cows that a fighting mob sprang up armed cap-a-pie who showered their missiles on the Royal Army who wounded them. It was the restraining force of Vasistha, the greatest store-house of soul force, that preven- ted them from killing the King's soldiers outright. Satyagraha is a most fine spiritual weapon. In my humble opinion in a satyagraha campaign unless the rank and file submit them- selves to the leadership of an expert in the science and use of it, they are likely to exceed limits."[115]

Tarakeswar satyagraha was mainly a religious movement launched against the removal of certain abuses in Hindu shrines. But it is quite significant that even the Mohammedans sympathized with the satyagrahis. They were welcomed by the Hindus too. It was reported that the Calcutta Khilafat Committee voiced its support in favour of the struggle. The committee was prepared, it was announced, to render every practical help to vindicate the principle involved in the struggle if called upon by 'the great Hindu community'.[116]

The leaders of the Mohammedan community heartily supported the movement. As Maulavi Abdul Hamed Deopuri observed in course of his speech at Mirzapur (now Sraddhananda Park) on 4 July 1924 that in the matter of religion when there was a general call for help and assistance the Hindus and Mohammedans should join hands and stand shoulder to shoulder on the common platform to save the religion in the country. It was admitted by him that from the standpoint of *fatwah* Mohammedans should not be allowed to enter the temple compound but they could help the Hindu brethren in dislodging the *Mohunt* from his post. The whole trouble, according to Maulavi Deopuri, would have been over long ago if the Government had not meddled in the affair. Finally, he appealed to all to help the movement.[117]

It was reported that a large number of Mohammedan youths had already come from Dacca and Tripura to offer satyagraha at Tarakeswar.[118] About 40 local Mohammedans came to offer satyagraha ; however they were entrusted with the duty of mobilizing men and collecting money.[119]

The BPCC took charge of the movement on 6 June 1924. It organized a committee for the proper functioning of the movement consisting of the following members : President : Deshabandhu C. R. Das ; Secretary : Lal Mohan Ghosh ; Members : Sasadhar Roy (President, Hindu Sabha), Pijush Kanti Ghosh (Secretary, Hindu Sabha), Girija Mohan Sanyal (Joint Secretary, Hindu Sabha), Panchanan Tarkaratna (President, Brahman Sabha), Mahamahopadhyay Lakshman Sastri (Secretary, Brahman Sabha), Benoy Bhusan Mukhopadhyay (Secretary, Bramhan Sabha), Surendra Mohan Ghosh, Basanta Kumar Majumdar, Amarendra Nath Bose, Srish Chandra Chatterjee, Satish Chandra Sarkar, Dr. J. M. Das Gupta, Dhara Nath Bhattacharya, Shyam Sundar Chakravorty, Swami Viswananda, Swami Satchidananda, Gour Hari Som, Tulsi Charan Goswami ; Treasurer : Madan Mohan Barman, Satkari Pati Roy, Anil Baran Roy.[120]

Dr Pratap Chandra Guha Roy undertook the responsibility for conducting the movement. An enquiry office and several other departments were opened for different purposes.[121] In Calcutta volunteers willing to join the movement were asked to register their names at 9 Russa Road.[122] The management of the temple was entrusted to a few volunteers of the Mahabir Dal and Congress who worked in excellent co-operation. All the religious rites were performed by them. *Bhog* was no longer sold to the highest bidder. The temple was made open to all by the volunteers. Money was no longer exacted from the people.

A satyagraha camp was set up for the recruitment of volunteers. An enquiry office was opened at the station. There was a medical and sanitary department in charge of Dr Ashutosh Das. It was reported that this department was very popular among the inhabitants of the locality and volunteers. On an average 30 patients came to the dispensary every day. The patients were treated free of cost. This department was also looking after the sanitary condition of the locality. It took precautions to prevent any outbreak of epidemic. Appeal was also made to the chemists and druggists to supply the medical camp at Tarakeswar with necessary medicines to save thousands of villagers from different diseases.[123]

There was also a *langarkhana* where on an average 300 men and women took their meals daily. Moreover, in order to popularize khaddar among the local people a sales office was opened at Tarakeswar by the organizers. A batch of volunteers regularly went to the villages to introduce khadi among the villagers.

There was a propaganda board which consisted of Gourhari Som, Bimal Chandra Ganguly, Dhara Nath Bhattacharyya, Benoy Kumar Basu, Brahmachari Jnanbhai, Ashesh Kumar Banerjee and Satya Charan Banerjee. It was the function of the members of the propaganda board to tour different places and hold public meetings there with a view to moulding public opinion in its favour.

A publicity board was also organized. Its duty was to collect correct information in all its detail. The reporters of the Calcutta Press and Associated Press were supplied with news by this board.[124] Sometimes inquiries were made by the committee to ascertain whether the pilgrims had experienced any ill-treatment or were made to pay illegal gratifications or whether they had any complaints or grievances against the arrangement made by the organizers.[125] Several distinguished personalities like Pandit Ramchandra Sastri, Kaviraj Sibnath Sen, Jitendranath Mitra of Burdwan, Bajroji Premji Bharucha from Bombay who was sent by Gandhi, Santosh Kumari Gupta, Surendra Mohan Ghosh of Mymensingh visited Tarakeswar to have first-hand impression of the satyagraha movement.[126]

X

Despite such extensive organizational activities the satyagraha movement at Tarakeswar during its last phase lost much of its tempo on account of paucity of human and material resources. The organizers were then searching for a settlement.[127] One might argue here that effort for an honourable settlement was an important criterion of satyagraha. But a careful analysis of the actual state of affairs shows that the settlement between the *Mohunt* and C. R. Das was arrived at not as a result of the former's conversion to the satyagrahis' point of view but rather it was the keen eagerness on the part of the latter that necessitated the settlement. Moreover, what is important was that the BPCC under the leadership of Deshabandhu Das directed the movement. It is to be noted in this connexion that the BPCC was at that time dominated by the Swarajya Party. It was held that C. R. Das assumed the charge to secure finance for the party. This point has been corroborated by Panchanan Chakravorty, a direct participant, who says that the settlement was arrived at to finance the Swarajya Party out of the income derived from the temple.[128] The attempt of the Swarajya Party to take political advantage of the situation brought for it 'certain unpopularity among particular sections of the community'.[129]

Finally, as regards the end-result of the movement R. C. Majumdar holds that the movement ended in a 'lamentable failure.'[130] We fail, however, to persuade ourselves to

8

subscribe to this view. For the purpose of satyagraha movement was to make the temple free from the corrupt practices of the *Mohunt*. As we have seen earlier it was judicially determined that a Receiver would take charge of the temple in place of the *Mohunt*. Thus it is evident that satyagraha was no longer required as its objects were fulfilled with the appointment of the Receiver. Gandhi correctly held : "The satyagraha was offered against the Mohunt or rather his methods. He is not in possession and the Court's order does not put him in possession. On the contrary, the judgment makes it clear that the Mohunt could not succeed, though he tried in gaining whole or partial possession.

"The object of satyagraha was to get rid of abuses in connection with the temple and to secure public entry to the Lakshmi Narain Temple. There is no question under the Court's order of any reversion to the old abuses or prohibition to temple entry. It is a matter of no moment to satyagrahis who has possession so long as the Temple management is pure and it is not the Mohunt who has the management."[131]

## NOTES AND REFERENCES

1. Cited in the editorial column, *Amrita Bazar Patrika*, 20.5.24, 4.

2. R. C. Majumdar, *History of the Freedom Movement in India*, III, 200. For details, see G.A. Sundaram, *Guruka Bagh Satyagrah* ; *Report of the Guruka Bagh Congress Enquiry Committee* ; H.N. Mitra (ed.), *Indian Annual Register*, I (1921-22), 144 (b)-(e).

For Gandhi's reaction to the Nankana tragedy, see *The Collected Works of Mahatma Gandhi*, XIX, 396-402, 422-5.

3. R.C. Majumdar, op. cit., 200.

4. *Forward*, 8.4.24, 4(3).

5. ibid., 25.4.24, 4(2).

6. Nabin-Elokesi affairs which took place in 1875 may be referred here. Nabin was a college student and Elokesi was his wife. Being persuaded by the *Mohunt* the parents of Elokesi forced her to go to the *Mohunt*. On learning this Nabin went to the *Mohunt's* house and out of indignation killed his wife with a 'dao'. For details, see Narendranath Bandyopadhyay, *Tarakeswar Satyagraha Samgram*, 32-3 ; Pramathanath

Sanyal Sastri, *Tarakeswar*, 32 and Sripantha, 'Mohanto-Elokesi Sambad,' in *Ananda Bazar Patrika*, Autumn Special, 1382 B.S., 27-37.

7. *Forward*, 10.4.24, 4(5). For details of the charges against the *Mohunt*, see Narendranath Bandyopadhyay, op. cit., 52-6.

8. The office-bearers of the Mahabir Dal were as follows : Founder—Swami Viswananda ; Commander—Swami Satchidananda ; Secretary—Makhan Lal Roy ; Assistant Secretaries—Durga Singh and Swabhab Brahmachari (alias Kalikrishna Ghosh). See Swarna Kumar Ghoshal, *Tarakeswar Satyagraher Itihas*, 14.

9. *Ananda Bazar Patrika*, 20.2.24.

10. ibid., 27.2.24, 3(6).

11. This refers to the open letter that Gandhi wrote to Akalis after the shooting of an Akali *Jatha*. The firing took place at Jaiton, on 21 February 1924, on a procession of Sikhs, including an Akali *Jatha* of 500 which had come all the way from Amritsar, after a march of over 3 weeks, to celebrate the anniversary of the Nankana incident in 1921. Gandhi advised Akalis to strictly adhere to non-violence 'in your special struggle about your Gurdwaras...' He asked them "to search yourselves and, if you find that you have not been true to the standard you set before yourselves, to cease further demonstration for the time being and perform the necessary cleansing process before beginning anew..." For the full text, see *The Collected Works of Mahatma Gandhi*, XXIII, 210-2.

12. *Amrita Bazar Patrika*, 28.2.24, 6(3).

13. *The Bengalee*, 9.4.24, 4(4).

14. *Amrita Bazar Patrika*, 2.3.24, 7(4).

15. *Ananda Bazar Patrika*, 3.4.24.

16. *Forward*, 8.4.24, 3(5).

17. ibid., 10.4.24, 3(5).

18. *Amrita Bazar Patrika*, 6.5.24, 6(3).

19. ibid., 20.4.24, 3(4).

20. *The Bengalee*, 9.4.24, 4(4).

21. *Ananda Bazar Patrika*, 13.4.24, 2(5-6).

22. *Amrita Bazar Patrika*, 16.4.24, 6(5).

23. *Forward*, 17.4.24, 6(3).

24. *Ananda Bazar Patrika*, 20.4.24, 2(4-5).

25. Narendranath Bandyopadhyay, op. cit., 83.

26. *Ananda Bazar Patrika*, 19.4.24, 2(6).

27. ibid., 24.4.24, 2(6).

28. ibid., 30.4.24, 2(6-7).

29. See note no. 24.

30. *Ananda Bazar Patrika*, 2.5.24, 3(4) ; *Amrita Bazar Partika*, 3.5.24, 5(2).

31. *The Indian Struggle 1920-1934*, 144.

32. *Ananda Bazar Patrika*, 2.5.24, 2(2).

33. ibid., 4.5.24, 2(4-5).

34. *Amrita Bazar Patrika*, 7.5.24, 5(5).

35. *The Bengalee*, 9.5.24, 4(7).

36. *Amrita Bazar Patrika*, 16.5.24, 6(2).

37. *Ananda Bazar Patrika*, 17.5.24, 2(1).

38. *Amrita Bazar Patrika*, 18.5.24, 5(4-5) ; *Ananda Bazar Patrika*, 18.5.24, 2(4-7).

39. *Amrita Bazar Patrika*, 18.5.24, 5(3-4) ; *Ananda Bazar Patrika*, 17.5.24, 2(1).

40. *Ananda Bazar Patrika*, 18.5.24, 2(5-6).

41. *Amrita Bazar Patrika*, 17.5.24, 5(2).

42. *Ananda Bazar Patrika*, 18.5.24, 2(7).

43. ibid., 17.5.24, 2(4).

44. *Amrita Bazar Patrika*, 18.5.24, 5(1-5).

45. ibid., 20.5.24, 5(1-2).

46. Quoted in Narendranath Bandyopadhyay, op. cit., 94-5.

47 & 48. See note no. 43.

49. *Ananda Bazar Patrika*, 21.5.24, 2(5).

50. For the full text of Swami Viswananda's appeal in this connexion, see *Amrita Bazar Patrika*, 18.5.24, 5(1).

For day-to-day account of the movement, see Swarna Kumar Ghoshal, op. cit., chs. III & IV.

51. *Amrita Bazar Patrika*, 21.5.24, 5(4).

52. *The Bengalee*, 21.5.24, 4(4) ; *Amrita Bazar Patrika*, 21.5.24.

53. *The Bengalee*, 22.5.24, 4(4) ; *Ananda Bazar Patrika*, 22.5.24, 3(1).

54. *The Bengalee*, 23.5.24, 4(4) ; *Ananda Bazar Patrika*, 23.5.24, 3(1-2) and *Amrita Bazar Patrika*, 23.5.24.

55. *The Collected Works of Mahatma Gandhi*, XXIV, 179-80.

56. *The Bengalee*, 31.5.24, 4(7).

57. *Amrita Bazar Patrika*, 31.5.24, 5(4) ; *The Bengalee*, 31.5.24, 4(7).

58. *Ananda Bazar Patrika*, 5.6.24, 2(7).

59. "This Conference expresses its sympathy with the Mahabir Dal who have launched Satyagraha under the leadership of the Swamis Viswananda and Satchidananda for management by a representative Hindu Committee to be elected by the Bengal Provincial Congress Committee of the Seva of Tarakeshwar, the temples, the palace, and Debutter properties and other moveable and immoveable properties standing in his and other persons' names by deposing the immoral and oppressive Mohunt Satish Giri, and his "Chela" Pravat Giri. This Conference requests the Bengal Provincial Congress Committee to take charge of and lead the movement and call upon the country to bring the movement to a successful issue with men and money."—H.N. Mitra (ed.), *Indian Quarterly Register*, 1924, I, 671.

60. *Ananda Bazar Patrika*, 7.6.24, 2(5). Also interview with Dr. Pratap Chandra Guha Roy, 3.9.71.

61. *The Bengalee*, 8.6.24, 4(7).

62. *Ananda Bazar Patrika*, 10.6.24, 3.

63. *The Bengalee*, 12.6.24, 4(4), 13.6.24, 5(5) ; *Amrita Bazar Patrika*, 12.6.24 and 13.6.24.

64. Swarna Kumar Ghoshal, op. cit., 33.

65. *The Bengalee*, 24.8.24, 5(1).

66. ibid., 26.8.24, 3(4).

67. *The Statesman*, 26.8.24, 6(3).

68. *The Bengalee*, 20.7.24, 6(4).

69. *Amrita Bazar Patrika*, 31.8.24, 6(1).

70. For the full text, see *The Bengalee*, 20.9.24, 4(6-7) and 6(4).

71. ibid., 6(4).

72. See note no. 69.

73. *The Bengalee*, 20.9.24, 4(6).

74. *Amrita Bazar Patrika*, 12.9.24, 4(4).

75. *Amrita Bazar Patrika*, 18.2.25, 7(2).

76. *The Bengalee*, 25.9.24, 5(7).

77 & 78. See note no. 74.

79. Swarna Kumar Ghoshal reports that the satyagraha was withdrawn on September 23, 1924. See Swarna Kumar Ghoshal, op. cit., 59.

80. *Amrita Bazar Patrika*, 12.3.25, 3(3).

81. ibid., 10.7.25, 3(4).
Meanwhile the *Mohunt* made a petition before the High Court praying to it for a stay-order against the decision of the District Court regarding the appointment of Receiver. [*Amrita Bazar Patrika*, 12.7.25, 6(5).] The High Court issued a rule to the effect. [*Amrita Bazar Patrika*, 14.7.25, 5(5).] Ultimately in its judgment the High Court sanctioned the appointment of Receiver only to the *debottar* property. This property included (i) properties over which a Receiver had already been appointed on 16 May 1924 consisting of the temple, the local market, the offerings made to the deity and the worship of the deity himself, and (ii) properties which had been treated as *debottar* so long. And the *Mohunt* would get back his personal properties. [*The Bengalee*, 9.1.26, 6(1).]

82. *The Collected Works of Mahatma Gandhi*, XXVII, 293.

83. *Amrita Bazar Patrika*, 9.7.25, 4(5).

84. *Ananda Bazar Patrika*, 6.3.24, 2(3-4).

85. ibid., 20.3.24, 4(2).

86. ibid., 20.2.24.

87. ibid., 13.4.24, 2(5-6).

88. ibid., 29.3.24, 5(5).

89. *Amrita Bazar Patrika*, 25.4.24, 8(1).

90. *Ananda Bazar Patrika*, 27.4.24, 2(4).

91. *The Bengalee*, 9.5.24, 6(3) and 14.5.24, 3(7).

92. *Ananda Bazar Patrika*, 11.5.24, 2(7).

93. *Amrita Bazar Patrika*, 15.5.24, 6(3).

94. ibid., 18.5.24, 5(1-5).

95.  ibid., 20.5.24, 5(1-2).

96.  *The Bengalee*, 21.5.24, 4(4).

97.  For the full text, see *The Bengalee*, 27.5.24, 3(5).

98.  "There were many arrests and a few lives were lost, either through rioting or police firing."—J. H. Broomfield, *Elite Conflict in a Plural Society*, 261.

99.  *The Bengalee*, 26.6.24, 5(7).

100. *Amrita Bazar Patrika*, 6.7.24, 5(3).

101. ibid., 8.7.24, 6(5).

102. ibid., 9.7.24, 5(6).

103. *The Bengalee*, 20.7.24, 4(1).

104. *Ananda Bazar Patrika*, 11.7.24, 2.

105. ibid., 13.6.24, 3(3-4).

106. *The Bengalee*, 20.7.24, 2(3).

107. *Amrita Bazar Patrika*, 25.9.24, 6(3-4).

108. ibid., 12.9.24, 11(5).

109. ibid., 4.5.24, 5(6).

110. ibid., 2.5.24, 6(5).

111. ibid., 17.5.24, 5(2).

112. ibid., 20.5.24, 5(1-2).

113. *Ananda Bazar Patrika*, 22.5.24, 3(2).

114. ibid., 25.5.24.

115. *The Bengalee*, 24.5.24, 3(5).

116. *Amrita Bazar Patrika*, 16.5.24, 6(2).

117 & 118.  ibid., 5.7.24, 6(1).

119. *Ananda Bazar Patrika*, 22.5.24, 3(1).

120. *Amrita Bazar Patrika*, 10.6.24, 8(2).

121. *Ananda Bazar Patrika*, 8.6.24, 2(5). Also interview with Dr. Pratap Chandra Guha Roy, 3.9.71.

Apart from the enquiry office, there were nine departments, namely, (1) Supervision of the ritual activities of the temple (2) Finance (3) Propaganda (4) Recruitment of volunteers (5) Volunteers (6) Recruitment of satyagrahis (7) Medical (8) Stores (9) Kitchen. See Swarna Kumar Ghoshal, op. cit., 30.

122. *Ananda Bazar Patrika*, 13.6.24, 3(3-4).

123. *Amrita Bazar Patrika*, 17.8.24, 6(6).

124. ibid., 6.7.24, 5(3) ; *The Bengalee*, 22.6.24. 5(6).

125. *Amrita Bazar Patrika*, 18.7.24, 3(4).

126. Narendranath Bandyopadhyay, op. cit., 83.

127. *Bengal Administration Report 1924-25*, xii—xiii.

128. Interview with Panchanan Chakravorty, 2.10.72.

129. *India in 1924-25*, 315-6.

"When he (C.R. Das) succeeded in patching up a compromise between the *mohant* and the *swami* in September, he was accused by both parties of dishonesty and self-interest. The episode served only to discredit him."—Broomfield, op. cit., 261.

130. R. C. Majumdar, op. cit., 201.

131. *The Collected Works of Mahatma Gandhi*, XXVII, 293.

## List of Satyagrahis

Baleswar Acharya, Jogendra Chandra Acharya, Rebati
Mohan Acharya, Kangali Adat, Krishnapada Adat, Amar
Adhikari, Balai Adhikari, Dhruba Adhikari, Hrishikesh
Adhikari, Jiban Adhikari, Kali Adhikari, Nirmal Chandra
Adhikari, Panchanan Adhikari, Rashbehari Adhikari, Suresh
Chandra Adhikari, Tulsi Charan Adhikari, Atul Aghuri,
Bholanath Aich, Jatindra Mohan Aich, Dulal Chandra Ash,
Haripada Bag, Jaladhar Bag, Nanda Bag, Netai Chandra
Bag, Kshudiram Bag, Subal Chandra Bag, Abala Bagchi,
Dharani Bagchi, Jagatjyoti Bagchi, Nakul Bairagi, Santosh
Bairagi, Bijoy Bairi, Ashutosh Bakshi, Priya Bakshi,
Kshitish Bal, Akinchan Banerjee, Anil Banerjee, Ashutosh
Banerjee, Balaram Banerjee, Bankim Banerjee, Basudeb
Banerjee, Batakrishna Banerjee, Bibhuti Banerjee, Bidhu
Banerjee, Bijoy Ratan Banerjee, Chandi Charan Banerjee,
Dhiren Banerjee, Dinabandhu Banerjee, Gobardhan Banerjee,
Gopi Banerjee, Jagadish Banerjee, Janaki Banerjee, Jnan
Banerjee, Kalachand Banerjee, Kali Banerjee, Kartik Banerjee,
Keshab Banerjee, Kishorilal Banerjee, Mukundalal Banerjee,
Nagen Banerjee, Nalini Banerjee, Nanda Banerjee, Nani
Gopal Banerjee, Naren Banerjee, Niranku Banerjee, Panchanan
Banerjee, Panna Banerjee, Paresh Chandra Banerjee, Phani
Banerjee, Phatik Banerjee, Prakash Banerjee, Prankrishna
Banerjee, Priyanath Banerjee, Satchidananda Banerjee,
Satyendranath Banerjee, Sudhir Chandra Banerjee, Taraknath
Banerjee, Tulsi Banerjee, Umapada Banerjee, Upen Banerjee,
Krishna Baral, Dulal Barma, Gopal Barman, Phatik Chandra
Baroli, Phani Basak, Bepin Behari Bera, Durgadas Bera,
Gobardhan Bera, Hari Bera, Kali Bera, Nabadwip Bera,
Paresh Bera, Tarini Bera, Abhay Bhadra, Jatin Bhadra, Kali
Bhadra, Jatin Bhakat, Narayan Bhakat, Jatin Bhandari, Chuni
Bhar, Panchanan Bhar, Purna Bhar, Vidyananda Bharati,
Krishnananda Bharati, Atul Bhattacharyya, Abhedananda
Bhattacharyya, Baman Bhattacharyya, Bhupati Bhusan
Bhattacharyya, Bibhuti Bhattacharyya, Bimal Chandra

Bhattacharyya, Dhiren Bhattacharyya, Ganesh Bhattacharyya, Gispati Bhattacharyya, Gopi Bhattacharyya, Hemen Bhattacharyya, Hrishikesh Bhattacharyya, Jajneswar Bhattacharyya, Jnanendra Bhattacharyya, Kalipada Bhattacharyya, Kanakeswar Bhattacharyya, Kanai Bhattacharyya, Manindralal Bhattacharyya, Pachu Bhattacharyya, Paran Chandra Bhattacharyya, Sasadhar Bhattacharyya, Suren Bhattacharyya, Tarak Bhattacharyya, Dhirendranath Bhowmik, Jogen Bhowmik, Kanai Bhowmik, Naren Bhowmik, Panchkari Bhowmik, Priya Bhowmik, Upen Bhowmik, Baidyanath Biswas, Chintaharan Biswas, Duryodhan Biswas, Dwijabar Biswas, Jiten Biswas, Kanailal Biswas, Nagendranath Biswas, Nirendranath Biswas, Nishikanta Biswas, Nityananda Biswas, Panchkari Biswas, Prabhas Biswas, Priya Biswas, Satish Biswas, Satya Biswas, Suresh Biswas, Naresh Bishnu, Ajit Kumar Bose, Amulya Bose, Anil Bose, Basudeb Bose, Becharam Bose, Bhupendranath Bose, Brajen Bose, Ganesh Chandra Bose, Gopal Bose, Hari Bose, Hem Bose, Jasoda Ranjan Bose, Kali Bose, Kanai Bose, Khagen Bose, Krishna Bose, Nishikanta Bose, Panchanan Bose, Paresh Bose, Peyari Bose, Phani Bhusan Bose, Prafulla Bose, Sailendranath Bose, Santosh Bose, Satin Bose, Satish Chandra Bose, Siddheswar Bose, Sreedamlal Bose, Sukumar Chandra Bose, Suren Bose, Tinkari Chandra Bose, Trailokya Bose, Upen Bose, Ashutosh Brahmachari, Bhagabananda Brahmachari, Jatindra Brahmachari, Paramananda Brahmachari, Sudhir Byapari, Ambika Chakravarty, Ananda Chakravarty, Atul Chakravarty, Biharilal Chakravarty, Bijoy Gopal Chakravarty, Biren Chakravarty, Byomkesh Chakravarty, Chittaranjan Chakravarty, Durgadas Chakravarty, Gobardhan Chakravarty, Gopal Chakravarty, Guiram Chakravarty, Haripada Chakravarty, Heramba Chakravarty, Jiten Chakravarty, Kali Chakravarty, Kamala Kanta Chakravarty, Kanailal Chakravarty, Keshabananda Chakravarty, Krishnapada Chakravarty, Kshitish Chakravarty, Nayantara Chakravarty, Nikunja Chakravarty, Panchanan Chakravarty, Pashupati Chakravarty, Prafulla Chakravarty, Satyananda Chakravarty, Satyendranath Chakravarty, Sukumar Chakravarty, Suren Chakravarty, Suresh Chandra Chakravarty, Kshudiram Chhal, Hari Charan Chanda, Jnaneswar Chandra,

Khadam Chandra, Nalini Chandra, Prabhas Chandra, Tara-
pada Chandra, Abinash Chatterjee, Adhar Chatterjee, Ajit
Kumar Chatterjee, Amulya Chatterjee, Anadi Chatterjee,
Ananta Chatterjee, Anath Chatterjee, Arabinda Chatterjee,
Baidyanath Chatterjee, Balai Chatterjee, Bhakti Bhusan Chatter-
jee, Birendranath Chatterjee, Braja Gopal Chatterjee, Byomkesh
Chatterjee, Chandi Chatterjee, Charu Chatterjee, Gopal
Chatterjee, Gopi Chatterjee, Gostha Chatterjee, Gourhari
Chatterjee, Haladhar Chatterjee, Haradhan Chatterjee, Hem
Chatterjee, Jagat Chatterjee, Jiban Chatterjee, Kalipada
Chatterjee, Kamakshya Chatterjee, Kanai Chatterjee, Kshudi-
ram Chatterjee, Kumud Chatterjee, Nanda Gopal Chatterjee,
Narayan Chandra Chatterjee, Nilmadhab Chatterjee, Nilratan
Chatterjee, Paban Chatterjee, Panchanan Chatterjee, Phelaram
Chatterjee, Pratap Chatterjee, Prabhas Chatterjee, Prabodh
Kumar Chatterjee, Purna Chatterjee, Radhaswami Chatterjee,
Ram Charan Chatterjee, Sadananda Chatterjee, Sarat Chandra
Chatterjee, Satya Chatterjee, Sitanath Chatterjee, Sudhir
Chatterjee, Suren Chatterjee, Sushil Chatterjee, Taraknath
Chatterjee, Ahindra Choudhury, Aswini Choudhury, Baladeb
Choudhury, Bangsa Gopal Choudhury, Biswanath Choudhury,
Gopal Chandra Choudhury, Jatin Choudhury, Jnanen Chou-
dhury, Nripen Choudhury, Panchanan Choudhury, Pramatha-
nath Choudhury, Promode Choudhury, Haridas Dandi Sannyasi,
Amulya Das, Ananda Das, Banchharam Das, Bibhuti Bhusan
Das, Bidhu Das, Binay Das, Birendra Chandra Das,
Chandi Das, Chiraranjan Das, Chunilal Das, Dasucharan Das,
Dhiren Das, Dulal Das, Durga Das, Gajendra Das, Gobardhan
Das, Gopal Das, Gour Das, Guiram Das, Haren Das, Hari-
bhusan Das, Haripada Das, Hrishikesh Das, Indu Bhusan Das,
Jagat Das, Jagatnath Das, Janaki Das, Jatindra Das, Jiban
Das, Jiten Das, Jogen Das, Kali Das, Kanai Das, Kangali Das,
Kartik Das, Krishna Das, Kunja Das, Mohanta Charan Das,
Nabin Das, Nagen Das, Narayan Das, Naren Das, Netai Das,
Nityananda Das, Panchanan Das, Panna Das, Phakir Das,
Prafulla Das, Prakash Das, Pranmohan Das, Pulin Das,
Purna Das, Sarat Chandra Das, Satish Chandra Das,
Satya Das, Subal Das, Subalak Chandra Das, Subodh Das,

Suresh Das, Sushil Das, Tarapada Das, Tulsi Chandra Das,
Upendranath Das, Kanailal Dasbairagi, Abani Das Ghosh,
Haripada Das Ghosh, Narottam Das Gupta, Sailendranath
Das Gupta, Sudhir Das Gupta, Amulya Ratan Datta, Anil Datta,
Bibhuti Datta, Bijay Datta, Bimal Datta, Bipin Datta, Dhani
Kanta Datta, Dharani Datta, Digen Datta, Dulal Chandra
Datta, Gajen Datta, Gopal Datta, Gour Datta, Haren Datta,
Haripada Datta, Hiren Datta, Hrishikesh Datta, Jiten Datta,
Jnanendra Datta, Jogen Datta, Kanai Datta, Keshab Datta,
Kshetra Mohan Datta, Manindra Mohan Datta, Matilal Datta,
Nityananda Datta, Nibaran Datta, Nemai Datta, Nakul Datta,
Panchanan Datta, Purna Chandra Datta, Radhanath Datta,
Satish Chandra Datta, Subodh Datta, Tarapada Datta, Nagen
Datta Gupta, Subodh Datta Gupta, Subodh Chandra Datta
Roy, Abodh Chandra De, Anukul Chandra De, Bipin Behari
De, Bishnupada De, Chandi Charan De, Deben De, Dhiren De,
Dinesh De, Gopal De, Hari Chandra De, Haridas De, Hemen
De, Hiralal De, Jaharlal De, Kali De, Kanai De, Krishna De,
Mahadev Chandra De, Nagen De, Nakul Chandra De, Narayan
Chandra De, Nepal De, Nilmani De, Netai De, Nityananda De,
Panchu Gopal De, Panna De, Sadhan Chandra De, Sagar De,
Sarat Chandra De, Satish De, Satya De, Sudhir Kumar De,
Suren De, Tinkari De, Upendra Chandra De, Girija Deb,
Kamini Deb, Nagendra Chandra Deb, Upen Debnath, Dwaraka
Debsarma, Hara Govinda Debsarma, Ashutosh Dhali,
Panchu Dhani, Gostha Dhar, Mathur Chandra Dhar, Parbati
Dhar, Bipin Dhara, Bishnu Dhara, Gopal Dhara, Kanai Dhara,
Krishnadhan Dhara, Jatin Dalui, Upen Dom, Ananta Ganguly,
Asit Ranjan Ganguly, Bhupendranath Ganguly, Nilratan
Ganguly, Surya Ganguly, Satish Chandra Garai, Purna
Chandra Gayen, Satisadhan Gayen, Ekkari Gheto, Amarendra
Ghosh, Amulya Ghosh, Balai Chandra Ghosh, Banbehari
Ghosh, Batakrisna Ghosh, Becharam Ghosh, Bhawani Prasad
Ghosh, Bhuban Mohan Ghosh, Bibhuti Ghosh, Bijay Ghosh,
Bishnu Ghosh, Biswanath Ghosh, Charu Ghosh, Deben Ghosh,
Dip Chand Ghosh, Durga Ghosh, Dwijen Ghosh, Ganesh
Ranjan Ghosh, Gostha Behari Ghosh, Gour Hari Ghosh,
Haralal Ghosh, Harendra Ghosh, Hari Ghosh, Jajneswar

Ghosh, Jatindra Mohan Ghosh, Jatindranath Ghosh, Jiban
Ghosh, Jatindralal Ghosh, Jnanendranath Ghosh, Jogesh
Ghosh, Kalipada Ghosh, Khagen Ghosh, Kshitish Ghosh,
Manmathanath Ghosh, Meghnad Ghosh, Mukundalal Ghosh,
Nagen Ghosh, Naren Ghosh, Nripen Ghosh, Panchanan Ghosh,
Phani Ghosh, Prabhas Ghosh, Prafulla Ghosh, Promode Ghosh,
Satya Charan Ghosh, Sajani Ghosh, Siddheswar Ghosh, Sisir
Kumar Ghosh, Sourin Ghosh, Sudhir Chandra Ghose, Suresh
Ghosh, Tara Ghosh, Tarak Ghosh, Tulsi Ghosh, Upen Ghosh,
Harihar Ghoshal, Jagatbandhu Ghoshal, Nanu Ghoshal, Phani
Galui, Santosh Gope, Anath Goswami, Bibhuti Bhusan
Goswami, Chidananda Goswami, Jiban Goswami, Jiten
Goswami, Kanai Goswami, Nitya Gopal Goswami, Phani
Goswami, Taraknath Goswami, Tulsi Goswami, Akshay Gouri,
Jatin Guchari, Nalinikanta Guha, Sudhir Guha, Sukumar
Guha, Kshitish Guha Thakurta, Kanta Guin, Anukul Gupta,
Bholanath Gupta, Jatin Gupta, Panchanan Gupta, Paresh
Gupta, Gour Hai, Batakrishna Haldar, Gour Haldar, Jugal
Haldar, Prafulla Haldar, Surendranath Haldar, Ashutosh
Hazra, Bhupati Bhusan Hazra, Bibhuti Hazra, Bipin Hazra,
Gopi Hazra, Krishna Hazra, Panchanan Hazra, Pramatha
Hazra, Kuria Hemran, Damodar Jairam, Anna Jana, Bishnu
Jana, Kishori Jana, Nagendra Jana, Satish Jana, Asutosh Jana,
Dibakar Kar, Dulal Kar, Jatin Kar, Kulendra Kar, Nagen
Kar, Tarak Kar, Tarini Kar, Phelu Karar, Tulsi Karar, Balai
Karmakar, Gobinda Karmakar, Jatin Karmakar, Kalipada
Karmakar, Paban Karmakar, Phatik Karmakar, Sannyasi
Karmakar, Tinkari Karmakar, Prankrisnhna Kayal, Manik
Chandra Khamari, Bisweswar Khan, Ganesh Khara, Tarini
Khara, Rajani Kanta Khotra, Ajit Kodal, Jatin Kolay, Kali
Kolay, Nalini Kolay, Panchanan Kolay, Tulsi Kolay, Adhar
Kshetri, Kanailal Kshetri, Bipin Kumar, Dhiren Kumar, Kalipada
Kumar, Kanti Chandra Kumar, Bibhuti Bhusan Kundu, Jiten
Kundu, Kanai Kundu, Karunamay Kundu, Paritosh Kundu,
Prafulla Kundu, Satkari Kundu, Tinkari Kundu, Panna Lāha,
Suren Laha, Krishna Lahiri, Chiranjib Lal, Ganesh Lal,
Abinas Maitra, Sreenath Maitra, Ananda Maity, Bhadreswar
Maity, Gour Maity, Hari Maity, Hiralal Maity, Jnanada Maity,

Kali Maity, Pijush Maity, Prasad Maity, Suren Maity, Basudeb
Majhi, Dulal Majhi, Guiram Majhi, Kalipada Majhi, Kanai
Majhi, Phanindranath Majhi, Santosh Majhi, Kumudbandhu
Majumdar, Satya Majumdar, Subodh Majumdar, Sudhansu
Majumdar, Jatindranath Malakar, Phukur Mali, Bibhuti Mallik,
Bhupati Chandra Mallik, Gobinda Mallik, Jiban Krishna
Mallik, Jnan Mallik, Kali Mallik, Naresh Mallik, Panchu
Mallik, Purna Mallik, Amulya Mandal, Banwari Mandal,
Bansarilal Mandal, Bishnupada Mandal, Chandi Mandal, Dulal
Mandal, Ekkari Mandal, Gobardhan Mandal, Gobinda Mandal,
Gostha Mandal, Harashit Mandal, Hiralal Mandal, Jogen
Mandal, Kali Mandal, Kanai Mandal, Krishna Mandal, Kush-
charan Mandal, Meghlal Mandal, Narayan Mandal, Nilmani
Mandal, Nitya Gopal Mandal, Panchanan Mandal, Rajendra
Chandra Mandal, Sunil Chandra Mandal, Tinkari Mandal,
Tulsi Mandal, Uma Mandal, Bholanath Manna, Gour Mohan
Manna, Haru Manna, Nilmani Manna, Phakir Manna, Prabodh
Chandra Manna, Sarat Chandr Manna, Suren Manna, Nagen
Matari, Jiban Mehta, Kalipada Mehta, Netai Misra, Patal
Chandra Misra, Basanta Mitra, Dhaneswar Mitra, Dharmadas
Mitra, Dhirendranath Mitra, Haren Mitra, Hem Mitra, Hrishi-
kesh Mitra, Indu Bhusan Mitra, Jiban Mitra, Nani Mitra,
Nilratan Mitra, Nripen Mitra, Pramatha Mitra, Pulin Mitra,
Sarasi Mitra, Anil Modak, Atal Modak, Kshudiram Modak,
Nitya Gopal Modak, Pulin Modak, Hari Modi, Ajay Mukherjee,
Amar Mukherjee, Ananta Mukherjee, Anil Mukherjee, Arabinda
Mukherjee, Asutosh Mukherjee, Bamapada Mukherjee, Basanta
Mukherjee, Bidhu Bhusan Mukherjee, Bibhuti Mukherjee,
Bijay Mukherjee, Binode Mukherjee, Birendra Chandra
Mukherjee, Birendranath Mukherjee, Dhirendranath Mukherjee,
Dulal Mukherjee, Haren Mukherjee, Haridas Mukherjee,
Jagatbandhu Mukherjee, Jatindra Mukherjee, Kali Mukherjee,
Kalikes Mukherjee, Kamal Mukherjee, Kishori Mohan
Mukherjee, Krishna Chandra Mukherjee, Lambodar Mukherjee,
Nagen Mukherjee, Nanda Mukherjee, Nirmal Chandra
Mukherjee, Panchanan Mukherjee, Panchu Gopal Mukherjee,
Paresh Mukherjee, Paritosh Mukherjee, Phani Bhusan Mukherjee,
Pramatha Mukherjee, Prankrishna Mukherjee, Promode

Kumar Mukherjee, Satya Chandra Mukherjee, Satya Charan
Mukherjee, Satya Ranjan Mukherjee, Satchidananda Mukherjee,
Subodh Mukherjee, Sudhansu Mukherjee, Sudhir Mukherjee,
Sushil Kumar Mukherjee, Tarak Mukherjee, Chatur Muram,
Atul Chandra Nag, Chandi Naik, Gopal Chandra Naik,
Nirapada Nan, Tridib Nanda, Haricharan Nandan, Ananda
Nandi, Anukul Nandi, Bijay Krishna Nandi, Gopal Nandi, Hem
Nandi, Indranath Nandi, Krishna Nandi, Lakshmi Narayan
Nandi, Nitya Gopal Nandi, Pasupati Nandi, Phatik Nandi,
Satish Nandi, Satya Nandi, Sudhir Nandi, Tirthapada Nandi,
Gopal Nath, Jiten Nath, Kanai Nath, Tarak Nath, Biren Neogi,
Dhirendranath Neogi, Harendranath Neogi, Chandrasekhar
Nyaz, Netai Padma, Bholanath Pagri, Bishnu Pakhira, Ajay
Pal, Amritalal Pal, Amulya Chandra Pal, Amulyadhan Pal,
Asutosh Pal, Banku Pal, Bimal Pal, Dasarathi Pal, Dinsaran
Pal, Ganesh Pal, Gourhari Pal, Hara Pal, Haran Pal, Jamini
Mohan Pal, Jatin Pal, Jiban Pal, Jitendranath Pal, Kalipada
Pal, Kanai Pal, Krishnapada Pal, Kshudiram Pal, Nagen Pal,
Narayan Pal, Narendranath Pal, Nibaran Pal, Panchanan Pal,
Prankrishna Pal, Suren Pal, Subodh Pal, Tinkari Pal, Upen
Pal, Chandrakanta Palit, Jnanada Ranjan Palit, Sudhir Chandra
Pan, Ganga Pandit, Gokul Pandit, Paresh Pandit, Panchu
Panja, Satish Chandra Parag, Basanta Paria, Satyananda Pari-
brajak, Abinash Pathak, Kanai Pathak, Tinkari Pathak, Nirmal
Chandra Patia, Baren Patra, Habul Chandra Patra, Nirmal
Patra, Panchanan Patra, Panna Patra, Sudhir Patra, Guiram
Paur, Badal Porel, Bijay Porel, Binode Porel, Haridhan Porel,
Bholanath Pramanik, Bishnu Pramanik, Dhanapati Pramanik,
Gour Pramanik, Kali Pramanik, Kartik Chandra Pramanik,
Natabar Chandra Pramanik, Santi Ram Pramanik, Satya
Pramanik, Dr Jatindranath Pratihar, Kumud Pratihar, Nibaran
Pratihar, Netai Chandra Rakshit, Etwari Ram, Narayan Rao,
Naresh Routh, Abinas Roy, Ananta Roy, Atul Chandra Roy,
Basanta Roy, Brajendranath Roy, Dasanan Roy, Dhirendra-
nath Roy, Dinesh Roy, Ganesh Roy, Girish Chandra Roy,
Gopal Roy, Haripada Roy, Harisadhan Roy, Harisankar Roy,
Jahar Roy, Jatin Roy, Jnansankar Roy, Indu Bhusan Roy,
Kali Roy, Khagen Roy, Khodan Roy, Kshitish Chandra Roy,

Kumar Krishna Roy, Nandalal Roy, Nani Roy, Narendralal
Roy, Narendra Prasad Roy, Niranjan Roy, Panchanan Roy,
Pasupati Kumar Roy, Patiram Roy, Prabhas Roy, Prafulla
Roy, Premananda Roy, Pulin Roy, Sasanka Sekhar Roy, Satish
Roy, Subodh Roy, Sudhir Roy, Sukumar Roy, Tarani Mohan
Roy, Tarini Roy, Jiten Roy Barma, Sudhansu Kumar Roy
Choudhury, Tarapada Roy Choudhury, Makhan Sa, Nagen
Sadhukhan, Panchanan Sadhukhan, Sudhir Sadhukhan, Gobinda
Saha, Hari Charan Saha, Hari Krishna Saha, Jogen Saha,
Kamal Kumar Saha, Nanda Saha, Nripen Saha, Panchu Gopal
Saha, Parshanath Saha, Pratap Saha, Radha Govinda Saha,
Tamal Saha, Bipradas Sahu, Upen Sahu, Saktiswarup, Banamali
Samanta, Gobardhan Samanta, Gour Samanta, Guiram
Samanta, Iswar Samanta, Jatin Samanta, Jugal Kishore Samanta,
Kalipada Samanta, Krishna Chandra Samanta, Kunja
Samanta, Nagendra Samanta, Patit Samanta, Surendranath
Samanta, Tarini Samanta, Upendranath Samanta, Haru
Santra, Jogendra Santra, Kali Santra, Kishori Mohan Santra,
Ajit Sanyal, Indu Bhusan Sanyal, Phani Sanyal, Asutosh Sarkar,
Bishnupada Sarkar, Chandi Sarkar, Gopen Sarkar, Harish
Sarkar, Khagendra Sarkar, Krishna Chandra Sarkar, Nani
Sarkar, Padma Sarkar, Prakash Sarkar, Purna Sarkar, Suren
Sarkar, Tarak Sarkar, Upen Sarkar, Digendra Sarma, Gouri
Sankar Sarma, Panchanan Sarma, Amulya Sasmal, Mahadev
Chandra Sasmal, Benoy Kumar Seal, Gopal Seal, Jagatnath
Seal, Nagen Seal, Narayan Seal, Nirapada Seal, Prasanna Seal,
Satish Seal, Syam Chandra Seal, Anadi Sen, Chandrasekhar
Sen, Indra ·Narayan Sen, Anil Sen Gupta, Gispati Sen Gupta,
Jatindranath Sen Gupta, Naresh Sen Gupta, Nibaran Sen
Gupta, Prafulla Sen Gupta, Sudhir Sen Gupta, Jogen Sen Roy,
Akshay Seth, Dibakar Seth, Kali Seth, Narayan Seth, Phatik
Seth, Abodh Gopal Shee, Brajendralal Singh, Anadi Sinha,
Brajen Sinha, Gopeswar Sinha, Gostha Sinha, Hemanta
Sinha, Jugal Sinha, Kanti Sinha, Nabal Sinha, Prafulla Sinha,
Tulsi Chandra Sinha, Jatin Sinha Barman, Balai Sinha Roy,
Balendra Sinha Roy, Gostha Sinha Roy, Janamejay Sinha Roy,
Jiban Sinha Roy, Keshab Sinha Roy, Nirapada Sinha Roy,
Prankrishna Sinha Roy, Prabodh Sinha Roy, Tarapada Sinha

Roy, Ajit Som, Biswanath Som, Haripada Som, Gopal Sur, Pramatha Surongi, Gadhadhar Swarnakar, Tinkari Swarnakar, Upen Talukdar, Kali Tarafdar, Ganesh Thakur, Jyotirmay Thakur, Pitambar Tripathi, Sankar Kumar Trivedi, Narayan Tudo.

> [Source : *Amrita Bazar Patrika, Ananda Bazar Patrika, The Bengalee,* and *Forward* 1924-1925 and Swarna Kumar Ghoshal, *Tarakeswar Satyagraher Itihas,* 66-74 ond 79-80.]

## CHAPTER V

# PATUAKHALI SATYAGRAHA

## I

COMMUNALISM RETARDED the liberation movement in India during its different phases. This was particularly evident in a series of communal riots which broke out after 1923. When the united action in the struggle against the alien government was a dire necessity, people belonging to the Hindu and Muslim communities engaged themselves in bitter inter-necine strifes. The British strategy of counterpoise was largely responsible for communal conflicts. Native vested interests also pursued their policy of promoting communal differences.[1] Nehru was quite right when he observed that Hindu and Muslim communalism was in neither case "even bonafide com-munalism, but political and social reaction hiding behind the communal mask."[2] A survey of the political history of India during the British rule, more particularly in this century, would reveal how the contagion of communalism perverted the social contents of the anti-imperialist people's movement.

After the withdrawal of the Non-co-operation Movement in 1922, and the failure of the Khilafat agitation on account of the secularization of Turkey, the nationalist activities in the country were reduced almost to a stalemate. Communalism reached its climax at that time. Communal riots broke out in different parts of the country and polluted the whole political atmosphere. Gandhi, an anti-communalist *par excellence,* was ruefully shocked by the turn of events. The citadel of Hindu-Muslim unity built by him 'tumbled down like a house of cards'.[3]

As against these ominous outbreaks efforts were also made jointly by both communities to put an end to this vicious monstrosity. Thus on December 1923 a Hindu-Muslim Pact was signed under the auspices of Bengal Provincial Congress Commitee.[4]

Yet the result was not as expected. On the contrary in 1925-26 the whole atmosphere of the country was vitiated by the outbreak of communal riots in different places. As a result the freedom movement receded to the background since no concrete measure could be devised to arrest the growth of this canker in the body politic of this country.

II

Patuakhali is a subdivision in the district of Backergunge (Barisal). The small town of Patuakhali, situated in the south of Barisal, was the headquarters of the subdivision. Though the Muslims formed the vast majority in the subdivision, the Hindus constituted the majority in the town.*

Patuakhali satyagraha was launched by the local Hindus with a view to asserting their 'time-honoured right' to music before mosque.[5] The local Mohammedans often objected to the processions with music led by Hindus when these passed by a mosque. On the other hand it was the demand of the Hindus that the roads were public, and therefore those must be open to any community for its free use, and the objection of the Mohammedans was unjust. The Hindus were, however, ready to stop music before mosque during prayer-time. To put it in another way, 'to assert the right to free use of the streets by Hindu processionists' was the ultimate object of Patuakhali satyagraha.[6]

Before Patuakhali satyagraha complete communal amity prevailed among the members of the Hindu and Mohammedan communities in the district. It is on record that in 1926

* Population of subdivision and town by religion and sex :

|  | Muslim | | Hindu | |
| --- | --- | --- | --- | --- |
|  | Male | Female | Male | Female |
| Subdivision | 292,569 | 279,781 | 53,625 | 44,020 |
| Town | 1,676 | 1,004 | 2,352 | 1,380 |

Source :   Provincial Table II, *Census of India 1931*, V (II), 312-3.

9

the Government of Bengal wanted to install a Union Board at Laukathi, a neighbouring village of Patuakhali, and collect tax for its maintenance from the villagers as it did in other places of Bengal. The inhabitants of this village, Hindus and Mohammedans alike, stood against this attempt in a body. Under the leadership of Satindra Nath Sen, Secretary, Barisal District Congress Committee, they resolved to orga- nize a movement against the Government. The Government resorted to all sorts of repressive measures but ultimately all those failed to defeat the movement. As a result the Union Board was withdrawn from Laukathi. This victory proved to the hilt the efficacy of communal unity. And since then Satindra Nath Sen had been recognized by all as the accredited leader of Pakuakhali.[7]

But Hindu-Muslim unity was not to the liking of either the reactionary vested interests of the Mohammedan community or the Government. They were up and doing to disrupt this unity. Communalism was to their hands to serve the purpose. This was substantiated by a subsequent series of events which occurred in Patuakhali town and other places adjacent to it. And all these account for the deteriora- tion of the cordial relations that existed between the two communities. The policy of 'divide and rule' pursued by the Government and the playing up of the unjust demands of the Mohammedans by reactionary leaders of their community forced the local Hindus to launch a satyagraha movement for the vindication of what they claimed as their 'inalienable right'.

The movement had its origin in the dispute over the location of Saraswati Puja of the Hindu students of the local H. E. School. As in the previous years the puja was to be held in the school building. But that year the Mohammedan students objected to it. The Hindu :students ignored the objection and held Sarswati Puja in the school premises. But the following morning the school premises were found completely burnt and also a chopped head of a cow was found on the very altar on which the puja was performed. Moreover, when the Hindu students wanted to lead a procession along public roads of Patuakhali town for immersion of the image of goddess Saraswati, local reactionary Mohammedan leaders raised objection to the proposal on the ground that 'while the procession would pass by the mosque, music must be stopped'. The local authorities sided with the Mohammedans and issued an order upholding the stand taken by them. Satindra Nath Sen, already famous for the Laukathi Union Board Boycott movement, proposed with a view to an amicable settlement that the Hindus should be allowed to hold a procession along all the public thoroughfares with music save at prayertime. The proposal did not find favour with the Mohammedans. However that year no procession was taken out.[8]

Meanwhile on May 13 a marriage procession was asked to stop its music while it was passing by a local mosque. Although the music was not played exactly before the mosque, the processionists stopped it to avoid a confrontation.[9] The usual practice was that music was stopped 30 to 40 cubits away from a mosque. But of late the Mohammedans were demanding that it should be stopped 400 cubits away from the mosque.[10] In protest a procession with music marched its way under the leadership of Satindra Nath Sen and the processionists stopped music for one minute while passing by the mosque. But on this occasion the Mohammedans did not oppose them.[11] Immediately after this incident the Deputy Magistrate called the local leaders of both communites and a committee of 8 persons—4 from each community—was formed to bring about peace in the town.[12] But ultimately no concrete measure was devised to solve the problem permanently.

Communalism with all its ugliness came to a limiting point of tension at Patuakhali on 30 August 1926 when a procession with music led by the Hindus on the eve of Janmastami festival was obstructed by the police near a mosque. The local authorities had earlier issued an order that no procession would be allowed to pass along public roads without licence and if there was any such procession, that would be declared illegal under section 30 of the Police Act. Accordingly the local Hindus applied for a licence for taking out a procession on the day of Janmastami festival. The licence was granted on the condition that music should stop before the local mosque, situated not by the District Board road along which the procession intended to pass, but by another municipal road about 60 to 70 cubits off.[13] From time immemorial the Hindus had been accustomed to take out processions along public roads. "This was for the first time in 1926 the right to take out procession was restricted."[14] Hence the Hindus felt much aggrieved by the Government order. Moreover the mosque situated by the main road was an abandoned one. The Government order to stop music before mosque at all hours appeared to the Hindus as an encroachment upon their civic right. They decided to violate the prohibitory order and accordingly on August 30 they organized a procession with music under the leadership of Satindra Nath Sen. When the procession reached the prohibited area the police obstructed its way. When the Hindus of the town heard this news they flocked in a body to the prohibited area. The Mohammedans also assembled there in large numbers. It was reported that some brickbats were hurled at the processionists. When the Hindus retaliated the Mohammedans took shelter in the mosque. Meanwhile the police came and tried to disperse the crowd but failed. Ultimately by the order of the Assistant Superintendent of Police about fifty persons were arrested.[15]

In fact, Patuakhali satyagraha began on and from that day. On the following day a similar procession was taken out and in the same manner it was obstructed by the police as a result of which eleven persons were arrested on the ground that the scheduled time for procession was over. Later, however, they were released on bail. The local Hindus thenceforth decided to continue satyagraha movement until their legal rights were recognized.[16]

The organization of satyagraha obviously demands men and money adequate enough to attain the end. The organizers of Patuakhali satyagraha were aware of this fact. They fervently appealed to the Hindus for help and support. The reaction of the Hindus was very much prompt in this respect. In a public meeting held on September 5 the Hindus of Patuakhali resolved to support the satyagraha movement wholeheartedly. The meeting also condemned the pro-Mohammedan

attitude of the Government officers who were in charge of
the affair and appealed to the Hindus of all parts of Bengal
to help strengthen the movement.[17] The Hindus of Barisal
even decided to institute a civil suit to assert their rights.[18]

Along with the organization of the movement efforts were
made to reach a solution of the problem. But nothing successful was achieved as the Mohammedans were not ready to
concede what was supposed to be a matter of right to the
Hindus.[19] The latter were however ready to settle the
question on condition that the Government should issue a
notification to the effect that music in procession was to be
stopped 'only in prayer-times before mosque' and this without
prejudice to the title suit that might be instituted to establish
the right.[20] For that purpose a telegram was sent by Pijush
Kanti Ghosh to the Governor on September 13 : "Hindus
willing to stop Satyagraha without prejudice to Civil Remedies
of the parties if notification in the terms of Calcutta regarding
music before ordinary mosque be immediately promulgated
here and pending prosecution dropped, early reply solicited."[21]
However the officiating Chief Secretary in reply informed him
that the Governor-in-Council was not prepared to issue such
an order and asked Ghosh to make any representations
which he might choose to make regarding the matter to the
District Magistrate.[22] At the outset, however, the local authorities seemed to be interested in bringing about an amicable
settlement of the dispute.[23]

Again on September 12 the Hindu leaders met the
Mohammedans and made overtures for a settlement to which
the latter declined to respond unless the proposals came through
the Government channel. The Hindus, on the other hand,
were of the view that the satyagraha movement could be
withdrawn only if the Mohammedans allowed them to lead
procession by the mosque with music excepting at prayer-time,
'pending the decision of the court in the civil suit' that was
going to be instituted shortly. But the Mohammedans did not
pay heed to the proposal.[24] Meanwhile the local administration issued fresh notice to the effect that an application should
be made two days in advance for taking out a procession.[25]

All these developments led the Hindus to intensify their struggle and the organizers of the movement began preparing themselves for the tasks ahead. In view of the new Government order served on September 15, they applied for licence for seven consecutive days.[26]    Already in a meeting on September 13 a satyagraha committee was formed with Nalinikanta Bandyopadhyay and Birendra Nath Sen ( brother of Satindra Nath Sen) as its President and Secretary respectively.[27]  Barisal Sadar, Bhola and Pirojpur came forward in aid of the satyagraha movement. A satyagraha committee was formed at Barisal with Sarat Kumar Ghosh as President and Nagendra Bijay Bhattacharyya as Secretary.[28]  A satyagraha camp was opened at Patuakhali.[29]   On and from September 2 four to five satyagrahis daily courted arrest.[30]

Meanwhile the Divisional Commissioner of Dacca came to Patuakhali to study the situation there.  On his return from Patuakhali on September 18 he met a deputation of the Hindu leaders which included Pijush Kanti Ghosh, Rai Bahadur Ganesh Chandra Das Gupta, Rasik Chandra Chakravorty, Chand Mohan Chatterjee, Sarat Chandra Guha and Gopal Chandra Biswas.[31]  They submitted a memorandum to the Commissioner setting forth their case for launching the satyagraha.  The memorandum *inter alia* stated :

"a)  Every subject has a natural right inherent in him to pass by a mosque, etc., in procession with music and it lay on those seeking to restrain its exercise to prove some law or custom having the force of law depriving him of the right. ...

b)  The right, however, must be exercised in such a manner as the Magistrate may not object to as dangerous to public safety.

c)  The prejudices of a particular sect ought not to influence the law. ...

d)  Where a custom is set up in derogation of such right, the custom must be proved to be valid and to constitute a valid custom it must be reasonable, certain and ancient. ...

e)  Where rights are threatened the persons entitled to them should receive the fullest protection the law affords them and circumstances admit of.  The authority of the Magistrate should be exerted in the defence of rather than in suspension of such rights, in the repression of illegal rather than an interference of (*sic*) lawful acts. If the Magistrate is satisfied that the exercise of a right is likely to create a riot he can hardly be ignorant of the persons from whom disturbances are to be apprehended and it is his duty to take from them security to keep the peace.

f) In affording special protection to persons assembled for religious worships or ceremonies the law points to congregational rather than private worship and it may fairly be required of congregations that they should inform the authorities of the hours at which they customarily assemble for worship in order that the rights of other persons may not be unduly curtailed.

g) If any impression is created in the minds of people that the authorities are powerless against the class from whom violence is apprehended against civil rights graver dangers are to be apprehended from refusing protection to the legitimate enjoyment of civil rights."[3][2]

The memorandum made out that the grievances of the Hindus were genuine. It was the duty of the police and the executive, the Hindu leaders held, to help them in the lawful exercise of their rights.[33]

The form of licence under sections 30 and 31 of the Police Act to the effect that music should be stopped near mosques at all times was, it was alleged, also inconsistent. For provisions of section 31 of the Police Act enjoined the police to maintain order and prevent obstruction in a public road caused by a procession or assembly *only during public worship and not at all times.* It was also inconsistent with section 30 on the ground that it was the duty of the police 'to regulate the extent of the music and not to stop it altogether'. "This form of the licence is responsible for the present unnecessary trouble in moffusil. There is no reason why the form of licence adopted by the Police Commissioner of Calcutta in consultation with local government should not also be adopted in moffusil," alleged the deputation.[34]

The Divisional Commissioner's reply to that was interesting.

He requested the leaders to withdraw the satyagraha movement since there was no possibility of an amicable settlement of the dispute. He also informed them that the Government had no interest in the matter. Then the leaders demanded that if the Government was not interested in effecting a nego-tiated settlement between the communities it should impose its own terms for an honourable settlement of the question affecting 22 crores of Hindus.[35]

It is important to note in this connexion that the deputation succeeded in impressing upon the Commissioner certain crucial points : (i) that the Hindus were compelled to resort to satyagraha, (ii) that it was the fittest case for Government intervention without which there was absolu-tely no possibility of resolving the crisis, (iii) that if the situation was not handled promptly by the authorities, there were chances of the satyagraha 'contagion' spreading and the people who were still hoping that something would be done by the Government being led into it, (iv) as it was an all-India question the satyagrahis were not willing to stop it without an honourable settlement of the matter and, finally, (v) the satyagrahis were absolutely non-violent and peaceful and never broke any existing law of the country, except the one interfering with their religious rights and so considered illegal by them.[36]

Still the Commissioner, it was reported, reaffirmed his earlier contention that the Government did not 'desire to to meddle in the affair'.[37]

This indifferent attitude of the Government exasperated the Hindus and hardened their attitude into a determination to confront not the Mohammedans but the Government itself whose 'sole aim seemed to be the preservation of law and order'. The Government was not interested in the justice or otherwise of the Muslim claim for ban on 'music before mosques' at any time of the day or of the Hindu citizens' demand.[38] Thus the whole issue was converted into a political one.

However in October 1926 the situation at Patuakhali was once again aggravated by an image-breaking incident at Chandpur, a village under the P.S. of Sutachipa. Only three Hindu families inhabited this village and that year they organized Durga Puja. On the day of immersion of the image of goddess Durga the Mohammedan boatmen refusing to assist the Hindus, the latter made their own arrangement for the purpose. Yet the Mohammedans blocked their way and attacked them when they protested against their action. They also broke the image into pieces and threw it into the river. It was reported that one Hindu was seriously injured by the Mohammedans. The police was duly informed but no prompt action was taken. It was alleged that the incident occurred as a result of a *maulavi's* malicious instigation against the Hindus.[39]

Meanwhile satyagraha was going on as usual. It was reported that four or five satyagrahis violated the prohibitory order and courted arrest regularly. On November 19, the 82nd day of the satyagraha movement at Patuakhali, Satindra Nath Sen, Kshitish Chandra Sen and seven other persons were arrested all on a sudden. It was reported that when the satyagraha and the arrests for the day were over, Sen and others were coming back. At that time a Mohammedan Inspector of Police under orders of the Hony. Magistrate arrested them on the ground that the time allowed by the licence was over. But they emphatically denied this allegation. They were, however, sent to the jail and they refused to be released on bail.[40] A case was filed against them and the local lawyers stood in defence. Ultimately in view of a settlement on December 6 they were released unconditionally by the order of the District Magistrate and the case against them was withdrawn.[41]

Accordingly on December 8 the SDO met the local Hindu leaders including Satindra Nath Sen for effecting a compromise 'without reference to outside interference and arbitration'.[42] The Hindus informed their inability to do so at this stage as the satyagraha at Patuakhali was not a local affair.[43] In a speech at a public meeting at Mirzapur (now Shraddhananda) Park on 16 January 1927 Satin Sen pointed out that the issue involved related to the right of the Hindus in taking out processions with music along public thoroughfares and unless there was a settlement of the issue on an all-India basis there could be no question of calling off the movement.

He also discussed at length the problem of Hindu-Muslim unity.[44]

Ten days after this meeting Muslim jailors and Hindu satyagrahis clashed inside the jail. It was reported that prior to this incident strained relations had developed between the two. The jailors were perturbed over the continuous influx of the satyagrahi prisoners in the jail. Moreover they felt annoyed at the songs and prayers performed by the Hindu satyagrahis. In retaliation the jailors forbade the Mohammedan prisoners to work for the satyagrahi prisoners. The Mohammedan prisoners also used to harass the satyagrahis in various ways. The satyagrahis had been demanding for a pretty long time the redress of their grievances, but it was alleged that nothing was done by the jail authorities to meet their demand.

On the very day of the event the jailor abused two satyagrahi prisoners when they were being taken to court. The satyagrahis reacted sharply. Then a Mohammedan prisoner threatened them which resulted in a hot exchange of words among the prisoners of the two communities. Immediately after that the Mohammedan prisoners attacked the satyagrahis with iron rods and other arms. A satyagrahi who was sleeping was seriously injured. It was reported that the satyagrahi prisoners organized themselves for defence and retaliation. In the meantime the jailor left the place and closed the jail gate. The satyagrahis felt insecure and cried out for help from the jail officials who were present at that time outside the jail gate. The situation was brought under control only when the SDO and other officers intervened.[45]

As this news spread over the town, people of both the communities gathered in large numbers at the jail gate. They were allowed to enter the jail. It was reported that meanwhile hundreds of armed Mahommedans from a neighbouring village attacked the Hindus assembled there. The Hindus also counter-attacked. As a result the Mohammedans retreated. A few persons were injured in the incident. The police patrolled the town that night and the SDO issued orders under section 144 Cr. P.C. prohibiting assembly of more than five persons and also public meetings. In spite of this prohibitory order several petty communal clashes took place in the town.[46] Both parties filed criminal cases against each other.[47] Subsequently, twenty satyagrahi prisoners were transferred to Barisal jail in order to avert further disturbances.[48]

Once again there occurred another incident which bitterly complicated the situation. As in the previous year there was some trouble at Patuakhali over the holding of Saraswati Puja by the Hindu students of Jubilee school. When the students were out in a procession with the image and reached the local Jubilee school, the police obstructed them. The School Committee had earlier resolved not to allow the Hindu students to hold Saraswati Puja in the school premises. But the students were determined to hold puja in their school. Therefore they were trying to enter the school campus by different ways. Ultimately they failed and most of the processionists left the place. Dr J. M. Das Gupta MLC was among the few who had not left and was taking note of the incident. Suddenly the police arrested all of them under section 144 Cr. P.C.. Dr Das Gupta felt aggrieved and refused to be released on bail. Others, however, were released on bail.[49]

Satyagraha was started at Patuakhali for the settlement of the question of music before mosques on a national basis. The satyagrahis intended to organize satyagraha in protest against the prohibitory orders of the Government at all places. The local authorities of Patuakhali prohibited procession with music in Laukhati on the eve of Dol festival. The local Hindus felt indignant at such an order and they sought the help of Satindra Nath Sen who responded immediately to the appeal. The local authorities issued orders under section 144 Cr. P. C. on March 16, 1927. Sen was invited to a tea-party hosted by the District Magistrate on March 18. In the presence of the Superintendent of Police the District Magistrate asked Sen about his reaction to the situation. In reply he categorically asserted that the Government order would be violated. Satin Sen was arrested under section 107 Cr. P.C. as he came out from the District Magistrate's bunglow.[50]

### III

It is to be noted in this connexion that the Mohammedans of Patuakhali from the very beginning took a hostile stand in this matter. Had they conceded the right of the Hindus, the whole trouble could have been avoided. Even when the satyagraha was just at a preliminary stage efforts were made for a compromise. At Barisal the Mohammedan leaders were approached by Sarat Chandra Guha, the Chairman of the Municipality, to pay a joint visit to Patuakhali for the purpose of bringing about a compromise. But they showed an indifferent attitude. Some of them had even said that they had already consulted the local Muslim leaders of Patuakhali and, therefore, there was no point in going there.[51] It had been a long-standing practice with the local Mohammedans to participate in Hindu festivals. But unfortunately during the satyagraha movement certain anonymous leaflets urging the Mohammedan villagers to boycott Hindu festivals had been circulated.[52] An anonymous letter was also sent to the Secretary, Satyagraha Committee, threatening the Hindus with dire consequences unless they left Patuakhali.[53] Public meetings were held to incite the simple Mohammedan villagers against the Hindus. In one such meeting on 12 December 1926 Maulavi Mojammel Haque, the principal speaker of the meeting, condemned the *Suddhi* and *Sangathan* movement as responsible for the present situation. He also challenged Swami Viswananda who was present in the meeting to answer certain questions, which led to a great commotion. However, thanks to the timely intervention by the police, nothing worse could happen. Later the Mohammedans demanded that music should be stopped before mosques at all times.[54] On 9 January 1927 the Mohammedans decided to take out a procession from Gaurandi to Patuakhali, a distance of 49 miles, to demonstrate their feeling against Patuakhali satyagraha.[55] However, the District Magistrate in apprehension of breach of peace warned the Mohammedan leaders not to take out such a procession. The leaders agreed to obey the directive.

Ultimately the obstinate stand taken by the Mohammedan leaders was responsible for an unfortunate massacre at Ponabalia, a place famous for a fair on the eve of *Sivaratri* festival. Each year pilgrims from different places came there to perform their rites on the eve of *Sivaratri*. In 1927 when the pilgrims began to come to that place for the said festival the Mohammedans, being provoked by an arrogant *maulavi*, declared a small hut standing by the District Board road as a mosque. Now the pilgrims had to pass along the District Board road with music on the eve of the festival. If there was to be a mosque by the road, they would have to stop music. Thus they were faced with a difficult situation when they heard the news of the Mohammedans' declaration. Meanwhile Satindra Nath Sen came to side with the pilgrims and the District Magistrate appeared at the place with his police force to study the situation. The District Magistrate was not ready to recognize the small hut as a mosque. He requested the assembled Mohammedans to disperse. The officers also pleaded with them to do so. But their persuasion proved to be of no avail. On the contrary the *maulavi* began to instigate the Mahommedans on the spot. As a result the police arrested the *maulavi*. They attacked the police with arms. As a consequence of that the police opened fire which resulted in the death of nineteen Mohammedans. Several others were seriously injured. Satindra Nath Sen severely criticized the Government action and indicted the District Magistrate : "You could well (have) avoided this measure if some preventive arrests were made earlier."[57]

IV

As stated earlier, the local administration from the very beginning sided with the unreasonable demands of the Mohammedans. Its main object was to curb the influence of the District Congress led by Satindra Nath Sen who was its Secretary. That was why it took the satyagraha movement as a challenge. By issuing prohibitory orders against the Hindus to prevent them from playing music before mosques at all hours of the day, the local authorities incurred displeasure of the Hindus who in protest resorted to satyagraha movement. The local officers were possessed with the idea that it was the Hindus and not the Mohammedans who were responsible for such a state of affairs. The Hindu case was 'so untenable in the official reports' that it was contemplated to station punitive police at Patuakhali and to make the Hindus liable for its maintenance, though the officials honestly believed that if any breach of peace was to take place it was more likely to come from the side of the Mohammedans.[58]

This intention to post the punitive police was announced by a Government Notification on 7 October 1926 : "In exercise of the powers conferred by Section 15 of the Police Act, 1861 (Act V of 1861), the Governor-in-Council is pleased to declare that the area within the local limits of the Patua-khali Municipality, ... in the district of Bhakarganj, has been found to be in a disturbed and dangerous state, and that the conduct of the inhabitants of the aforesaid areas has rendered it expedient to increase the number of police by the appointment of an additional force to be quartered in the said areas at the cost of the inhabitants thereof, subject to any orders which may be passed exempting any person or class or section of the inhabitants." It was also notified that the proclamation would remain in force for a period of six months.[59] After this proclamation the local adminis-tration used to hold out threats of punitive taxes. It was reported that through the manager of a local zamindar the Government asked the local shopkeepers and tenants "to wash their hands clean of satyagraha and to keep aloof from it", if they liked to be exempted from the threatened punitive tax.[60]

The expenses for maintaining the punitive police from September 1926 to February 1927 in Patuakhali town amounted to Rs. 12,155 and the same was sought to be realized exclusively from the 552 Hindus.[61] The Hindus appealed to the Govern-ment for exemption but the appeal went unheeded. A seven days' notice was served for the realization of such taxes. Only a few persons, it was reported, paid the taxes.[62] The Government then threatened that unless the punitive taxes were paid within three days (from March 24 to March 27), properties of the tenants would be attached.[63] The tenants ignored this ultimatum and consequently the police attached their properties.[64] The attached properties were later sold by auction to realize the taxes.[65]

What was more strange was that as soon as the satyagraha movement started, only Mohammedan officers were placed in charge of the Patuakhali subdivision. The ground for this action stated by Mr A. N. Moberly in the Bengal Legislative Council was follows : "Local conditions render it desirable at present to place a Mahommadan officer in immediate charge of the subdivision."[66] This argument could not convince anyone of the impartiality of the Government in the matter. However, on 19 January 1927, the Goverment issued another communique notifying that it would in no way tolerate the 'intoxicated devotion to religion on the part of Hindus.' Rather it cherished the hope that the Hindu leaders would refrain from violating the prohibitory order and endeavour to solve the problem by means of deliberation failing which they might resort to civil court.[67]

To reinforce its stand the local authorities applied all sorts of repressive measures to defeat the satyagraha movement. Oppression continued galore. The inhabitants did not dare to help the satyagrahis.[68] More than two thousand satyagrahis were arrested and sentenced to imprisonment and fine. The entire government apparatus was directed against the movement. Even a telegram sent by the satyagrahi leaders for outside help was suppressed by the local telegraph authorities under the direction of local administration.[69] Orders under section 144 Cr. P.C. were issued by the local authorities at its own sweet will to disallow picketing and public meetings.[70] A police picket was also posted at the satyagraha office to prevent the satyagrahis from using it.[71] The students who enthusiastically joined this movement were even threatened with expulsion from the school by the Divisional Inspector of Schools.[72]

The satyagrahis were not safe even in jail. The jail authorities maltreated the satyagrahi prisoners. The warders and other convicts even assaulted them.[73] The satyagrahis were denied the right of reading Gandhi's speeches and writings.[74] The student satyagrahis were not allowed even school-books.[75] Satyagrahis were not supplied with sufficient warm clothes in winter.[76] As a result some suffered from fits of fever, but proper medical aid was not given to them.[77] Meals served in the jail were not at all satisfactory.[78]

Moreover local judicial authorities whimsically increased the amount of security for the arrested satyagrahis. The security amount was raised from Rs. 500 to Rs. 700 for each satyagrahi. It was alleged that although section 32 of the Police Act was bailable, yet the court refused to grant bail at a security of less than Rs. 500. As a result persons having no sufficient property could not bail out the satyagrahis. It was alleged that previously the amount of security was only Rs. 50. Now it was increased to Rs. 700. An appeal was made to the District Magistrate to intervene in this matter.[79] But the District Magistrate showed no interest.

Meanwhile in September 1927 another incident occurred. On the 12th evening Maulavi Abdul Halim Chaudhury while returning home from his office was attacked by a man from behind. The *maulavi* lodged a complaint with the local police. Several persons were arrested on suspicion but the *maulavi* could not identify any of them as the assailant. Consequently a final report was submitted under sections 147/307, I.P.C.[80]

The Government, it is to be noted, had adopted a new technique since October 1927. The satyagrahis as usual entered the prohibited area for satyagraha. But no arrest was made by the police any further.[81] Sometimes the police, it was reported, escorted the processionists through the prohibited area.[82] However, on October 19 a batch of satyagrahis was arrested and that was the single case of arrest since the adoption of the 'new policy'.[83] Prohibitory orders were still in force. The adoption of the new technique by the Government led many to assume that in this way the Government recognized the right of the Hindus and the object of the movement was said to have been gained.[84] But the assumption was not valid as it was the clear-cut stand of the satyagrahis that under the circumstances until the restrictions on music before mosque in the licence were withdrawn and unrestricted processions were allowed or the Mahomedans came to honourable terms with the Hindus there could not be any question of discontinuing the satyagraha.[85]

On the other hand the Mohammedans took offence against the Government action allowing the Hindus to pass in a procession with music by a mosque.[86] They called a strike though it was not successful.[87] It was reported that later on even the punitive tax was imposed on them.[88] Meanwhile Mr Donovan, who came in place of Mr Blandy, endeavoured for a compromise but the Mohammedans refused to accept the compromise terms of satyagrahis.[89]

On 10 February 1928 Maulavi Samsuddin Ahmed, Assistant Secretary of the Bengal Provincial Congress Committee, came to Barisal with a view to finding out a compromise formula. He met the leaders of both the communities and even requested Satindra Nath Sen to withdraw the satyagraha movement. The compromise formula was : (1) that the Hindus could pass with religious processions at all times of the day ; but music of any procession other than religious must be stopped before mosques during prayer-time and (2) that the Mohammedans could perform *korbani* (cow-slaughter for religious sacrifice) in duly covered areas.[90] On March 18 a sub-committee was formed to see that the satyagraha, postponed for the time being, might not be launched again and that complete amity between the two communities prevailed.[91] Several meetings were held in the meantime with the Government, satyagrahi leaders and the Mohammedans participating in the negotiation with a view to settling the dispute. But all efforts failed. As a result almost after two months the satyagraha movement started anew on 14 May 1928.[92]

Finally, on July 7 in a public meeting the members of all communities unanimously agreed to the following terms of settlement :

"(1) that every member of the public has the right to take processions with music along all public thoroughfares throughout the district at all hours subject to the statutory power of the Magistrate regarding control of such processions,

(2) that every community will strive to promote and maintain good feeling amongst all classes of the people,

(3) that the original of this agreement and declaration will remain in the office of the District Magistrate to

10

be permanently preserved—authenticated copies of which may be available to any member of the public on payment of cost and one original copy will be supplied to each of the communities joining in this agreement."[93]

The number of signatories was 65.[94] The cases against twenty-three satyagrahis were withdrawn 'in view of but not part of the settlement.' The cases against Satindra Nath Sen were, however, not withdrawn.[95]

Thus Patuakhali satyagraha ended in success and it, as Nirmal Kumar Bose observes, "did not leave a trail of bitterness between the Hindu and Muslim leaders of Backergunge. They had measured their strength against one another, and at the end of the satyagraha had come to recognize and respect one another."[96]

## V

The success of a movement depends, in the first place, upon organization and secondly, on the leadership. These two factors were mainly responsible for the success of Patuakhali satyagraha. "The organization of the satyagrahis in Patuakhali had been perfected with care, the leadership was also unified ; while, the feeling that the Muslim demand was unjust became so widespread that it helped to consolidate the unity of the Hindus still further."[97]

The movement at Patuakhali was organized to direct the action of satyagraha and to provide for self-defence.[98] It has already been stated that immediately after the commencement of satyagraha propaganda was launched to draw the attention of local people to the issue in question. This had the desired effect. Prompt response came from the people. Committees were formed in different parts of the district to strengthen the movement. They collected money and recruited volunteers in aid of the satyagraha.

But at the outset the number of participant-satyagrahis was small. Hence it was decided that a satyagrahi, when released on bail, should again court arrest.[99] But after some time a large number of persons came to join the movement. Therefore the organizers decided that they would not bail out the satyagrahis with effect from 30 September 1926.[100]

Along with the organization of the movement arrangements were made to publicize the issue all over India. It was expected that for the recognition of an important and immemorial public right which was denied to the Hindus of Patuakhali the movement would 'receive the support of other Hindus all over the country.'[101] This expectation was not belied. A provincial committee in aid of the movement was formed in Calcutta.[102] It did its best to support the movement by contributions in cash and kind and also by recruiting satyagrahis. Several distinguished persons were members of this committee : President—Sarala Devi ; Vice-Presidents—Durga Charan Banerjee, Jatindra Nath Basu, Hirendra Nath Dutta, Ghanashyam Das Birla ; Secretaries—Amarendra Nath Chatterjee and Dr Jatindra Mohan Das Gupta. Many important personalities were also included in the committee.[103] The satyagrahi leaders went to Gauhati to consult national leaders at the All-India Congress Committee session. There they met Pandit Madan Mohan Malaviya, Pandit Jagat Narayan Lal, Lala Duni Chand, Dr Moonje, Dr Rajendra Prasad and others. All the leaders expressed their sympathy for the movement and requested the Satyagraha Committee to carry on the fight to establish the right of the Hindus. There the representatives tried to elicit the opinion of the leaders on the question of arbitration.[104]

Meanwhile, it was reported, the District Magistrate proposed to the Satyagraha Committee, Patuakhali, for setting up of an arbitration board to settle the dispute. The leaders approached by the satyagrahi representatives favoured the proposal but at the same time warned them against 'showing any disposition to yield at all.'[105]

As a result of this propaganda, help in the form of material and human resources began to pour in, volunteers from different parts of the country joined to strengthen it. Besides the different districts in Bengal, help also came from Hyderabad, Jamalpur, Simla, Maharashtra, Punjab, Kanpur, Benaras, Dehra Dun, Bihar, Karimgunj, Gauhati, Jabalpur, Prayag and other places. Prominent leaders like Dr Moonje, Dr J.M. Das Gupta, Piyush Kanti Ghosh, Makhan Lal Sen, Padmaraj Jain and others came to Patuakhali. Efforts were made by Rash Behari Bose from Japan to help finance the movement.[106] What is more interesting is that the contemporary dailies played an important role in vindicating the cause of the Hindus—*Amrita Bazar Patrika*, *Ananda Bazar Patrika*, *Forward*, *The Bengalee*, *Atmasakti*, *Nayak* deserving special mention in this connexion.[107] Women and students did not lag behind ; they also participated in the movement.[108]

Almost all the non-violent techniques were adopted in this movement. A satyagraha office was opened in a room of the local Town Hall. Hunger-strikes were resorted to in protest against the maltreatment of the jail authorities.[109] The students went on strike against the rustication of certain students of the local school on 1 December 1926.[110] The organizers also participated in Constructive Programme. Workers of Abhoy Ashram came from Calcutta to sell *khaddar* to satyagrahis.[111] Moreover, the organizers made fervent appeal to the people for the removal of untouchability.[112]

As stated earlier, besides organizational activities, the organizers of the movement arranged for legal defence of the satyagrahis. For this purpose the local lawyers came forward to help them.[113] Abani Chandra Banerjee, Bar-at-Law came from Calcutta to defend the satyagrahis' cases.[114] After the arrest of Satindranath Sen, Manmatna Nath De went to Calcutta to approach B.C. Chatterjee, the renowned counsel of that time, who, it was reported, agreed to defend the case of Mr Sen under sections 107 and 114 Cr. P.C..[115] Accordingly, Mr Chatterjee came to Barisal on June 18, 1927[116] and appeared before the SDO's court.[117]

Now to turn to the leadership aspect. It goes without saying that Satindranath Sen was the accredited leader of the movement. The movement achieved complete success only due to his indomitable spirit. From the beginning he stood by the side of the Hindus in asserting their rights. The local authorities arrested him on 18 March 1927. This, they expected, would lead to the withdrawal of the movement. Sen

was sentenced to execute a bond of Rs. 5,000 with two sureties
of Rs. 2,500 each "to keep the peace for the period of one
year." In default he was to be imprisoned for that period or
till the execution of bond.[118] An appeal was made against
this order to the District Judge by Indu Bhusan Sen and
Manmatha Nath De. The appeal was granted and Satindra
Nath Sen was released on a surety of Rs. 500.[119] In this
Appeal Judgment the District and Sessions Judge reduced the
amount by demanding a personal security of Rs. 500 with two
sureties of Rs. 250 each for keeping the peace for a period of
one year in default to undergo one year's simple imprisoment.
On 27 Septemher 1927 Sen surrendered to the court to serve one
year's simple imprisonment.[120] He was sent to the Presidency
Jail the next day.[121] However on appeal before Mr Justice
Canunaide of the Calcutta High Court, Sen was released on a
bail of Rs. 500.[122] But during the pendency of his appeal
against the order Sen was further arrested under section 110
Cr. P.C.. Against this action of the Government Manmatha De
preferred a motion with the High Court.[123] The motion was
moved by J.M. Sen Gupta who pointed out the atrocities and
zulums that were being perpetrated at Patuakhali by the local
and district authorities. In his judgment Mr Justice C.C.
Ghosh remarked : "So long the High Court exists in the
country it is not going to tolerate any zulum, that may be
brought upon by anybody to anybody. It is our bounden duty
when it is brought out to take notice of it."[124] Satindranath
Sen on being acquitted came to Barisal.

## VI

Patuakhali satyagraha was launched against the unjust
demands of the local Mohammedans as put forward by their
reactionary leaders and as supported later by the Government.
It was the policy of the Government to aggravate communal
tension so that the freedom movement 'receded to the background.'[125] And that was why the movement to them was a
'notorious' one.[126] Instead of making any attempt to solve
the problem of music before mosques, the Government adopted
measures to frustrate the movement. But ultimately all its

efforts failed and victory was achieved by the satyagrahis led by the Congress. Nevertheless it is to be noted in this connexion that although the feeling of Hindu brotherhood contributed much to the strength of the organization of satyagrahis yet the fact remains that it was reinforced by 'a factor which was not the result of non-violence'. Rather "it sprang from the sentiment that the Hindus were threatened by the unjust demands of the Muslims, who were rightly, or wrongly, being favoured by the British."[127]

Whatever might be the factor that contributed to the victory of the satyagraha at Patuakhali, we have some reservations as to the 'non-violent' nature of the movement. For by satyagraha we mean "a way of conducting 'war' by means of non-violence."[128] And what is non-violence ? Non-violence means "the exercise of power or influence to effect change without injury to the opponent."[129] But the attitude of the leadership was not in keeping with the spirit of unadulterated satyagraha. Its strategy during the movement was to combat the opponents by adopting the same method as the latter followed. In other words violence was fought by violence, though for defensive purposes.[130] As a result it is not non-violence, but organized effort of the satyagrahis to adopt the 'tit for tat' principle that made people courageous to confront the opponents.[131] Moreover, at least in two cases in the movement, the criterion of strict non-violence was not adhered to. It may be recalled that on 26 January 1927 the satyagrahi prisoners retaliated against their opponents with arms hurled at them by the latter. Outside the jail also a large number of Hindus returned tit for tat to the Mohammedans who at first attacked them. These two incidents at least reveal that there was a wide gap between the principle of non-violence professed by the leaders of Patuakhali satyagraha and their practice of the same.

It had been suggested[132] that Patuakhali satyagraha was not communal in character as it was directed against the policy of the Government. True, considered from that point of view it was an anti-Government movement. But the question is whether the movement was conducted along non-violent lines and whether the participants in the movement proved themselves true satyagrahis by their conduct. For satyagrahis are required to observe a code of discipline when a communal conflagration breaks out. The code as enunciated by Gandhi is as follows :

1. No civil resister will intentionally become a cause of communal quarrels.

2. In the event of any such outbreak, he will not take sides, but he will assist only that party which is demonstrably in the right. Being a Hindu he will be generous towards Mussalmans and others, and will sacrifice himself in the attempt to save non-Hindus from a Hindu attack. And if the attack is from the other side, he will not participate in any retaliation but will give his life in protecting Hindus.

3. He will, to the best of his ability, avoid every occasion that may give rise to communal quarrels.

4. If there is a procession of satyagrahis they will do nothing that would wound the religious susceptibilities of any community, and they will not take part in any other processions that are likely to wound such susceptibilities.[133]

Judged by the above criteria it is doubtful whether Patuakhali satyagraha can be called a satyagraha in the true sense of the term.

## NOTES AND REFERENCES

1. A. R. Desai, *Social Background of Indian Nationalism,* 315 ; Wilfred Cantwell Smith, *Modern Islam in India,* 211. For an objective analysis of the communal problem, see Asoka Mehta and Achyut Patwardhan, *The Communal Triangle in India.*

2. Jawaharlal Nehru, *An Autobiography,* 459.

cp. "...the Hindus, Muslims and the British Government constitute the three arms of the communal triangle. From other considerations also, the question assumes a triangular shape. The political arm of the triangle is generally best known, since it is the most obvious. But complex problems do not always admit of simple and cut-and-dry explanations. While the political aspect has an importance all its own, it is by no means the only aspect of the communal problem. There are other forces whose influence must be adequately appraised. One such is the sociological basis of the communal problem. The other is the irrational factor..."—Asoka Mehta and Achyut Patwardhan, op. cit., 7-8.

3.  R.C. Majumdar, *History of the Freedom Movement in India*, III, 282.

4.  ibid., 281-2.

The main provisions of the Bengal Pact were as follows :

1.  Representation in the Legislative Council on the population basis with separate electorates.

2.  Representation to local bodies to be in the proportion of 60 to 40 in every district—60 to the community which is in the majority and 40 to the minority.

3.  Fifty-five per cent of the Government posts should go to the Muslims.

4.  No music should be allowed before the mosque.

5.  There should be no interference with cow-slaughter for religious sacrifices but the cow should be killed in such a manner as not to wound the religious feeling of the Hindus.

For the full text, see H.N. Mitra (ed.), *Indian Quarterly Register*, 1924, I, 63 ; Maulavi Abdul Karim, *Letters on Hindu-Muslim Pact*, Appendix A. For further reading, J.H. Broomfield, *Elite Conflict in a Plural Society*, 245-6 ; Leonard A. Gordon, *Bengal : The Nationalist Movement 1876-1940*, 194-8 ; V.V. Nagarkar, *Genesis of Pakistan*, 132-4 ; Maulana Abul Kalam Azad, *India Wins Freedom*, 18 ; M. R. Jayakar, *The Story of My Life*, I, 346 ; Subhas Chandra Bose, *The Indian Struggle*, 145 ; Maulavi Abdul Karim, *Letters on Hindu-Muslim Pact*, 1-10.

For the resolution passed at Serajgunge Conference in favour of the Bengal Pact 1924, see *Indian Quarterly Register*, 1924, I, 669-70.

For Maulana Akram Khan's Presidential Address at Serajgunge, see *Indian Quarterly Register*, 1924, I, 665-8.

5.  For details about the 'unrestricted right to play music on the King's highway', see V.V. Nagarkar, op. cit., 162 ff.

6.  N.K. Bose, 'Patuakhali Satyagraha for Civil Rights,' in *Point of View*, 14.10.72, 10 ; Nirmal Kumar Bose, *Lectures on Gandhism*, 28-30.

7.  Interview with Manmatha Nath De, 1.7.73.

For an account of the Laukathi Union Board Boycott movement, see Asutosh Mukhopadhyay, *Mrityunjayee Satin Sen* (in Bengali).

8.  See note no. 7.

9.  *Ananda Bazar Patrika*, 19.5.26, 11(I).

10.  ibid., 18.5.26, 9(5).

11.  ibid., 19.5.26, 11(1).

12.  ibid., 18.5.26, 9(5).

13.  *The Bengalee*, 4.9.26, 4(6).

14.  See note no. 7.

15.  *The Bengalee*, 1.9.26, 5(4) ; *Ananda Bazar Patrika*, 1.9.26, 3(4).

16.  *Ananda Bazar Patrika*, 3.9.26, 7(4).

17.  *The Bengalee*, 10.9.26, 4(5) ; *Ananda Bazar Patrika*, 9.9.26, 8(4) and 10.9.26, 8(2).

18.  *Ananda Bazar Patrika*, 10.9.26, 3(3).

19. ibid , 14.9.26, 3(5).
20. *The Bengalee*, 15.9.26, 4(3).
21. ibid., 21.9.26, 5(6) ; *Ananda Bazar Patrika*, 20.9.26, 10(5).
22. *The Bengalee*, 26.9.26, 5(2).
23. *Ananda Bazar Patrika*, 11.9.26, 4(5).
24. ibid., 16.9.26, 3(4) ; *The Bengalee*, 16.9.26, 4(4).
25 & 26. *Ananda Bazar Patrika*, 17.9.26, 3(3) ; *The Bengalee* 17.9.26, 4(5).
27. *Ananda Bazar Patrika*, 15.9.26, 7(4).
28. ibid., 16.9.26, 3(4) ; *The Bengalee*, 16.9.26, 4(4).
29. *The Bengalee*, 8.9.26, 5(6).
30. *Ananda Bazar Patrika*, 11.9.26, 4(5).
31. ibid., 20.9.26, 10(5).
32, 33 & 34. *The Bengalee*, 21.9.26, 5(6).
35. *Amrita Bazar Patrika*, 8.10.26, 4(4).
36. *The Bengalee*, 1.10.26, 4(3).
37. *Amrita Bazar Patrika*, 8.10.26, 4(4).
38. See note no. 6.
39. *Amrita Bazar Patrika*, 29.10.26, 5(1) ; *Ananda Bazar Patrika,* 29.10.26, 3(1).
40. *The Bengalee*, 25.11.26, 4(5).
41. *The Bengalee*, 7.12.26, 5(3) ; *Ananda Bazar Patrika*, 7.12.26, 3(1).
42. *The Bengalee*, 10.12.26, 4(4) ; *Ananda Bazar Patrika*, 10.12.26, 5(1-2).
43 & 44. *The Bengalee*, 17.12.26, 4(4).
45. *Ananda Bazar Patrika*, 31.1.27, 10(4-5).
46. ibid., 28.1.27, 3(1-3).
47. ibid., 31.1.27, 5(5).
48. ibid., 5.2.27, 3(5).
49. ibid., 7.2.27, 3(1-3)
50. Asutosh Mukhopadhyay, op. cit., 92-3.
51. *The Bengalee*, 12.9.26, 4(7) ; *Ananda Bazar Patrika*, 13.9.26, 5(4-5).
52. *Amrita Bazar Partika*, 5.11.26, 5(1) ; *Ananda Bazar Patrika*, 5.11.26, 3(3).
53. *Ananda Bazar Patrika*, 14.6.27, 3(5).
54. ibid., 14.12.26, 3(5) ; *The Bengalee*, 14.12.26, 4(5).
55. *Amrita Bazar Patrika*, 18.12.26 ; *The Bengalee*, 18.12.26, 5(5).
56. *Ananda Bazar Patrika*, 11.1.27, 3(1-2).
57. Asutosh Mukhopadhyay, op. cit., 90.
58. *The Bengalee*, 1.10.26, 4(3).
59. ibid., 8.10.26, 5(2).
60. *Amrita Bazar Patrika*, 5.11.26, 5(1) ; *Ananda Bazar Patrika*, 5.11.26, 3(3).
61. *Ananda Bazar Patrika*, 24.2.27.
62. ibid., 4.3.27, 3(3).
63. ibid., 25.3.27, 3(3).
64. ibid., 5.4.27, 3(5) ; 8.4.27, 3(4).

65. *Amrita Bazar Patrika*, 6.12.27, 3(5).

66. *Bengal Legislative Council Proceedings*, 13.12.27, XXVII, 74.

67. *Ananda Bazar Patrika*, 22.1.27.

68. *Amrita Bazar Patrika*, 6.4.28, 9(7).

69. *The Bengalee*, 8.9.26, 5(6).

70. *Ananda Bazar Patrika*, 5.4.27, 3(5).

71. ibid., 28.3.28, 3(5).

72. *Amrita Bazar Patrika*, 20.10.26, 3(2).

73. *Ananda Bazar Patrika*, 15.12.26, 3(3).

74. *Amrita Bazar Patrika*, 30.10.26, 4(5) ; *The Bengalee* 23.10.26, 6(5) and *Ananda Bazar Patrika*, 30.10.26, 4(5).

75. *Amrita Bazar Patrika*, 30.10.26, 4(5).

76. ibid., 5.11.26, 5(1) ; *Ananda Bazar Patrika*, 5.11.26, 3(3).

77 & 78. *Amrita Bazar Patrika*, 11.11.26, 5(5) ; *Ananda Bazar Patrika*, 11.11.26, 3(1).

79. *Amrita Bazar Patrika*, 22.10.26, 5(2).

80. *Bengal Legislative Council Proceedings*, XXVII, 30-1.

81. *The Bengalee*, 12.10.27, 4(3).

82. ibid., 18.10.27, 4(4).

83. *Ananda Bazar Patrika*, 22.10.27, 8(4).

84. *Amrita Bazar Patrika*, 14.10.27, 4(2).

85. *The Bengalee*, 23.10.27, 4(4-5).

86. ibid., 26.10.27, 3(2).

87. *Ananda Bazar Patrika*, 27.10.27, 3(3).

88. ibid., 2.11.27, 4(5).

89. *The Bengalee*, 22.11.27, 3(6).

90. *Ananda Bazar Patrika*, 15.2.28, 11(2).

91. ibid., 20.3.28, 3(4).

92. *Amrita Bazar Patrika*, 17.5.28, 3(5).

93. *Bengal Legislative Council Proceedings*, XXXIII, 28.

94. *Amrita Bazar Patrika*. 8.7.28, 5(7).

95. *Bengal Legislative Council Proceedings*, XXXIII, 38.

96 & 97. See note no. 6.

98. Asutosh Mukhopadhyay, op.cit., 82-3.

99. ibid., 79.

100. *Ananda Bazar Patrika*, 27.9.26, 3(4).

101. *The Bengalee*, 29.9.26, 4(3).

102 & 103. *Ananda Bazar Patrika*, 17.12.26, 6(4).

104. *The Bengalee*, 31.12.26, 4(7). The All-India Hindu Mahasabha at its Special Session at Gauhati passed, among other things, the following resolution on 29.12.26 : "This Mahasabha expresses its sympathy with the suffering of the Satyagrahis of Patuakhali who have been sent to jail for asserting in a peaceful manner their right of taking out processions with music on a public street. The Mahasabha trusts that the Hindus of other parts of India will lend every legitimate support to

their brethren of Patuakhali to enable them to continue their Satyagraha until their right is fully vindicated and recognised."—*Indian Quarterly Register*, 1926, II, 357.

105. *The Bengalee*, 31.12.26, 4(7).

106. *Ananda Bazar Patrika*, 10.3.27, 3(4).

107. ibid., 1.10.26, 6(2).

108. ibid., 24.9.26, 4(4) and 25.9.26, 3(3).

109. *The Bengalee*, 18.11.26, 7(4).

110. ibid., 2.12.26, 4(5).

111. *Ananda Bazar Patrika*, 25.9.26, 8(3).

112. *The Bengalee*, 11.12.26, 4(5).

113. *Amrita Bazar Patrika*, 27.11.26, 3(4) ; *Ananda Bazar Patrika*, 27.11.26, 7(1).

114. *Amrita Bazar₁Patrika*,, 30.10.26, 9(3-4) and 11(5-6).

115. Interview with Manmatha Nath De.

116. *Ananda Bazar Patrika*, 20.6.27, 10(3).

117. ibid ; *Amrita Bazar Patrika*, 3.7.27, 5(5) ; 10.7.27, 5(4-5) and 21.7.27, 10(3-5).

118. *Amrita Bazar Patrika*, 31.7.27, 12(4).

119. *Ananda Bazar Patrika*, 1.8.27, 11(5).

120. *The Bengalee*, 28.9.27, 5(1).

121. ibid., 30.9.27, 4(4).

122. ibid., 29.9.27, 4(3).

123. See note no. 115.

124. *The Bengalee*, 26.6.28, 4(4).

125. Statement of Binode Kanjilal, Dinesh Sen Gupta and Adhir Banerjee as recorded by Miss S. Ghosh on 30.6.72.

126. *India in 1929-30*, 385.

127. See note no. 6.

128. Nirmal Kumar Bose, *Studies in Gandhism* (1972), 109.

129. Joan V. Bondurant, *Conquest of Violence*, 9.

130. Asutosh Mukhopadhyay, op. cit., 82-3.

131. Nirmal Kumar Bose regarded Patuakhali satyagraha as 'nonviolent.' See *Lectures on·Gandhism*, 30.

132. *Atmasakti*, 10.12.26, 1(2-3).

133. *Young India*, 27.2.30, in M. K. Gandhi, *Satyagraha*, 80-81 ; *The Collected Works of Mahatma Gandhi*, XLII, 493.

## List of Satyagrahis

Anileswar Banerjee, Brajanath Banerjee, Dhiren Banerjee, Sunil Chandra Banerjee, Jajneswar Banik, Jnaneswar Barik, Haralal Basu, Hiralal Basu, Phanindra Krishna Basu, Rajendra Basu, Ramani Ranjan Basu, Sukumar Basu, Suraj Kumar Basu, Indu Kumar Bose, Jitendranath Bose, Rajendranath Bose, Birendranath Bhattacharyya, Dhirendranath Bhattacharyya, Harendranath Bhattacharyya, Indubhusan Bhattacharyya. Nalini Ranjan Bhattacharyya, Pramathanath Bhattacharyya, Ramkrishna Bhattacharyya, Bholanathji, Kali Charan Bhora, Mohanlal Bhuinya, Mukundalal Bhuinya, Bihari Biswas, Jatindranath Biswas, Nagendranath Biswas, Sivadas Biswas, Atulchandra Brahmachari, Sankarananda Bramhachari, Bijay Gopal Chakravarty, Bipin Behari Chakravarty, Braja Gopal Chakravarty, Jyotish Chakravarty, Kalikanta Chakravarty, Kripanath Chakravarty, Krishnadas Chakravarty, Manoranjan Chakravarty, Purna Chandra Chakravarty, Ram Kanta Chakravarty, Surendra Chakravarty, Amulyadhan Chatterjee, Dhirendranath Chatterjee, Indu Bhusan Chatterjee, Jogen Chatterjee, Khagendranath Chatterjee, Manindra Chatterjee, Nripendranath Chatterjee, Phanilal Chatterjee, Sadananda Chatterjee, Benoy Kumar Chatterjee, Surendra Chandra Choudhury, Suresh Chandra Choudhury, Ananta Kumar Das, Asutosh Das, Atul Chandra Das, Basanta Kumar Das, Bholanath Rajak Das, Bimal Chandra Das, Bireswar Das, Chand Mohan Das, Chintaharan Das, Chittaranjan Das, Debendranath Das, Dhirendranath Das, Dinesh Chandra Das, Ganesh Chandra Das, Gopal Chandra Das, Haripada Das, Hem Chandra Das, Hemanta Kumar Das, Jagadish Das, Jitendranath Das, Kanailal Das, Kartik Chandra Das, Lalit Mohan Das, Makhanlal Das, Mohini Mohan Das, Manoranjan Das, Nakul Chandra Das, Nityananda Das, Prakash Chandra Das, Priyanath Das, Satyaranjan Das, Sitanath Das, Sitaram Das, Subal Chandra Das, Sudhir Kumar Das, Sukharanjan Das, Dr J. M. Das Gupta,

Rishikesh Das Gupta, Santi Ranjan Das Gupta, Bankim Chandra Datta, Debendranath Datta, Madhusudan Datta, Nagendra Datta, Narayan Datta, Hemanta Kumar De, Nibaran Dhopi, Benode Lal Dolui, Mohini Ganguli, Manomohan Ganguli, Rameswar Ganguli, Rebati Mohan Ganguli, Suresh Chandra Ganguli, Swami Ganesananda, Abinas Chandra Ghosh, Jyotish Chandra Ghosh, Khagendranath Ghosh, Mahim Chandra Ghosh, Nagendranath Ghosh, Pramatha- nath Ghosh, Sailendra Kumar Ghosh, Sukomal Ghosh, Hirendranath Ghoshal, Dinendranath Guha, Subodh Chandra Guha, Sukumar Guha, Susil Kumar Guha, Upendra- nath Guha, Jatadhar Jha, Bholanath Jogi, Swami Kamala- pati, Swami Kamalapuri, Benode Kanjilal, Mahideo- prasad Kapur, Haridhar Kar, Haripada Kar, Balaram Karmakar, Harendralal Karmakar, Matilal Karmakar, Mano- ranjan Karmakar, Ramkrishna Karmakar, Krishnamurti, Narayan Chandra Kundu, Pandit Madhusudan. Mahabali, Manoranjan, Mithulalji (Kanpur), Mithulalji (Jabalpur), Jitendranath Majumdar, Rangalal Majumdar, Sailendra Majumdar, Sasi Majumdar, Subodh Majumdar, Binay Krishna Mandal, Brajendra Mitra, Dharmadas Mitra, Asutosh Mukherjee, Haradhan Mukherjee, Haridas Mukherjee, Manohar Mukherjee, Niharranjan Mukherjee, Panchkari Mukherjee, Susil Mukherjee, Hara Chandra Nag, Haran Chandra Nag, Jamini Kanta Nandi, Jatindranath Nath, Swami Niranjan- ananda, Abhay Charan Pal, Gopal Chandra Pal, Haralal Pal, Jogendranath Pal, Mangal Chandra Pal, Manoranjan Pal, Ramani Pal, Ramkrishna Pal, Satyaranjan Pal, Sreemanta Pal, Satyanarayan Panchagni, Mahabir Pande, Prasad Pande, Sahadeo Pande, Sarban Pande, Ayodhanath Pathak, Ramen- dranath Pramanik, Janaki Prasad, Sibananda Prasad, Siddha Prasad, Sitanath Puri, Mahendranath Putatunda, Bholanath Rajak, Raja Ram, Jitendranath Roy, Manindranath Roy, Niharranjan Roy, Amarnath Roy Choudhury, Anantanath Roy Choudhury, Haripada Roy Choudhury, Sadananda Roy Choudhury, Surya Kumar Roy Choudhury, Brajendra Saha, Dinendranath Saha, Gouranga Mohan Saha, Hiralal Saha, Sitanath Saha, Syamlal Saha, Ramdeo Sahay, Dhunder Sahu,

Kedarnath Samaddar, Khagen Samaddar, Matilal Samaddar, Satish Caandra Samaddar, Amulya Charan Sarkar, Bholanath Sarkar, Jamini Kanta Sarkar, Nani Gopal Sarkar, Madhusudan Sarma, Ramsingh Sashi, Dhiren Sen, Kshitish Chandra Sen, Manoranjan Sen, Satindranath Sen, Surendranath Sen, Bidhubhusan Sen Gupta, Sudhir Kumar Sen Gupta, Kshudiram Sethi, Ananta Kumar Sil, Umakanta Sil, Ananta Kumar Simlai, Ramkamal Singh, Ramswarup Singh, Satiram Singh, Bireswar Som, Ramdayal Sukla, Rajanikanta Tantradhar.

[Source : *Amrita Bazar Patrika, Ananda Bazar Patrika* and *The Bengalee* 1926-28.]

## CHAPTER VI

# MUNSHIGANJ KALI TEMPLE SATYAGRAHA

## I

UNTOUCHABILITY IS AN inhuman institution in Hindu society. Hardly any society has ever condemned a section of it to physical segregation as the Hindu society has been doing over the ages. The mere touch of an untouchable is considered a sin. Untouchability thus, as Gandhi put it, is 'the greatest blot on Hinduism'.[1] The practice of untouchability also hindered the progress of India's freedom movement to a considerable extent. So Gandhi gave top priority to anti-untouchability campaign with a view to enabling the Hindu society to present a united front to the alien rule. The aim of the anti-untouchability campaign was primarily and essentially humanitarian. But that does not mean that it was in any way less significant in the context of the national liberation movement. Indeed, how could the country march forward in its struggle for swaraj with such a vast mass of the toiling people left beyond the pale of society? As Gandhi observed, "Swaraj is a meaningless term if we desire to keep a fifth of India under perpetual subjection, and deliberately deny to them the fruits of national culture. We are seeking the aid of God in this great purification movement, but we deny to the most deserving among His creatures the rights of humanity. Inhuman ourselves, we may not plead before the Throne of deliverance from the inhumanity of others."[2]

Denial of the right of temple-entry to the so-called untouchables had been a long-standing practice with the high caste Hindus. But as Gandhi observed, "Temple-entry is the one spiritual act that would constitute the message of freedom to the 'untouchables' and assure them that they are not outcastes before God."[3] Moreover, to him, it is the "persecutors who are unknowingly defiling their own religion by keeping out of public temples men who are at least as honourable as they claim to be themselves and are willing to abide by all the ceremonial rules observable by Hindus in general on such occasions. More than that no man has any right to impose or expect. The heart of man only God knows. An ill-dressed Panchama may have a much cleaner heart than a meticulously dressed high caste Hindu."[4]

Among the disabilities of the untouchables sought to be removed was the denial of the right of temple-entry to them. Even the British Courts in India had recognized this evil custom, "so much so that certain acts done by untouchables as such came to be offences under the British Indian Penal Code."[5]

The question was how to eradicate this evil—by using force or violence ? To Gandhi, the only means could be satyagraha which, he always insisted, was a weapon to be used "in all fields of life and against friend and foe, relative and stranger, one and many, individuals and institutions."[6] Indeed a few satyagraha movements were launched in India against the sin of untouchability. In 1924 Vykom satyagraha was launched with a view to removing 'the prohibition upon the use by untouchables of roadways passing the temple.' That was a serious 'disability' on the part of the untouchables since they had to take a long, circuitous route to reach their dwellings.[7] Gandhi himself participated in the movement, though at a later stage. Over the question of temple-entry, two important satyagrahas were launched in 1929—one at Poona, popularly known as Parvati Satyagraha[8] and the other at Munshiganj of Bengal. However, for the present we are concerned only with Munshiganj Kali Temple-entry satyagraha launched in Bengal in 1929.

## II

Munshiganj is a subdivisional town in the district of Dacca. Since the establishment of the subdivisional headquarters at Munshiganj, the Kali temple was founded there by public subscription, the local legal practitioners taking the initiative. On November 1928, a *Namasudra* went to take *caranamrita* and he was reported to have accidentally touched the priest for which he was insulted by the priest. That event caused a commotion among the local *Namasudras* who organized a big meeting to protest against such maltreatment. People from different parts of Bengal attended the meeting and passed a resolution condemning the action of the priest.[9]

No further unpleasant consequences followed the incident but the local *Namasudra* community could not forget the insult meted out to one of its members and they practically boycotted the high caste Hindus. After the fifth session of the Bengal Provincial Hindu Conference at Dacca was over, some of the local *Namasudra* leaders were reported to have approached Swami Satyananda of the Hindu Mission. On their invitation Swami Satyananda alias Kalyan Kumar Nag, Pandit Satindranath Vidyabinode, Rai Saheb Binode Behari Sadhu, Brahmachari Amal Krishna and some other workers of the Hindu Mission arrived at Munshiganj on 29 August 1929 and held a large public meeting in the evening at the Kalibari Natmandir under the presidentship of Jnanendra Chandra Mitra, a local pleader. In that meeting Swami Satyananda delivered a very instructive and inspiring speech dwelling mainly on *suddhi*, *sangathan* and removal of untouchability from Hindu society.[10] A resolution asserting the rights of free access and worship in respect of the Kali temple which was claimed to be a public place of worship was moved and passed before that large gathering by an overwhelming majority in spite of the opposition of some orthodox Brahmins. Hundreds of non-Brahmins then and there enlisted themselves as satyagrahis in response to the Swami's appeal.[11]

Thus it was decided to launch the satyagraha movement on 30 August 1929.[12] The immediate aim of the movement was to assert the *Namasudras*' right to enter the Kali temple at Munshiganj. And the ultimate aim was 'to assert the inherent right of every Hindu to enter and offer Puja irrespective of caste and creed in the place of public worship' by removing the 'blot' of untouchability from Hindu society. Swami Satyananda, the accredited leader of the movement, stated : "It is admitted by all that Hindu social structure as exists at present require reform and untouchability is one

11

of the evils which must be eradicated at once. The question
arises as to how to remove this evil and raise the depressed
classes. Everybody has got his likes and dislikes in food
and drink. Removal of untouchability cannot mean compulsory
interdining and intermarriage. In a country like India religion,
religious rites and festivals are the true bonds of union among
the people. If the depressed classes get the right of free
access to all places of public worship and can sit side by
side with the high class Hindus the caste prejudice will be
mitigated to a great degree. I think this is the most elementary right of every member of a religious community. So
I have begun with the assertion of this right by the depressed
classes and temple-entry is the first step towards its realization." The Swami explained categorically that he was not
a destroyer of Hindu religion and society. He did not intend
to change the existing management of the Kali temple or
to disturb its existing arrangement in any way. The only
thing he wanted was that those who used to offer prayers
from outside would go inside the temple and offer *puja* and
*anjali* to the deity.[13]

### III

As scheduled, the satyagraha started on 30 August 1929.
At 10 a.m. Swami Satyananda along with his co-workers
and several *Namasudras* went to the Kali temple for offering
*puja*. The temple was strongly cordoned by a posse
of constables and the door of the temple was under double
lock. The Swami and his party waited there till the evening
but could not enter the temple as the door was not opened
for the day. A large crowd assembled in the street to witness
the satyagraha but occasionally it was dispersed by the police.
In the evening S. C. Bose ICS, the SDO of Munshiganj,
met Swami Satyananda at the Kali temple and had a long
discussion with him regarding the situation.[14] The SDO had
also a discussion with Dr Mohini Mohan Das MLC who
arrived that evening.[15]

On 12 September 1929 the President of the Hindu Mission,
Calcutta, wrote a letter to Jamnalal Bajaj, the Convener of

the Anti-Untouchability Committee of the AICC, informing the latter of the satyagraha launched at Munshiganj and soliciting his opinion and help in that connexion. Bajaj wrote in reply that 'the existing conditions did not warrant starting satyagraha at once and the question of temple-entry was a delicate matter that needed special handling.' "There was danger of creating internal jealousy among the various Hindu communities and jeopardizing unity." Finally he opined that if satyagraha was to be resorted to at all, the caste Hindus should take the initiative.[16]

But the upper caste Hindus did not come forward. The Munshiganj Bar Association, composed of high caste Hindus, was, in fact, in charge of the management of the temple. It was not eager to recognize the untouchables' right of temple-entry. As a result the satyagraha continued. Now the satyagrahis adopted a new technique. Leaving the temple-gate, they came to the local Bar Association Hall on 28 September and lay down before its door, thereby preventing the members of the Association from entering or coming out of the hall. Later, however, they were persuaded to leave the place.[17]

The movement gained momentum with the arrival of Prof Nripendra Chandra Banerjee, a government college teacher, on the scene. He was elected President of the Temple Committee which was formed to manage the affairs of Munshiganj Kali temple at a meeting held on 13 October 1929 at Kewar village, three miles away from Munshiganj. Surendra Chandra Majumdar was elected Secretary of the said committee. The meeting which was to be held had been postponed due to the promulgation of section 144 Cr. P. C. prohibiting any public meeting within the radius of two miles of Munshiganj.[18]

In pursuance of the resolution adopted in the meeting at Kewar village, satyagraha was offered on 14 October under the leadership of Swami Satyananda and Prof Nripendra Chandra Banerjee by about 2,000 volunteers, most of them being *Namasudras*.[19] Earlier the leaders informed the SDO that the satyagraha would start at 2 p.m. They also assured him that it would be absolutly a peaceful 'show' and advised him to remain neutral.[20]

Just at 2 p.m. the satyagrahis stood in rows of four in the vicinity of the satyagraha office and after receiving instructions from the leaders they went towards the temple in a disciplined manner with flower offerings in hand. In front of the temple a posse of police constables stood blocking the way. Satyagrahis in batches assembled there and that continued for nearly half an hour when, it was said, the police suddenly charged the satyagrahis with lathis and dispersed them forcibly. As a result a large number of people and satyagrahis suffered injuries. Immediately a meeting of the satyagrahis was called by Prof. Banerjee but before the meeting could formally start, it was once again forcibly dispersed by the orders of the SDO.[21] Meanwhile when Prof. Banerjee was dictating a message for the Press to one of his co-workers, he was put under arrest along with Surendra Chandra Majumdar.[22] Both of them were arrested under section 114 Cr. P. C.[23] and were taken to the temple-compound and presented before the Subdivisional Magistrate.[24] It is to be noted in this connexion that Prof Banerjee was one of the first prominent Congressmen in Bengal to be jailed in 1929.[25] At the moment of his arrest Prof. Banerjee requested Swami Satyananda and other leaders and workers to carry on the fight non-violently.[26]

As a result of the arrest of Prof. Banerjee there prevailed a tense excitement all over Munshiganj. Three security bonds of Rs. 5,000/- were demanded of each of the two arrested leaders who were put in jail.[27] Both Prof. Banerjee and Mr Majumdar refused to accept release on those terms.[28] But Haripada Banerjee (brother of Prof. Banerjee and a lawyer by profession) moved the SDO on their behalf to rescind the orders and release them on personal recognizance bonds. Prayer was also made for dispensing with their personal attendance in the court at the time of trial in view of the sedition cases which were pending against Prof. Banerjee in different courts and of the indifferent condition of Mr Majumdar's health due to tubercular attack.[29] But the petition was rejected by the SDO.[30]

In view of the situation created by the arrest of Prof. Banerjee and Mr Majumdar, Srish Chandra Chatterjee, Nalini

Kishore Guha, Madan Mohan Bhowmik and others came from Dacca and held an informal conference with Swami Satyananda and other leaders and local people. The conference held, among other things, that the satyagraha was in principle an absolutely peaceful move and had all along been so in actual practice. It also decided that constitutional propaganda would be carried on throughout Bikrampur emphasizing the peaceful character of the movement and held that governmental inference was absolutely uncalled for. It also blamed the Government for all complications that had arisen in the situation.[31] It was also reported that Subhas Chandra Bose, the BPCC President, took keen interest in the movement and asked other Congress leaders to hold an enquiry.[32]

## IV

Arrest of the leaders could not depress the fighting spirit of the satyagrahis. On the contrary, it gave a fresh impetus to the movement. The volunteer corps had been largely reinforced. The people gave warm reception to Swami Satyananda and Hindu Mission workers when they sought for public support.[33]

Finding no way for settling the dispute Swami Satyananda sent urgent letters to Subhas Chandra Bose and Kiran Sankar Roy requesting them to pay a visit to Munshiganj without delay as the situation demanded their presence. The Swami thought that in view of the 'unbending attitude of the orthodox party' the technique of the movement required a change.[34]

November 1929 onwards the situation began to take a serious turn. On 8 November at about 11 a.m. when several satyagrahis found the main gate of the temple open and entered there, they were forcibly removed by the priest and the guards. In the course of the scuffle the satyagrahis received minor injuries.[35]

On 10 November, the day of Jagaddhatri Puja, when the local *muktears* were entering the temple compound for performing *pujas*, a *Namasudra* satyagrahi attempted to get in there but was obstructed by a Nepali guard at the gate. An exchange of hot words was followed by a scuffle in the course of which the said satyagrahi slapped the Nepali guard on the face. At this the satyagrahi was forcibly taken inside the temple compound and mercilessly belaboured. The following morning when one of the guards went to the local market, he was, as the report went, assaulted by some unknown persons. As a sequel to that incident the OC of the local thana served warning notices under section 154 IPC on Swami Satyananda and two of his workers as well as on the President of the Munshiganj Bar Association, the priest of the temple and two Nepali guards.[36]

The situation took an ugly turn on 13 November. At about 4 p.m. eight satyagrahis, finding the gate of Kali temple kept open, entered the compound to offer worship to the deity. As soon as they entered inside the temple, the Nepali guards bolted the gate from within and informed the orthodox pleaders. The satyagrahis apprehending some mischief wanted to come out and repeatedly asked the guards to open the gate to which the latter did not respond. As a result they had to remain confined there till some pleaders together with a number of orthodox people ran into the temple-compound and began forthwith to assault them indiscriminately. Five of the satyagrahis managed somehow to escape from their grips but the remaining three who were mere boys could not come out. It was alleged that the boys were 'kicked, fisted, slapped and pushed' by the pleaders and the guards so mercilessly that the boys fell prostrate on the ground almost unconscious. At that stage some of the pleaders began to trample them under their feet with shoes on. As a result of this brutality the boys received severe injuries all over their body.[37] When the OC received the news he hastened to the temple and rescued the boys from wrongful confinement. He brought them to the thana and gave them first aid. The SDO also went to the place immediately and visited the injured boys personally in the thana. After an *ejahar* was taken, the injured boys were sent to the hospital for treatment.[38]

Meanwhile a large crowd gathered on the street. Swami Satyananda also went there. On seeing him a Brahmin began to abuse him in filthy language and the Swami was threatened with assault. Later a relation of the priest aimed a blow at the Swami's head with a bamboo pole and a pleader began to push him towards the gate for forcibly taking him into the temple compound, the purpose being to assault the Swami. But now some among the crowd intervened and snatched away the bamboo poles and prevented the pleader from pushing the Swami towards the gate.[39]

Even the *Namasudra* women were not allowed to enter the Kali temple. On 17 November more than five hundred *Namasudra* women with babies in their arms came out in a procession from the residence of Swami Satyananda and proceeded to the Kali temple. When they reached the temple-gate they requested the priest to open the gate and allow them to offer their *pujas*. But the priest refused to do that. Being disappointed, the *Namasudra* women went back to the place from where they started. The procession was led by the wife of Dr Mohini Mohan Das MLC.[40]

## V

At the very initial stage of the movement the leaders tried to arrive at an amicable settlement of the dispute. Swami Satyananda, for example, made the following appeal to the members of the Munshiganj Bar Association : "I request you to reconsider the just demands of the millions of your brethren who are participating in your culture for centuries and the great principle involved in the present satyagraha movement here. It is neither a local affair, nor a sectarian question. It is not a struggle between Brahmins and non-Brahmins. It is an all-India movement and it has sanction of *sastras* and support of the greatest men of India such as Mahatma Gandhi, Madan Mohan Malaviya, Maha-mahopadhyay Pramatha Nath Tarkabhusan, Dr B. S. Moonje, Mr N. C. Kelkar and G. D. Birla. ...I beg further to add that in making your mind (*sic*) you will kindly take into consideration...the pangs of untouchability so keenly felt by the majority of our people, the irresistible forces of the time and the dangerous activities of the enemies of Hindu religion and Hindu culture who are eager to swallow us any day. I

believe you will not fail to support the cause for which
satyagraha is going on at the door of Kalibari."[41]

This rather long extract will show how eager and sincere
was the satyagrahi leadership to arrive at an amicable settlement.

The provincial leaders also took an active part in effecting an amicable settlement. On 28 October J. M. Sen Gupta
paid a short visit to Munshiganj. There he convened a
meeting of the representatives of the satyagrahis, leaders
of the Bar and of the Congress to discuss the terms of compromise. Swami Satyananda, Matilal Basu Choudhury, Bhuban
Mohan Choudhury, Mohini Mohan Das, Durga Mohan
Bose, Sailendra Banerjee, Jnan Chandra Mitter, Hem Chandra
Sen and Uma Charan Sen were, among others, present in the
meeting. Swami Satyananda then handed to J. M. Sen Gupta
a letter from Subhas Chandra Bose and a note with
some suggestions from Prof. Nripendra Chandra Banerjee
regarding the compromise. But the suggestions of Prof. Banerjee
were not acceptable to the orthodox Hindus. Sen Gupta,
therefore, himself suggested a compromise formula but that
also was not acceptable to them. Finally, Sen Gupta recommended arbitration by Subhas Chandra Bose and Lalit Mohan
Das. That proposal too was rejected.[42] Ultimately Sen Gupta
left Munshiganj assuring the satyagrahis of their success and
asking them to remain non-violent.[43]

Another attempt was made by Swami Viswananda of
Tarakeswar fame[44] during his visit to Munshiganj. In a
statement to the Associated Press on India on 19 November
he said that he was much grieved to find acute dissensions
among the different sections of the Hindu community, especially in that part of the country where the Hindus constituted
only 30% of the total population. In his opinion all Hindus
had equal rights to worship the goddess Kali. Her worshippers
were not pure Vedic Brahmins who ate neither fish nor meat
but *tantrics* among whom there is no caste distinction. He
challenged the orthodox Brahmin leaders to quote texts from
the *sastras* to prove that Vedic Brahmins were allowed to
take meat and fish and that there was any untouchability
among the *tantrics*. Swami Viswananda regretted the uncom-

promising attitude of some of the pleaders and said that
'by putting fences round the temple compound they were preventing other touchable Hindus from worshipping the goddess'.
He hoped that the Government would not remain indifferent
to a matter which interfered with the personal rights of the
worshippers.[45] During his stay at Munshiganj he approached
the orthodox Brahmin leaders individually and appealed to
them to be generous and humane to the 'untouchables'.
Swami Viswananda thus made an earnest effort to effect an
amicable settlement which was ultimately frustrated.[46]

Another provincial leader who took keen interest in the
matter was Padmaraj Jain, Secretary of the Bengal Provincial Hindu Sabha. Jain held conferences with the two contending parties and suggested to them certain terms and conditions
for the settlement of the dispute.[47] But his efforts also ended
in failure owing to the opposition of some of the pleaders
of the Munshiganj Bar.[48] It was then decided to move
vigorously and for that purpose it was resolved to form a
satyagraha committee under the auspices of the Dacca District
Hindu Sabha. Jain left for Dacca and there he held an
informal meeting with the leading gentlemen of the town.[49]

## VI

On 10 December morning when about half a dozen satyagrahis were sitting before the gate of the Kali temple, thereby
obstructing the passage of the priest, the guard kicked a
satyagrahi who immediately returned a blow. Consequently
a criminal case was instituted by the priest before the Deputy
Magistrate as a sequel to which Swami Satyananda and five
of his workers were summoned under sections 143 and 341
IPC.[50] In consequence of the morning incident a *Namasudra*
satyagrahi was forcibly dragged into the temple compound
in the afternoon and was severely assaulted there. On receiving
this information the Inspector of Police hastened to the
temple and rescued the satyagrahi. He also brought the man
to the local thana and after recording his statement sent him
to the hospital for medical examination and treatment.[51]

After that nothing serious happened. But on the day of

*Sivaratri* Mr Hodson, the SP, visited Munshiganj for the second
time since the beginning of the movement. He inspected the
local Kali temple. A large number of people assembled at
the gate of the Kali temple for offering *puja*. As the gate was
closed, nobody could enter the temple. The satyagrahis as usual
sat before the gate. Later, S. C. Bose ICS, the SDO, and
Dharmadas Bhattacharyya, ASP, went to the Kali temple, had
the gate opened and allowed the satyagrahis and other people
to go inside the temple compound. Thus everything passed
off smoothly.[52]

While the movement continued efforts were made to arrive
at a compromise. Once again Swami Satyananda fervently
appealed to the members of the Bar Association : "The most
memorable fight for India's complete Independence has begun
and I hope the members of the Munshiganj Bar Association
will not fail to take advantage of this great occasion to do
justice to millions of their untouchable brethren struggling
for emancipation from the curse of untouchability. India
holds you responsible for the unholy act of closing the gates
of the local Kali temple against your own brethren."[53] He
pointed out how untouchability had ruined India irreparably
and how it had sapped the foundation of humanity and
degraded the whole population morally and spiritually. In
his opinion no sacrifice was equal to 'the task of purging
the society of this monstrous evil.' "May I hope that this
appeal will not fail to evoke your sincere sympathy for the
cause and persuade you to join hands with me to remove
this great evil once for all," he concluded.[54]

But the reactionary members of the Bar turned a deaf ear
to all these appeals. At this stage Swami Satyananda announced
that he would have recourse to aggressive measures from
6 April if negotiations for a compromise fell through.[55] And
a few days after this statement a number of satyagrahis
attacked the Kali temple and entered the compound by forcibly
opening the gate in spite of resistance by the temple guards.
However, the police brought the situation under control.[56]

The movement took a new turn abruptly from 16 May.
The local Youngmen's Association consisting of the Hindu

boys of the higher castes formulated certain terms of settlement
about the temple-entry affair in order to put an end to the
impasse. They requested the contending parties to accept
those terms. But their attempt at an amicable settlement
failed. Thereupon six boy-members of the Association belonging
to the orthodox high caste Hindu families started hunger-
strike from 16th morning. They lay down at doors of the
houses of orthodox pleaders and in the temple compound
to effect an amicable settement between the parties. They
resolved not to take any food unless the parties came to terms.
Swami Satyanada and another *Brahmachari* also went on
sympathetic hunger-strike.[57]

The hunger-strike had a tremendous impact on the local
people. When the high caste Hindus remained obdurate after
sixty hours' hunger-strike by the boys, Swami Satyananda and
others, ladies of their families intervened. On 17 May morning
about 200 ladies with the help of the members of the Youth
Association removed all barriers with hammers, axes and saws
and threw open the door of the temple to Hindus of all classes
amidst shouts of *Bande Mataram* in the presence of 2,000
spectators. The gentlemen did not then offer any resistance.[58]

Thus the Kali temple-entry satyagraha at Munshiganj which
lasted for 261 days had 'a strange ending.'[59]

## VII

Let us now examine the stand taken by the high caste Hindus
to defeat the satyagraha movement. We have seen earlier how
every attempt at an amicable settlement had been frustrated by
the obstinate attitude of the members of the Munshiganj Bar
Association. Even when an arbitration board with the SDO
as its President was set up with a view to settling the dispute
amicably its efforts failed owing to the unyielding attitude of
the orthodox high caste Hindus.[60]

On 5 September 1929 the Bar Association held a meeting on
a requisition by seventeen pleaders of the Association. The
purpose was to discuss and consider the grave situation arising
out of the satyagraha movement launched by Swami Satyananda. It was resolved in the meeting that the "Bar Associa-

tion while recognizing the right of entry into the rooms of
Kali's temple in the Kalibari of Munshiganj by the Brahmins,
Kayasthas, Vaidyas, Tilis, Karmakars, Gopes and other touchable communities of the Hindus, is of opinion that the
Namasudras and other untouchable communities have not the
aforesaid right as not being sanctioned or recognised by any
local usage or custom."[61]    About 70 members of the Association attended the meeting.[62]

While opposing the resolution Manoranjan Banerjee, a
pleader of Dacca who came at that time to study the satyagraha situation, pointed out that the resolution of the
Munshiganj Bar Association recognized the right of entry of
several classes of Hindus into a temple which was formerly
confined to the Brahmins alone and thereby proved that they
were ready to move with the time. He, therefore, requested
them to modify the resolution so as to include all Hindus.[63]
A contemporary daily observed that by passing the resolution
the Bar Association indirectly admitted the Kali temple to be
a place of public worship but excluded the Namasudras by
styling them untouchables, thereby throwing an open challenge
to that depressed community and putting off the prospect of
any amicable settlement.[64]

A sharp difference of opinion developed among the members
of the Bar Association on the question of the right of admission
into the temple, seventeen members of the Association submitting a requisition to the Secretary to hold an emergent
meeting once again to remove all sorts of misconception and
misunderstanding in order to define in clear terms the relationship of the Bar Association with the Kali temple.[65]

A strange thing is to be noted in this connexion. While the
ceremony of purification of the goddess Kali was performed by
the high caste orthodox Hindus,[66] Mohammedan guards
were brought to thwart the satyagrahis' attempt to enter the
temple.[67]   In the afternoon of 1 October when the satyagrahis
sat before the gate, Matilal Bose, President of the Munshiganj
Bar Association, asked the Mohammedan guards to remove
the satyagrahis forcibly. The guards however refused to do
that. Then the President himself with the help of another

junior pleader assaulted the satyagrahis indiscriminately and drove them out of the temple compound. As a result of their refusal to carry out orders the Mohammedan guards were dismissed.[68]

The high caste Hindus at Munshiganj resorted to all means, fair or foul, to foil the satyagrahis' attempt. The temple compound was fenced with strong bamboo posts and iron wires turning it into almost a prison-house.[69] They also instituted several criminal cases against the satyagrahis.[70] Since the visit of J. M. Sen Gupta police guards were totally withdrawn from the gate of the temple. Then the President of the Bar Association brought some upcountry men to guard the gate.[71] It was also reported that the orthodox high caste Hindus invited Mahamahopadhyay Panchanan Tarkaratna to visit Munshiganj on behalf of Brahman Mahasabha and support their cause against the satyagrahis.[72]

Once again the members of the Bar Association found themselves divided. Now the issue centred round the management of temple-property. The priest of the temple was a paid employee of the Association which was 'the trustee and Manager of the temple-properties on behalf of thh public.' All other incidental costs for maintaining the temple-properties were borne by the Association, its members setting apart one anna per *vakalatnama* for meeting the expenses. All the buildings and structures of the temple were built by the Bar at an enormous expense for which a sum of Rs. 500 was due to the local loan office. A large section of the pleaders realizing the situation had sent a requisition to the Secretary of the Bar Association for holding an emergent meeting to take early steps for protecting the rights and interests of the Association.[73]

Moreover, when the movement ended in success, the high caste Hindus did not support the removal of the age-old social evil but neither did they offer any obstruction when the gate was thrown open to the untouchables including the *Namasudras*.

## VIII

Munshiganj Kali temple-entry satyagraha was purely a socio-religious movement. But the alien government meddled in it on the pretext of maintaining 'law and order' in the town. Of course, it tried earlier to effect a peaceful settlement through an arbitration board. But that did not ultimately succeed.

When 30 August 1929 was announced as the date for launching satyagraha an order under section 144 Cr. P. C. was served on Swami Satyananda, Brahmachari Amal Krishna, Rai Saheb Binode Behari Sadhu, Dr Mohini Mohan Das and others prohibiting them from entering the Kali temple, holding any meeting and taking out any procession.[74] After the expiry of the period section 144 Cr.P.C. was promulgated for the second time. Now the order prohibited the holding of any meeting within the radius of two miles from the Kali temple. As a result a meeting of the untouchables which was to be held had been postponed and it was decided by the untouchables to hold the same later in a village three miles away from Munshiganj.[75]

To avoid any breach of the peace in the town a fresh batch of police was brought from Dacca to guard the temple round the clock.[76] A conference was also held in the SDO's bungalow to study the situation and to devise means for preserving peace and order.[77] The constables used to guard the temple and no outsiders except the police officers were allowed to enter the temple compound. They did not even allow the President of the Brahman Mahasabha, Sailendra Chandra Banerjee, to enter the temple compound on 3 September which caused great indignation among the high caste Hindus. Owing to the order under section 144 Cr.P.C. not more than five persons were allowed together on the street in front of the temple. Further, not more than five customers were allowed at a time to enter the tea and stationery shops situated opposite the temple.[78]

However, after a few days the number of police guards was reduced from four to one[79] and during the visit of J. M. Sen Gupta to Munshiganj the police force was totally withdrawn.[80] The police sometimes set satyagrahis free even after they managed to enter the temple.[81]

Senior police officials also visited the place to study the situation and take proper measures for handling the same. Thus on 9 September 1929 E. Hodson, the SP of Dacca, came to

Munshiganj. He inspected the actual place of occurrence and had free conversation with the satyagrahis at the temple-gate. He also visited the satyagraha office and had discussion with Jibanlal Chatterjee, an ex-detenu, and other leaders of the movement.[82] In the evening a conference was held at the local thana. Mr Hodson, Mr S. C. Bose, the SDO, the President of the Bar Association and others attended it and discussed the measures to be adopted to protect the temple and prevent breach of the peace.[83] The SP visited Munshiganj once again on the day of *Sivaratri*.[84] At the same time Dharmadas Bhattacharyya, the ASP, helped the satyagrahis by allowing them to enter the temple to offer their *pujas*.[85]

It was alleged that the police had maltreated the satyagrahis. Even when Swami Satyananda had been lying ill at the District Board dak bungalow he was served with a notice asking him to vacate the bungalow within four hours but the Swami refused to leave in that state of health.[86] When Prof. Nripendra Chandra Banerjee was taken to Jessore for his trial under section 124 (A), he was denied travel by first class. Prof. Banerjee had earlier notified to the local authorities that being a member of the AICC and also a college teacher he would refuse to travel except by first class. But he was forced to travel by inter class. While boarding the steamer for his journey to Jessore he demanded that undertrial political prisoners should be given facilities to travel by first class and he asked his countrymen "to realize the baneful consequences of untouchability in society and to fight social evils as strongly as the alien Government."[87] However, Surendra Chandra Majumdar who was arrested along with Prof Banerjee was released for his ill health.[88] Sometimes the wounded satyagrahis, when taken to the hospital, were treated but their names were not entered in the hospital register.[89] The Government also threatened to levy punitive taxes to meet the expenses for keeping police guard at the temple-gate.[90]

## IX

It goes without saying that the success of a movement depends largely on organization. In Munshiganj Kali temple-

entry satyagraha organizational activities were divided into four
parts : (i) recruitment and maintenance of volunteers, (ii)
campaign of satyagraha, (iii) legal defence, and (iv) propaganda.

(i) The leaders of the movement made an extensive tour to
enroll volunteers for the satyagraha movement. The *Namasudras* in different districts of Bengal were asked by wire to
send men and money for continuing satyagraha to a successful
termination.[91] The *Namasudra* leaders from different districts
came to Munshiganj in the evening of 1 September and held
a meeting in which they unanimously decided to continue
the satyagraha at any cost unless their just grievances were
redressed.[92] Several leading members of the *Saha, Subarna-
banik* and other so-called untouchable communities approached
Swami Satyananda to join the movement.[93]

(ii) Swami Satyananda visited different villages and held
discussions with all sections of the Hindu community in those
places. He had been assured of wide support from the villagers
for the movement.[94] On 16 September 1929 Swami Satyananda addressed an important meeting at Dacca Coronation
Park held in support of Munshiganj satyagraha. He held
that the temple in question was a public property and common
sense dictated that every Hindu irrespective of caste should
have the right to enter it. But it was a pity that orthodox Hindus
at Munshiganj stood in the way of removing this nasty social
evil. The meeting was also addressed by Nalini Kishore Guha,
Manoranjan Banerjee, Dr Mohini Mohan Das and others. It
resolved to support the satyagraha and to censure the Munshiganj Bar Association for its attempts to frustrate the honest
efforts of the satyagrahis and their supporters for the removal
of the social evil. It further resolved to condemn the Government for its interference in a purely religious matter.[95] In
another meeting of the depreseed classes Swami Satyananda
appealed to the Congress to take up the cause. He said that
there were one crore and sixty lakhs of untouchables in Bengal
and added that unless the Congress took up the cause of this
vast multitude of people for ameliorating their deplorable
condition in society, the Congress could not claim to be a
national organization.[96] Later two resolutions were passed

requesting the local, provincial and All-India Hindu Mahasabha and also the local and Provincial Congress Committees
to lend their active support with men and money to the temple-
entry satyagraha.[97]

(iii) Arrangements for legal defence were made for the
arrested satyagrahis. Thus when notices under section 144
Cr. P. C. were served on seven Hindu Mission workers, Dr
Mohini Mohan Das MLC and Ganesh Chandra Chatterjee
appeared before the court and Srish Chandra Chatterjee, a
pleader of Dacca, appeared for them.[98]  Similarly, J. C. Gupta
Bar-at-law was engaged to defend Prof. Nripendra Chandra
Banerjee and Surendra Majumdar who were arrested under
section 107 Cr.P.C. .[99]

(iv) Adequate propaganda is an integral part of satyagraha.
Hence the leaders with a band of volunteers made extensive
propaganda tours in order to rouse public opinion in favour of
the movement. Several meetings were held in the course of that
tour since 10 December.[100]  It was reported that the propaganda squad carried posters and flags and toured the villages
on foot with *kirtan* and band. Everywhere it received warm
reception. While addressing public meetings the leaders
emphasized the problem of temple-entry in particular and the
removal of untouchability in general. This type of propaganda
work was a new thing to the locality and it roused tremendous
enthusiasm among the villagers. Every evening lantern lectures
were also arranged.[101]  Several meetings were also organized
in different districts of Bengal. At Comilla,[102] Rajshahi[103]
and Bogra[104] public meetings were held and addressed by
Swami Satyananda and other leaders of the movement. People
who attended these meetings expressed their support for the
movement. Propaganda was also made in Chittagong where
Swami Satyananda was received by Surya Kumar Sen, Secretary
of the District Congress Committee.[105] At Noakhali also a
similar meeting was held.[106]  Reports of those meetings were
published regularly in the contemporary dailies.

From a scrutiny of the material, it seems that the Congress
as an organization was not involved in the movement, though
some of the important Congress leaders and local Congress

workers actively participated in it. That was why Swami Satyananda appealed to the Congress to take up the issue.[107]

## X

Due to extensive propaganda, the movement drew whole-hearted support from different parts of Bengal. Several meetings and conferences were organized outside Munshiganj in support of the movement. Thus many high caste Hindus of Bikrampur living in different districts in Bengal sent letters to the leaders of the satyagraha movement expressing their support and sympathy for the depressed classes.[108]

Several distinguished persons visited Munshiganj to study the situation arising out of the satyagraha movement. On 6 September 1929 Manoranjan Banerjee, Pratul Chandra Ganguly MLC, Nalinikishore Guha, Editor of *Banglar Bani*, and Dr Mohini Mohan Das MLC came from Dacca to study the situation at Munshiganj. They had discussions with the members of the Bar Association of Munshiganj regarding the satyagraha and requested them to settle the issue amicably. They also asked the satyagrahis to remain non-violent and requested them not to stand in the way of amicable settlement honourable to both sides.[109] The Secretary of All Bengal Namasudra Association, Bharat Chandra Sarkar, visited Munshiganj and assured Swami Satyananda of his whole-hearted support.[110] Rajani Kanta Basak, Managing Director of Dhakeswari Cotton Mills, Sibesh Chandra Pakrashi and Prafulla Chandra Raha of the Dacca Hindu Mahasabha also came to Munshiganj. They had also talks with the orthodox members of the local Bar. During the discussion they specially stressed the need of settling internal disputes in view of the existing political situation.[111] Earlier we have seen that J. M. Sen Gupta, Padmaraj Jain and Swami Viswananda also visited Munshiganj and tried their best to effect an amicable settlement.[112]

Several meetings were organized outside Munshiganj to express sympathy with the movement. The Dacca District Namasudra Association held a big meeting at Regent Park, Dacca on 21 October 1929 under the presidentship of Birat

Chandra Mandal. Swami Satyananda was invited to address the meeting. The Association further asserted that every Hindu had the right to enter any Hindu temple which was a place of public worship and requested the Government "to take necessary steps to protect this right in connexion with the satyagraha movement at Munshiganj Kali temple."[113] The Dacca Hindu Sabha also held a meeting at Coronation Park of Dacca under the presidentship of Harendra Kumar Ghosh to discuss the right of entry into the public temples of all classes of Hindus. Swami Satyananda, Manoranjan Banerjee, Prafulla Chandra Raha and Surendra Kumar Saha addressed the meeting. Resolutions supporting the movement, condemning the police action and congratulating Prof. Nripendra Chandra Banerjee and Surendra Chandra Majumdar on their arrest were adopted.[114] In another meeting of the untouchables, Rajani Kanta Das, Secretary of the All-Bengal Washermen's Association, assured the *Namasudras* of their support.[115] In a meeting of the Untouchability Removal Committee of the Dacca District Hindu Sabha, a District Satyagraha Committee was formed with Manoranjan Banerjee and Prafulla Ranjan Saha as its President and Secretary respectively to carry on necessary activities in connexion with Munshiganj satyagraha.[116]

It is to be noted in this connexion that women took active part in the movement. They took out a procession led by the wife of Dr Mohini Mohan Das MLC to the temple. They had, however, to return as they were not allowed by the priest to enter the temple. More than 500 *Namasudra* women joined the procession.[117] Eventually the satyagraha movement came to an end owing to the direct interference of the high caste Hindu women.[118]

## XI

Munshiganj satyagraha was rightly directed against the high caste Hindus who had been denying the untouchables 'just' right to enter the Kali temple.[119] The satyagrahis were justified in claiming that as the temple was a public property, every Hindu should have the right to enter it.[120] That the temple

was a public property was evident from the statement of Rai
Bahadur Ramesh Chandra Guha, Honorary Magistrate and
zamindar of Bajrajogini (Bikrampur) and also the son of the
founder of the temple : "I do not think it a temple for the
private worship of our family or of anybody else. And certainly
we do not now, nor did we before claim it as a private
property. My father founded the temple for the public and
since then it has been a place of public worship." He continued
to state that he could confidently say that "my father never
meant the Munshiganj Kali temple for any particular class or
sect or person, high or low."[121]

Gandhi said that he had absolutely no desire that temples
should be opened to Harijans "until Caste Hindu opinion is
ripe for the opening. It is not a question of Harijans asserting
their right of temple-entry or claiming it. They may or may
not want to enter that temple even when it is declared open to
them. But it is the bounden duty of every Caste Hindu to
secure that opening for Harijans."[122] Munshiganj satyagraha
presents a different picture. The movement was brought to an
end not by the 'conversion' of the high caste Hindus, nor by
the initiative of the Bar Association. Rather they were reluctant to allow the *Namasudras* to enter the Kali temple. As has
been seen above, the upper caste ladies with the help of the
members of the Young Association removed the barriers while
the gentlemen remained aloof.[123]

A pertinent question arises here : can the Munshiganj
temple-entry satyagraha be called a satyagraha in the Gandhian
sense ? It appears from the above discussion that Munshiganj
satyagraha measures up to the greater part of the satyagraha
principle. The leaders always stressed the need to conduct the
movement in a non-violent manner. The satyagrahis were
always prepared for self-suffering. Indeed, the success of the
movement was due in a large measure to the pressure exerted
by the young boys who resorted to hunger-strike in order to
effect a 'change of heart' in the high caste Hindus. The leadership was always insistent upon observing non-violence. It
might be mentioned in passing that when the President of
Munshiganj Bar Association assaulted the satyagrahis, one

satyagrahi tore himself away from the President's grip.   As a result he was declared unfit to be a satyagrahi and was sent home by Swami Satyananda.[124]   Alongside of the movement, the satyagrahis devoted themselves to nursing cholera-stricken patients.[125]   Moreover, the leadership was always eager to arrive at an amicable settlement and tried its best to persuade the upper castes to recognize the untouchables' right to temple-entry.[126]   And we know that 'negotiation' is one of the leading principles of satyagraha.

But there is the other side of the shield.   There were lapses as well.   Despite the leadership's efforts to remain non-violent, satyagrahis sometimes could not restrain themselves and grossly violated one of the essential canons of satyagraha.   We know that to be a perfect satyagrahi a person has to observe certain codes of discipline.   For example, he 'will harbour no anger' but 'will suffer the anger of the opponent.'   In so doing he 'will put up with assaults from the opponent, never retaliate.'[127]   But on 10 October 1929 a satyagrahi slapped a Nepali guard on the face.[128]   Again on 10 December when the temple guard kicked a satyagrahi, who among others, obstructed the priest's passage at the temple-gate, the satyagrahi returned a blow.[129]

At times even the leadership could not restrain itself.   Thus when the prospects of settling the dispute seemed to be remote, Swami Satyananda threatened that he would adopt 'aggressive measures' from 6 April 1930 if negotiations for a compromise fell through.[130]   It may be mentioned here that a few days after the statement of the Swami, a number of satyagrahis attacked the Kali temple and entered the compound by forcibly opening the gate in spite of resistance by the guards.[131]   Moreover legal defence which is against the satyagraha principle was resorted to.[132]   These events demonstrate the minus side of the satyagraha.   But on the whole the movement was non-violent.

## NOTES AND REFERENCES

1, *Young India*, 27.4.21, 135 ; *The Collected Works of Mahatma Gandhi*, XIX, 569.

2. ibid., 25.5.21, 165 ; *The Collected Works of Mahatma Gandhi*, XX, 136.

3. *Harijan*, 11.2.33, 5 ; *The Collected Works of Mahatma Gandhi*, LIII, 264.

4. *Young India*, 11.3.26, 95 ; *The Collected Works of Mahatma Gandhi*, XXX, 93-4.

5. *The Collected Works of Mahatma Gandhi*, LIII, 262.

6. R. R. Diwakar, *Saga of Satyagraha*, 146.

7. Joan V. Bondurant, *Conquest of Violence*, 46.

For details of Vykom Satyagraha, see Joan V. Bondurant, op. cit., 46-52 ; Nirmal Kumar Bose, *Studies in Gandhism* (1972), 87-90 ; *Lectures on Gandhism*, 30-5 and Krishnalal Sridharani, *War Without Violence*, 93-5.

8. For Parvati Satyagraha, see *Indian Quarterly Register*, 1929, II (July-December), 278-9 and R. R. Diwakar, op. cit., 147.

9 & 10. *The Bengalee*, 5.9.29, 3(6).

11. *Amrita Bazar Patrika*, 31.8.29, 3(7) ; *The Bengalee*, 5.9.29, 3(6).

12. *Indian Annual Register*, 1930, I (January-June), 18.

13. *Liberty*, 8.9.29, 12(5).

14. *The Bengalee*, 1.9.29, 4(5) ; 5.9.29, 3(6) ; *Liberty*, 1.9.29, 8(4).

15. *The Bengalee*, 5.9.29, 6(1).

16. *Indian Quarterly Register*, 1929, II (July-December), 278.

17. *The Bengalee*, 1.10.29, 6(1).

18. ibid., 10.10.29, 4(5).

19 & 20. *Amrita Bazar Patrika*, 16.10.29, 8(4) ; *Liberty*, 15.10.29, 11(5).

21. *Amrita Bazar Patrika*, 16.10.29, 8(4) ; *Liberty*, 15.10.29, 11(5). See also Nripendra Chandra Banerji, *At the Cross Roads 1885-1946*, 192.

22. Nripendra Chandra Banerji, op. cit., 193.

23. See note no. 19.

24. Nripendra Chandra Banerji, op. cit., 193.

25. ibid., 194.

26 & 27. See note no. 19.

28 & 29. *Liberty*, 16.10.29, 5(6) ; *Amrita Bazar Patrika*, 17.10.29, 3(6).

30. *Liberty*, 17.10.29, 7(7) ; *Amrita Bazar Patrika*, 17.10.29, 3(6).

31 & 32. *Liberty*, 18.10.29, 8(3) ; *Amrita Bazar Patrika*, 18.10.29, 3(3).

33. *Liberty*, 22.10.29, 7(6) ; *Amrita Bazar Patrika*, 22.10.29, 3(2).

34. *Liberty*, 2.11.29, 7(6) ; *Amrita Bazar Patrika*, 2.11.29, 3(7).

35. *Amrita Bazar Patrika*, 10.11.29, 10(5) ; *Liberty*, 10.11.29, 6(2).

36. *Liberty*, 15.11.29, 6(4) ; *The Bengalee*, 15.11.29, 5(6) and 5(1).

37, 38 & 39. *The Bengalee*, 17.11.29, 7(3).

40. *Liberty*, 21.11.29, 7(3) ; *Amrita Bazar Patrika*, 21.11.29, 3(5).

41. *Amrita Bazar Patrika*, 29.9.29, 2(7) ; *The Bengalee*, 29.9.29, 8(5).

42 & 43. *Amrita Bazar Patrika*, 31.10.29, 11(3) ; *Liberty*, 31.10.29, 7(6).

44. See Chapter IV.

45. *Liberty*, 23.11.29, 8(4) ; *Amrita Bazar Patrika*, 23.11.29, 2(2).

46. *Liberty*, 24.11.29, 6(1).

47. *Liberty*, 29.11.29, 6(2).

48. & 49. ibid., 4.12.29, 7(5) ; *Amrita Bazar Patrika*, 4.12.29, 11(5).

50 & 51. *Liberty*, 12.12.29, 8(6).

52. *Amrita Bazar Patrika*, 2.3.30, 6(1).

53. & 54. ibid., 18.3.30, 12(3).

55. *Liberty*, 6.4.39, 9(4).

56. *The Bengalee*, 8.4.30, 3(3).

57. ibid., 18.5.30, 8(3).

58. ibid., 18.5.30, 5(4-5) ; *Indian Annual Register*, 1930, I (January-June), 18 ; Interview with Badal Chatterjee, 28.9.76.

59. R. R. Diwakar, op. cit., 147.

60. *The Bengalee*, 5.9.29, 3(6) ; *Liberty*, 1.9.29, 8(4).

61. *Amrita Bazar Patrika*, 10.9.29, 6(3) ; *The Bengalee*, 13.9.29, 3(5).

62. *The Bengalee*, 13.9.29, 3(5).

63. *Amrita Bazar Patrika*, 8.9.29, 3(3) and 10.9.29, 6(3).

64. *The Bengalee* 13.9.29, 3(5).

65. *Liberty*, 26.9.29, 8(6).

66. *The Bengalee*, 2.10.29, 5(5).

67. *Amrita Bazar Patrika*, 5.10.29, 3(2).

68, 69 & 70. *The Bengalee*, 10.10.29, 4(5).

71 & 72. *Amrita Bazar Patrika*, 10.11.29, 10(5) ; *Liberty*, 10.11.29, 6(2).

73. *Liberty*, 18.2.30, 6(7).

74. *Amrita Bazar Patrika*, 31.8.29, 3(7) ; *The Bengalee*, 1.9. 29, 4(5) and 5.9.29, 3(6).

75. *The Bengalee*, 2.10.29, 5(5). See also note no. 18.

76. ibid., 1.9.29, 4(5) ; *Liberty*, 1.9.29, 8(4).

77. *The Bengalee*, 5.9 29, 3(6).

78. *Amrita Bazar Patrika*, 8.9.29, 3(3) ; *The Bengalee*, 13.9.29, 3(5).

79. *The Bengalee*, 19.9.29, 7(4).

80. See note no. 71.

81. *The Bengalee*, 1.10.29, 6(1).

82 & 83. *Amrita Bazar Patrika*, 12.9.29, 3(2) ; *Liberty*, 12.9.29, 8(6).

84 & 85. See note no. 52.

86. *Amrita Bazar Patrika*, 6.9.29, 9(4).

87. ibid., 26.10.29, 3(2).

88. ibid., 14.12.19, 3(2).

89. ibid., 16.10.29, 8(4) ; *Liberty*, 15.10.29, 11(5).

90. *The Bengalee*, 13.9.29, 3(5) and 13.4.30, 4(7).

91. ibid., 5.9.29. 3(6).

92. *Amrita Bazar Patrika*, 4.9.29, 3(6).

93. ibid., 6.9.29, 9(4).

94. *Liberty*, 17.9.29, 10(6).

95. *Amrita Bazar Patrika*, 18.9.29, 3(2).

96. & 97.　ibid., 22.3.30, 2(4).

98.　*Liberty*, 7.9.29, 5(4) ; *The Bengalee*, 13.9.29, 3(5).

99.　*Liberty*, 22.10.29, 7(6) ; *Amrita Bazar Patrika*, 22.10.29, 3(3).

100.　*Liberty*, 12.12.29, 8(6) ; *Amrita Bazar Patrika*, 14.12.29, 3(2).

101.　*Liberty*, 15.12.29, 8(4).

102.　ibid., 31.1.30, 5(6).

103.　ibid., 11.2.30, 9(7).

104.　ibid., 12.2.30, 5(5).

105.　*Amrita Bazar Patrika*, 21.1.30, 9(4).

106.　ibid., 28.1.30, 3(7).

107.　See note no. 96.

108.　ibid., 12.9.29, 3(2) ; *Liberty*, 12.9.29, 8(6) and 26.9.29, 8(6).

109.　*Amrita Bazar Patrika*, 8.9.29, 3(3) and 10.9.29, 6(3) ; *The Bengalee*, 13.9.29, 3(5).

110.　*Liberty*, 22.10.29, 7(6) ; *Amrita Bazar Patrika*, 22.10.29, 3(3).

111.　*Liberty*, 23.10.29, 3(4) ; *Amrita Bazar Parika*, 23.10.29, 3(4).

112.　See note nos. 42-9.

113.　*Liberty*, 24.10.29, 8(3).

114.　*Amrita Bazar Patrika*, 2.11.29, 3(7).

115.　*Liberty*, 4.12.29, 7(5).

116.　*Amrita Bazar Patrika*, 14.1.30, 8(5).

117.　See note no. 40. Also interview with Dakshina Ranjan Basu, 8.11.76.

118.　See note no. 58.

119.　*Amrita Bazar Patrika*, 11.12.29, 7(3).

120.　In fact, as a contemporary daily observed, there were three different parties who claimed absolute right of management of the Munshiganj Kali temple. They were the priests, the Bar Association and the Hindu public in general. See *The Bengalee*, 10.10.29, 4(5).

121.　*Liberty*, 26.9.29, 8(6).

122.　*Harijan*, 23.2.34, 10.

123.　See note no. 58.

124.　*The Bengalee*, 10.10.29, 4(5).

125.　*Liberty*, 14.11.29, 6(5).

126.　For the efforts made by the leadership to effect an amicable settlement, see section V of this chapter.

127.　*Young India*, 27.2.30, in M. K. Gandhi, *Satyagraha*, 79 and *The Collected Works of Mahatma Gandhi*, XLII, 491.

128.　*Liberty*, 15.11.29, 6(4) ; *The Bengalee*, 15.11.29, 5(6) & 5(1).

129.　See note no. 50.

130.　*Liberty*, 6.4.30. 9(4).

131.　*The Bengalee*, 8.4.30, 3(3).

132.　See note nos. 98 & 99.

## Chapter VII

## MAHISHBATHAN SALT SATYAGRAHA

### I

AFTER THE DECISION of the Congress to suspend mass civil disobedience in February 1922 the efficacy of satyagraha was seriously disputed. A section of the Congress leadership and radical intelligentsia and the newly emerging left groups were not convinced of the 'compelling power' of the Gandhian technique.[1] On the other hand, Lord Irwin, the then Viceroy, shortly after his arrrival from England, issued a statement on 31 October 1929 wherein he said that "the natural issue of India's Constitutional progress" was "the attainment of Dominion Status."[2] But unfortunately the Viceroy did not act according to the declaration. Hence Gandhi and the Congress leadership, realizing the remote possibility of attaining the Dominion Status for the country, declared Purna Swaraj (Complete Independence) as its goal which was later endorsed by the All-India Congress Committee at its Lahore session in December 1929. It was also decided there that 26th of January should be celebrated all over India as Independence Day. The Lahore Congress also resolved to "launch upon a programme of Civil Disobedience including non-payment of taxes, whether in selected areas or otherwise..."[3] Time seemed ripe to Gandhi to organize a non-violent campaign. And he came forward to pursue the programme of Civil Disobedience.

Evidently it was Gandhi's intention to initiate the Civil Disobedience movement by breaking the prevailing Salt Act, for, to him, this particular act was severely injurious to the Indian people. "History has no instance of a tax as cruel as the salt tax."[4] The salt tax, according to Gandhi, was "unjust and evil."[5] Condemning the cruel incidence of this taxation upon the poor people, Gandhi wrote in a letter to Lord Irwin, "I regard this tax (the salt tax) to be the most iniquitous of all from the poor man's standpoint. As the independence movement is essentially for the poorest in the land the beginning will be made with this evil. The wonder is that we have submitted to the cruel monopoly for so long. It is, I know, open to you to frustrate my design by arresting me. I hope that there will be tens of thousands ready, in a disciplined manner, to take up the work after me, and, in the act of disobeying the Salt Act to lay themselves open to the penalties of a law that should never have disfigured the Statute-book."[6] He considered the action of the Government with regard to the salt tax illegal as it stole 'the people's salt' and forced them to pay heavily for the 'stolen' article. At the same time he expressed the hope that the conscious people would have "every right to take possession of what belongs to them."[7] Earlier, in his famous Eleven Point programme, he suggested certain reforms including abolition of the salt tax.[8]

Ultimately, on 12 March 1930, in pursuance of the Civil Disobedience programme Gandhi began his historic march towards Dandi to violate the Salt Act.[9] While endorsing the step taken by Gandhi and hoping that the whole country would respond to his call to implement the programme, the AICC also urged the Provinces to 'concentrate on a civil breach of the Salt laws'.[10]

On 6 April Gandhi launched the Salt Satyagraha. Immediately after the breach of the Salt Act he stated, "Now that the technical or ceremonial breach of the Salt Law has been committed, it is now open to anyone who would take the risk of prosecution under the Salt Law to manufacture salt wherever he wishes, and wherever it is convenient. My advice is that workers should everywhere manufacture salt, and where they know how to prepare clean salt, make use of it and instruct the villagers likewise, telling the villagers at the same time that they run the risk of being prosecuted. In other words, the villagers should be fully instructed as to the incidence of the Salt Tax, and the manner of breaking the laws and regulations connected with it so as to have the Salt Tax repealed."[11]

In response to Gandhi's appeal preparations were made in other parts of the country with a view to spreading the movement on an all-India scale. Rajagopalachari in Tamil-nad, Vallabhbhai Patel for the whole of Gujarat, Jawaharlal Nehru in the United Provinces, Satish Chandra Das Gupta in Bengal and Gopabandhu Choudhury in Utkal (Orissa) were entrusted with the responsibility of organizing the movement in their respective fields of action.[12]

## II

Before we start analysing the course of action followed in the movement, it would be advisable for us to trace the evolution of salt monopoly enjoyed by the British imperialist regime in Bengal, for it will enable us to comprehend the whole matter objectivly.[13]

In the early days of the East India Company, along about 330 miles of sea-coast from Balasore ( now in Orissa) to Chittagong (now in Bangladesh ), and over an area of about 7,000 square miles, 12,000 *khallaries* ( salt-manufacturing plants ) yielded over 30 lakh maunds of salt every year. Over 45,000 *mullangees* ( salt-makers), besides inferior workmen and superior traders, earned their living by serving this industry. Out of the said 30 lakh maunds of salt, 20 lakhs were consumed in Bengal by a population of 10 million, and the rest was exported to Bihar and other parts of India.

During the Nawabship of Mir Kasim, the East India Company demanded free trade in salt which they claimed as their privilege obtained from Furrokh Sher in 1717. But Mir Kasim turned down this demand, and abolished 'all customs or duties whatsoever on salt, whether the trade was carried on by the English Company or native merchants or others.' This led the Company to introduce a new plan that might serve its interests.

After the acquisition of *Dewany* in 1765, Clive made a plan which enabled the "exclusive Company or Society" of European servants to enjoy the profits of the concern instead of salary. A Regulation was also passed in September 1766 allowing them to sell salt to the natives at as much as Rs. 200 per hundred maund. It also ensured that the *mullangees* would get advance to help defray the initial expenses. But the plan did not interest the Court of Directors. It, on the contrary, ordered that 'none but Indians should be concerned in the inland trade in salt.' By a new Regulation it fixed a duty of as much as 50 per cent. on the value of the salt manufactured.

In 1772 Warren Hastings prepared a scheme of farming, designed to let out the salt manufactories in farm for 5 years. His object was also to improve the revenue, but it was not fulfilled. With the expiry of the said period, however salt *mahals* were let out to the zamindars and other wealthy men 'on annual leases on payment of a ready money-rent, including duties.' Thus the salt was left to the disposal of the lessees, leaving the revenue condition all the same. This experiment did not prove satisfactory. The system of leases was abandoned in 1781 and in its place European salt agents were appointed. These Agents used to perform the following functions : (i) they moved about in the interior of the salt-area, (ii) advanced money to the *mullangees* for carrying on their work, (iii) took delivery of the entire production on payment to them, and finally (iv) sold the salt to wholesale dealers at the rate of Rs. 200 per hundred maund. Ultimately, this system achieved success. Thus on account of the encouragement from the Government and also of the adoption of certain measures to better its conditions, the salt industry flourished rapidly till 1817. "What was more important from the national point of view was that over a million persons, as manufacturers, workmen and labourers must have found employment and a living in this industry of the country."

But from 1817 the condition began to worsen due to the retrograde policy of the Company. At first a duty of Rs 3-4-0 was levied on imported salt but it was gradually reduced to Rs 3, Rs 2-12-0 and Rs 2-8-0. On the contrary nothing was done to improve the method of salt manufacture. As a result the whole industry suffered a tremendous set-back, thereby compelling Bengal to depend for her salt on Liverpool, Germany, Aden, Muscat, Jedda, Bombay and Madras. The financial condition of Bengal was also adversely affected by the policy of the Company since the provincial revenue suffered a sharp decline.

The salt trade monopoly was subjected to severe criticism. Yet it was allowed to continue. It was argued that when the

Company "constituted the Government of the country, a monopoly could be justified only so far and so long as it aimed at regulating and developing the industry on a sound footing for the benefit of the people governed. But when this objective was lost there could not be any justification for continuance of the monopoly : it only strangled private enterprise and thus eventually brought about the ruin of this industry in Bengal."

III

As soon as Gandhi announced his intention of launching civil disobedience campaign on national scale, steps were taken by the Bengal Congress leaders to chalk out a programme of action having regard to the peculiar needs and circumstances of the province. People were asked to organize satyagraha movement in six coastal districts of Bengal, namely, Chittagong, Noakhali, Barisal, Khulna, 24 Parganas and Midnapore.[14] However, Mahishbathan, a small village in the district of 24 Parganas, was chosen as the main field of action[15] where satyagraha was to be directed by the Council of Civil Disobedience, Bengal.[16]

Mahishbathan, known for its brine, is adjacent to Salt Lake, a place under the P.S. of Rajarhat and the subdivision of Barasat in 24 Parganas. Most of the people of this village were very poor and some were so poor that they had no capacity to buy even salt.[7]

Mahishbathan satyagraha, it is to be noted, was a part of a greater movement, namely, the Salt Satyagraha launched on an all-India scale. As a natural consequence its objectives were quite identical with the general ends sought to be secured by Gandhi, namely, immediate repeal of the Salt Act and ultimate attainment of Purna Swaraj, the method of achieving these ends being civil disobedience with Salt Satyagraha as one of the items of the programme. According to Gandhi, the 'nefarious' monopoly of salt as enjoyed by the British Government was detrimental to the interests of Indian people as it deprived the people of a valuable easy village industry, involved wanton destruction of property that nature produced in abundance, the destruction itself caused more national expenditure, and fourthly, to crown this folly, an unheard-of tax of more than 1000 per cent. was extracted from a starving people.[18] Moreover, as Bondurant shows, the revenue realized from the Salt Tax amounted at that time to $ 25,000,000 out of a total revenue of about $ 800, 000,000.[19] Hence Gandhi wanted to deprive the British Government of its 'illegitimate' and 'cruel' monopoly of salt. His aim was to get the Salt Tax abolished. "That is for me one step, the first step towards full freedom."[20]

The Council of Civil Disobedience, Bengal started campaigning in favour of the impending struggle, namely, satyagraha at Mahishbathan. People were being informed by the Council of the objectives and commencement of satyagraha by means of meetings, etc.[21] For this purpose, *Satyagraha Sambad*, a cyclostyled organ of the Council, edited by Satish Chandra Das Gupta, used to be published.[22] In response to an appeal made by the Council people in large numbers began to gather at Sodepur to enrol themselves as satyagrahis. Sodepur, a place 13 miles away from Mahishbathan, was the base camp of the movement. The Bengal Provincial Congress Civil Disobedience Committee also organized two camps at Mahishbathan to strengthen the Salt Satyagraha there.[24]

A satyagrahi had to take the following pledge drawn up by the Council of Civil Disobedience, Bengal :

"I promise to fulfil the following conditions and desire to be a satyagrahi :

(i) I have become a member of the Congress in 1930 ;

(ii) I shall wear *khaddar* at all times ;

(iii) For the sake of my country I am ready to go to jail and undergo all other sufferings and penalties that may be inflicted on me ;

(iv) I pledge satyagraha for the attainment of Purna Swaraj. I shall always remain non-violent ;

(v) I am ready to obey the orders of the Council of Civil Disobedience ;

(vi) In case I am prosecuted for political offence, I shall not resort to self-defence.[25]

## IV

Ultimately, on 2 April 1930, Dr Indranarayan Sen, a prominent Congress leader, with six volunteers reached Mahishbathan.[26] They took shelter at National School, Mahishbathan, selected as the 'war camp of the civil soliders'. The school was organized during the Non-co-operation movement and was financed by Lakshmi Kanta Pramanik, a local zamindar and also a civil resister for several years in connexion with the Union Board taxes.[27] Through public meetings the satyagrahis informed the villagers of the movement that was to be organized immediately, and sought their help for the purpose.[28] Satish Chandra Das Gupta decided to make over the office of the President of the Council of Civil Disobedience, Bengal, to Jatindra Mohan Sengupta on his release from Rangoon jail. On 5 April with a band of 29 satyagrahis[30] he proceeded from Sodepur to Mahishbathan. In a message to the countrymen Das Gupta said : "If we are arrested on the 6th of April, our work will be rendered easy ; we shall then have to march up in hundreds and fill the jails of the Government. When this happens before villagers the desire for Swaraj will also grow in their minds and they themselves will then follow our path. This will ultimately bring about the end of the salt-tax law as well that of the foreign government in the future.[31] He also outlined the programme to be followed for widening the basis of the movement. "Batches of satyagrahis will have to be formed, who will be able to guide their own work and depend upon themselves in case of emergency, and then to send them out to the field. One party of satyagrahis must be sent out each day ; and no two of them must follow the same route. When the satyagrahis reach a suitable village they will go on manufacturing salt. When the people of the village are ready only two or three satyagrahis will remain in the village and the leader of the satyagraha party will then start for another village after filling up his ranks with new volunteers from that village. The residents of each village must be told that it is their duty to manufacture salt from salt-earth wherever that is possible and preserve the salt for their own use at home. If the police come on enquiry, the householder should tell them that he possesses the salt of his own manufacture but that the police will have to find it out for themselves. If they propose to search the house they should be allowed to do the same and the householder should bear cheerfully any loss or harassment which might come in its train." Finally, he cherished the hope that it was in that way that they would be able to turn the salt tax satyagraha into a mass movement.[32]

Accordingly, on April 6, the day when Gandhi broke the Salt Act, Satish Chandra Das Gupta along with other volunteers started the Salt Satyagraha at Mahishbathan by manufacturing salt there. Thus the Salt Act was violated in Bengal. The actual field of action was Narikeltala Chawk ( $1\frac{1}{2}$ miles away from the war camp ) and a 'Daha Bari' ( a reservoir in which the water was filtered ) had been kept ready beforehand for the manufacture of salt.[33]

The process of salt extraction which the satyagrahis learnt from the local villagers was as follows. Two earthen wares were placed one over another. The lower vessel was kept empty and the top one having a few small holes in its bottom was filled with the saline earth scraped from the soil. After the top vessel was full of saline earth, the scrapings were rammed in order to make it a compact body on which thereafter water was poured. This water dissolved the salt and was allowed to percolate through the holes into the lower vessel. In this way, the bottom vessel became full of extracted brine which was brought to the main camp at Mahishbathan for boiling it over the fire. When the aqueous part of the brine was evaporated, it took the shape of salt crystals.[34]

It was reported that five seers of salt were manufactured on the first day.[35]

After violating the Salt Act, Satish Chandra Das Gupta declared that they were inclined to do three things : (i) they would continue to prepare salt until they were arrested ; (ii) in order to widen the basis of the mass movement, they would extend their activities to the neighbouring villages ; and finally ; (iii) if the police stood in their way, they would resort to hunger strike. And they would not 'budge an inch from their resolve'.[36]

As already stated, due to the increase in the number of enthusiastic satyagrahis, the movement was extended to other parts of the village of Mahishbathan. It was also strengthened by the participation of the people of the surrounding villages.[37] Satyagrahis broke the Salt Act also at Port Canning, Haroa, Taki, Hasnabad (all are in the district of 24 Parganas) under the auspices of Mahishbathan organization. Volunteers were also recruited from Arambagh (in the district of Hooghly).

The Salt Act could be violated in three ways : (i) by manufacturing salt wherever there were facilities for doing so, (ii) by possessing, purchasing and selling the contraband salt, and (iii) by hawking, or by carrying away the natural salt deposits on the seashore.[38] Satish Chandra Das Gupta declared that in urban areas the Salt Act would be violated by means of selling the contraband salt. For this purpose certain instructions were circulated by the Council of Civil Disobedience, Bengal. In the first place, local organizations were to inform the Magistrate and the SDO of the place where they were going to sell the contraband salt, with details of route, time and the names of satyagrahis who would break the law. Secondly, satyagarahis should have small packets of salt with them during its sale. And finally, satyagrahis were advised to stop the sale, if there were any 'apprehension of disorderliness'. People who were eager to purchase the contraband salt were also requested not to assemble by the roadside but to remain in their houses where the satyagrahis would call on them to offer salt for sale. If the satyagrahis were arrested or maltreated by the police, the people, the Council requested, should remain perfectly non-violent.[39]

It was reported that immediately after the violation of the Salt Act at Mahisbathan, contraband salt was sold at the price of Rs 5 to Rs 25 per *tola* [40] and the rest was used by 400 satyagrahis in the camps of Sodepur and Mahishbathan.[41] In Calcutta the people enthusiastically purchased it from the office of the Council of Civil Disobedience, Bengal at 2 College Square. At Burrabazar also people showed keen interest.[42] The whole move at once received momentum by the participation of Jatindra Mohan Sen Gupta, President, Council of Civil

13

Disobedience, Bengal.[43]   Even ladies under the leadership of Urmila Devi ( sister of Deshabandhu Chitta Ranjan Das ) took active part in selling the salt produced by the satyagrahis.[44]

People gathered in large numbers to see how the satyagrahis violated the law.[45] Some people were so moved by the zeal with which the satyagrahis organized the movement that they enrolled themselves as volunteers.  It was reported that about 3,000 villagers participated in the movement.[46]   Even students and women were not lagging behind.  All Bengal Students' Association sent satyagrahis to strengthen the movement.[47]   In support of the movement women organized meetings and courted imprisonment by violating the Salt Act.[48]

While the movement was going on people remained absolutely peaceful, patient and non-violent.  Sometimes satyagrahis saved the earthen pots full of hot extracted brine used in salt manufacture even at the risk of burns.[49]   That the people or satyagrahis were non-violent is evident from the reaction of a villager.  Asked what they would do when the police treated them brutally, the villager firmly answered :  "Come what may, we are not going to give way to violence.  That will be our undoing.  We are pledged to follow Mahatma Gandhi's sacred rule of non-violence."[50]

Several distinguished personalities visited the place.  Among them were J.M. Sen Gupta, President, Council of Civil Disobedience, Bengal, Jadabendra Nath Panja, Secretary, District Congress Committee, Burdwan,[51] Acharya P.C. Ray, Narasinha Das Bajoria, Rangalal Janodia, J.C. Gupta, Rajshekhar Basu, Prabhudayal Himmatsinka, Padmaraj Jain, Baldeo Das Jhunjhunwala and Haridas Haldar.[52]   Urmila Devi also visited the satyagraha camp at Mahishbathan.[53]

The local villagers provided financial support to the movement.[54]  It can, however, be assumed  that income from the sale of their salt was also  spent for meeting the expenses of the movement.

Certain measures like economic boycott[55]  and resignation from Government offices[56]   were resorted to by the satyagrahis as an alternative form of Civil Disobedience.  It was reported that a cloth-merchant stopped selling foreign clothes.[57]   In a meeting under the presidentship of Urmila Devi the speakers urged the people to boycott foreign goods.[58]

The satyagraha movement suffered a temporary set-back during the rainy season since it was not possible to manufacture salt at that time. Soon it was revived during winter but operational activities were not so intense as before. However, for the last time, salt was manufactured on 24 February 1931 and ultimately, the movement was withdrawn as a result of the Gandhi-Irwin Pact, 1931.[59]

## V

Gandhi was not contented with merely launching a satyagraha movement ; he also wanted to rouse in the minds of the common people a sense of self-reliance, consciousnss, initiative and discipline. That was why he introduced the Constructive Programme, along with the Civil Disobedience programme. He wrote : "...my handling of Civil Disobedience without the constructive programme will be like a paralysed hand attempting to lift a spoon."[60] Again, "Civil Disobedience, mass or individual, is an aid to constructive effort and is a full substitute for armed revolt. Training is necessary as well for Civil Disobedience as for armed revolt. Only the ways are different. Action in either case takes place only when occasion demands. Training for military revolt means learning the use of arms ending perhaps in the atomic bomb. For Civil Disobedience it means the Constructive Programme."[61] In short, constructive programme is a platform of action for the building up of strength of the people at the bottom.[62]

Constructive programme includes introduction of spinning wheel, use of hand-spun cloth, rural reconstruction, prohibition, etc. The satyagrahis at Mahishbathan adhered to all these.[63] As a part of the constructive programme Lakshmi Kanta Pramanik, a local zamindar, introduced *charkha* on a wide scale among the villagers. In the rural areas of Krolberia and Bagusaptagram ( villages adjacent to Mahishbathan ) Prabhat Mohan Bandyopadhyay, Kumud Chandra Sarkar and Abinash Chandra Bain, among others, taught the villagers how to make *charkha* out of bamboo without any cost. In this way they helped the villagers to be self-sufficient by spinning clothes for themselves.[64]    Along with the manufacture of salt, carding and spinning by means of *takli* and *charkha* became a regular feature of the camp-life of the satyagrahis.[65]    The satyagrahis also persuaded the local people to adhere to prohibition.   Even the nibs of toddy (fermented juice of the palmyra) were destroyed in some places where the people did not respond to  the appeal of the satyagrahis.   In these places satyagrahis had been maltreated and even assaulted by the villagers who were addicted to toddy.   The satyagrahis, however, ultimately won them over. The local villagers also took the initiative in pursuing the constructive programme.[66]

## VI

To the British Government the Salt Satyagraha was "nothing less than to cause a complete paralysis of the administrative machinery".[67]    Hence it tried its utmost to suppress the movement.   Initially, however, the  police  did not do any harm to the satyagrahis.   On the first day some Government officials visited the place for reconnaissance.[68]    It was learnt that a high Indian official of the Intelligence Branch from Simla was also present there for reconnoitering.[69]

Subsequently, the Government let loose repression on the satyagrahis.[70]    But its persistent attempts to persecute them could not compel their surrender.[71]

Arrests were also made by the police.   Satish Chandra Das Gupta, Lakshmi Kanta Pramanik  and Roy Chand Dugar were sentenced respectively to 2 years, r.i., $1\frac{1}{2}$ years' r.i. and Rs 1000/- fine or in default further r.i. for six months, and 6  months'  r.i. for violation of section 9(a) of the Salt Act (Act  XII,  1882).[72] On 11 May 1930 the police attached some of Lakshmi Kanta Pramanik's articles in default of fine imposed on him.[73]

Finally, the movement came to an end as soon as the Gandhi-Irwin Pact was signed in March 1931.[74]    It was agreed that Civil Disobedience would be "effectively discontinued and reciprocal action would be taken by the Government."[75]

But the result was not so hopeful as was expected. The aspirations with which the people started the movement were not fulfilled. The Salt Act was only partially modified. It was notified that in order to give relief to certain sections of the poorer classes, the Government was prepared "to extend their administrative provisions, on lines already prevailing in certain places, in order to permit local residents in villages immediately adjoining...where salt can be collected or made, to such villages, but not for sale to, or trading with, individuals living outside them."[76]

## VII

Thus it is evident that when the satyagraha was about to reach its end, the Gandhi-Irwin Pact dealt it a tremendous blow and the people had to reel back. To recapitulate, the Salt Satyagraha was launched to abolish the Salt Act. "The first step towards freeing ourselves from such oppression is to seek the abolition of the salt tax. We shall violate the salt tax law to such an extent that we shall be prepared to suffer whatever the penalty we may have to face—be it imprisonment, flogging or any other."[77] The Congress leaders also held the same view. They declared : "No solution would be satisfactory unless it recognized the right of India to secede from the British Empire, gave India complete national government responsible to the people,—including control of defence forces, economic control, and covering all the eleven points[78] raised in Mahatma Gandhi's letter to the Viceroy...If the foregoing terms were acceptable to the British Government, the Civil Disobedience Movement would be called off, but picketing of foreign cloth and liquor shops would continue—and also salt manufacture, but not raids on salt *depots*."[79] Surprisingly enough, the Gandhi-Irwin Pact evaded all these issues. The retreat perpetrated through the Pact acted as a stunning blow to the people who with their indomitable spirit flung themselves against the oppressive measures of the British Government.

## NOTES AND REFERENCES

1. Krishnalal Shridharani, *War Without Violence*, 120-1.
2. R. C. Majumdar, *History of the Freedom Movement in India*, III, 322.
3. B. Pattabhi Sitaramayya, *The History of the Indian National Congress*, I, 357.
4. *The Collected Works of Mahatma Gandhi*, XLIII, 144.
5. ibid., 156.
6. ibid., 7.
7. *The Collected Works of Mahatma Gandhi*, XLII, 501.
8. For Eleven Point Programme, see *The Collected Works of Mahatma Gandhi*, XLII, 434.
9. For a 'case history' of the Salt Satyagraha, see Gene Sharp, *Gandhi Wields the Weapon of Moral Power*, 55-219. See also Joan V. Bondurant, *Conquest of Violence* : 88-102 ; Nirmal Kumar Bose, *Studies in Gandhism* (1972), 91-7 ; R. R. Diwakar, *Saga of Satyagraha*, 169-73 ; K. Shridharani, op. cit., 122 6 : Dennis Dalton, 'Dandi March,' in *Seminar* 194, 17-28. For source material, see N. R. Phatak (ed.), *Source Material for a History of the Freedom Movement in India* : *Mahatma Gandhi*, III (III) : 1929-1931.
10. B. Pattabhai Sitaramayya, op. cit., 385.
11. ibid., 387-8.
12. Joan V. Bondurant, op. cit., 89.
13. This section has been based upon Rai M. N. Gupta Bahadur, *Analytical Survey of Bengal Regulations*, 353-60.
14. *Ananda Bazar Patrika*, 19.3.30, 3(4).
15. *Liberty*, 28.3.30, 5(2).
16. In a conference held on 11 March J. M. Sen Gupta announced the formation of All Bengal Civil Disobedience Council. The conference was attended by Amarendra Nath Chatterjee, J. C. Gupta, Hemanta Kumar Bose, Santosh Mitra, Suresh Chandra Majumdar, Satish Chandra Das Gupta, Dr P. C. Ghosh, Dr P. C. Guha Roy and others. The main function of the Council was, according to J. M. Sen Gupta, 'to formulate general policy and to direct and regulate the programme of action having regard to the peculiar needs and circumstances of the province.'

*Liberty*, run by the rival group of Sen Gupta, published the news with the comment : "It was, however, alleged that in view of Gandhi's instruction and repeated requests that the decisions of the Working Committee of the AICC and the instructions of the Provincial Committee should be followed, it was somewhat surprising how J. M. Sen Gupta, an ex-President of the BPCC, had thought it fit to form a separate body and to issue an appeal without even consulting the BPCC which under the constitution is the only authority to decide all these matters in the province."—13.3.30, 8(4-5).

The BPCC, it may be noted in this connexion, was then dominated by the Bose group. For Bose-Sen Gupta group-rivalry in Bengal politics, see references under note 5 of Chapter III (Bandabila Union Board Boycott Movement).

17. *Amrita Bazar Patrika,* 7.4.30, 1(2) and 2(5).

18. *The Collected Works of Mahatma Gandhi,* XLIII, 168.

19. Bondurant, op. cit., 89.

20. *The Collected Works of Mahatma Gandhi,* XLIII, 27.

21. *Amrita Bazar Patrika,* 4.4.30, 3(6).

22. Prabhat Mohan Bandyopadhyay, 'Deshapremik Nandalal,' in *Desh,* Baisakh, 1373 B. S., 269.

23. Interview with Satish Chandra Das Gupta, 20.5.72.

24. *Amrita Bazar Patrika,* 13.4.30, 3(2).

"At the special general meeting of the Bengal Provincial Congress Committee held on March 16, a strong sub-committee of the BPCC was formed with Sj. Satish Chandra Das Gupta as President to carry on the satyagraha campaign launched by Mahatmaji. All funds for satyagraha will be raised, received and controlled by the sub-committee. The sub-committee has also been empowered to carry on negotiations for the purpose of concerted action with other bodies contemplating C. D. in Bengal."—*Liberty,* 17.3.30, 1(3). As a result of group-rivalry in Bengal Congress, two committees were set up in Bengal to launch satyagraha movement—one consisting of some prominent Congressmen headed by J. M. Sen Gupta and another appointed by the BPCC. Regarding the formation of two committees we quote a statement issued by Satcowripati Roy on the basis of the latter's interview with Jawaharlal Nehru and Gandhi. "Regarding the two committees Nehru opined that he would not understand how there could be a committee which was not organised either by a PCC or a DCC or any other Congress Committee to carry on the work. He admitted that it was quite possible for certain individuals to form a group of themselves and to break the Salt Act. Certainly any Congress Committee could not prevent them. But if such a group, he continued, consisted of provincial Congressmen such as members of the PCC and if that group wanted to work even without consulting the Congress Committees their conduct was undoubtedly deplorable. Gandhi also regretted the situation and appealed to both the contending parties either to forget or even suspend for the present what appeared to him to be their "family quarrel'."—*Liberty,* 27.3.30, 6(6-7).

While Nehru openly lent his support to the BPCC Committee Gandhi hoped for an amicable settlement.

In a letter to Satis Chandra Das Gupta dated March 17, 1930 Gandhi wrote : "I saw in the newspapers that Bengal has appointed you dictator. Is it true ? If true, have you been appointed by both the factions or only one ? Whatever it may be, I, know that your love will put everything right."—*The Collected Works of Mahatma Gandhi,* XLIII, 89.

Satish Chandra Das Gupta, it may be noted here, because of his political affiliation with the Sen Gupta group, led the satyagraha sponsored by the Council of Civil Disobedience, Bengal.

25.   *Ananda Bazar Patrika*, 19.3.30, 3(5). (translated)
26.   *Ananda Bazar Patrika*, Autumn Number, 16.10.31, 89.
27.   *Amrita Bazar Patrika*, Satyagraha Special, 7.4.30, 1(2).
28.   See note no. 26.
29.   *Amrita Bazar Patrika*, 5.4.30, 5(1).
30.   ibid., 6 4.30, 5(2) ; *Ananda Bazar Patrika*, 7.4.30, 7(2). For the names of satyagrahis, see Appendix I.
31.   *Amrita Bazar Patrika*, 5.4.30, 5(1).
32.   ibid., 6(5).
33.   See note no. 26.
34.   See note no. 23. Also *Compass* (a Bengali weekly), IX (45), 989-91.
35.   *Amrita Bazar Patrika*, 8.4.30, 6(1).
36.   ibid, 7.4.30, 1(2).
37.   See Appendix III.
38.   *The Collected Works of Mahatma Gandhi*, XLIII, 46-7.
39.   *Amrita Bazar Patrika*, 10.4.30, 3(7).
40.   See note no. 26.
41.   *Ananda Bazar Patrika*, 9.4.30, 5(1).
42.   *Amrita Bazar Patrika*, 9.4.30., 4 (6-7).
43.   ibid., 13.4.30, 3(1) ; *Ananda Bazar Patrika*, 12.4.30, 5(4).
44.   *Ananda Bazar Patrika*, 14.4.30, 3(4).
45.   *Amrita Bazar Patrika*, 16.4.30, 3(6).
46.   ibid., 20.4.30., 6(6-7).
47.   ibid., 12.4.30, 3(6) and 14.4.30. 3(4).

The ABSA (1928-34) "took a leading part in the Civil Disobedience movement initiated in 1930 and 1932..."—Amarendra Nath **Roy**, *Students Fight for Freedom*, 9. For details about the ABSA, see the above-mentioned book.

48.   *Ananda Bazar Patrika*, 14.4.30,3(4-5) and Autumn Number, 16.10.31, 89-91.
49.   *Amrita Bazar Patrika*, 12.4.30, 3(6).
50.   ibid., Satyagraha Special, 7.4.30, 1(1-2).
51.   ibid., 10.4.30, 3(6).
52.   *Ananda Bazar Patrika*, 14.4.30, 4(5).
53.   *Amrita Bazar Pataika*, 11.4.30, 3(2).
54.   ibid., 13.4.30., 3(1) ; *Ananda Bazar Patrika*, 14.4.30, 11(2).
55.   *Ananda Bazar Patrika*, 14.4.30, 3(4-5).
56 & 57.   *Amrita Bazar Patrika*, 15.4.30. 6(1-2).
58.   See note no. 55.
59.   *Ananda Bazar Patrika*, Autumn Number, 16.10.31, 89-91.
60.   M. K. Gandhi, *Constructive Programme*, 30.
61.   ibid., 5.

62.  Buddhadeva Bhattacharyya, *Evolution of the Political Philosophy of Gandhi*, 327.

63.  Sourendra Kumar Basu, *Gandhipanthay Gramgathan*, 50.

64.  Satish Chandra Das Gupta, *Khadi O Charkhar Katha*, 71.

65.  *Amrita Bazar Patrika*, 8.4.30, 6(1-2 ).

66.  *Satyagraha Sambad*, 8.5.30., 1 ; 9.5.30, 1 ; 12.5.30, 1-2 ; 12.6.30, 1 ; *Ananda Bazar Patrika*, 29.4.30. 9(2) ; Sourendra Kumar Basu, op. cit., 50-5

67.  Joan V. Bondurant, op. cit., 89.

68 & 69.  *Amrita Bazar Patrika*, Satyagraha Special, 7.4.30., 1(2).

70.  ibid., 12.4.30., 3(6-7).

71.  ibid., 10.4.30., 5(6-7) ; 11.4.30. 3(2-3) ; *Ananda Bazar Patrika*, 9.4.30., 5(1).

72.  See note nos. 22 and 26.  For the list of satyagrahi prisoners, see Appendix II.

73.  *Satyagraha Sambad*, 12.5.30., 2.

74.  For a recent study on the subject, see Sumit Sarkar, 'The Logic of Gandhian Nationalism : A Study of the Gandhi-Irwin Pact (March 1931)' (mimeo.), Nehru Memorial Museum & Library, New Delhi, 1976.

75.  B. Pattabhi Sitaramayya, op. cit., I, 438.

76.  ibid., 441.

77.  *The Collected Works of Mahatma Gandhi*, XLIII, 106.

78.  See note no. 8.

79.  Cited in *India in 1930-31*, 85.

## Appendix I

### First Batch of Satyagrahis

Susil Kumar Banerjee (Howrah), Kali Kinkar Bardlu (Jia-gunj), Sourindra Basu (24 Paraganas), Chandra Prakas Bose (Calcutta), Rabindranath Bose (North Calcutta), Debendranath Bhattacharyya (North Calcutta), Ram Kumar Bhoalka (Burrabazar), Ram Taran Bhuratia (Burrabazar), Kripanath Brahma (24 Paraganas), Subal Chandra Chanda (North Calcutta), Satish Chandra Das Gupta (Leader, Council of Civil Disobedience), Agam Nath Datta (Howrah), Nanda Gopal Datta (Kalighat), Satyapal Dhublay (Burrabazar), Roy Chanderji Dugar (Burrabazar), Haricharan Ganguli (North Calcutta), Amiya Ranjan Ghosh (Council of Civil Disobedience), Kalobaran Ghosh (Howrah), Ajit Kumar Mallik (Howrah), Ramkrishna Mishra (Burrabazar), Haridas Mukherjee (Jessore), Mahabir Prasad Poddar (Burrabazar), Tarapada Pramanik (North Calcutta), Sambhu Prasadji (Burrabazar), Rampada Ram (Jiagunj), Janardan Roy (Burrabazar), Pasupati Roy (Berhampore), Bhabatosh Sen (North Calcutta), Anil Ranjan Sen Gupta (Barisal), Sibnath Sukla (Burrabazar). •

[Source : *Amrita Bazar Patrika*, 6.4.30, 5(2) and *Ananda Bazar Patrika*, 7.4.30, 7(2)]

## Appendix II

### List of Satyagrahi Prisoners

Alhadi Dasi, Am Dasi, Bhuti Dasi, Brajeswari Dasi, Budimani Dasi, Chamatkari Dasi, Dolai Mishi, Durgamani Dasi, Gatimani Dasi, Gopaswami Dasi, Karunamani Dasi, Matimani Dasi, Mukta Dasi, Padmamani Dasi, Ramani Dasi, Sabitrimani Dasi, Mara Dhali.

Bhupendra Mohan Acharya, Abinash Badyi, Adwaita Badyi,

Balai Badyi, Dwarik Badyi, Nibash Badyi, Sundar Badyi, Bipin
Chandra Baishnab, I. M. Baksh, Amarendranath Banerjee,
Bholadas Banerjee, Bibhuti Bhusan Banerjee, Krishnapada
Banerjee, N. L. Banerjee, Bansidhar, Binode Narayan Barua,
Bikasendu Basu, Sudhir Chandra Basu, S. R. Bose, Tarak Nath
Bose, Benode Bihari Bhadra, Gouripada Bhattacharyya,
Subhendu Bhattacharyya, Subodh Chandra Bhattacharyya,
Adhar Chandra Biswas, Asutosh Biswas, Chintamani Biswas,
Lakshmi Kanta Biswas, Pasupati Biswas, Sachindranath Biswas,
Bijay Krishna Chakravarty, Gouranga Chakravarty, Krishna
Chandra Chakravarty, Rammohan Chakravarty, Ramapada
Chakravarty, Sankari Chakarvarty, S. N. Chatterjee, Gokul
Chandra Chaturvedi, Gokul Chandra Cholia, Gouripada
Choudhuri, Atul Krishna Das, Narayan Chandra Das, Niranjan
Chandra Das, Kshitish Chandra Das Gupta, Bhupati Chandra
Datta, Bibhuti Datta, Jatindra Mohan Datta, Anath Bandhu
De, Tarit Kumar De, Anukul Dhali, Badri Prasad Dhali, Meher
Dhali, Satish Dhara, Indubilas Ganguli, Aditinandan Ghatak,
Amiya Ranjan Ghosh, Balaram Ghosh, Bishnupada Ghosh,
Kalipada Ghosh, Pasupati Ghosh, Pritam Narayan Ghosh,
Pasupati Ghosal, P. K. Goswami, Arun Kumar Gupta, Madhu-
kar Gupta, Ananda Prasad Haldar, Niranjan Hazra, Sukhdeo
Singh Jadab, Ram Chandra Jam, Baranchhi Kalwar, Balai
Chandra Kara, Kalilal Kayastha, Adya Khan, Rajnarain Lal,
Bhikshula Mahato, Srish Chandra Mahato, Mahavir, Nirmal
Kumar Maitra, Sankaracharya Maitra, Panchu Majhi, Bibhuti
Bhusan Majumdar, Nakul Chandra Majumdar, Abad Mandal,
Abhimanyu Mandal, Akrur Mandal, Akshay Mandal, Ashu
Mandal, Babu Mandal, Badal Chandra Mandal, Bhadrendar
Mandal, Bhusan Chandra Mandal, Bhutnath Mandal, Bipin
Mandal, Birupada Mandal, Bishnupada Mandal, Charupada
Mandal, Dukhiram Mandal, Dulal Mandal, Gadadhar Mandal,
Gokul Mandal, Ganesh Mandal, Haran Mandal, Haripada Man-
dal, Ishan Chandra Mandal, Jadunath Mandal, Jatiram Mandal,
Jharuram Mandal, Kartik Mandal, Kiran Chandra Mandal,
Laharaddi Mandal, Lakshmi Narayan Mandal, Mahendra Man-
dal, Manik Mandal, Manyadhar Mandal, Mathur Mandal,
Mohan Mandal, Muktaram Mandal, Naba Kumar Mandal,

Nandalal Mandal, Panchanan Mandal, Panchu Mandal, Prahlad Mandal, Prananath Mandal, Prankrishna Mandal, Priya Nath Mandal, Radhakrishna Mandal, Rajendra Mandal, Rajeswar Mandal, Ramdas Mandal, Sanat Mandal, Sannyasi Mandal, Shironam Mandal, Srinibas Mandal, Chandi Charan Mitra, Harihar Mitra, Jiteswar Mitra, Ishab Molla, Majehar Molla, Saroj Prasad Mukherjee, Tarak Nath Mukherjee, Brajanath Roy Mandal, Behari Naskar, Binode Behari Naskar, Gobardhan Naskar, Hari Chandra Naskar, Haripada Naskar, Jatindranath Naskar, Jogendranath Naskar, Kali Krishna Naskar, Krishna Naskar, Kshirod Naskar, Nitai Naskar, Panchu Naskar, Raghunath Naskar, Rakhal Chandra Naskar, Sitanath Naskar, Tarak Chandra Naskar, Kailash Nath, Syampada Nath, Manik Chandra Pal, Ram Chandra Pal, Bidyadhar Pande, Jadabendranath Panja, Pyarilal Pathak, Asoke Chandra Pramanik, Bhusan Chandra Pramanik, Budhiswar Pramanik, Dip Chandra Pramanik, Dulal Chandra Pramanik, Hangsaman Pramanik, Jaganath Pramanik, Kalipada Pramanik, Kamala Kanta Pramanik, Kunja Behari Pramanik, Lakshman Pramanik, Lakshmi Kanta Pramanik, Lal Chand Pramanik, Nilkantha Pramanik, Panchanan Pramanik, Rajyeswar Pramanik, Santosh Kumar Pramanik, Sudhir Pramanik, Sundar Pramanik, Tapeswar Pramanik, Utthanpada Pramanik, Ramkrishan, Ramkrishnaji, Ramnarayan, Sheonandan Ram, Daha Roy, Krishnadas Roy, Sukhendranath Roy, Umesh Chandra Roy, Kanailal Saha, Akshay Sardar, Bijay Sardar, Hriday Sardar, Karnadhar Saddar, Mahendra Sardar, Mati Sardar, Phani Sardar, Hazarilal Sarkar, Rajendra Mohan Sarkar, Rakhal Chandra Sarkar, Sindhu Sarkar, Harinarayan Sarma, Murari Mohan Sarma, Syam Sundar Sarma, Bishnupada Sen, Dr Indranarayan Sen, Amarendranath Sen Gupta, Prabhat Kumar Sen Gupta, Hari Gobinda Shah, Madho Singh, Mahabir Singh, Prithwi Bahadur Singh, Sahadeb Singh, Kedar Nath Sinha, Meghnad Sinha, Kunja Tarafdar.

[Source : *Amrita Bazar Patrika* and *Ananda Bazar Patrika* 1930-1931.]

## APPENDIX   III

Following is the list of the neighbouring villages of Mahishbathan where the activities of Salt Satyagraha were extended.

Baguihati, Bagusaptagram, Bhatpota, Bhojerhat, Byaonta,
Chandiberia, Chandiswar, Dwivaj, Ghanimaghi, Ghuli, Hati-
sala, Jagatpur, Jatragachi, Jyangra, Kantala, Kanthalberia,
Kariadanga, Kharamba, Krisnapur, Krolberia, Kulberia,
Mahishgoth, Maricha, Narayantala, Nayapati, Saintala, Sukh-
pukur, Sulanggari, Tarunia, Thakurdari.

[By courtesy :   Prabhat Mohan Bandyopadhyay]

## APPENDIX   IV

### Branches of Mahishbathan Satyagraha Camp

| Centre | Captain | Number of Satya-grahis at the Centre |
|---|---|---|
| 1. Thakadari | Atul Das | 4 |
| 2. Canning | Amulya Chatterjee | 6 |
| 3. Homra | Tarapada Banerjee | 2 |
| 4. Pyanabad | Ushanath Roy Choudhury | 6 |
| 5. Sarangabad | Bhabatosh Sen Gupta | 9 |
| 6. Bhangore | Nirmalya Roy | 9 |
| 7. Mahishbathan | Umesh Chandra Ghose | 3 |
| 8. Berachapa Haroa | Nibaran Chandra Banerjee | 6 |
| 9. Husainbad | Santosh Kumar Bagchi | 12 |
| 10. Lakshmi-kantapur | Krishnadhar Chakravarty | 5 |
| 11. Bamanghata | Abani Nath Basu | 14 |
| | Total | 76 |

[ Source :   *Amrita Bazar Patrika*, 22.4. 30, 3(5) ]

## CHAPTER VIII

## BRIKUTSA TENANTS' SATYAGRAHA

BRIKUTSA IS A small village under the Sadar subdivision in the district of Rajshahi. The majority of the population were Mohammedans while the zamindar was a Hindu. Higher caste Hindus like Brahmins also inhabited the village. The general agricultural condition of the village was satisfactory thanks to the existence of a good irrigation system ensured by a stream and a bog adjacent to it.[1]

In 1931 the tenants of Brikutsa launched a satyagraha against the corrupt zamindar of the village. A near-famine condition prevailed when the movement started.[2] The tenants who were in severe economic distress were much aggrieved at certain malpractices perpetrated for a long time by the zamindar. But they could not protest against this injustice out of fear of oppression by him.[3] Their main grievances which were largely economic[4] may be stated as follows :

1. In the absence of any registration office in the village, the transfer of property of the villagers was transacted through the zamindar. In such cases, the sellers had to write what was known as *istaphanama* to the zamindar, which, when executed, enabled the zamindar to take the property in his own hand and the purchasers were asked to pay money as *nazar*.[5]

2. For *khariz dakhal* (replacing the name of the deceased owner of the land by that of the legal heir) the estate levied as much money as was the annual rent of the land.

3. Transfer of land was followed by an enhancement of rent. But the prevailing law was that enhancement of rent should not be made more than once in fifteen years.

4. In pursuance of a long-standing custom in the estate the zamindar used to levy tax on the tenants on the occasion of marriage in their families.

5. Besides, a sum of money (amounting to Rs 25,000 approximately), collected by way of subscription from the villagers

for the establishment of a school, was deposited with the zamin-dar. But the zamindar, showed no interest whatsoever in hand-ing over this fund to a public committee. Of course, a com-mittee was there but ·that was represented by men selected by the zamindar himself and not by the villagers.[6]

6. Moreover, apart from the rent, the villagers were to pay a certain amount of money as *abwab* to the zamindar. This collection was illegal.[7]

Initially, the tenants were not in a position—both organiza-tionally and psychologically—to oppose the zamindar. Though they wanted to have their grievances redressed, they themselves did not dare to stand up to him. Naturally they sought help from the local Congress Committee, the only organization which, in their opinion, could stand on their behalf against the injustice of the zamindar.[8]

However, the issue was for the first time taken up by Pravas Chandra Lahiry, Secretary, Rajsahi District Ryot Samiti.[9] Pre-vious to that he made an appeal to the zamindar and the tenants to come to an amicable settlement. He also stressed the point that in case of any direct confrontation between the zamindar and the tenants, he would unhesitatingly side with the latter.[10] By a letter dated 11 June 1931 he intimated the zamindar, Panchanan Banerjee, of certain allegations made to him by the tenants against certain officers of the estate, and demanded the zamindar's immediate intervention.[11] Protesting against the allegations Binay Krishna Ghose, Manager of the Brikutsa estate, brought a charge of defamation of the officers of the estate against Pravas Chandra Lahiry and requested the President of the Bengal Provincial Congress Committee to send a representative to inquire into the matter.[12] He also served a show-cause notice on Mr Lahiry.[13] Meanwhile on 16 June Satish Chandra Das Gupta approached by some rela-tions of the zamindar came to Brikutsa to inquire into the grievances of the tenants.[14] Certain written statements of the ryots bearing out the grievances were presented before him by Pravas Chandra Lahiry. The eldest son of the zamindar, Bireswar Prasad Banerjee, was also present there.[15] An enquiry committee was formed with Das Gupta and Lahiry respectively as its President and Secretary.[16] Subsequently, when the inquiry was over, Satish Chandra Das Gupta suggested certain terms of compromise duly approved by the tenants. Those were also endorsed by the eldest son of the zamindar.[17] The terms, *inter alia*, were as follows :

1. The system of *istaphanama* in the transference of rights over lands by the tenants by gift or by sale should be abolished and the documents should be registered under the Acts of Government.

2. For *khariz dakhal* the estate should not be allowed to receive more than a rupee. The legal heirship should be settled according to *Shariat* by the *maulavis*. In case of any disputes over the judgement of *maulavis*, their heirship should be settled by pious and disinterested arbitrators. In the case of Hindus arbitrators should settle their heirship.

3. Enhancement of rent in case of transference of land should be stopped.

4. The zamindar should have no right to try cases of dispute among contending tenants and to fine anybody for the same. Also, in criminal or civil suits, neither the officers of the estate nor the headmen of the village (as in such cases they acted as supporters of the zamindar) shall have any right whatsoever to arbitrate. Settlement should then be entrusted to arbitrators selected by the contending parties themselves. In other words, the zamindar should not be allowed to make profit by acting as an arbitrator in such cases of disputes.

5. Officers, *paiks*, elephants, *mahuts* etc., while on tour, should not be billeted on the tenants. Matrimonial taxes should also be abolished.

6. The zamindar should not have any right to collect *nazar* for allowing tenants to dig wells or ponds or to cut down trees on their land. (Even after the passing of the Tenancy Act, the tenants were not allowed the right to do any of these things.)

7. Complaints regarding heavy rents of lands should be inquired into by an impartial committee which should fix up the rents after inquiry.

8. The moneys due to the Provident Fund and the Game Fund of the school should forthwith he deposited in the said

funds. The loans of the school should immediately be liquidated
from the school fund lying in the hands of the zamindar. The
documents in regard to money belonging to the school fund
which the zamindar was rolling back into it as loans from
himself, should be transferred to the school committee.[18]

It was stated that nothing contained in these terms was illegal.[19] Finally, on 17 July 1931 Satish Chandra Das Gupta
handed over the compromise formula to Bireswar Banerjee
who asked for one month's time for their final confirmation by
his father, Panchanan Banerjee, the zamindar of Brikutsa. By
a letter written from Benaras on the 11th August to Mr Das
Gupta, the zamindar's son informed him : "A few days back,
father started for Calcutta and a talk with you regarding our
zamindary (Brikutsa) will end all disputes."[20]

Unfortunately the zamindar did not turn up accordingly to
meet Das Gupta and set aside all the terms of the proposed
compromise.[21]

Now there was no way open to the tenants other than to
launch a movement against the zamindar. In a meeting held
on 18 August under the chairmanship of Md. Ismail Sardar
they resolved to organize a movement against the oppression
of the zamindar. They also decided to adhere to the principle
of non-violence. They further stated that the door for honourable compromise would always be open to the zamindar. In
the same meeting they authorized Pravas Chandra Lahiry to
take necessary action to protect the tenants' cause during the
crisis.[22]

Thus began the first phase of the movement.[23] Pravas
Chandra Lahiry organized several meetings to launch a movement, and ultimately, an enthusiastic response came from the
tenants. They were also urged to pay no taxes to the zamindar
until their grievances were redressed by him. Later on Mr
Lahiry was arrested on 10 October, 1931.[24]

So long the local Congress Committee had been organizing
the movement. All on a sudden the Brikutsa estate was transferred to the Court of Wards. Thus started a new phase of
direct confrontation between the Government on the one hand
and Congress and the tenants on the other.[25] Now realizing

14

the importance of the issue involved in the movement, the Rajshahi District Congress Committee came forward to organize it in a more systematic way.   In a meeting held on 13  October 1931 the executive  committee of the District Congress Committee resolved  to take  charge  of  the Brikutsa  movement  and accordingly, Manas Gobinda Sen, Secretary of the Rajshahi District  Congress Committee, was authorized "to take up  the work left unfinished  by Sj. Pravas Chandra Lahiry."[26]   According to Mr Sen, the presence  of some landlord members in the executive  committee  of the  District Congress  Committee made  it very difficult  to pass the resolution.   However, at last, they  agreed  to  the  proposal, though  reluctantly, and  thus ensued the second stage of the Brikutsa tenant  movement.[27] The Natore Congress Committee also joined the movement.[28]

The characteristics of the strategy  that was followed at  this stage  of  the movement  may be noted here.   In the first place, publicity was carefully avoided since that would,  as they held, destroy the spontaneity of the tenants' initiative by allowing the outsiders to strengthen the  movement.   Secondly, all financial assistance  from  outside  was  refused.   On  the contrary, more stress was laid on the self-reliance of the tenants.   Nothing was spent for the movement even from the  District  Congress  fund. Thirdly, emphasis was laid on  the  recruitment  of  satyagrahis from within the village. Even the proposal of the Bengal Provincial  Congress Committee to help the movement was not accepted by  the  organizers.   Finally, means  was  given  the  utmost importance. Attainment of ends  by  any  means was—fair  or foul—was strictly avoided. The leadership insisted more on the method that was to be followed in the movement.[29]

Finally,  no-rent  campaign  was  organized by the leadership and as a result, the big *jotdars* withdrew  from  the  movement while  the  poorer  tenants  enthusiastically responded to it.[30] However, after some days Manas Gobinda Sen was arrested  on 12 December 1931.[31]

After the arrest of Mr Sen, Prabhat Mohan Bandyopadhyay undertook the responsibility of leading the movement but on 10 January 1932 he was also arrested[32] under a special Ordinance issued by the Government.[33]

The Brikutsa tenants' movement, as stated earlier, was initially a matter of confrontation between the zamindar and the tenants. When the Congress took up the cause of the tenants, the zamindar sought help of the Government. This confirms the lesson of history that the ruling class and imperialism never look to the interests of the poor. Hence it was only natural that the district administration of Rajshahi would come forward in defence of the zamindar since the zamindory in India formed the social base of the imperialist rule. When the authorities of the Rajshahi district administration, under the magistracy of Mr Pinnel, an experienced ICS officer, realized that the tenants of the Brikutsa estate were determined to stick to their demand, they appeared on the scene under the cloak of Court of Wards. Thus they threw down the gauntlet before the Congress and the tenants. They had recourse to various repressive measures. The police arrested several leaders of the movement. Pravas Chandra Lahiry was sentenced to one year's simple imprisonment.[34] Moreover, we learn from his brother's letter that he was again arrested under the Criminal Law Amendment Act just after his release from jail.[35] Manas Gobinda Sen, Sankaracharya Maitra, Atul Chandra Chakravarty, Nagendranath Majumdar and Ramani Sarkar were arrested and each was sentenced to one year's simple imprisonment.[36] Prabhat Mohan Bandyopadhyay who was also arrested was sentenced to two months' imprisonment.[37] The satyagrahis did not put up any defence at their trial. The prisoners were maltreated in jail and they went on hunger-strike in protest against the supply of the ordinary 'file-diet' to them.[38]

As a sequel to the tenants' resolve not to pay any rent till their grievances were redressed properties of the tenants were attached and put on auction. But the villagers took no part in it. It was reported that the immovable property of the Secretary of Konabalia Congress Committee was attached for non-payment of rent. The properties attached were taken to the *kutchery* at Brikutsa for auction. But none came forward to bid. Then the attached property worth Rs. 100/- was sold to zamindar's men at the nominal price of Rs 5.[39] It was also reported that certain tenants of Talgharia in Brikutsa estate

were prosecuted under sections 180 and 183 of IPC for resis
tance to process and rescuing the attached cattle in Talgharia.[40]

It is to be noted in this connexion that Mr Pinnel, the District Magistrate of Rajshahi, adopted a new technique to thwart
the movement. He met the tenants in their homes and his wife
cultivated the peasant women. Thus he was able to gain sufficient popularity among the tenants. He advised them not 'to
pay any heed to Congressmen but acquaint Government officers
with their difficulties.' But, according to Manas Gobinda Sen,
the tenants did not oblige the British Magistrate by doing so.
As against this method of public relations of Mr Pinnel, Congressmen exhorted the people to stick to their guns. Eventually
their firmness paid and they came out victorious in their struggle against the Government. Nirmal Kumar Bose observes that
when the tenants were impressed by the behaviour of the said
District Magistrate, "the Government took swift steps in order
to meet all the demands which the Congressmen had helped
them in formulating. The result was that the peasantry did not
gain the feeling that they had fought their way to victory. Instead the feeling gained ground that everything had happened
through the generosity and sympathy of officers who represented
the Government."[41]

On the contrary, according to Pravas Chandra Lahiry and
Manas Gobinda Sen, the intensity of the movement compelled
the Government to yield to the tenants' demand.[42]

It appears from our interviews with the leaders of the movement that Brikutsa tenants deserved full credit for their hard-
earned victory.

The Brikutsa tenants' movement was organized completely
by means of non-violent method. The tenants never took the
law into their own hands. Moreover, the Gandhian constructive programme was effectively pursued by the organizers during the movement. They urged the tenants to use *khaddar,*
*charkha* etc. which, they believed, would generate self-reliance
in the people. The tenants favourably responded to this
appeal.[43]

As stated earlier, the majority of the tenants at Brikutsa
were Muslims while the zamindar was a Hindu. Thus there

was every chance that the movement, whatever the end proposed and the means adopted, might be converted into a communal one. And communalism is a well-known device to divert the attention of the people from the real problem. Hence it was imperative for the organizers to take into account all these factors. In fact, much of the success of the Brikutsa tenants' movement was due to the competence of the leadership to make the people realize that the mill of exploitation grinds all people alike irrespective of religion, caste or creed. Fortunately, the leadership was able to bring home this fundamental social truth to the tenants. That is why, despite all sorts of provocation from the opponents, the tenants succeeded in standing unitedly against the zamindar. And an all-in Hindu-Muslim unity against the offensive of the landlord-Government combine could thus bring victory to the tenants.

## NOTES AND REFERENCES

1. Interviews with Manas Gobinda Sen, 6.9.71, and Pravas Chandra Lahiry, 12.9.71.

2. *Ananda Bazar Patrika*, 23.7.31, 11(5).

3. Interview with Manas Gobinda Sen.

4. Interview with Prabhat Mohan Bandyopadhyay, 4.1.72.

5. *Advance*, 16.10.31, 9(5).

6. ibid., 8.9.31, 9(4-5).

7 & 8. See note no. 3.

9. See note no. 1. Also *Ananda Bazar Patrika*, 23.7.31, 11(5).

10. *Ananda Bazar Patrika*, 23.7.31, 11(5).

11-14. See note no. 6.

15. ibid., 18.7.31, 5(6) ; *Ananda Bazar Patrika*, 18.7.31, 5(6). See note no. 6.

16. *Amrita Bazar Patrika*, 11.10.31. 6(5).

17-21. See note no. 6.

22. *Ananda Bazar Patrika*, 21.8.31, 6(1).

23. Manas Goibnda Sen has classified the course of the Brikutsa tenants' movement under three stages.

24. *Advance*, 11.10.31, 7(4) ; *Ananda Bazar Patrika*, 11.10.31, 4(6).

25. *Advance*, 16.10.31, 9(5).

26. ibid., 17.10.31, 8(2).

27. See note no. 3.

28. *Advance*, 7.11.31. 9(3).

29 & 30.   See note no. 3.

31.   *Advance,* 13.12.31, 9(2) ; *Ananda Bazar Patrika,* 13.12.31, 3(4).

32.   *Ananda Bazar Patrika* 12.1.32, 3(3-4).

33.   On 4.1.32 the Government issued four new Ordinances.

34.   *Advance,* 24.12.31, 7(4) ; *Ananda Bazar Patrika,* 24.12.31, 7(1)

35.   *Advance,* 2.6.37, 11(4).

36.   *Ananda Bazar Patrika,* 17.1.32, 4(6) and 24.12.31, 7(1) ; Advance, 24.12.31, 7(4).

37.   See note no. 4.

38.   See note no. 26.

39.   *Ananda Bazar Patrika,* (*Special issue*), 21.12.31, 4(3).

40.   *Amrita Bazar Patrika,* 17.1.32, 10(5),

41.   N. K. Bose, *Studies in Gandhism* (1972), 165.

42.   See note no. 1.

43.   Interview with Pravas Chandra Lahiri.

## CHAPTER IX

## ARAMBAGH SETTLEMENT BOYCOTT

DURING THE PERIOD 1928-33 Indian economy developed in the complex and contradictory context of the overproduction crisis which engulfed the world capitalist system. As imperialist powers in their bid to grapple with this crisis endeavoured to pass the buck to the dependent and colonial countries, the exploitation of the toiling masses increased. In India the impact of the world capitalist crisis of this period was intensified by its own agrarian crisis which had caused further deterioration of its economy. The crisis hit Indian agriculture most severely. Although the prices of farm-produce fell sharply, the prices of manufactured goods did not fall at the same rate owing to the policy of the foreign monopolies. This widened the gap between the prices of manufactured goods and agricultural produce, which enabled British finance capital to intensify its exploitation of the people of India and amass still more enormous profits.[1]

It was the peasantry which suffered most due to the crisis. They were already groaning under the crushing burden of abject poverty. Miserable material conditions caused by different factors like heavy indebtedness to the village money-lenders, low agricultural returns, etc. characterized their life.[2] The Agricultural Credit Department of the Reserve Bank of India in a survey undertaken in 1937 noted that owing to the great depression the burden of this indebtedness had become "much more crushing than could be judged from a comparison of the growth of its volume in rupees."[3] The Bengal Jute Enquiry Committee recorded the 'desperate position' of the peasants in Bengal in its Report of 1934 on the variations in purchasing power between 1920-21 and 1932-33. According to the estimates given in the Report the total value of marketable crops in Bengal fell from an annual average of Rs. 724 million for the decade 1920-21 to 1929-30, to Rs. 327 million in 1932-33, whereas monetary liabilities actually rose from Rs. 279 to Rs. 283 million. It meant a fall in the 'free purchasing power' of the cultivators from Rs. 445 to Rs.44 million.[4]   During this period the gold ornaments, the traditional form of savings, "were drained from the peasantry to stave off bankruptcy, and served to maintain the annual tribute from India when the exports of goods could no longer cover it.   Between 1931 and 1937 no less than £ 241 million of gold was drained from India.   But this 'distress' gold could only avail a section, and could not serve to put off the evil day for more than a limited period."[5]

In a statement prepared for presentation to Parliament the Government of India admitted the impoverished condition of the agriculturists.[6]   "Everything is against him (the peasant). Because he is a cultivator, he must borrow to secure his crop. Because his holding is small and has to support than it can feed, he must increase his borrowing to keep those persons alive while the crop is in the ground... As the debt grows, the repayment of it becomes more difficult—until at last some calamity comes upon him, repayment of it becomes impossible, and he sinks into a state of chronic indebtedness from which death alone can release him."[7]   All these statements unmistakably suggest the ruin of the peasantry.   The necessity of a movement for security of tenure and rent reductions was now felt.   The Government promulgated new tenancy acts.   True, they met some of the peasants' demands, but they did not touch the basis of exploitation which ground down particularly the poorer sections of the Indian peasantry.   Thus the Bengal tenancy acts of 1928 and 1930 "granted the right of security of tenure to certain categories of sub-tenants (ryots and sub-ryots) paying fixed rents in cash.   But metayers, though they often provided the seed, plough and draught cattle, far from being given security of tenure, were not even recognized as tenants. This worsened the position of one of the main sections of the Bengal peasantry."[8]

Arambagh Settlement Boycott movement in Bengal was launched in 1931-2 against one of such tenancy acts which reinforced the settlement operations at Arambagh.   Arambagh is a subdivision of the Hooghly district.   The place is distinctly rural in appearance and has no large trade or industry.[9]   Apart from its importance in other respects, Arambagh is well known for its glorious tradition of participating in the movements against the alien ruler. The people of Arambagh played an important role in different phases of the struggle for freedom. It may be mentioned here that the people of Arambagh also fought against the zamindari oppression. For instance, in 1926-27 the people of Arambagh organized a movement against a zamindar who forcibly extorted from the people a certain sum of money as *abwab*. In 1928-29 they took part in the Simon Commission Boycott movement organized on a national scale. In 1930 when the Salt Satyagraha was launched Arambagh did not lag behind.[10] Besides organizing the movement in their locality the people of Arambagh also sent a batch of volunteers to Mahishbathan to reinforce the satyagrahis there.[11] Prafulla Chandra Sen was one of the leaders of the Salt Satyagraha at Contai.[12]

A survey of all these movements, which is well beyond the scope of the present study, will bear testimony to the intense nationalistic feeling and pro-struggle attitude of the people of Arambagh. And it is no wonder that they would not tolerate the settlement operations started by the Government in Arambagh subdivision in November 1931 particularly when they were groaning under severe economic hardship because of the low prices of farm-produce.[13] The prices of paddy, jute and other crops went down to such a level that the peasants were losing heavily by cultivation. They could not sell their produce at economic rates and therefore were unable to meet the dues of landlords and *mahajans*.[14] They could hardly pay rents to zamindars and meet other liabilities ; they were also heavily indebted. The prospect of the standing crops was anything but bright—the yield that year was, as it had been apprehended, abnormally low and the prices were still going down. Thus the people were reduced almost to a famine condition. Instead of providing relief works for them the Government introduced settlement operations thereby prejudicially affecting peasants' interests. This action was also said to have affected the zamindars as they had to bear their share of settlement expenses though their collection of rent was less than 30 per cent.[15] With a callous indifference to the suffering of the peasants the Government determined to go on with settlement operations. It was reported that the settlement was to be done at the cost of the tenants and the landlords who were unable to realize their dues from the peasants.[16] The people would be liable to pay a considerable sum in the shape of stamps for the settlement of disputes that might arise in the course of settlement operations. Moreover the peasants were forced to maintain the settlement officials. They were also asked to clear bushes, jungles and valuable trees at their own expense.[17]

Prior to the launching of the movement appeals were made to the Government for the suspension of the settlement work. It was reported that about 115 applications were sent to the authorities with prayers to that effect.[18] The tenants urged the Government to reduce the rents payable by them in accordance with clause 38(1) of the Bengal Tenancy Act as amended in 1929.[19] The main contention of the peasants was that they were unable to bear the costs of settlement work.[20]

But all these appeals were of no avail. The Government started settlement operations in the teeth of vehement public opposition. The people had then no alternative to organizing themselves against the Government. They resolved to resort to non-violent direct action.

The whole issue was taken up by Prafulla Chandra Sen, the accredited Congress leader of the subdivision. Later the Hoogly DCC endorsed his action. In its executive committee meeting held on 21 November 1931, the DCC resolved, *inter alia*, to protest against the settlement operations at Arambagh that put a heavy burden on the people and also to entrust Prafulla Chandra Sen and Gour Hari Som, Secretary of the DCC, to take necessary action for mitigating the suffering of the people in consultation with the BPCC.[21] In protest against the settlement operations the tenants of Arambagh subdivision observed a complete *hartal* on 27 November. On that day shops were closed and *hats* (bi-weekly bazaars) were not held. Even a *jatra* could not take place as the audience did not turn up and the annual *Rash mela* at several places were put off till the withdrawal of *hartal*. Public meetings were also held in all important villages.[22] A workers' conference was held on 12 December 1931 at Syampur, a village under Arambagh subdivision. The conference was presided over by Dr Asutosh Das M. B. (of Haripal). The object of the conference was to consider the situation arising out of the severe economic distress and settlement operations at Arambagh. Several hundreds of villagers attended the meeting. Prafulla Chandra Sen, who had toured the villages to study the situation, described the state of affairs before the people present at the meeting. He asked the villagers to organize themselves and establish Congress committees to fight against the *zulum* of the settlement officials. He added that the villagers where Congress committees were active had made a determined bid to resist such *zulum*. The meeting was addressed by Panchanan Bose (of Khadi Mandal), Bijay Kumar Bhattacharyya (of Burdwan), Bhupendra Narayan Sen and Maulavi Zainuddin Muhammad.[23]

Apart from these agitational activities, the organizers engaged themselves in constructive programme. They organized a *pathsala* (lower primary school) for the poor students of the villages. Efforts were also made to introduce *charkha* and the villagers were urged to use *khaddar*. One of the important activities of the organizers in relation to the constructive programme was the removal of untouchability. The organizers did their best to promote communal harmony.[24] It may be mentioned in this connexion that in a public meeting held on 15 December at Syampur, Maulavi Zainuddin Muhammad urged the local Muslims to help the settlement boycott movement. They were also requested to join the Congress and to boycott foreign cloth.[25] The volunteers also carried propaganda campaign in favour of prohibition.[26]

It has been already stated that the Government turned a deaf ear to the people's demands and forcibly started settlement operations. For this purpose *amins* and *kanungoes* were posted in Arambagh subdivision to the 'utter dismay' of the distressed peasantry. This action of the Government clearly proved, as Prafulla Chandra Sen observed, that the Government had lost all sense of proportion, for nothing else could account for "its foolish and cruel project of commencing settlement work in places where the people are in dire need of economic and medi-cal relief."[27]  Besides this, the tenants were forced to feed the settlement officials. Summonses were served to harass the people. Moreover several complaints of highhandedness of settlement officials were reported.[28]  It was also reported that settlement officials now and then oppressed the people. Some-times they even threatened to shoot people.[29]  The police used to beat the peasants when they prevented settlement officials from performing their duties.[30]  Those who were unwilling to pay rents were arrested by the police and their properties attached. Later on the properties were put on auction but could not be sold as nobody came forward to bid at the auc-tion. The arrested persons were sentenced to imprisonment as they refused to be released on bail.[31] Attempts were made to arrest Prafulla Chandra Sen. News reached the villagers that Mr Healy, the settlement officer, would come on elephant to arrest Prafulla Babu. While the officer seated on the elephant was about to approach the village he was surrounded by nearly three to four thousand men and thus the attempt to arrest Mr Sen was frustrated. It is to be noted here that the people had adopted a novel technique by boycotting settlement officials socially. As a result the officials had to quit bag and bag-gage.[32]

Ultimately the movement took such an intensive form that the Government had to suspend the settlement work. This resulted in complete victory for the organizers of the movement. What characterizes the movement under review is that it was non-violent all through. As to its social content it may be designated as a multi-class movement since both the tenants and the zamindars who were equally affected by the settlement operations participated in it. However, later on it merged in the Civil Disobedience movement of 1932.[33]

## NOTES AND REFERENCES

1. V. V. Balabushevich and A. M. Dyakov (eds.), *A Contemporary History of India*, 175.
2. "Agricultural capital is supplied mostly by the village money

lender. The agriculturist is almost always poor, and he usually cultivates his land with capital borrowed from the money-lender, on which he has to pay high—sometimes exorbitant—rates of interest. The practice of borrowing money is almost universal. It is frequently a part of the bargain that the produce should be delivered to the money-lender at a certain price, which is always below the market rate. Sometimes the cultivator becomes heavily indebted, and the debt often runs through the life of the borrower and inherited by his heirs."—Pramathanath Banerjee, *A Study of Indian Economics*, 143-4.

3.  ibid., 368.

4 & 5.  R. P. Dutt, *India Today*, 243.

6.  *India in 1930-31*, 156.

7.  Quoted in K. S. Shelvankar, *The Problem of India*, 41.

8.  V. V. Balabushevich and A. M. Dyakov (eds.), op. cit., 176.

9.  *Census 1961, West Bengal, District Census Handbook, Hooghly*.

10.  Interview with Prafulla Chandra Sen, 9.3.74.

11.  See Chapter *VII*.

12.  Interview with Satish Chandra Das Gupta, 20.5.72.

13.  *Advance*, 11.11.31, 9(1) ; *Liberty*, 12.11.31, 4(1).

14.  *Advance*, 13.11.31, 9(2).

15.  See note no. 13.

16.  See note no. 14.

17 & 18.  *Advance*, 5.12.31, 9(2) ; *Ananda Bazar Patrika*, 8.12.31. 11(2).

19 & 20.  See note no. 14.

21.  *Advance* 24.11.31, 4(3).

22.  See note no. 17.

23.  *Advance*, 18.12.31, 9(2) ; *Ananda Bazar Patrika*, 25.12.31, 2(6).

24.  See note no. 10.

25.  *Advance*, 18.12.31, 9(2).

26.  See note no. 10.

27.  *Advance*, 11.11.31, 9(1).

28.  See note no. 17.

29.  *Ananda Bazar Patrika*, 9.4.32, 7(4).

30.  ibid., 8.5.32.

31, 32 & 33.  See note no. 10.

## Chapter X

## DAMODAR CANAL TAX SATYAGRAHA

IN THE LATE 1930s serious popular discontent gathered force in the canal areas of the river Damodar over the question of the Bengal Development Act and the levy imposed thereunder. A movement crystallized and awakened the unsophisticated villagefolk of Burdwan. To understand its nature it is necessary to go deep into the history of the Damodar Canal.

Till the close of the 18th century the river Damodar had been connected, on either side, with a number of spill-channels, streams and watercourses and had served the purpose of irrigation in the whole of the Burdwan Zamindary. A cess called 'poolbundy'[1] was levied on the ryots of the riparian areas to meet the cost of repair and maintenance of the banks of the river. When the Burdwan Raj was relieved of its responsibilities and liabilities to maintain the poolbundy works at the end of the 18th century, the Government admitted its obligation to keep the watercourses, spill-channels, streams, dykes, pools, tanks and their embankments, etc. in a proper state. Eventually, however, the Government was found to have failed to keep its promise and worked in the opposite direction. After taking over the poolbundy works, it thoroughly strengthened the left embankment and made it watertight. As a result its innumerable spill-channels were closed, and subsequently, the zamindars and tenants, according to Sir William Willcocks, made numerous secret breaches through the embankment. In the period between 1856-59 the Government cut off 20 miles of embankment on the right side of the Damodar with a view to protecting the E. I. Railways and the G. T. Road and left the right embankment unrepaired. All this accelerated the silting up of the river bed, reduced the sectional area, and indirectly caused the death of the live channels. Sir William Willcocks called them satanic chains of the Damodar which doomed the once healthy and prosperous tract to malaria and dire poverty.[2]

To fulfil a part of its obligation and to compensate the people of Burdwan and Hooghly the Government opened the Eden Canal in 1881 and the Damodar Canal in 1933. The Damodar Canal Project as sanctioned by the Secretary of State in 1921 was intended to irrigate nearly 200,000 acres of rice-producing area every year (140,000 acres according to a press report) in 379 villages. The canal was expected to supply water to the Eden Canal also for irrigation of at least 24,000 acres in addition to the area then supplied by the Eden Canal. The expenditure to be incurred for the purpose was estimated to be about Rs 73 lakhs, but the actual cost rose up to about 1 crore of rupees and a quarter. The construction of the canal started by 1926-27 and the new canal began supplying water for irriga-tion in May 1932, but it was formally opened at Rondia head-works, some 30 miles away from Burdwan, by the Governor of Bengal on 22 September 1933. It was practically completed in 1935-36. Then the area served by it stood at 134, 464 acres extending over 297 villages.[3]

After the formal inauguration of the canal the Government began to think of realizing a part of the capital expenditure by imposing a canal tax on the ryots who derived benefit from the canal. At first it wanted to collect the canal tax through a lease system by appointing mukhia in each village. The tax being heavy the ryots refused to execute any lease to get the canal water. As a result, the Government thought it proper to impose a compulsory levy by means of a suitable legislation.[4] With that end in view on 18 February 1935 Khwaja Nazimuddin, Minister-in-charge of Irrigation, introduced the Bengal Development Bill, 1935 which provided for the improve-ment of land in Bengal and imposition of a levy in respect of increased profit resulting from improvement works constructed by the Government.[5]

As the Bill referred to above became the cause of a bitter popular struggle against governmental high-handedness it is necessary for us to acquaint ourselves with the object, nature and scope of the aforesaid bill. The object of the bill, according to the Minister introducing the Bill, was to tide over the finan-cial difficulty which prevented the Government from taking up works undoubtedly necessary for the prosperity of the province and to enable complex and far-reaching schemes of improvement to be undertaken with the knowledge that so far from being a burden on the provincial resources they would prove remunerative. In accordance with the spirit of the Bill, the cost of the scheme financed by the Government out of loan-funds should be met by means of tax levied at a flat rate on the total area benefited and provisions for appointment and realization should be made as elastic as possible. The principle was that the Government should be entitled to recover a portion of the increased profits which accrued to private individuals and companies from land of any description, whether used for agriculture or not, owing to works undertaken at the cost of the State and which they would not have otherwise enjoyed. The principle was applicable to areas where schemes for the improvement had only recently been carried into effect, as well as to areas where such schemes were to be undertaken in future.[6]

As regards the nature and scope of the Bill, the Minister said that when the Government had improved the outturn of land it should be allowed to take back for itself at least half of the net increase. In his opinion, it was a fair proposition : "I shall give you a rupee if you give me back eight annas." The Bill, it was argued, would not only compel the ryots to pay up to half of their increased profits, but also would enable them to make increased profits by taking advantage of the improvements. The Minister in justification of his stand said that during years of normal rainfall the people did not take the canal water, rather they treated the irrigation canal as an insurance against a failure of the monsoon. It was imposible, he said, to finance irrigation works by recoveries only in years when the moonsoon failed, and if the people regarded the irrigation works as an insurance they ought to pay every year for that insurance. It was not unreasonable, he argued, that the people who possessed lands were under a moral obligation to society to develop these lands in the best possible way ; and in the malarious tracts of the delta when anyone refused to take advantage of flood irrigation he was actually encouraging malaria or not helping in its eradication. He emphasized that if individuals were allowed to act in accordance with their sweet will, the scheme simply would not work. That was why the Bill proposed that if any man indulged in the luxury of keeping land underdeveloped, he should at any rate pay as the man who co-operated in the improvement by cultivating his land. In his opinion it could hardly be regarded as a harsh measure. Further, he observed that not more than half the net increase in outturn was the maximum levy to be imposed under the Bill. As the yield of the lands varied, there would have to be a full inquiry before the rate of any improvement levy was fixed, and the idea would be to fix it at such a rate as to leave the payer substantially better off. The improvement levy would not be a tax in the ordinary sense, but so far as it could be called a tax, it would be "what the Government is looking for—a tax that would not hurt anybody but benefit everybody." He admitted that the Bill did not specify the classes of persons who would be liable to pay the improvement levy ; it left this to be determined by rule. There was a risk in such an attempt of allowing certain persons who had no real benefit from improvement. So it was intended to determine after a full inquiry, when any area was taken up for improvement levy, what particular classes in it ought to be paid out of the profits due to the improvement and so it should be paid by persons who got the benefit. As regards the question of assessment, he observed that the Government wanted to estimate the average outturn before and after improvement. As regards the period for which an assessment would hold good, he said that it would be convenient alike to the Government and to the assessees if the rate did not vary too often, but until the conditions returned to normal the rate might have to be revised (according to fluctuations in prices) at comparatively short intervals, perhaps every year. The questions of assessment and revision were to be left to a process of trial and error and to be governed by rules. Another most important feature of the Bill was the provision that the civil court should not interfere. The Government feared that a court might, at any stage, on some nice point of law declare some action illegal and throw the whole, or a large part, of the cost of a scheme of improvement upon

15

the provincial revenues. There was also a risk that it might pass orders which could paralyse administration and be fatal to an improvement scheme. These were the problems facing the province ; and it was therefore necessary to steer clear of these difficulties by providing for special appeal authorities to deal with all disputes which might arise in connexion with the scheme. Hence the Government asked for wide and drastic powers. The non-interference by civil courts, the rule-making power, the assessment by executive authority and the refusal to recognize as a matter of course the right to compensation were some of the provisions of the Bill which some members of the Legislature opposed.[7] The Bengal Development Bill was, however, finally passed on 3 October 1935.

Even a cursory reading of the Bengal Development Act, 1935 would suggest that though certain provisions of the Act were sugar-coated, it was, in essence, detrimental to the interests of the poor cultivators. The difficulties facing the Government as regards the costs of construction, maintenance and establishment of the Damodar Canal were attempted to be overcome by bringing the canal area under the operation of the above-mentioned Act. Within the area notified as benefited by the canal, water was supplied, though no application was made under section 74 of the Bengal Irrigation Act and the Government imposed a levy at the rate of Rs 5-8-0 per acre per year irrespective of the benefits derived or likely to be derived from the irrigation facilities of the canal.[8]

## II

The primary motive behind the canal tax agitation was, of course, political. It was aimed at stimulating resistance against the colonial rule. Secondarily, the movement was based on the grievances of the local peasantry burdened with a heavy rate of improvement levy. The Bengal Development Act, 1935 and the tax rate imposed thereunder—these two being clearly inter-linked—together sowed the seeds of agitation and disaffection among the cultivators of the canal area.[9]

Shortly after the Bengal Development Bill was proposed, the drastic provisions of the Bill stirred the members of the

Burdwan Bar Association and other literate people of the town. Later when a heavy burden of tax was imposed under the enactment it had a crushing effect on the already famished peasantry. The National Congress was then lying low in the district. The illiterate rural masses are wont to attribute their miseries to an unkindly providence. To rouse the inert and sluggish peasantry and to give some relief to their mute and inglorious life a dozen members of the Bar came forward. They formed an association, namely the Burdwan District Raiyats' Association, with D. P. Chaudhuri and Balai Chand Mukopadhyay as President and Secretary respectively, to fight the regressive measures as embodied in the aforementioned Act and to agitate against the canal tax.[10]

In the initial phase the Burdwan District Raiyats' Association organized a meeting on 27 July 1935 in the Burdwan Town Hall in protest against the Bengal Development Bill which was yet to be adopted as an enactment by the Legislature. The meeting was presided over by Sir Nalini Ranjan Chattopadhyay. Sir Bijoy Prasad Sinha Roy, while delivering speech, said that "we have assembled here to criticize this Bill, not to protest against it." Then Abdus Sattar, Secretary, District Congress Committee, opposed Sir Bijoy Prasad and said that "we have assembled here to protest against the Bill, not only to criticize it." He emphasized that the Bill must be revoked. Sriharsa Mukhopadhyay, president of the reception committee for the meeting, supported Abdus Sattar and voiced the opposition of the general masses towards the Bill.[11]

When the Government enacted the Bill in October 1935 in utter disregard of public opinion, the Raiyats' Association decided to hold public meetings and publish pamphlets explaining to the people the motive of the Government and the effect of the legislation.[12]

On 20 December 1935 a mass meeting attended by the peasants of about 500 villagers of the Damodar Canal area was held under the auspices of the Raiyats' Association at Bangsagopal Hall with Md. Yasin in the chair. The meeting adopted a number of resolutions repudiating the figures regarding estimates of the produce of lands in the pre-canal and post-canal days and protesting against the improper application of the Development Act and the rules framed thereunder. The meeting also decided to send copies of the resolutions to the District Magistrate, Burdwan, the Member, Board of Revenue, the Member-in-charge of the Irrigation Development, Bengal, and to the Governor of Bengal.[13]

Three months earlier the Congress had started its election campaign in Burdwan. Though the Congress had not yet formed any separate organization exclusively meant for the canal tax agitation, the Congress leaders discussed canal tax issues at several election meetings with an eye to the ensuing election. The campaign continued till the end of January 1937. The Congress propaganda no doubt helped the people of the canal area to form a definite opinion about the Bengal Development Act and the tax imposed in accordance with its provisions.[14]

The Raiyats' Association organized another meeting which was presided over by Netai Gupta and addressed by Jadabendra Nath Panja at Sodya on 31 January 1937. It is interesting to note that this was attended by the members of the Krishak Samiti.[15]

By the beginning of February the agriculturists of the canal area were seriously affected on account of the enforcement of the Development Act. The Government started harassing poor cultivators for the realization of the canal tax and began to recover the arrears of taxes by notice of demand, certificate procedure and the like.[16]

As regards the grievances of the cultivators in the Damodar Canal area an informal discussion took place on 10 February in the Burdwan Raj Palace with the Maharaja in the chair. Besides the two Kumars the following gentlemen attended on invitation : Durga Pada Chaudhuri, Balai Chand Mukhopadhyay, Prafulla Kumar Panja, Mahadeva Roy, Lakshman Kumar Chattopadhyay, Helaram Chattopadhyay, Secretary, Krishak Samiti, Maulavi Golam Mortuza and S. N. Batabyal. The President and the Secretary of the Burdwan District Raiyats' Association described in detail how the improper application and misuse of the Bengal Development Act, 1935 by the officials concerned had caused great hardship to the ryots who had failed to get any relief even on repeated representations to the Government authorities. Further, they pointed out that the imposition of the development tax at the rate of Rs 5-8-0 per acre had badly hit the tax-payer. Thereafter the Maharaja suggested that a public protest meeting should be held with Maharaj Kumar Uday Chand Mahatab as president to formulate the grievances of the ryots in the form of resolutions and place them before the Government for consideration. The Kumar would meet such officers as he might think necessary in order to get their grievances redressed and would propose in the provincial Assembly such amendments to the Bengal Development Act, 1935 or table such resolutions as might be necessary for the purpose. In the meantime, the Maharaja urged, the present gentlemen should send through him a formal representation to the District Magistrate of Burdwan for the purpose of mitigating the rigours of the executive proceedings for the realization of the arrears of the canal rates. [17]

On 14 February 1937 about one thousand representatives of the cultivators of the Damodar Canal area attended a conference held at the Town Hall Maidan under the presidentship of Niharendu Dutta Mazumdar to decide their future course of action in view of the Government demand of Rs 5-8-0 per acre as development tax. The president referred in his speech to the miserable condition of the peasantry in India and the crushing burden of taxes on their shoulders. He characterized the canal tax as exorbitant and unjust and urged for unity among all sections of the people to give vent to their feeling and to make their demands effectively felt by the Government. [18] The resolutions passed at the conference were as follows : That in the opinion of the conference the principles underlying the Bengal Development Act and sections thereunder were arbitrary, opposed to the interests of the *prajas* and *krishaks* in general in the sense that they had been placed outside the jurisdiction of the civil court so that the application of the Act might make the executive officers all-powerful and give them absolute, arbitrary and unfettered authority which was sure to be used to oppress the ryots ; that an estimate of the surplus produce of lands in the Damodar Canal area made by the officials of the

Irrigation Department was devoid of logic and was not based on facts ; that the amount of paddy produced in the canal area did not admit of a taxable surplus after the deductions for payment of rent to the zamindar and expenditure on cultivation ; that the conference recorded strong protest against the remarks made by the Collector of Burdwan that the cultivators were ready to pay at $\frac{1}{4}$ rate of the canal tax, and that the Government be requested to appoint a committee of inquiry to investigate how the Eden and the Damodar Canal might be best utilized for the benefit of the local people.[19]

On 24 February 1937 a meeting attended by about three thousand people was held at Bhatar bazaar under the auspices of the Raiyats' Association. This meeting too resolved to fight the canal tax.[20]

By the end of the month the working of the canal system embittered the people at large and a vast number of villagers of the non-canal areas submitted petitions to the canal authorities requesting the latter not to extend branch canals to their areas.[21] It was also learnt that about 40,000 certificates had even been prepared for the realization of the canal dues.[22]

On the first day of March 1937 the Raiyats' Association organized another meeting of the cultivators of the canal area at the Town Hall Maidan under the presidentship of Maharaj Kumar Uday Chand Mahatab. The Maharaj Kumar said that though there might be differences of opinion as regards the utility of the canal, there could not be any doubt as to the fact that the canal rate was excessive. He urged the cultivators to send petitions to the Divisional Commissioner praying suspension of the issue of certificates and assured the audience that he would support their cause so long as they would fight through legal means. Then Bankim Mukhopadhyay, an important leader of the Communist Party of India, said that they did not want to adopt any illegal course, but at the same time the Government should proceed in a legal way ; if the Government remained obstinate and intractable and did not submit to people's legitimate demands, the people must surely be prepared for a bitter fight. The meeting resolved that since there had been no development, and no increased outturn of lands situated in the

Damodar Canal area, no improvement levy as such could be imposed under the Bengal Development Act, 1935 ; that the improvement levy had been fixed solely with reference to heavy and extravagant capital expenditure and costs, etc. incurred by the Government in the construction and maintenance of the said canal without any regard to the paying capacity of the agriculturists and actual benefit, if any, derived by them ; that the improvement levy as assessed by the Government was totally illegal, unjust, unreasonable and contrary to facts and opposed to natural justice ; that the scheme and provisions of the Bengal Development Act were too drastic and arbitrary and were prejudicial to the interests of the peasants and cultivators in general inasmuch as the Act made no provision for considering the objections or grievances of the cultivators in respect of their liabilities and amount of assessment, and moreover, by shutting out the jurisdiction of the civil court, the Act had placed the entire canal administration under the control of a few executive officials of the Government ; that with a view to redressing the above grievances of the people, the scheme, principle and the provisions of the Bengal Development Act ought to be thoroughly revised and recast as early as possible and the newly elected members of the Bengal Legislature advised accordingly to urge for early amendment of the Act.[23]

Apart from the meetings organized by the local organizations, the citizens of Calcutta convened a meeting at Albert Hall on 9 May 1937 under the presidentship of Santosh Kumar Bose MLA. The meeting unanimously demanded a joint enquiry committee consisting of official and non-official members to probe the grievances of the cultivators of the canal areas in the districts of Burdwan and Hooghly regarding the imposition of canal taxes under the B. D. Act and urged that pending the report of the enquiry committee the realization of arrears of canal tax by the Government by means of attachment or otherwise be kept in abeyance. In his speech Santosh Kumar Bose emphasized that for a proper understanding of the situation arising out of the Government's efforts for realizing canal dues it was necessary to look at the question in its proper perspective. It was true that the Government had spent a huge sum of money

for the construction of the canal.   But it arbitrarily decided to
impose a levy at an exorbitant rate upon all  lands  commanded
by the canal, irrespective of any consideration of the  actual benefit derived or likely to be derived  from the canal water by the
cultivators.   It was suggested by many that the method of flood
irrigation was necessary for improving the  productive power of
the land  and  also  useful  in  coping  with  malaria.   But the
Government refused to take all those suggestions into consideration and tried to throw the whole burden  of  the  tax  on  the
shoulders  of  the  tenants  whose  paying  capacity had already
been strained to the limit.   The speaker demanded that an
impartial inquiry should  be made and alternative methods of
assessment be explored.   Meanwhile, he said, the order for realization of the arrears of canal tax should be revoked. Pramatha
Nath Bandyopadhyay MLA, Sukumar Dutta MLA and Bankim
Mukhopadhyay also addressed the audience and demanded an
immediate inquiry into the grievances of the peasants. Among
others present were Kamal Krishna Roy  MLA,  Hemanta
Kumar Bose, Mahendra  Chandra  Sen,  Balai Chand Mukhopadhyay, Sailendra Nath Roy, Panchanan Roy, Satindra Mitra,
Abdus  Sattar,  Dasarathi  Tah,  Basantalal  Murarka  and
Kalipada Mukhopadhyay.   The meeting unanimously resolved
that the imposition  of the levy under the B. D. Act at the high
rate of Rs 5-8-0 per acre irrespective of the  benefit derived
or likely to be derived  was inequitable, unjust and oppressive
and caused hardship to the poor peasantry of the canal area.[24]
    Meanwhile with the intensification of  people's agitation
against the canal tax the  Government officials at the local  level
began to resort to repressive measures like the issue of certificates and attachment of movable properties for the  realization
of arrears. According to a report dated 24 April 1937, a large
number of certificates were issued for the realization  of  arrears
of tax in the  canal area, and seven cows and calves of Gostha
Muchi of Samsore were attached and kept in the village pound.
It was also learnt that movable properties of the inhabitants of
Bhatar, Palar, Natun Gram, etc. were liable to be  attached  as
thirty days had expired from the date of issue of the certificates.[25]
The officials of the Canal Development also attached and seized

one calf, one bullock, two buffaloes and five cows for the realization of Rs 133-5-0 from Panchanan Maitra and Dharmadas Maitra of the village of Mahuagram and kept the attached animals in the municipal pound. But these repressive measures failed to cow the aggrieved peasantry and break their morale.[26]

In the middle of May 1937 the Burdwan District Krishak Conference was held at Ghuskara under the presidentship of Muzaffar Ahmad. The conference lent its support to the resolutions passed at the meeting of the representatives of the cultivators and tenants of the Damodar Canal area at the Burdwan Town Hall Maidan under the presidentship of Niharendu Dutta Mazumdar MLA on 14 February 1937 and also to those adopted in a meeting called by the Raiyats' Association at the same place on 1 March 1937 under the presidentship of Maharaj Kumar Uday Chand Mahatab MLA. It expressed its deep resentment at the forcible collection of taxes, assessed on the basis of wrong data by Government servants, by issuing certificates, attaching movables, etc. and applying the old repressive policies, and drew the attention of the Government to the fact that the dissatisfaction amongst the cultivators was growing more and more serious and urged it to immediately appoint a non-official enquiry committee, reduce the assessed tax and remit the unrealized tax in proportion to the tax so reduced.[27]

In the foregoing paragraphs we have refered to the proceedings of the several meetings organized mainly by the Burdwan District Raiyats' Association. Apart from these, a kisan conference presided over by Niharendu Dutta Mazumdar was held on 13 June in the district of Burdwan. The conference dealt with the canal tax movement.[28] Further, the first meeting of the All India Kisan Committee, held on 14 July at Niyamatpur in Gaya district (Bihar), endorsed the criticisms levelled against the Bengal Development Act by the local peasantry which were supported by the Bengal Kisan Conference. It strongly condemned the action of the Government in repressing the peasantry of the villages adjacent to the canal area, the wholesale attachment of the properties of the defaulters and the delay in settling the issue.[29]

Besides, Balai Chand Mukhopadhyay, Secretary of the Raiyats' Association, issued statements from time to time drawing
the attention of the members of the Bengal Legislature as well as
of the Ministers to the serious situation created by the imposition of the 'improvement levy' in the canal area and demanding
an open inquiry into the actual state of things. The Government, on the other hand, characterized in its communique's
those meetings and deliberations as 'mischievous machinations
of designing agitators from Calcutta.'[30]

The Burdwan District Congress, which had so long kept quiet
or had not actively intervened, took up the matter seriously
only in the middle of 1937. Jadabendranath Panja, in accordance with the resolutions of the District Congress Committee,
appointed an enquiry committee on 9 June 1937. The committee first met in Calcutta on 12 June and it was decided that it
would inquire how far the Damodar Canal was helpful to the
people concerned for the purpose of irrigation and whether
the assessment was just and the ryots were in a position to
pay for the benefit, if any, derived from the canal. J. N.
Bose was appointed President, Priya Ranjan Sen, Secretary
and Hemanta Kumar Dutta, Assistant Secretary of the
committee.[31]

On 25 June, for the first time, at the invitation of Maharaja
Srish Chandra Nandy, Minister-in-charge of Communications
and Works, a representation was made on behalf of the cultivators of the Damodar Canal area by Abul Hashem MLA, Balai
Chand Mukhopadhyay, Radhagobinda Hati, Advocate, Maulavi Fakir Mandal and others. The deputation pointed out that
the Damodar Canal had done some good to the people but the
Government should reduce the rate of the canal tax ; otherwise
Burdwan would turn into a 'second Midnapore'. (The reference
is here to the Contai Union Board Boycott movement.-B.B.)
The Minister gave them a patient hearing for three hours and
promised to give early relief to the cultivators of the canal
area.[32] However, the Canal Kar Pratikar Samiti[33] held that
the members of the deputation were pro-establishment and
hence could not truly represent the interests of the suffering
peasants. It observed that the resolutions adopted in the meet-

ings at the Burdwan Town Hall on 14 February and 1 March should be taken as their charter of demands.[34]

Realizing the gravity of the situation the Government issued a press communique' on the Damodar Canal issue which was published on 10 August 1937. The communique' refuted the allegations of the agitators that the increase in the value of outturn had been overestimated and was not so much as to justify the charge of Rs 5-8-0 per acre. Referring to Townend Report dated 10 March 1937 it defended the methods employed in estimating the pre-canal and post-canal yield and in fixing the rate of assessment. It said that the Government accepted the principle of assessment under the Bengal Development Act as scientific and was satisfied that the charge of Rs 5-8-0 which was as a rule much less than half the value of the excess produce due to irrigation, was fair and equitable. It, however, admitted that much hardship was caused to the cultivators as the assessment for 1934-35 was made very late and the rates had, therefore, to be paid in the following year. In order to give some relief, it said, the Government had decided to grant a remission of four annas in the rupee on the demand for the year 1936-37.[35]

On 16 August Balai Chand Mukhopadhyay, once again issued a statement refuting the arguments put forward by the Government in its defence in the above-mentioned press note. He tried to draw the attention of the members of both the houses of the Legislature to the utter helplessness of the poor cultivators of the canal areas who on several occasions prayed, but in vain, to all the powers that be, ranging from the canal *zamadar* and the District Magistrate to their Excellencies, the Viceroy and the Governor, and the Hon'ble Ministers. He once more appealed to the members of the said legislative bodies to compel the Government to hold an open inquiry into the matter.[36]

In response to these appeals Pramathanath Bandyopadhyay moved two cut motions in the Bengal Legislative Assembly on 28 August to discuss the appalling conditions of the people living in the canal areas. He said that the canal project was intended to serve two purposes—one of supplying water to the area under irrigation and the other of fighting malaria. The canal was also expected to distribute 'liquid gold' all round. But its actual operation belied all those hopes and expectations. True, the canal project cost the Government of Bengal a sum of Rs 124 lakhs and the Government of India raised a loan at a high rate of interest to meet the capital expenditure. But, Pramatha Nath Bandyopadhyay said, Sir Otto Niemeyer's report enabled the Government of Bengal to liquidate all those obligations to the Government of India with certain exceptions and so far as the capital which was borrowed from the Government of India and the interest charge on that capital were concerned, they had been written off. Therefore, he observed, the plain position was that under section 12 of the B.D. Act the people of the locality were bound to pay levy only for the maintenance, establishment and the repair charges of the canal area. Thus, even for fiscal purposes, he said, it was not necessary to continue the levy at the rate of Rs 5-8-0 per acre in the canal area. He maintained that it was an intolerable burden on the peasantry. He refused to regard the question as a local one because Mr Townend said that the Damodar Canal area was the testing ground for the whole of Bengal. For all these reasons, he said, the question should receive serious consideration from the Government, the area should be surveyed and the grievances of the peasantry carefully ascertained. He requested the Ministers concerned to visit the area and settle the issue so as to alleviate the distress of the canal area. Then the Maharaj Kumar of Burdwan intervening in the debate said that though the Government had proposed to give some concessions to the people for paying up their arrears the actual trouble remained there. He suggested that the Irrigation Minister should at his earliest convenience visit the area, hear the grievances direct from the people and try to come to some sort of settlement. He also demanded that no further expansion of the Damodar Canal should be undertaken until proper inquiry was made and the present question of levy settled. Thereafter Banku Behari Mandal spoke in support of the motion. He said that the oppression prepetrated by the certificate officials for the realization of the canal rate had become so much severe that the

Damodar Canal was 'now...a menace' to the people of Burdwan. He urged the Minister-in-charge of Irrigation to consider the case of the cultivators, reduce the tax and extend the time for the payment of arrears of taxes. As regards the appointment of the enquiry committee he said that it should consist of non-official members along with some members of the Cabinet. Among others who supported the cut motion moved by P.N. Bandyopadhyay were Al-Haj Maulana, Dr Sanaullah, Adwaita Kumar Majhi, Abul Hashem and Bankim Mukhopadhyay. Thereafter F. C. Brasher spoke on behalf of the European group and opposed the motion. In reply Maharaja Srish Chandra Nandy of Cossimbazar, Minister-in-charge of Irrigation, assured the House that the Government had decided to appoint an enquiry committee with the Premier as its Chairman to examine the Damodar Canal issue in all its aspects and submit a report at the earliest opportunity. Premier A. K. Fazl-ul-Huq admitted in his speech that there had been a widespread agitation in the canal area against the B.D. Act and the tax-rate imposed under the same. Since the question was a complicated one, he observed, nothing could be done except by appointing a committee to investigate the matter. As regards the personnel of the committee, he assured the House that the Government would consult the leaders of various groups before it came to a final decision. At last the motion was withdrawn in view of the assurance given by the Premier.[38]

On 31 August 1937 about 1,000 cultivators from the villages of Sodya, Simpra, Korori, Saligram, Chakundi, Bora, Hatgobindapur, Bongram, Palsa, Nabastha, Bhodhpur, Begut, Kuchut, Faridpur, Bakalsa, Bararuntia, Jarui, Ataghat, Tajpur, Sukur and twenty other villages of the Damodar Canal area arrived in the town and entered the court compound to impress upon the collector the fact that they were unable to pay the canal tax at the present rate and the arrears thereof. As he was not present, the cultivators approached the Sadar Subdivisional Officer and urged him to contradict the Government communique' on increased outturn. The Subdivisional Officer, while regretting his inablity to do so, assured that he would place before the Government through the Collector their demands regarding reduction of the canal tax, suspension of certificate orders pending the publication of the report of the enquiry committee and inclusion of a sufficient number of their representatives in that committee. The cultivators then met the Revenue Officer and requested him to stop executing certificates till the next harvest. The Revenue Officer said that he could defer it up to September 30 after which a fresh order from the Government was required for suspending the execution till the next harvest. Afterwards the cultivators went out in a procession shouting different slogans along several thoroughfares of the town.[39]

During the next two months no fruitful attempt was made to settle the canal issue except a few statements and counter-statements by the Government and the Congress Committee.[40] It was on 11 November 1937 that a conference regarding the Damodar Canal dispute was held at Writers' Building and attended by Sir B.P. Sinha Roy, Maharaja Srish Chandra Nandy, Maharaj Kumar U.C. Mahatab MLA, Adwaita Kumar Majhi MLA and some other gentlemen from Burdwan. Sir B. P. Sinha Roy said that he would like to have a fresh discussion with the gentlemen present with a view to arriving at a solution of the problem. He was ready to conduct a fresh crop-cutting experiment in such a manner as would win support from all quarters. In this experiment, he said, four villages from each union would be selected and the lands classified before crop-cutting in the presence of the villagers. The only object of this experiment would be to find out the actual increase in outturn. He agreed to accept the pre-canal yield as six maunds per *bigha* and hoped that the people would not refuse to pay 50 per cent. of the average increase in outturn. Then Balai Chand Mukho-padhyay said that the cost of cultivation actually left no margin of profit to the cultivators to pay the canal tax. He also observed that the Government was trying to make profit instead of doing any good to the cultivators and since the Government had been still persisting in applying the B.D. Act, it was useless to discuss the matter any further. He asserted that the pre-canal yield was not less than eight maunds per *bigha* on

average. At this stage Maharaja Srish Chandra Nandy brus-
quely remarked that the cultivators might be heavily indebted,
but the Government was not concerned with their miseries.
Thereafter Sir Bijoy Prasad requested the representatives of the
cultivators to ask the people of the canal area to pay off the
canal tax. In reply Sri Kumar Mitra said that they could not
ask the people to do so unless the Government gave them
substantial relief immediately. At last Sir Bijoy Prasad and
Maharaja Nandy assured them that they would soon visit the
canal area to make an on-the-spot study of the situation.[41]

On 25 November Maharaja Srish Chandra Nandy and Sir
Bijoy Prasad came to Burdwan and went to a village, about 17
miles away from the town, where they met about 6,000 agriculturists and discussed with them the Damodar Canal issue
in detail. The local people complained of the high rate of canal
tax which, they said, they were not in a position to pay because
of the fall in the prices of agricultural produce. But they
intimated their willingness to pay a reasonable rate. They all
accepted the suggestion of the Ministers relating to a fresh
crop-cutting experiment to determine the actual outturn and
agreed to co-operate with the local officials to make the
experiment a success. The Ministers asked them to make a part
payment of the arrears of taxes pending the crop-cutting
experiment and final decision regarding the canal tax, so that
they might not have to pay a heavy sum at a time. The
Ministers said that the part payment might be made at a lower
rate to be shortly announced by the Government and necessary
adjustment would be made against next year's payment. The
Ministers also assured that the crop-cutting experiment would
be conducted in their presence and with their help. Later the
Ministers visited Galsi and met 7,000 people and held a
discussion on the same line.[42]

Balai Chand Mukhopadhyay said in a statement on behalf of
the Raiyats' Association on 6 December that the Government,
instead of determining the average yield of per-canal days from
the pre-canal settlement records, old registered deeds and
decrees of civil courts, had this time quite arbitrarily assumed
the average of per-canal yield to be six maunds per *bigha*. The

Government by proposing a new crop-cutting experiment
following a curious method of chance lottery in the classification of lands and making this experiment on the current
year's crop would be taking advantage of an exceptionally good
year of bumper harvest.  He regarded it as a matter of regret
that the authorities of the Revenue and Irrigation Departments,
instead of making an earnest endeavour to arrive at an honourable settlement, appeared to be confusing the real issue.[43] The
same day an almost similar statement was issued by Jadabendranath Panja, President Burdwan District Congress Committee.[44]

It was reported on 16 December that the Government after
dragging its feet for a long time had, in pursuance of the
assurance given in the last session of the Bengal Legislative
Assembly, appointed an enquiry committee with Mriganka
Bhusan Roy, Revenue officer, as Secretary.[45]  The first meeting
of the newly appointed Damodar Canal Enquiry Committee
was held on 15 December, Sir B.P. Sinha Roy presiding in
the absence of the Premier.  During the long discussion it
was pointed out that because of the irrigational facilities
the canal areas were yielding a crop which was 50 per cent.
more than the amount the cultivators used to get in the
pre-canal days and hence the rate was to be fixed on the basis
of that increased outturn.  The Government was, however,
prepared to consider the question in all its aspects and ready to
fix the rate at Rs 3 per acre.  But the Government had to
accept Townend Report as the basis of calculation although by
its own admission it had no intention to regard the said report
as infallible.  One of the members of the committee asserted
that the levy should be imposed only to meet the maintenance,
establishment and repair charges for the canal, since the
capital expenditure incurred for the construction of the canal
had been paid off by the Government of India on the latter's
acceptance of Otto Niemeyer's Report.  However, it was finally
decided that a few sites would be selected and the committee
would visit those places in order to ascertain facts and figures.

On 17 December Balai Chand Mukhopadhyay made a statement of behalf of the Raiyats' Association.  Referring to the
official enquiry committee and its first conference he said that

the task of the committee would be difficult and hazardous in view of its restricted and undefined scope and terms of reference. He resented the Ministers' decision to stick to their previous stand and their refusal to consider whether the cultivators had any actual capacity to pay the high rate of canal tax or not. [47]

In the last week of December the Government announced its decision relating to *ad interim* relief. A press note issued on 23 December said that it might take some time for the enquiry committee "to submit its report and for Government to consider it and to reach a decision thereon. To prevent an accumulation of arrears, it has been decided by Government that three-fourths of the demand should be collected now as an 'ad interim' measure pending their final decision on the subject. As the demand has already been reduced from Rs 5-8-0 to Rs 4-2-0 per acre by the grant of a rebate of 25 per cent, the collection be made at the rate of Rs 3 per acre which approximates to three-fourths of the demand after deducting the rebate." The communique' further added that "... the above concession and the rebate will be admissible to those who pay up their dues by the end of February, 1938." [48]

The Government decision to give some 'ad interim relief' to the cultivators of the canal area was criticized by Balai Chand Mukhopadhyay and Jadabendra Nath Panja. Their point was that when the Government had decided to hold an inquiry and start fresh crop-cutting experiment, it should not urge the cultivators to pay the arrears of canal tax at the rate of Rs 3 by the month of February 1938 pending the report of the enquiry committee. The Government should await report of the said committee and concede the demands of the agriculturists. [49]

By the the first week of January 1938 the Damodar Canal authorities were reported to have finished their crop-cutting experiments. Balai Chand Mukhopadhyay lodged his protest against the irregular and unreliable methods and procedures adopted by the authorities concerned in the matter. He said that crops of several plots of land were cut and measurement thereof taken by Government officials without letting the respective owners or cultivators know anything about the matter.

16

The final measurement or weighting was not done in the presence of local men. Hence, he observed, the aggrieved cultivators could not have any confidence in the experiments made in such a perfunctory and surreptitious way and the data or figures collected by such wrong and improper devices could not be relied upon for a fair and correct estimate of the increased outturn.[50]

On 29 January twelve of the eighteen members of the Damodar Canal Enquiry Committee including Sir B. P. Sinha Roy, Maharaja Srish Chandra Nandy, J. N. Bose, B.B. Mandal, A. Majhi, Maulavi A. Hashem and Maulavi N. Ahmed visited Khana junction, about 12 miles west of the Burdwan town. There Sir B. P. Sinha Roy addressed about 1,000 people and explained to them the purpose of their visit. Jadabendra Nath Panja, President, District Congress Committee and a resident of the area, submitted a memorial on behalf of the local cultivators. The members of the enquiry committee then went to a village, Balgona, where Chandra Sekhar Konar submitted on behalf of 2,000 cultivators a memorial similar to that of Mr Panja. Netaipada Gupta of Saligram placed before the members of the enquiry committee an account of the production of the last five years ( 1339 B.S. to 1344 B.S.) to show that the cultivators earned no profit from the canal. The memorial submitted by the inhabitants of the villages affected by the improvement levy may be summarized as follows :

"...There is no increase in the outturn of paddy owing to irrigation from the canal. ...The crop-cutting experiment at the last harvest season was vitiated by the fact (i) that the lands were not classified according to the quality of the soil, (ii) that the plots in which crop-cutting operations were held were not selected in the presence of the villagers concerned, (iii) that crop-cutting was mostly made without notice to the owner of the field and in his absence, (iv) that in some cases crops were cut from a larger area than the standard one of 11 × 9 ft. and (v) that no allowance was made for the boundary ridges (ayils) of the fields and the inevitable wastages of the produce in reaping, stocking, carrying and storing the paddy. At least one sixteenth should be. deducted from gross produce for the last item." The memorial also said that "the total cost of the construction of the canal was met by the loan from the Government of India. With the inauguration of the provincial autonomy, on the basis of Sir Otto Niemeyer's report, the Government of India remitted the loan, thereby exempting the Bengal Government from the payment of the cost of construction. The Government now can demand at the utmost the most reasonable maximum cost of maintaining the canal in proper condition." But, the memorial continued, "... the whole cost of maintaining the canal cannot be equitably charged upon the impoverisned peasants alone, inasmuch as one of the objects of the Damodar Canal is to mitigate the strength of the flood, which may even endanger the city of Calcutta. Having regard to these facts, the East Indian Railway, the Grand Trunk Road, Burdwan-Katwa Light Railway, the Bengal Nagpur Railway, the city of Calcutta, towns and other vested interests which are benefited...should be made to contribute to the cost." The memorialists admitted that the "only benefit the peasants derive from the canal is some sort of insurance against the uncertainty of rains—against drought which occurs occasionally at an interval of 7 or 8 years." The memorialists, therefore, prayed that "the Committee may be pleased to recommend to the Government of Bengal...that the agriculturists holding not more than two acres of land may be exempted from the levy ; that the minimum rate may be levied upon your Memorialists adjudged by your Committee on due consideration of facts set forth in the memorial ; that arrears outstanding may be adjusted to the altered rate ; and that steps may be taken to have proper drainage for the low lands so as to save them from utter ruin."[51]

To the said committee Kiron Chandra Dutt submitted a separate memorandum since he could not agree to the points contained in the memorial of Jadabendra Nath Panja. He made out seven points in his memorandum. : "No development tax should by levied on Burdwan people even if they have got benefit by the Damodar Canal or even if their lands have improved. The estimate of the 'increased outturn' of land in the Damodar Canal area is... arbitrary and too high. The supply of water is not regular and scientific and great mischief is being done ; comparativly lower 1st class Sali lands are becoming waterlogged and the high lands do not get water—no water is available where it is necessary and it is supplied where there is superfluity of it. Owing to the defect in the system the quantity of silt carried in the canal water is negligible whereas on the other hand quantity of sand is so large that sand carried by the canal water deteriorate them. There has been no improvement at present. The cultivators at present in the canal area have no taxable surplus after defraying their necessary costs and they have no paying capacity and the authorities while assessing overlooked the economic condition of the cultivators and considered only the heavy expenditure of the department ; and the system is expensive out of all proportion. The procedure of assessment in the Act is not according to the fixed principles of public finance and opposed to the interests of the peasants."[52]

On 4 February 1938 a meeting of the official enquiry committee was held in Sir B. P. Sinha Roy's room in the Assembly House, Calcutta. After considering the facts and figures collected from the cultivators the committee arrived at the conclusion that the average increased outturn per acre was four maunds of paddy and six *pans* of straw. Sir B.P. Sinha Roy said that the cultivators were getting Rs 6 as profit per acre and hence they should pay Rs 3 as improvement levy. However, he said that the cost of maintenance of the canal system was Rs 320,000 per annum, and unless Rs 2-10-0 was paid to the Government as tax per acre to enable it to meet the establishment costs, it would not be possible to allow 15 per cent. remission for fields which became waterlogged and those which did not receive adequate supply of water. It was learnt that P. N. Bandyopadhyay and Maulavi Abul Hashem could not accept the figures supplied by the Government about the results of crop-cutting experiment.[53] Abul Hashem later submitted a note of dissent and upheld the arguments as contained in Kiron Chandra Dutt's memorandum.[54]

Both Jadabendra Nath Panja and Balai Chand Mukho-padhyay later protested against the decision of the Government to fix the canal tax at Rs 2-10-0 acre. Mr Mukhopadhyay said that the cultivators were agreeable to pay Rs 1-8-0 per acre for the only benefit they derived from the canal as a drought insurance. He asked the people not to lose heart but to take a bold stand and resolutely assert their rights against the arbitrary decision of the Government.[55]

On 14 February a big meeting was held at the Burdwan Town Hall Maidan under the presidentship of Umapada Roy of Sodya. In their speeches Sukumar Bandyopadhyay, Sambhu Nath Konar, Chandra Sekhar Konar, Pramatha Nath Bandyopadhyay and Aswini Kumar Mandal explained the attitude of the Bengal Government towards the canal tax agitation and exhorted all to stand united and fight back every unjust move of the Government.[56]

The Congress Canal Levy Enquiry Committee finalized its report by the end of February. On examination of the pre-canal accounts of agricultural produce, settlement records, decrees of *bhag chas* suits in law courts, results of crop-cutting experiments, quinquennial reports, figures available from other governmental publications and records and the evidence collected from the peasants, the committee came to the conclusion that "the Damodar Canal has not, to any appreciable extent, increased the productivity of the area served by it. ...the yield per acre was about 24 maunds before the canal and the same is the average even after the canal." The Report admitted : "There is, however, a general consensus of opinion that the canal is really useful in years of drought. Therefore, if any levy can at all be imposed on the cultivators of the canal area, it can only be on the basis of drought insurance benefit." But the committee held that "On the whole...for the purpose of levy on the ground of drought insurance, we may proceed on the basis that there is drought in one year in course of six years, and that once in six years there is half failure of crop." It further pointed out that the benefit might, therefore, be calculated at half the full crop, i.e., twelve maunds of paddy per acre. Distributed over six years it came upto 2 maunds of paddy per acre, half of which might be charged for according to the Development Act Rules. Therefore, the Report said, "The levy per year then amounts to the price of one maund of paddy and one maund (*sic*) of straw, the price being calculated according to the current rates each year in January. But in view of the fact that a large number of assessees are owners of holding not exceeding one acre, and also that the cost of cultivation in relation to the falling price of paddy is disproportionately high along with the high rent the cultivator has to pay, the Committee thinks it desirable that such cultivators ( with holding not exceeding one acre) should be exempted from the levy." The committee admitted no question of realizing the capital expenditure for the canal, because the Government of India exempted the Government of Bengal from repaying the capital borrowed from the former in accordance with Sir Otto Niemeyer's report. It only considered the question of running expenses for the canal. On this point the Report said : "The levy which we are now recommending (viz. the price of one maund of paddy and one maund (*sic*) of straw per acre in January which in the present year comes to about Re. 1 and 8 as.) may not be sufficient for the purpose. But it is quite obvious from the history of the Damodar Canal project that the canal was never meant for irrigation purpose alone. It was intended 'inter alia' that the canal should protect the railways, the Grand Trunk Road, the Burdwan town, the port of Calcutta etc. by moderating the strength of the Damodar flood." The Report, therefore, recommended : "...there are important beneficiares other than the cultivators of the canal area. In all fairness and justice, if more money has to be raised for the purposes of maintaining the Damodar Canal, Government should look to those beneficiaries for making good the deficiency, if any, rather than overtax the poor cultivators for benefit which may in a sense be said to be problematical."[57]

In the second week of May the Government issued a communique on the modification of canal rates. It said : "After due consideration Government have accepted the recommendations of the Committee and reduced the rate for the levy under the Bengal Development Act for the years 1936-37 and 1937-38 to Rs. 2-9 per acre to afford the cultivators some relief on account of the present low price of paddy and to enable them more readily to pay off the accumulated arrears of the levy. ...In view of the very great misconception prevalent in the area commanded by the Damodar Canal regarding the imposition of compulsory levy under the Bengal Development Act, Government have decided to reintroduce the system of voluntary irrigation through leases under the Bengal Irrigation Act. On account of the prevailing low price of agricultural produce the rates of the kinds of leases have been modified. ...The chief reduction is in the rate for an annual lease which is now Rs. 4 per acre instead of Rs. 4-8."[58]

A few days before the publication of the above press note, Balai Chand Mukhopadhyay called the decision of the Government on the modification of canal rates anomalous and inscrutable. He condemned the 'shop-keeper's policy' adopted by the Government. Instead of giving any relief to the famished peasantry, said Mukhopadhyay, the Government had poured ridicule on their helpless condition.[59] Jadabendra Nath Panja also blamed the Government decision to collect the canal tax at a rate absolutely beyond the paying capacity of the peasants.[60]

From the middle of May through the next two months several protest meetings were organized in villages like Hatgobindapur, Galsi, Mandalgram, Karuri, Kulgarh, Kuchut-Dharmarajtala, Belgram, Baroshibtala, Uragram, etc. Those meetings were addressed by Jadabendra Nath Panja, Bankim Mukhopadhyay, Abdus Sattar, Sasthi Das Chaudhuri, Manas Gobinda Ghatak, Abdullah Rasul, Pramatha Nath Bandyopadhyay, Sachindra Das Adhikari, Chandra Sekhar Konar, Helaram Chatterjee, Dasarathi Tah, Mahendra Khan, Jahed Ali, Gobinda Dutta, Ashutosh Hazra, Mahaprasad Konar, Narayan Mandal, Balai Deb Sharma, Golam Mahabul, Nakul Chandra Dutta, Aja Kumar Kesh, Balai Chandra Haldar, Kartik Chandra Ghosh, Choudhury Ali Saheb, Phelaram Mandal and others. They all exhorted the people of the canal area not to bow down to the Government decision and take canal water by signing lease deeds at a high rate. They urged the people to carry on their agitation until their legitimate demands were fulfilled.[61]

The Government, on the other hand, since the publication of the press note in which it declared its decision to reduce the improvement or rather the compulsory levy to Rs 2-9-0, had kept quiet and hoped that the people would happily agree to its decision and pay up their arrears. The local peasants, however, considered the Government decision arbitrary and refused to sign lease forms. At last the Government broke the dreadful silence and began to issue certificate notices for the realization of arrears of taxes. In consequence, it was reported in October 1938, the peasants of the canal area had marched to the office of the District Collector to lodge their complaints against the coercive measures adopted by the canal authority.[62]

By the beginning of the following year the Government had started attaching movable properties of the defaulters of the canal area. On 12 January 1939 eight attached cows of the village of Kadra had been kept in the village pound of Ausha. The peasants divided in several groups had been trying to resist the attachment operations. The cultivators were determined to launch a satyagraha movement and continue their agitation till all their demands were fufilled. On the other hand, the Government had decided to send a large contingent of Gurkha soldiers and deploy them on patrol duty in order to bring the situation under control.[63]

Within a month the satyagraha movement began to take shape. In a statement Manoranjan Hazra, member, Bengal Provincial Congress Committee and Kisan Sabha, appealed to the people of Bengal for help. He said that for several months the people of the canal area had been vigorously protesting against the imposition of a high rate of canal tax and, at present, finding to their exasperation that the Government had miserably failed to fulfil the demands of the poor peasantry, they had resorted to satyagraha.[64]

According to a report dated 15 February, Rabi Mazumdar, Secretary, Volunteers' Division of Bengal Provincial Kisan Sabha, said that at Aushagram a satyagraha camp had been set up to conduct the campaign in a peaceful and non-violent way. About fifty satyagrahis had been keeping watch on the pound by turns so that the police authorities could not take out the attached cattle to put the same on auction. He also reported that seventeen thousand certificates had so far been issued and a huge posse of soldiers had been kept ready. But even in the face of all the repressive measures the satyagrahis remained un-daunted in spirit and unflinching in determination. The culti-vators had expressed their readiness to pay the canal tax at the rate of Rs 1-8-0. But they were determined to resist any move of the Government to collect the tax at a higher rate. The peasant women, under the leadership of Nanibala Samanta, took an active part in the movement. [65]

Bankim Mukhopadhyay observed in a statement that the Government had promulgated section 7 Cr. P. C. and ordered the police to attach movable properties of the defaulters. On 15 February, he said, a procession of peasants was scheduled to be taken out, but the local authorities prohibited it under section 144. In the face of this provocation the peasant leaders decided to postpone the holding of the procession. [66]

On 16 February Pramatha Nath Bandyopadhyay moved an adjournment motion in the Legislative Assembly to discuss the serious situation arising out of the notification No. 656 P, dated the 10th February 1939, of the Government of Bengal, extend-ing the provision of section VII of the Criminal Law Amend-ment Act of 1932 to the whole of Burdwan district, excluding Asansol subdivision, and the promulgation on 13 February of section 144 Cr.P.C. in certain parts of the district. In the said notification the Government stated that "the arrears in that area come up to about Rs. 542,000 and the collections amounted to less than Rs. 32,000 only. The result has been practically a stopp-age of all collections and...that the stoppage in the collection has been due to political agitation of an undesirable type involving the boycottt of officials. It is for this reason that Government have been obliged to despatch armed police and motor lorries and buses for the purpose of removing properties attached of the tenantry who are either unable or unwilling to pay. They have also promulgated section 144 prohibiting public meetings and they have called in (*sic*) their assistance section 7 of the Criminal Law (Amendment) Act of 1932." Pramathanath Bandyopadhyay requested the Minister concerned to put a halt to the 'policy of terrorization' and settle the dispute with the tenantry. [67]

An emergency meeting of the executive committee of the

Burdwan District Congress Committee held on 19 February adopted a resolution strongly condemning the Government policy of letting loose repression on the people of the district. The meeting demanded immediate release of all persons arrested in this connexion and repeal of all repressive measures. In another resolution it protested against the false propaganda carried on by the Government that the Congress had started a no-tax campaign. The meeting also reiterated its stand on the canal tax issue and urged the people to pay their arrears.[68]

On 21 February eighteen volunteers were arrested from the Ausha satyagraha camp.[69] Arrests were also made in other parts of the canal area and a reign of terror prevailed.[70]

Till the middle of 1939 the satyagraha movement continued unabated and the police could not demoralize the illiterate masses of the canal area. However, even such a heroic and long-protracted struggle failed to compel the Government to reduce the tax to Rs 1-8-0. As a result the people subsequently accepted the Government rate of Rs 2-9-0 and paid the arrears.[71] The Government, on its part, released the convicted persons and thus ended the movement.

### III

An attempt will be made here to make an analytical review of the organizations which actively participated in the movement and their differences regarding the formulation of the demands of the peasantry and the methods they followed in the course of the movement.

It is on record that the Burdwan District Raiyats' Association first plunged into the agitation and took up the issue in right earnest. The reason was that the pleaders and advocates who were doyens of the Association had landed interests in the canal area and naturally they got alarmed about the possible financial drain when the Government decided to impose a heavy burden of compulsory levy on the ryots of the canal area.[72] They admitted the utility of the canal and never decried the scheme as such. What they wanted to achieve through their agitation by means of 'appeals' and 'prayers' was to persuade the Government to reduce the canal tax to a rate within the paying capacity of the ryots. The Association, at the initial stage, tried to 'keep aloof from the Congress for fear of government repression, which, it thought, 'would scare away the peasants from uniting for a common cause.'[73] The Raiyats' Association held several public meetings at the Burdwan Town Hall Maidan and in different villages of the canal area. The members of the Association established contact with the masses through direct personal approach and propaganda by means of publishing pamphlets and booklets and also by issuing appeals and statements in newspapers. With a view to attracting their attention to the grievances of the peasants they visited the members of the Legislature and furnished them with facts and figures.[74]

The Congress actively joined the movement after its defeat in the elections,[75] and stood by the side of the peasants till its acceptance of the modified rate of canal tax fixed by the Government. The Congress first appointed an enquiry committee on 9 June 1937 to investigate the grievances of the ryots arising out of the canal levy. The Congress Enquiry Committee took the trouble of going to the rural areas for an on-the-spot study. The committee submitted its report in the first week of March 1938. In accordance with the report the Congress advised the cultivators to accept the canal as a drought insurance and to pay one maund of paddy and one *pan* of straw per acre.[76] Moreover, the Congress organized meetings and demonstrations and its leaders issued appeals to the Government for reduction of the canal rate and published statements on several occasions in newspapers either ventilating the grievances of the local cultivators or refuting Government communique's which always defended the canal scheme and the rate imposed under it. Further, the Congress MLAS moved cut motions compelling the Government to appoint an enquiry committee to investigate the canal issue. The Congress Working Committee during its session in Calcutta from 26 October to 1 November 1937 adopted resolutions sympathizing with the Damodar Canal tax agitation.[77] The Bishnupur Conference of the Provincial Congress Committee also expressed its full sympathy with the canal tax movement.[78] On 28 May 1938 Subhas

Chandra Bose came to Burdwan and next day he discussed the canal tax issue with the local Congress workers and urged them to see to it that the peasants did not sign the lease forms. He also asked them to launch a vigorous movement against the unjust tax imposed on the poor cultivators.[79]   Not only did the Congress Working Committee and its leaders sympathize with and lend support to the canal tax agitation, its other wings too supported the cause of the local peasants. The Burdwan District Krishak Conference which was held in the first week of June 1938 in the village of Kasipur under the presidentship of Prafulla Chandra Sen of Arambagh condemned the Government policy of imposing compulsory bettement levy on the poor peasants. The conference resolved that the canal tax should not be more than Rs 1-8-0 and the peasants with small land-holding be exempted from payment of canal tax.[80]

Nevertheless, from the material at our disposal, we can safely observe that the Congress did not urge the local people to launch any satyagraha movement or no-tax campaign against the Government when the latter had refused to accept the rate recommended by it. Finally, when the Government in utter disregard of the popular sentiment intensified repression, the Congress only issued statements in protest and its MLAs appealed to the Government for an early settlement of the dispute, and strangely enough it denied any connexion with the satyagraha movement and advised the people to pay the arrears at the rate fixed by the Government.

The Krishak Samiti [81] which mainly conducted the satyagraha movement differed both from the Raiyats' Association and the Congress in respect of the issues and the goal of the movement. Before we dwell on those points, we should add a few words on the justification behind 'its co-operation with the Congress'.[82]   The members of the Krishak Samiti constituted the 'left wing' of the Congress. They tried to press the canal issue on the Congress leadership soon after the Congress defeat in the election and persuaded it to form a joint platform.[83]   As the two differed from each other in their political convictions and moorings the organizational progress of the newly formed Canal Kar Pratikar Samiti suffered to a great extent. On many occasions the left-wing Congressmen and the Communists had to fall in with the Congress leadership, because they wanted to pursue a policy of 'united front'[84] with the Congress with a view to giving the latter a 'national revolutionary orientation'[85] and to widen their mass base through it. However, in the middle of 1938 the Congress-Krishak Samiti alliance broke down on account of intransigence of both the parties.[86]

The Communists or the leaders of the Krishak Samiti formulated the issues of the movement in a slightly different way. To quote one of them : "The Burdwan Canal Tax Movement was based on the stand that availability of irrigation was to be there as a matter of course. As a matter of fact, it was claimed that there had been an irrigation system prevailing when the British established their regime. If the system broke down, it was maintained that such breakdown was due to the failings of the administration and the landlords in commission and omission. So whatever irrigation arrangement was being made now was a belated compensation and a meagre compensation at that for damages that had already been done. Hence no levy was due from the ryots."[87] But the Congress Enquiry Committee considered the canal useful as a drought insurance and its Report did not say a single word on the damage done to the peasants by the administration. For that reason, the Congress Enquiry Committee could fix the canal rate equal to the price of one maund of paddy and one *pan* of straw—which was then Rs 1-8-0. But it was not unknown to the members of the said committee that the price of paddy fluctuated, and if the price rose up the peasants were to pay more. The Krishak Samiti understood the real implication of the Congress decision and declared that it was ready to accept the rate of Rs 1-8-0 but would not accept any rate in terms of agricultural produce as suggested by the Congress and reiterated this stand in several meetings.[88] When members of the Krishak Samiti found to their utter consternation that the Government would not budge an inch from its decision of Rs 2-9-0 and the Congress had tacitly accepted the rate, they started satyagraha movement.[89] They asked the people to surrender their movable goods on demand by the executive officials for collection of arrears. They exhorted the people to refuse payment at the rate of Rs 2-9-0. Their volunteers kept vigil on the pound guards so that they could not get out from the villages with the attached animals and goods to put them on auction. They even foiled the Government officials' attempt to sell the attached articles by auction by giving 'no-bid' calls.[90]

## IV

Now we will deal with the attitude of the Government and the measures it adopted to curb the movement and the reaction of the people to them.

It becomes obvious from our chronological narration of the events of the movement that the Damodar Canal tax agitation was present in a nascent form even when the Bengal Development Act was not finally passed. At the initial stage the Government did not attach any importance to the movement and, accordingly, refrained from taking any stern measures against the agitators. Several meetings took place in Burdwan to voice the protest of the ryots against the Bill till its final passage in October 1936. When in the beginning of 1936 the vast area adjacent to the Damodar Canal was notified as 'improved' by the canal and a rate of Rs 5-8-0 per acre was fixed, the Burdwan District Raiyats' Association came to the fore and initiated a movement against the application of the drastic provisions of the Bengal Development Act to the canal area. They organized meetings, published pamphlets and contacted peasants to express their resentment against the high rate of canal tax. From the last quarter of 1936 till the end of January 1937 the Congress was busy with the election campaign and, side by side with its propaganda in election meetings, the Congress leaders tried to explain to the peasantry the far-reaching implications of the Development Act and urged the people to agitate against the imposition of compulsory 'improvement' levy. On February 13 the Congress appointed the Damodar Canal Levy Enquiry Committee to probe the grievances of the ryots and fix an equitable rate of tax. Now these hectic activities of the Raiyats' Association and the Congress made the Government realize the gravity of the situation. Accordingly, it arranged to send Ministers and officials to the affected areas to mobilize the support of the local people in favour of the Development Act and the canal scheme. Meanwhile the Krishak Samiti joined the movement and began to co-operate with the Congress. As a result the movement gained added strength and momentum. In the Bengal Legislative Assembly the Premier and the Minister of Communications gave an assurance to form an enquiry committee after a cut motion was tabled by a Congress MLA on behalf of the people of the canal area. The local peasants submitted several memoranda to the Ministers for the redress of their grievances. The Government earlier announced a 25 per cent. rebate and was now compelled to reduce the tax to Rs 3-0-0. After a good deal of vacillation it also appointed enquiry committee which soon began to work, though not in a satisfactory manner. By the first week of March 1938 the Congress Enquiry Committee published its report and recommended a levy equal to the price of one maund of paddy and one *pan* of straw per acre. Later, the official Enquiry Committee fixed the improvement levy at the rate of Rs 2-9-0 per acre. But this partial fulfilment of the demand of the poor peasants could not dissuade them from launching a satyagraha movement even against the reduced rate. They refused to sign lease forms and pay the modified rate. The villagers happily parted with their possessions when attached and refused to participate in the subsequent auction. Once a cobbler's cow was attached in Bhatar. Under the leadership of the Krishak Samiti nearly five to six thousand peasants encircled the area so that the Government officials could not go out of the villages with the attached goods. Nine cows belonging to a Brahmin of the village Kandra ( Sadar P.S. Burdwan ) were attached and taken to a village named Aula situated in the Nabastha area for sale. Thousands of peasants intercepted the Government party with cows, set up camps and started satyagraha. The peasants boycotted the canal officials. The volunteers organized picketing. The Government, on its part, unleashed repression. Section VII of the Bengal Criminal Law Amendment Act of 1932 ( otherwise known as Anderson Act or the Black Act ) was enforced in Burdwan district, and section 144 Cr. P.C. promulgated everywhere. On 14 February 1939 about fifteen to twenty thousand peasants under the leadership of the Krishak Samiti assembled from all sides to enter the town of Burdwan to violate section 144 in protest against the policy of attachment. In the face of the Government's provocative measures and the lukewarm attitude of the Congress, the Krishak Samiti controlled the peasants and sent them back home in a disciplined way. That night eleven lorry loads of the military personnel raided the village of Aushagram. They marched inside the village singing the tune of an infantry band. They beat the villagers and collected money from them. The attached cows were brought under military escort to the Burdwan Revenue office for auction. The peasant volunteers picketed before the office. The local executive officials issued seventeen thousand certificates in all and indiscriminately attached movable properties of the defaulters and put them on auction. The volunteers who organized picketing and resistance were arrested and sentenced to six months' imprisonment under clause 7 (2) of the B.C.L. Act. Even in the face of these repressive measures the satyagraha workers continued their agitation till the middle of 1939 when the movement fizzled out for reasons more than one.[91]

## V

Before we conclude we may divide the Damodar Canal Tax movement into two stages. The first stage started with the introduction of the Bengal Development Act and the imposition of the compulsory canal levy of Rs 5-8-0 thereunder. The next stage began with the launching of the satyagraha movement by the Krishak Samiti. In so far as the aim of the Raiyats' Association and also of the Congress was to compel the Government to reduce the canal rate to an acceptable minimum, the movement was succesful in the first stage. The Government was forced to institute an inquiry, modify the canal rates, withdraw the compulsory levy and reintroduce the lease system. But since it was the goal of the Krishak Samiti in the second stage to bring down the canal rate to Rs 1-8-0 it was, no doubt, a failure. The failure may be partially attributed to the fact that though the Congress urged the people not to sign the lease form for taking canal water at the rate of Rs 2-9-0 for a few months and condemned the repressive measures of the Government, it did not provide any organizational support to the satyagraha movement. Its lukewarm attitude and half-hearted participation in the later stage damped the spirit of the local people. The left-wing, on the other hand, stuck to their decision even when they realized that they had no sufficient mass base to carry on the movement without Congress support. However, the Damodar Canal Tax movement considered as a whole was partially successful.[92] It goes to the credit of the organizers of the satyagraha movement that they set in motion the politically inert peasants and taught them to remain alert, even when engaged in a movement, about the leadership which was often guided by its own class interests. Finally, it must be recorded that the Communists, while committed to an ideology of their own, adopted the non-violent technique of satyagraha, for it proved the most effective weapon in a particular historical context.

## NOTES AND REFERENCES

1. "The charge of clearing the tanks and canals, the repairs of their banks, those of rivers and causeways is known under the denomination of POOLBUNDY." *Fifth Report*, vol. II, p. 98, cited in the Memorandum submitted by Kiron Chandra Dutt, p. 5. See Appendix I.

2. Sir William Willcocks, *Lectures on the Ancient System of Irrigation in Bengal and its Application to Modern Problem*, 23-4. See also the Memorandum submitted to the Damodar Canal Enquiry Committee by Kiron Chandra Dutt of Burdwan on the 29th January, 1938 (Appendix I) ; the Humble Memorial of the People of the Trans-Damodar Area for Relief Measures (Appendix II).

3. *Report of the Damodar Canal Levy Enquiry Committee*, Burdwan District Congress Committee, 1939, 2-3. Though we have accepted the figures as contained in the said Report, they are not similar to those given by the Government in Townend Report, and the Press Notes published in *Amrita Bazar Patrika*, 7.9.37, 14(3) and *Hindusthan Standard*, 12.5.38, 5(6-7).

Mr H. P. V. Townend was the Rural Development Commissioner, Bengal.

4. Interview with Hemanta Kumar Dutta, 21.11.71.

5. Nripendra Nath Mitra (ed.), *Indian Annual Register*, 1935, I (January-June), 176.

6. Statement of Objects and Reasons, *The Calcutta Gazette*, Part IV, 14 February, 1935, 49.

7. *Proceedings in Council*, XLV, 7 March 1935, 79-90, cited in the *Bengal Acts*, 951-6.

8. See note no. 4.

9. Interview with Niharendu Dutta Mazumdar, 27.10.72.

10. Interview with Durgapada Chaudhuri, 22.11.71. See also note no. 4.

11. Interview with Santosh Mandal, 4.11.71. See also *Vardhaman Varta* (a local Bengali weekly), 17.7.39.

12. See note no. 4.

13. Proceedings of different meetings and conferences were made available to us by Mr Kiron Chandra Dutt.

14. *Vardhaman Varta*, 17.7.39. Also interview with Santosh Kumar Mandal.

15. *Vardhaman Varta*, 17.7.39.

16. *Advance*, 12.2.37, 13(4) ; 14.2.37, 13(4).

17. ibid., 12.2.37, 13(4) ; 13.2.37, 7(1).

18. ibid., 19.2.37, 13(4-5).

19. Resolutions adopted by the peasants' conference. See note no. 13. See also *Advance*, 19.2.37, 13(4-5) and *Congress Socialist*, II(17), 1.5.37, 21(1-2).

20. See note no. 15.

21. *Advance*, 3.3.37, 13(5).

22. ibid., 4.3.37, 15(1).

23. From the proceedings of the meeting held on 1 March 1937. See note no 13. See also note no. 22.

24. *Amrita Bazar Patrika*, 10.5.37, 2(7).

25. *Advance*, 29.4.37, 12(2) ; *Amrita Bazar Patrika*, 27.4.37, 13(4).

26. *Advance*, 15.5.37, 12(1).

27. From the proceedings of the Burdwan District Krishak Conference. See note no. 13. See also note no. 15.

28. *Congress Socialist*. II(25), 26.6.37, 22(2).

29. N. G. Ranga (ed.), *Kisan Handbook*, 33-4.
Later also the AIKC in its Tripuri meeting held on 7-8 March 1939 "greeted the Kisans of the Damodar Canal area of Burdwan district (Bengal) in their heroic struggle against the excessive canal tax imposed on them in the face of police and military terror, and wished it complete success."—M. A. Rasul, *A History of the All India Kisan Sabha*, 48.

30. *Amrita Bazar Patrika*, 9.4.37, 12(4) ; *Advance*, 14.4.37, 13(3).

31. The committee consisted of the following members : JatindraNath Bose MLA, Atul Chandra Gupta Advocate, Pramatha Nath Bandyopadhyay Bar-at-law, Dr Prafulla Chandra Ghose, Jadabendra Nath Panja, President, Burdwan District Congress Committee, Priya Ranjan Sen,

Lecturer, Calcutta University and Mr Hemanta Kumar Dutta Pleader, Burdwan. See *Advance*, 11.6.37, 6(4) ; 13.6.37, 10(5) and *Report of the Damodar Canal Levy Enquiry Committee*, 2.

32. *Amrita Bazar Patrika*, 15.6.37, 7(1). For the Memorandum to the Minister of Communications and Works, see Appendix III.

33. A decision was arrived at in a meeting held in the village of Sodya to form a Canal Kar Pratikar Samiti with all sorts of people and groups affected by the imposition of the canal rate. However, a dispute cropped up as to the nature and composition of the organization. The Communists and the Krishak Samiti workers who represented the leftward tendency within the Congress held that the doors of the organization should be thrown open to all who were agreed to fight for the cause of the affected peasantry irrespective of their political conviction and party affiliation. The District Congress leadership, on the other hand, insisted on its control over the organization and demanded that the Samiti should owe allegiance to the Congress and be affiliated to it. A convention to chalk out the programme of the Canal Kar Pratikar Samiti of the Congress was called at the Bangshagopal Town Hall Maidan. The Communists and the Krishak Samiti workers had to agree to the Congress proposals and enrolled themselves in large numbers as members of the Congress-sponsored Kanal Kar Pratikar Samiti. As many as fifteen committees were formed under the leadership of the District Krishak Samiti and Communist workers. Three other committees owing allegiance to the official Congress leadership were also formed. —Interview with Syed Sahedullah, 16.2.72.

34. *Advance*, 13.6.37. 10(5).

35. *Amrita Bazar Patrika*, 10.8.37, 10(5-6).

36. ibid., 24.8.37, 8(7) ; *Advance*, 19.8.37, 11(2-3).

37. The Government of India Act, 1935 provided for a scheme of federal finance. Certain heads of revenue were made entirely federal. Certain others were made entirely provincial and a few other heads of revenue were made partly federal and partly provincial. A fourth category of taxes was to be administered by the Federal Government, but the proceeds were to be transferred to the provinces, subject to surcharges for federal purposes in cases of emergency.

Sir Otto Niemeyer was appointed by the Secretary of State to recommend the proper distribution of the proceeds of share of the income-tax and of the export duty on jute to the provinces, as also the subventions to be paid to the different provinces. His recommendations were adopted by an Order-in-Council.

In accordance with the recommendation of Sir Otto Niemeyer, the debts due from the provinces to the centre were consolidated or cancelled, either wholly or in part, and the balances held by the Central Government were decentralized. See Pramatha Nath Banerjee, *A Study of Indian Economics*, 262-3.

This Pramatha Nath Banerjee was the Minto Professor of Economics of Calcutta University and was not the same person as Pramatha Nath Bandyopadhyay referred to in the text.

38. *Extracts from Bengal Legislative Assembly Proceedings*, Second Session LI, 3-4, 20.8.37-30.9.37, 721-37. See also *Advance*, 29.8.37, 9(1-2).

39. *Advance*, 2.9.37, 5(5).

40. *Amrita Bazar Patrika*, 7.9.37, 14(3) ; 9.9.37, 6(4) ; *Advance*, 10.9.37. 12(2).

41. *Hindusthan Standard*, 12.11.37, 5(3) ; *Advance*, 18.11.37, 12(4). For the reaction of the District Congress Committee, see *Advance*, 26.11.37. 12(2).

42. *Amrita Bazar Patrika*, 27.11.37, 10(6).

43. *Advance*, 8.12.37, 11(3).

44. ibid., 9 12.37, 8(5) ; *Hindusthan Standard*, 9.12.37, 13(2).

45. The committee consisted of the following members : the Hon'ble Abul Kasem Fazl-ul-Huq, Premier, the Hon'ble Nalini Ranjan Sarkar, Minister of Finance, the Hon'ble B. P. Sinha Roy, Minister of Revenue, the Hon'ble Maharaja Srish Chandra Nandy, Minister of Communications and Works, the Collector of Burdwan, Nizamuddin Ahmed MLA, Jatindra Nath Basu MLA, Maharaj Kumar Uday Chand Mahatab MLA, P. N. Banerjee MLA, Adwaita Kumar Majhi MLA, Banku Behari Mandal MLA, Maulavi Abul Hashem MLA, Maulavi Md. Abul Rashid MLA, Maulavi Abdul Quasem MLA, Khan Bahadur Alfazuddin Ahmed MLA, Khan Sahib Maulavi S. Abdur Rauf MLA, Maulavi Abdul Wahab Khan MLA, Mr David Hendry MLA. See *Amrita Bazar Patrika*, 16.12.37, 2(7). The report of this committee was not published.

46. *Hindusthan Standard*, 17.12.37, 5(7).

47. *Advance*, 20.12.37, 12(5).

48. *Hindusthan Standard*, 24.12.37, 5(7).

49. ibid., 31.12.37, 13(4) ; 6.1.38, 13(3) ; *Amrita Bazar Patrika*, 31.12.37, 10(3) ; *Advance*, 2.1.38, 2(5) ; 7.1.38, 6(5) and *Ananda Bazar Patrika*, 6.1.38, 11(7).

50. *Advance*, 5.1.38, 8(3).

51. *Hindusthan Standard*, 1.2.38, 13( 6-7) ; *Ananda Bazar Patrika*, 31.1.38, 5(6-7) and *Advance*, 1.2.38, 9(4).

52. Memorandum submitted by Kiron Chandra Dutt of Burdwan on the 29th January, 1938, 1. See Appendix I.

53. *Hindusthan Standard*, 8.2.38, 13(5).

54. For extracts from the Note of Dissent, see Appendix IV.

55. *Hindusthan Standard*, 10.2.38, 13(3) ; 13.2.38, 15(2).

56. ibid., 16.2.38, 13(4).

57. *Report of the Damodar Canal Levy Enquiry Committee*, 8-10. See also *Hindusthan Standard*, 4.3.38, 4(6) ; 11.3.38, 6(2-3) ; 12.3.38, 6(2-3) ; *Advance*, 5.3.38, 6(4) and *Amrita Bazar Patrika*, 4.3.38, 10(2).

58. *Hindusthan Standard*, 12.5.38, 5(6-7) ; *Vardhaman Varta*, 9.5.38, 1 & 3.

59.  *Advance*, 28.4.38, 6(7) ; *Hindusthan Standard*, 28.4.38, 4(4).

60.  *Vardhaman Varta*, 2.5.38, 1 & 2 ; *Hindusthan Standard*, 14.5.38, 3(7) and *Advance*, 15.5.38, 8(5).

61.  *Vardhaman Varta*, 23.5.38 ;  6.6.38,  4 ; 20.6.38, 3 ; 4.7.38, 1 & 2 ; 11.7.38, 2.

62.  ibid., 24.10.38, 4.

63.  ibid., 13.2.39, 4.

64.  *Jugantar*, 14.2.39, 4(1).

65.  ibid., 15.2.39, 7(6-7).

66.  ibid., 16.2.39, (4-5).

67.  *Extracts from Bengal Legislative Assembly Proceedings*, LIV(1-2), Sixth Session, 15.2.39-7.3.39, 99-103.

68.  *Vardhaman Varta*, 27.2.39, 3.

69.  ibid., 27.2.39, 2.

70.  ibid., 6.3.39, 4-5 ; 27.3.39 ; 3.4.39 ; 10.4.39.

71.  ibid., 4.12.39.

72.  Interview with Santosh Mandal ;  Helaram Chattopadhyay and Sivaprasad Dutta (3.11.71).

73.  Interview with Durga Pada Chaudhuri.

74.  See note no. 4.

75.  Interviews with Santosh Kumar Mandal ; Syed Shahedullah.

76.  *Report of the Damodar Canal Levy Enquiry Committee*, 10.

77.  *Indian Annual Register*, 1937, II, 326.

78.  *Ananda Bazar Patrika*, 28.1.38, 13(4).

79.  *Vardhaman Varta*, 6.6.38, 1 & 3.

80.  *Advance*, 8.6.38, 8(4) ; *Vardhaman Varta*, 4.7.38, 2.

81.  The Burdwan District Krishak Samiti was formed in a meeting held in May 1933 at Hatgobindapur under the presidentship of Dr Bhupendra Nath Dutta.  Helaram Chattopadhyay was the Secretary of the Samiti.  See M. A. Rasul, *Krishak Sabhar Itihas*, 79-80.

82.  Interviews with Helaram Chattopadhyay and Sivaprasad Dutt ; Syed Sahedullah.

83.  See note no. 75.

84.  Interview with Syed Shahedullah. For an analysis of CPI's policy of United Front with the Congress, see Gene D. Overstreet and Marshal Windmiller, *Communism in India*, 166-70 ; L.P. Sinha, *The Left Wing in India*, 418-26 and M. R. Masani, *The Communist Party of India*, 59-66.

85.  See note no. 9.

86.  See note no. 15.

87.  Interview with Syed Shahedullah.

88.  Interview with Helaram Chattopadhyay and Sivaprasad Dutt.

89.  cp. "The Congress leaders who had been carrying on the agitation felt that, *with their present stre gth of organization*, it would be wise to strike the bargain at that point.  The pressure of the Government for the realization of water-rates was great, and there were also signs of waver-

ing and indecision among the peasants, for the latter did not belong to one class, but ranged from a fairly prosperous section to those who possessed no land. If a settlement could be arrived at at this point, it would at least lead to *a sense of success* among those who had tried to resist. A consultation was held in the Congress office, when the senior members pleaded for acceptance of the Government offer. The younger Leftists were however determined to stick to the lowest demand. Eventually the negotiations failed." (italics in original) See Nirmal Kumar Bose, *Lectures on Gandhism*, 27.

90. Interviews with Santosh Mandal ; Helaram Chattopadhyay and Sivaprasad Dutt ; Niharendu Dutta Mazumdar ; and Syed Shahedullah.

91. Interviews with Helaram Chattopadhyay and Sivaprasd Dutt ; Santosh Mandal. See also Md. Abdullah Rasul, *Krishak Sabhar Itihas*, 79-80.

92. Dr. Binay Bhushan Chaudhuri, however, holds a different view : "The peasants won a *complete* victory in the Damodar Canal area." (emphasis added) See his 'Agrarian Movements in Bengal and Bihar, 1919-1939,' in B. R. Nanda (ed.), *Socialism in India*, 217.

APPENDIX I*

*Memorandum submitted to the Damodar Canal Enquiry Committee by Kiron Chandra Dutt of Burdwan on the 29th January, 1938.*

On an analysis of the demands and complaints of the people of the Damodar Canal area as expressed in their resolutions and memorandums submitted to the Government and those expressed through local and Calcutta newspapers I come to the following 7 points :

1st. :  No development tax should be levied on Burdwan people even if they have got benefit by the Damodar Canal or even if their lands have improved.

2nd. :  The estimate of the "increased outturn" of land in the Damodar Canal area is not based on facts neither that of pre-canal days and the assessment is arbitrary and too high.

3rd. :  The supply of water is not regular and scientific and great mischief is being done ; comparatively lower 1st. class Sali lands are becoming waterlogged and the high lands do not get water—no water is available where water is necessary and it is supplied when there is superfluity of it.

4th. :  Owing to the defect in the system the quantity of silt carried in the canal water is negligible whereas on the other hand quantity of sand is so large that sand carried by the canal water deteriorate them.

5th. :  There has been no improvement at present.

6th. :  The cultivators at present in the canal area have no taxable surplus after defraying their necessary costs and they have no paying capacity and the authorities while assessing overlooked the economic condition of the cultivators and considered only the heavy expenditure of the department ; and the system is expensive out of all proportion.

7th. :  The procedure of assessment in the Act is not accord-

* Appendices I-III are verbatim and unabridged reproductions, with obvious typographical errors corrected.

ing to the fixed principles of public finance and opposed to the interests of the peasants.

I will place 1st, 2nd, 5th and 7th points together :

Irrigation was practised in ancient India during the Hindoo as well as Muhammadan period, and the districts of Burdwan, Howrah and Hooghly were not exceptions, on the contrary they were placed in a better position, nay perhaps the best position. In this my short memorandum I will not go to detail.

## Land Tax in Akbar's Time

"Some soils produce crops almost spontaneously ; whilst others require the greatest exertion of labour and skill. *Much depends upon the vicinity or distance of water* ; and the neighbourhood of cities ought also to be a matter of consideration. So that it behoveth the officers of Government, in their respective districts, to attend to every one of those circumstances, that the demands of the state may be fixed accordingly."[1]

1. Aini Akbari, translation by Francis Gladwin, vol. I, p. 238.

At that time lands were divided for taxation purpose into Pooloj, Perwoty, Checher and Benjor according to productive capacity.

Vide Ibid., p. 244.

In Akbar's time there was no separate tax for irrigation. At that time 'diminutions were allowed constantly to be made from the gross rental on account of the damages sustained by extraordinary drought, inundation, war, pestilence or famine.'

Vide Fifth Report, vol II, p. 181.

The 'Amilguzzar' (or the Collector of the Revenue) in Akbar's time was instructed by the Government to be the immediate friend of the husbandman to exert himself to bring back lands having fallen waste into cultivation and to see that the arable lands are not neglected. When any village was cultivated to the highest degree of perfection by the skilful management he was rewarded proportionate to his merit. During Akbar's time 'there were thirteen variety of taxes'. In those 13 taxes there is no mention of irrigation tax though there were irrigation. The inference is

Vide Aini Akbari, vol. I., pp. 261-62.

Vide Aini Akbari, p. 248.

that *during Akbar's time and before him irrigation facilities were taken into account when land tax was assessed.*

## Land tax from after Akbar's time uptil 1760 A. D.

The Jumma Kumul Toomary or more perfect standard account of the imperial revenues of Bengal, settled finally by Sujah Khan in the year 1722 A. D., "was not the original amount framed by Todar Mal, and specified in the Ayini Akbari, but a repeatedly enlarged, corrected, practical scheme of the finances improved by actual surveys, hustobood accounts, or *particular local investigations* in course of near a century and half, and exhibiting accurately minute, regular, authoritative, proportionate standard assessments of territory, that hath been formed."[2]

2. Fifth Report, vol. II, p. 192.

At that time i.e. 1722 A. D. "Burdwan formed of the Circars of Shereefabad, Madarun, Peschush, the greater part of Selimabad, with a portion of Satgong, and including the rich zemindary of Burdwan as then granted, one-third of Beerbhoom, and the whole of the tributary districts of Bishnepoor and Pacheet, &c., 61 perganahs in all, was assessed at Rs. 2,244,812."[3] This was a huge amount of increase in comparison with Akbar's time. "The increase of the old rent during the above period was done by gradual improvement of the lands, and *from the yearly hustobood accounts of their real produce,* or periodical investigations, set on foot for the purpose of ascertaining such produce."[4] The above Jumma Toomary of Sujah Khan for the year "1722 A. D. was the famous established rentroll which in the fourth quarter of the 18th century during the rule of the East India Company" was indispensably necessary throughout Bengal, in granting Zemindary Sunnuds, ascertaining all fiscal divisions of lands and above all, in equalizing on the several districts any new demands of revenue, as well as judging of the equity of old."[5]

3. Ibid., pp. 188-89.

4. Ibid., p. 190.

5. Ibid., p. 192.

In the 'Eahtiman' or Zemindary trusts, in the annual settlement, exclusive of Jaggeers, showing the proportion of the royal standard assessment, at first instituted in the Government of Jaffir, and confirmed by Sujah Khan in the year 1728 A. D., Burdwan is mentioned as "the enlarged, compact and fertile Zemindary in grain, cotton, silk and sugarcane"[6] and was bestowed on Maharaja Keereetchand and it consisted of 57 pergunnas and was known as Chuckla Burdwan comprised with Circurs Sheereefabad, Midarun, Selimabad, Peshcush, Satgram, Circur Satrgam in Chuck of Hooghly and pergunnath Munhur Shahy Sheereefabad in Chuck Moorsheedabad and in the same year i.e. 1728 A.D. it was assessed at Rs. 2,047,506.

6. Ibid., p. 194.

Vide Ibid., pp. 410-12.

Vide Ibid., p. 194.

In 1149 A. B. i.e. 1742 A. D. annexations from Zemindary of Aruh i.e. Kubazpoor, Circur Selimabad, Jaggeer Circur, Raipoor Kootwally Satgaon, the annexations of the Zemindary of Govindez with 14 pargannas and that of the Zemindary of Jaggernaut Persad with 4 Pargannas made the revenue Rs. 2,306,126 and Muscoorat deductions Rs. 54,280 making the total net Ausil Jumma of the Zemindary in 1167 i.e. 1760 A. D. Rs. 2,251,306 and the Abwabs to the same date Rs. 829,933 and Towfeer on Jageer Circur Rs. 19,166 making the total Ausil and Abwab* in 1760 A. D. Rs. 3,100, 435 ; besides that there appears to have been Keffyet or profit unknown to the Musalman Government.

Vide Ibid., pp. 411, 412.

*In the category of Subhadary Abwabs there is no irrigation tax.

### Subsequent Period

On the 27th September 1760 A. D., Burdwan Chuckla was ceded to the East India Company by Nawab Mir Muhammad Kasim Khan, Governor of Bengal and it was confirmed by a Sunnud dated 11th October 1760 A. D. and was estimated to yield a clear net revenue of Rs. 3,175,391 free of all Sebundy, Muscoorat and all Mofussil charges. At that time Burdwan Zemindary "comprising 5174 B. Square miles was like a garden in a desert, deemed wonderfully productive."[7],, The territor surrendered in conformity to the grant, comprehended simply

Vide Ibid., p. 257.

7. Ibid., p. 235.

the jurisdiction of Raja Tilukchand, second in descent from Keereetchand, the first acknowledged legal occupant of Burdwan,"[8] i.e. the territory of Keereetchand "enlarged by the five pergunnahs of Bundelgaut, etc. and eleven lesser ones of Arseh, etc., in the Chuckla of Hooghly together with the foreign annexation of Bahmnibhoom from Orissa, in addition to interior dependencies of Chunderconah."[9] At this time "it was assessed at a standard considerably higher than that of any other Zemindary jurisdiction of the Subah."[10] Dissatisfied with the collections of 1760-61 Burdwan Zemindary was farmed out 'in violation of the financial practice of the Mogal Government for a period of 3 years to irresponsible farmers' with the result that the revenue was increased from 'Rs. 3,175,391 to Rs. 3,858, 429'.

8. Ibid., p. 248.

9. Ibid.
10. Bengal D.G., vol. XXIII, p. 145. Vide also Fifth Report, vol. II, pp. 98, 408. Vide Ibid., 144, 145 ; also Fifth Report, p. 409.

"In 1172 i.e. 1765 A. D. Mr. Verelst's financial operations commenced, and after various regulations, Hustobood investigations and improvements, for 5 years,"[11] the revenue in 1771 A. D. "was 4,328,509 Rs. which was inclusive of the profits forthcoming from the Dewey Mahals appropriated to the Ranny's use and estimated to amount to about 180,000 Rs. additional ; at the same time the articles of incumbrance with which it was or could regularly be charged under the denomination of Serinjamy Mofussil, were 1st. Salieneher Moshaireh of the Zemindar Rs. 230,000, 2nd Muscoorat reduced to half a lac and thirdly "POOLBUNDY" ordinary expenses 50,000 Rs. more ; —in all making an object of 330,000 Rs. proper to be deducted from the gross, to ascertain the net effective income of the state from the whole district."[12] This is the highest in comparison with any other district in Bengal or throughout the whole of Hindusthan.

The conclusion drawn from the above revenue History of Bengal from after Akbar's time down to 1770 A. D. is that no separate item of irrigation tax was realized from the Zemindar of Burdwan by the Government and that lands were assessed according to productive power taking into consideration irrigation facilities and that the Zemindary was assessed at an abnormally high rate.

In the year 1771 A. D. we see for the first time that the East India Company gave the Burdwan Raj credit of Rs. 50,000 for "POOLBUNDY". It is an expense of the Government.

What is POOLBUNDY ?  *"The charge of cleaning the tanks and canals, the repairs of their banks, those of rivers and causeways is known under the denomination of POOLBUNDY."*[13]

13. Fifth Report, vol. III, p. 98.

The Government was under the obligation to do the above works and they realized it and realized rightly, but they entrusted the Burdwan Raj with the above works, so they granted the Raj Estate a credit of Rs. 50,000 from their Juma in 1771. "The Raj Estate having fallen in arrears of revenue the Government took charge of the Estate for several years and entered into a contract with Mr. Fraser for the repair of the embankments of the rivers. The contract expired in 1783 A. D. and the Government then decided to make a settlement with the Raja as being more agreeable to the Zemindari consititution and granted the Raj Estate a credit of Rs.60,001 for the POOLBUNDY charges."[14]

14. Bengal D. G., vol. XXIX, p. 164.

Thus it is evident that the obligation which the Government owed to the people was transferred to the Burdwan Raj for an annual price of Rs. 60,001 ; so in Sir John Shore's minute in the statement of Zemindary charges of Burdwan for the year 1793 we find POOLBUNDY to be Rs. 60,001 and it is meant to defray the expense on that item by the Government.

Now let us see why the Government was under the obligation to perform the POOLBUNDY works.

The following Abstract of a Ryot's account taken in the year 1781, will show the mode in which this is done.

"Rent of 7 begas 12 cottahs 7 chattacks of land, of various produce, calculated at a certain rate per bega according to its produce, extracted from an account of demands and payments, called

| | Rs. | A. | G. |
|---|---|---|---|
| Hissawb | | | |
| Korcha ··· ... ... | 14 | 0 | 8 |

*ABWAB   CESSES :*

| | | | | |
|---|---|---|---|---|
| Chout at 3/16 per rupee | 2 | 10 | 0 | 0 |
| POOLBUNDY, a half month's demand of Jama | 0 | 9 | 7 | 2 |
| Nuzzerana one month's or ½ | 1 | 2 | 15 | 0 |
| Mangun one month's or ½ | 1 | 2 | 15 | 0 |
| Fouzdarry 3/4 of one month's amount or 1/16 | 0 | 14 | 5 | 0 |
| Company's nuzzerah one month & a quarter | 1 | 7 | 0 | 0 |
| Batta, one anna per rupee | 0 | 14 | 0 | 0 8 12 2 2 |

Total.................22  12    10    2

Khelaat at 1 anna &
half p' each rupee of
the above sum          ...      ...    2    2    1    2

Total Jumma  ...  24  14  12  0"

Vide Fifth Report, vol. II, p. 85. Vide Minute of Sir John Shore, dated 18th June 1789 A. D.

From the above abstract it is evident that at least in 1781 the "ryots are paying POOLBUNDY to the 'Zemindar'. We know that after the permanent settlement the ryots' 'ausil' and 'abwab' was consolidated" into one neat sum. That the ryots of Burdwan pay 'POOLBUNDY' which is now consolidated in their ausil juma ; and this is more confirmed from the statement of ryots of Burdwan Zemindary in November 1859 made before Mr. C. P. Hobhouse, Collector of Burdwan, who stated that they pay cess for POOLBUNDY.

Vide Bengal D.G., vol. XXXIX, p. 164.

Reg. 1 of 1793 ; also Fifth Report, vol. II, p. 136.

Vide The Canals & Flood Banks of Bengal Inglis, p. 261.

The Government never shook off that obligation, rather they accepted it and accepted rightly.  So a Regulation for Repairs of Dykes and Pools, recorded on the 11th February 1791 and a Regulation concerning Tanks, recorded on 21st. October 1791, illustrate how the then Government accepted the obligation.  In the above Regulation of the 11th February 1791 we find that the Collector of Burdwan was the most interested. Further the Regulation XXXIII of 1793 was passed. It was a Regulation for re-enacting, with modifications, the Rules passed on the 11th. February and 21st. October 1791 for repairing the embankments kept in repair at the public expense ; and for encouraging the digging of Tanks or Reservoir, and watercourses, and making embankments.  Section 7 of Regulation recorded on the 11th February 1791 runs thus :

"Resolved, that the Board of Revenue be directed to communicate the above Resolutions to the *Collector of Burdwan*, and to such other Collectors as are, or may be, entrusted with the charge of POOLBUNDY of their district, and they authorize *the Collector of Burdwan to make such disbursements, under the above Regulation as may be requisite for POOLBUNDY of his district until the estimate or the total expense of the work to be performed, shall have been completed.*"

The Regulation of the 25th October runs as follows :

"Resolved that the several Collectors and Resident at Benares be vested with a discretionary power *to open any tanks or reservoirs* that are private property for the *purpose of watering the crops on the lands paying revenue to Government* under the following restrictions." etc.

The reason of the high assessment of Burdwan is not far to seek ; in the year 1786, James Grant in his historical analysis describes Burdwan as "the most compact, *best cultivated*, and in proportion to its dimensions, *by far the most productive in annual rent* to the proprietory sovereign which, under British administration, not only of all such districts within the soubah of Bengal but compared to any other equal magnitude throughout the whole Hindusthan."[13]

13. Vide Fifth Report, vol. II, p. 407.

Speaking of Tanjore and Benares Mr. Grant says of Burdwan "they cannot at all be brought in competition with Burdwan." Sir John Shore in his minute also held the same view.  It was the 'overflow' irrigation system of the Damodar with its connected streams and watercourses on both sides which made Chuckla Burdwan such fertile, wealthy and prosperous.

"The River Damodar was such better placed irrigation than the Ganges." The whole Chuckla of Burdwan i.e. the tract on both sides of the Damodar on the south up to Dwarakeswar and Rupnarayan and on the north up to Ganges, were connected with spill channels, streams and watercourses. This served the purpose of irrigation in the whole of the Burdwan Zemindary. The Gangan or Behula, Kunti or Kana Nadi, Saraswati, Kana Damodar, Madaria Khal, Bessia, Mundeswari, Kana Dwarakeswar, Naya Sari Banka, Khari, Nunia, Sigaroon, Tamla, Gangur, all Devkhal sall of them being spill channels, watercourses, or streams of the Damodar or connected with its streams served a purpose of overflow irrigation throughout the whole district of Burdwan including the present Damodar Canal area. These streams or water-courses run through the low-embankments of the Damodar and served the purpose of 'flood water irrigation' and fed the Dykes, Pools, and tanks also with flood water. It had been necessary to regulate them in proper repair so the ryots were levied with a cess called 'POOLBUNDY' which the Government had ultimately taken to keep the above irrigation process in tact ; for this the Government made provision in the three Regulations above mentioned and took the responsibility to fulfil their obligation to the people. For the same reason they made 'POOLBUNDY' allowance for Bishnupur, Murshidabad, Nadia, 24 Parganas, Midnapur and Jessore in 1793.

Vide D.G., vol. XXIX & vol. XXIII ; also Royal Commission on Agriculture Evidence Bengal ; also Eden Canal Project Stodard's note. Also Willcocks, various reports and minutes recorded by Govt. Engineers, Civil officers between the years 1851 & 1888 ; also see Tassinsmap, map prepared by Rennel and also the map of the Damodar tract prepared by De-Bourble in 1853, etc. See also the old survey maps of the villages by the Govt.

Though the Government admitted their obligation and undertook to keep the watercourses, spill channels, streams, dykes, pools, tanks, embankments, etc. in proper state but as a matter of fact they failed to fulfil their obligation and promise and practically worked in the opposite direction. How I shall show later on.

I have mentioned that in 1793 the Government made a
contract with Burdwan Raj whereby the Burdwan Raj was made
answerable to the Government. This agree-
ment was confirmed by Regulation I of 1793.
The Burdwan Raj Estate occasionally entered
into contract with Europeans for the execution
of the POOLBUNDY work i.e. with Mr. Marriot in 1800.  The
appointment of Mr. Marriot was at first questioned by the Board, which subsequently allowed advances to be made to him.  At that
time neither the Government nor the European contractors
knew how to utilize the flood water and keep
up the embankments nor did they know how to
control the flood water and use it for the purpose of cultivation.  The result was that their
neglected state necessitated the formation of a
special committee to take care of them.  The
Burdwan Raj Estate petitioned the embankment committee to take over Rs. 60,001 and
carry out the POOLBUNDY work which was thrust upon it.
This was finally allowed by Government.  (in the year 1809 )*

*Vide Embank-
ment Manual
1907.*

*Vide D.G., vol.
XXIX, p.164.*

*\* The bracketed
portion added
after the
Memorandum
was submitted
to the
Enquiry
Committee.*

Thus the Burdwan Raj was relieved of its responsibility and
the liability to maintain the POOLBUNDY works reverted to
the Government and the Government is bound to perform its
obligations towards the tenants and Zemindars of Burdwan.
When the Government took over the works it thoroughly strengthened the left embankment and made it watertight and cut
off 20 miles of embankment on the right side of the Damodar
in the period between 1856-59 with a motive of protecting the
E.I. Railway line and the Grand Trunk Road.  The Grand
Trunk Road which was always breached in old times by Damodar floods was much raised.  When the left embankment was
strengthened its innumerable spill channels of which I have
mentioned below or rather canals were closed and the E. I.
Railway line and the raised Grand Trunk Road made second
and third embankments respectively.  These have been called
by the great irrigation expert Sir William Willcocks satanic
chains of the Damodar and they have doomed the once healthy

and prosperous tract between it and the Hooghly to malaria and comparative poverty. These are facts well established and admitted by the Government ; the old records of the Government will prove this.

Thus the present Damodar and Eden Canal area was deprived of its fertility, though the tenants were paying tax as POOLBUNDY for the irrigation facility.

From the old records of the 'Eden Canal Project' it appears that *the Government in order to compensate the people of Burdwan and Hooghly opened the Eden Canal,* and it will also appear from the same records that *the Bengal Government opposed taxation for water of the Eden Canal to be used for irrigation purpose.* The fact is that the Bengal Government fully realized that the supplying of water even for irrigation would be merely a lawful compensation for the loss to the tenants by the overt act of the Government. It will also appear from the old records that both Zamindars and tenants are demanding compensation from the Government all along. The grounds on which compensation was not allowed to the Zamindars for the mismanagement of the left embankment and the abandonment of the right embankment of Damodar by the Government, were arbitrary and against the principles of justice and equity. The Lieutenant Governors, Commissioners, Collectors, Government Engineers all for a long period of time realized the legitimate rights of the Zamindars and Talukdars and tenants to get compensation for the wrong done by the higher continuous watertight embankment on the left side of the Damodar and abandonment of the right side. From laws then current and subsequent legislation it is clear that they are entitled to compensation either in cash money or remission in rent or revenue. The Zamindars did not get remission from the Government so they could not grant remission to the tenants generally.

The result is that the present Damodar Canal area people though paying tax for irrigation from time immemorial their facilities were obstructed by the Government causing deterioration in the soil and poverty to the people ; they did not get either remission of rent or compensation.

18

## Permanent Settlement for the Ryots

On the 16th August 1769 the Bengal Government desires Collector to impress upon the raiyots that "our object is not increase of rents or accumulation of demands, but solely by fixing such as are legal, explaining and abolishing such as are fraudulent and unauthorised, not only to redress the raiyots' present grievances, but to secure him from all invasions of his property." Warren Hastings wrote on 1st November 1786 "many other points of inquiry will also be useful to secure the raiyots the permanent and undisputed possession of their lands, and to guard them against arbitrary exactions." On the 12th April 1786, the Court of Directors wrote : "It is entirely our wish that the natives ('raiyots or subjects') may be encouraged to pursue enjoyment of the profit of their industry ; and that the Zemindars and raiyots may not be harassed by increasing debts either public or private, occasioned by the increased demands of Government." Sir John Shore in his minute expressed the same view. The Court of Directors on the 19th September 1792 approved the views of Sir John Shore and the Regulation I of 1793 was also for a permanent settlement for raiyots ; on the 15th January 1819 the Court of Directors deliberately re-affirmed "we fully subscribe to the truth of Mr. Sisson's declaration that the faith of the state is to the full as solemnly pledged to uphold the cultivator of the soil in the unmolested enjoyment of his long-established rights, as it is to maintain the zemindar in the possession of his estate, or to abstain from increasing the public revenue permanently assessed upon him."* From all the papers, regulations and Acts of the Government I assert that in 1793 by Regulation I, by Puttah Regulation, etc. *permanent setttlement was made not only with the Zemindars but also with the ryots, the agrarian class.* The intention that by the arrangement of 1793 the ryots' rent should be as permanently settled as the zemin-

Colebrook's Digest, p. 180.

E.I. Revenue Selections, vol. I, p. 455.

Report of Select Committee of 1810, p. 158.

Report of Select Committee, 1810, APP 12A, p. 172.

*Sess, 1831-32 vol. XI, p. 101.

dar's at the amount obtaining in 1793 was a well-known and
established fact and on that understanding Mr.

Revenue Selec-   H. Colebrooks urged in 1812 that "measure
tions, vol. I,   should be adopted late as it now is, to reduce
p. 263.          to writing a clear declaration and distinct
record of the usages and rates according to which the ryots of
each pergunah or district will be entitled to demand the renewal
of their pottahs, upon any occasion of a general or partial
cancelling of basis."

## Obligation of the State to the People

The Court of Directors on the 9th May 1821 asserts "so long
as the rights of the inferior classes of the agricultural popula-
tions shall remain unprotected, the British
Sess. 1831-32.   Government must be considered *to have fulfil-*
vol. XI, p. 101.  *led very imperfectly the obligations which it owes*
*to its subjects.*" It will be superfluous to quote here many
other declarations of the Government regarding its obligation
towards ryots; but I shall only state here that the Government's
right to interfere for securing the ryot was expressly reserved.

As shown before that there were spill channels connected
with the Damodar on its both banks which supplied the whole
of the Burdwan district and most parts of Hooghly and
Howrah we have also got the fact that the Government after
taking over the charge of the embankments made them watertight on the left and with it we have got the number of innnu-
merable breaches in the earlier part of the 19th century of
which Sir William Willcocks has said secret breaches. The
people of Bengal could not give up their ancient custom smoothly and really the holders and cultivators of land made cuts
and watercourses through the embankments. For this special
legislation had to be made. So Regulation XXXIII was modified by Regulation VI of 1806. Sections 12 and 13 of the above
Regulation were enacted for the above purpose. Clause I of
Section 12 of the above Regulation will be instructive :

Reg. VI of 1806, Section 12, Cl. I. Material injury and in-
convenience having been sustained from the abuse of the powers
exercised by the holders and cultivators of land, in making cuts

and watercourses through the embankments : the following
rules have been established for general observance with respect
to the point.

Now we shall not hesitate to concur with
Willcocks　　　Sir William Willcocks that 'the breaches were
generally secretly made by the holders and cultivators of land.'

There in Regulation VI 1806 we see provision for cuts,
watercourses and sluices *through the embankments.* The Government was passive all along as regards those works.

Only in 1881 the little Eden Canal and in 1934 the Damodar
Canal were opened to fulfil a part of that obligation which the
Government owe to the peasantry of Burdwan and Hooghly.

In this connection let me quote a few lines from Colebrook's
Digest vol. 3, p. 500 : "Immediately connected with the security and collection of the land revenue as well as the private
rents of land, is the seasonable repair of the embankments
constructed on the side of the large rivers, and other rivers, in
which the water rises to a considerable height in the rains, to
prevent inundation. Although the landholders and farmers with
whom a settlement has been concluded by a clause in their
engagements, have been generally made answerable for the
repair of embankments within the limits of their estates, or
farms, this responsibility has never been understood to include
certain embankments, which (to use the terms of the preamble
to Regulation XXXIII of 1793) have been considered as public
works and have been kept in repair at the expense of Government in consequence of their great extent, and the damage to
which districts and places for the projection of which they have
been constructed would be liable from inundation, in the event
of their not receiving the necessary annual repairs." The importance of providing for the due repair of the public embankments referred to induced the Governor-General-in-Council to
pass a regulation on July 1791."

In spite of the above Regulation the Government was
unable to control the Damodar.

Para 6 of No. 40 dated 16th March 1867 from the Governor-
General-in-Council to the Secretary of State for India will be

relevant in this connection. "The floods of the Damodar have been for years a source of trouble. The Government had long ago entered into agreement with the Zemindars to keep up the embankments. Year after year the embankments were repaired, and year after year they were breached. The floods let suddenly on the land, after being for a time held up by the embankments, were more disastrous than if they had spread quietly over the country from the first. At last in 1851, Colonel Beadle ( then Lieutenant ) suggested that the Government was attempting an impossibility, and that the lower channels of the river would not carry off between the embankment the volume of water which in floods poured down from the upper courses of the river. Surveys were made and levels were taken, and on these being submitted to calculation it was proved that Colonel Beadle's *notion* was correct and that no practicable height embankments, and no practicable width of channel left between the embankments, would suffice to carry off the floods. And, ultimately, the Government adopted his proposal to throw down the embankments of the right bank of the river, in order to save the left from flood."

An extract from the report by Captain Garnault on the Damodar and Hooghly canal project dated 12th October 1869 will also throw some light on the point : "In 1852 a very able note was written by Mr. Ricketts a' propose of some enquiry connected with the embankments. ...In this note reference was made to a proposition by Lieutenant Beadle, the Acting Secretary to the Millitary Board, for abandoning the embankments and render the more important interests on the side viz., *the town of Burdwan, the Grand Trunk Road and the East Indian Railway safe from floods.*"

I have mentioned already that the right embankment was abandoned in the year 1855-56 and from that time the left embankment was made higher, continuous and watertight and the overflow flood irrigation on the north side of the Damodar was completely stopped and the right side was burdened with heavy pressure of floods devastating the southern side which at present is increasing each year. The left side of the Damodar has deteriorated to an abnormal state by the higher watertight continuous embankments ; the pools, dykes and tanks of this side are not fed with flood water and the streams and the small rivers of this side became stagnant and offensive pools, much choked with rank and decomposing vegetation and other organic matter, and highly insalubrious ; the silt has been prevented from spreading over the surrounding country and the natural drainage has been interfered with whereby the fertility on the one hand is lowered and the incidence of disease raised to a serious extent ; and the subsoil water to a greater depth ; the effect was that the productivity of the soil was decreasing year by year and this I will establish by the out-turn of crops from the year 1788-89 to the present day.

### Out-turn in 1788-89

In 1788-89 'the valued medium rent of all the lands of Burdwan was estimated at 2 rupees per bigha,'[1] 'at the established rate of the rebba or $\frac{1}{4}$ of the yearly gross produce.'[2] On the 18th of April 1788, the Collector of Burdwan reported that 'rice sold at Burdwan at 25-28 pucca seers a rupee, at Mandalkote at 20-24 pucca seers, and Sheogarh at 25 pucca seers.'[3] It means near about average pucca one maund ten seers of paddy per rupee. The inference deduced is that in 1788-89 the average gross out-turn of paddy in the Burdwan district was in the vicinity of 30 maunds average per acre.

1. Fifth Report, vol. II, p. 416.
2. Ibid., p. 272.
3. Burdwan D.G., p. 110.

### Out-turn in 1869

During the Damodar Canal project of the last century there were enquiries to find out the actual out-turn of crops in the Burdwan District. At last at the instance of the Government of India W. E. Ward Esqr., Offg. Collector of Burdwan, made a thorough enquiry from the ryots, talukdars, zemindars, etc. very minutely. I insert here the statements of his findings which was sent to the Commissioner of the Burdwan Division on *26th December 1869* and subsequently which was transmitted to the Lieutenant Governor

The bracketed portion inserted after the memorandum was submitted.

of Bengal, which finally was submitted to the India Government. I note here that the statement set forth below was never disputed by the India Government or the Bengal Government. (On further careful scrutiny I find that it was accepted by the India Government.)*

### Extract from the enquiry report of the Collector of Burdwan in the year 1869

### Statement of crops grown in the Burdwan District

| Name of crops sown | Date of sowing | Date of Cutting | Estimated profit per bigha |
|---|---|---|---|
| Amun or hoy-montic paddy | In Ashar, if there be rain i.e. about 15th June | In Aughran-Pous, from 15th Nov. to 15th Dec. | Rs. 16-8-0* |

*This crop, of course, requires much water, the more the better, although according to the best authorities, the water should not cover more than three-fourths of the stalk. Amun is sown on Sali lands only ; never on Sona. The profits shown in column 4 are on a bigha of average 1st class Sali lands, and have been calculated as follows.

|  | Rs. | A. | P. |
|---|---|---|---|
| Gross produce of paddy *per bigha 15 mds.* @ 1¼ mds. per rupee      ...  ...  ... | 10 | 0 | 0 |
| Ditto of straw, 15 pons, @ 6 pons the                    rupee | 2 | 8 | 0 |
|  | 12 | 8 | 0 |
| Deduct cost of cultivation and reaping and storing      ...      ... 3/- | | | |
| Rent      ...      ...      ... 3/- | 6 | 0 | 0 |
| Net profit | 6 | 8 | 0* |

The profit derived from this crop, as grown on *Sali 3rd*

*class*, of which the greater portion of this district is composed, may be cultivated as follows :

. Gross produce per bigha, 8 mds. @ .

| | | |
|---|---|---|
| 1½ mds. the rupee ... ... ... | 5 5 0 | |
| Ditto of straw 8 pons @ 6 pons the rupee | 1 5 0 | |
| | 6 10 0 | |

Rs. A. P.

Vide Selections
from the Re-
cords of the Ben-
gal Govt. No. I,
pp. 300 to 310.

| | Rs. | A. | P. |
|---|---|---|---|
| Deduct Rent ... ... | 1 | 4 | 0 |
| Labour if em-
ployed in cultiva-
tion and storing ... | 2 | 8 | 0 |
| ... ... | 3 | 12 | 0 |
| Net profit ... | 2 | 14 | 0 |

*Ryots who water their own lands and cut out their own crops and do not employ labour for that purpose will reap a greater profit.

See Commissioner of Burdwan's No. 13 dated 25th June 1870 (General No. 1675).

### Out-turn of winter rice (unhusked) per acre in pounds from 1917-18 to 1926-27 average

### DISTRICT BURDWAN

| Year | lbs. | Year | lbs. |
|---|---|---|---|
| 1917-18 | 2093 | 1922-23 | 1916 |
| 1918-19 | 1609 | 1923-24 | 1572 |
| 1919-20 | 1958 | 1924-25 | 2278 |
| 1920-21 | 1779 | 1925-26 | 1516 |
| 1921-22 | 2212 | 1926-27 | 2302 |

Total of 10 years from 1917-18 to 1926-27 is 19235 lbs. i.e. the average out-turn per acre is 1923½ lbs. ; taking 82⅖ lbs. equal to 1 maund we get 23⅓ maunds per acre. (Vide Report on the crop-cutting experiments during the quinquennium from 1917-18 to 1921-22 and report on the same for the years 1922-23 to 1926-27. Both submitted by the Director of Agriculture published from the Bengal Secretariate Book Depot.)

The average out-turn of winter rice in India as we find from the Imperial Gazetteer of India vol. III  published in 1907 is 2400 lbs. i.e. 29 maunds per acre.

At the same time from the Provincial  Gazetteers of India, Bengal, volume I, we find, "the yield per acre of cleaned rice is estimated at 11·02 cwt. for winter rice in the rich  rice swamps of East Bengal  the result is at least half as much again.  Un-husked rice yield about three-fifth of its weight as cleaned rice." So in Bengal the average yield per  acre at that time was 25 maunds of paddy.

Besides out-turn let me show other effects ; for this I quote a few extracts from the report of the Council of the Indian  Institute  of Economics for 1932-33.  The Hon'ble Mr. Naliniranjan Sarkar, Minister of Finance, was  the President of  the above Institute when the report was published.  "The detour of the Damodar towards the west in 1770 and the interference of natu-ral drainage by  Railway and river embankments have brought about widespread waterlogging and the greater part of Burdwan and Hooghly districts is characterized by overgrown vegetation burying the homesteads of the decadent  population.  In many areas of *Burdwan, Nadia, Jessore and Murshidabad*,  again, the subsoil water  level has fallen, causing a marked reduction of the aman area.  The high land becomes too dry to be valu-able, while there are wide marshes at low  levels which  do not drain and in which water lies all year round.  Generally speak-ing, it is the combination of these two factors, the  high subsoil water and the jungly and moist conditions of the villages which so seriously increase the malaria rate.  A closed  river  with  its legacy of marshes, pools and depressions choked with weeds and the jungle with its moist nooks and corners which are inad-dequately exposed  to sunshine exhibit the optimum conditions for the breeding and multiplications of the anopheles.  When the rivers silt  up  and  no longer flow freely, the district is at once changed for the worse and presently is blacklisted with the most malarious in the  province.  Burdwan has suffered this degradation.  In all malaria-stricken tracts there are old water-courses which have silted up ; the natural drainage of the coun-try is disturbed, and the  whole place is waterlogged.

'Crops irrigated with the rich  red  water of the  flood have a vigour and stamina, enabling them to withstand the early failure of the monsoon which the anaemic crops deprived of the red water cannot possess. The anaemic plants and anaemic men and cattle go together.'*

Burdwan is a district showing a great shrinkage of cropped area. It was described as an exceedingly healthy tract, the 'garden of Bengal' at the time of the British conquest. Only 39·1 p.c. of the cultivable area is being cropped now, as compared with 54 p.c. in 1921 and more than 80 p.c. a few decades ago. Depopulation and physical breakdown due to malaria and decline of soil fertility have led to a shrinkage of cultivation in Burdwan and Hooghly unprecedented in agricultural history.

### Comparison of agriculture, health and population movement in Burdwan and Hooghly

|  | Cropped area at the end of the last century | Cropped area 1901-2 | Cropped area 1931-32 |
|---|---|---|---|
| Burdwan | 1248300 | 1128300 | 742100 |
| Hooghly | 541400 | 491300 | 293900 |
|  | Percentage variation of cropped area | Incidence of Malaria 1930 | Percentage variation of population |
| Burdwan | -40 | 53.4 | 3.7 |
| Hooghly | -45 | 46.6 | 6.2 |

There is no equal in decrease of cropped area in any part of the world. It increased in Noakhali by 152 per cent, in Dacca 57 p.c., Bakarganj 21 p.c., Mymensingh 19 p.c., Faridpur 13 p.c., and Tippera by 11 p.c. and decrease in Nadia 7 p.c., Murshidabad 14 p.c., Jessore 31 p.c., Burdwan 40 p.c. and 45 p.c. in Hooghly.

It is needless to comment on the above figures, but I shall ask you to compare a statement set forth below : Extract from the Budget Speech of Lord Curzon, Viceroy and Governor-General of India, on 27th March 1899. "We are all familiar with the aphorism about the service of the Statement who can make two blades of grass grow where only one grew before, and in India we do not need to be reminded of the direct and almost immediate benefit to the agrarian class that results from an increase in the area of cultivation." But in Burdwan and Hooghly i.e. the Damodar area, is not one or more blades of grass destroyed where it grew two ? I think nobody can dare to dispute this.

Again let us take into account the Agricultural Statistics for the year 1935-36 as prepared by the Director of Agriculture, Bengal.

|   |   | BURDWAN Acres | HOOGHLY Acres |
|---|---|---|---|
| 1. | Area according to professional survey (net area), also by village papers | 1,700,334 | 768,135 |
| 2. | Not available for cultivation | 441,779 | 276,390 |
| 3. | Culturable waste other than fallow | 242,408 | 75,340 |
| 4. | Current fallows | 552,647 | 193,405 |
| 5. | Net area sown during the year | 463,500 | 223,000 |
|   | Total | 1,700,334 | 768,135 |

Now let us see the economic condition of the people of the Burdwan district which I have collected from the Report of the Board of Economic Enquiry Committee which was published in the supplement to the Calcutta Gazette dated 24th January 1935.

According to the findings of the Board 23 p.c. of the agricultural families are not in debt at all. 43 p.c. are in debt less than two years income (Class A). Total debt Rs. 27 crores. 16 per cent in debt less than four years' income (Class B). Total debt 23 crores. Those whose principal debts exceeded the latter figure must be regarded as insolvent ( Class C ).

The total indebtedness is in the neighbourhood of Rs 97 crores. But it is the principal debt. Interest is not taken into account by the Board. Let us see the position of the district of Burdwan.

## District Burdwan

| Average earner | Average dependants | Average family size | Average land in acres |
|---|---|---|---|
| 1·80 + ·04 | 4·32 | 6·12 + ·11 | 6·06 + ·16 |

### 1928 Average ( in Rupees )

| Income | Expenditure | Surplus | Debt |
|---|---|---|---|
| 272 + 8 | 276 + 8 | —4 | 138 + 15 |

### 1933 Average ( in Rupees )

| Income | Expenditure | Surplus | Debt |
|---|---|---|---|
| 156 + 6 | 197 + 7 | —41 | 219 + 13 |

### Average p.c.

| No Debt | A. Class | B. Class | C. Class |
|---|---|---|---|
| 24·5 + 1·3 | 40·2 + 1·5 | 18·8 + 1·2 | 16·5 + 1·1 |

### 1933 Average Debt in each class (in Rupees)

| A. | B. | C. | A B C |
|---|---|---|---|
| 186 | 312 | 521 | 290 |

### Percentage Debt in each class

| A. | B. | C. |
|---|---|---|
| 34·1 | 26·7 | 39·2 |

### Families in thousands

| A. | B. | C. | Total | Total debt in lakhs |
|---|---|---|---|---|
| 47 | 22 | 20 | 89 | 2,57 |

So from 1928 to 1933 the surplus of Burdwan has become Rs. —41 in place of Rs.—4, and debt from 138 + 15 to 219 + 13 in the same period. No district throughout the whole province decreased its surplus in such a huge proportion within this short interval. Most prosperous throughout the whole of Hind-oostan indeed ! Ought not the name 'Vardhaman' ( vernacular of Burdwan, which means prosperous ) be replaced by Asta-man ( vernacular meaning vanishing ) ?

Now is there any doubt that works of POOLBUNDY was done in the opposite direction ? The Government failed to fulfil its obligation : now I will boldly assert that by the opening of the present Damodar Canal the Government has only fulfilled a part of that obligation which it owed to the tenants and zemindars, and for which the Government had all along been taking water tax for a few centuries from the tenants through the zemindars. So the present canal area is already taxed and it ought not to be taxed twice on the same article ; this will be double taxation and against the principles of public finance. Again let me take into consideration the Development Act and its applications in the present Damodar Canal area. We know the motive which prompted the Hon'ble Khwaja Nazimuddin the then Irrigation Minister to introduce the Development Bill which he thought was for the welfare of Bengal but at the same time I must confess that perhaps the department concerned specially the Department of the Director of Land Records did not bring to the notice of the Hon'ble Minister the old papers of this district and he had to rely merely on the reports of the Irrigation Department Committee of 1930, which did not consider at all the revenue administration of the province and neither took evidence on the point from experts and so was fallacious so far at least their recommendation as regards finance and taxation are concerned. There is also reason to believe that the Development Act was based on the 9th recommendation, Chapter V of the Indian Taxation Enquiry Committee 1924-25.

There the recommendation was for "a guarantee of supply newly given" ; but in the Damodar Canal Area the supply is not newly given. Moreover the Director of Land Records did not point out to the then Irrigation Minister the data of outturn in pre-canal days and the Hon'ble the then Irrigation Minister, nay, the whole House of the then Council were under the impression that no such data were available. I as a lay man have supplied you with some very convincing data of outturn from published Government Records. Had the then Director of Land Records been a little more responsible he could have furnished the then Irrigation Minister with many

more data and had it been so done I believe that the Hon'ble
Sir Khwaja Nazimuddin would not have thought of the application of the Development Act at Damodar and Eden Canal
areas.

In the Development Act it is nowhere stated from what
period the calculation is to be made in order to find out the
improvement, on the other hand from the instructions to
Kanungoes by the Government for carrying out the survey in
the Damodar Canal area for the preparation of a record with a
view to assessment of improvement levy it is laid down, "It
is therefore necessary to obtain from experienced cultivators
in villages opinion regarding the following points : ...(2) in
how many years out of *every ten* was it possible to grow paddy
on land of each sort etc." From this it is evident that that it
was the intention of the Government to take into account the
out-turn of old times as far as could be gathered in order to
ascertain the actual improvement. I have placed that of
1788-89, 1869 and of 1917 to 1927.

The Canal authorities have stated that the average out-turn
has become 23·65 maunds per acre by the Damodar Canal.
From the data I have submitted, if the Government now levy
any improvement tax it will be unfair, inequitable, and doing a
great injustice to the most agrarian class of my district.

In conclusion I again boldly assert that the 1st., 2nd., 5th.
and 7th. points raised by the canal area people are quite just,
proper and reasonable and based on established facts and that
the Government from this very day ought to suspend the realization of Development Tax. I also mention in this connection
that the points I have placed are admitted by Goverment. If
the Government wants to dispute any one of the points I place
myself to be cross-examined before this impartial committee, at
the same time I may be allowed to examine him who disputes
my statements. Let me further add that the people of Burdwan
fully realize the principle of Kautilya's Artha Sastra that "all
undertakings require money" but at the same time they know
that the capital invested on the present Damodar Canal area
has been wiped out from the account according to new financial adjustments. The people of Burdwan are in a position to

show whence money is to be found for all those works. If the Government does not care to take our advice we shall say as the last recourse that let the Government spend for Burdwan the amount which they derive from Burdwan. With the above recommendation I humbly submit this memorandum before this impartial Committee from whom Burdwan is anxiously waiting for getting justice.

**Kiron Chandra Dutta**

Bolgona Camp
District Burdwan
The 29th January, 1938.

APPENDIX   II

To
His Excellency the Right Hon'ble
SIR JOHN ANDERSON P.C., G.C.B., G.C.I.E.,
Governor of Bengal.

*The humble Memorial of the People of the*
*Trans-Damodar area for Relief measures.*

Most Respectfully Sheweth :

1. That before 1793 the River Damodar was deep and used to overflow both the banks in the high floods—the surplus water being promptly drained through the living channels on either side, after flushing the country and enriching the soil.

2. That subsequently two marginal embankments were constructed, one on each side, to restrict this beneficial overflow, with an eye to certain other interests and in 1840 the outlets for the bunds were also closed.

3. That these marginal bunds accelerated the silting up of the river bed, thus reducing the sectional area, by and by, and indirectly helped the death of the living overflow channels, thus thrown into disuse, and subsequently gagged by cross bund obstructions and shortsighted encroachments.

4. That the restricted sectional area being thus unable to cope with the discharge, there were several breaches every now and then and from 1858, the right embankment was left unrepaired, till eventually in 1882, this embankment down to Sonergeria was completely removed under Government orders.

5. That the inevitable effect of the abandonment of the right embankment, which was only partially done, was to force a very large fraction of the Damodar flood through the gap thus created, with the result that the natural spill channels on the right bank became overburdened and rapidly scoured and deepened in section, also the natural bank of the river hitherto covered by embankment was left at the mercy of the flood current which created uncontrolled furrows and spill channels and undesirable places.

6. That the excess flood began in consequence to force new openings on the unprotected right side, in front of prosperous villages situated at about......* level than the natural bank itself.

7. That the most dangerous of these openings was the one opposite Kumirkola which devasted practically the whole of the Khandaghose Thana in......*

8. That the uncontrolled onrush of the flood spills began to create disasters to crops, villages and homesteads in Thanas Raina, Khandaghose and other areas situate on the right bank and necessitated the erection of ring bunds on the river side of those villages, of which the one in front of Kumirkola breach was constructed by Government at a cost of nearly Rs. 18,000/-, as a result of representations of the public.

9. That the disastrous floods of 1913 caused great havoc and the Kumirkola bund was completely washed away with ruinous consequences. Later on, a representative deputation led by the Maharajadhiraja Bahadur of Burdwan waited on His Excellency the Earl of Ronaldshay, the then Governor of Bengal, and His Excellency was graciously pleased to visit the affected areas in order to obtain a first-hand knowledge of the situation brought about by the floods with a view to taking suitable steps to stop recurrence of such devastations in future.

* not decipherable.—B.B.

Unfortunately no attempt was made to revive or maintain the Kumirkola bund and the actions taken by Government have not in any way mitigated the ravages of the floods.

10. That the trans-Damodar people are thus allowed to be ruined year after year and their humble representations have unfortunately failed to attract the sympathy of the benign Government up-to-date.

11. That the abnormal flood of the current year, exceeding all previous records in that area, forced several new openings in the right bank, even above the Kumirkola Breach—the foremost of the new openings being the one at Bibirbagan, about 2 miles west of Khandaghose.

12. That though the highest flood level of the current year in Khandaghose was over 3′ higher than that of the Great Flood of 1913—the water level being 9′ above the Thana and the Inspection Bungalow compound, the level in Burdwan side was lower by about 1′-6″ than that of 1913.

13. That the area inundated was over 300 sq. miles, as shown in light blue in the annexed map covering about 500 villages and rendering over 21,000 people homeless and though the casualty was not very high owing to the flood having reached most of the places in the date time, the death of cattle was about 600 and the total estimated loss about 20 lakhs.

14. That about 6 sq. miles yet remain waterlogged owing to the absence of any outlet thus helping the spread of malaria, cattle disease and other epidemics and rendering some rich fields unfit for cultivation, besides making all communications almost impossible.

15. That it is believed that the volume of water brought down the Damodar river during the flood of August last was not less than that of the 1913 flood and the permanent obstruction, created by the Anderson Weir, has by raising the flood levels above the weir forced a very large volume of water over the right bank through the Bodai Nullah and this volume, considerably reinforced by the spills entering through the new breaches at Bibirbagan and Bhasnan, is the root cause of incalculable damage done to the right bank whose fall across country from the river is nothing less than 2′ per mile and the steep

gradient is capable of general terrific current over the area and in channels and hollows between high lands.

16.  That villages Bhasnan and Bibirbagan being situated at the right of the river, the unrepaired breaches in the right bank at those villages were exposed to the direct onrush of the Damodar current and two deep channels 100′ wide and 400′ wide have been formed for some length inland and those channels carried a terrific current with coarse sand to the areas in Khandaghose Thana.

17.  That the fall from Bibirbagan bank to the Debkhal feeding the Dwarkeswar river near Sahspur Railway station on the Bankura Damodar River Railway being over 2′ per mile as mentioned above, the water through the new breaches jumps down with a tremendous rush only to be obstructed by the B. D. R. Railway embankment having an opening not calculated for this extra water at all,—the result being that the villagers near the Railway line remains under about 20′ of water for days together.

18.  That were it not for the fact that about ¾th mile of the Railway embankment was washed away, the people would have been killed in numbers.

19.  That your Excellency's humble memorialists are fully conscious of the tremendous magnitude of the Damodar flood problem and the difficulty of devising and executing remedial measure for coping with the problem as a whole but believing that substantial protection to life and valuable property can be given effect to by the adoption of measures within the financial capacity of Government and that such measures will give results commensurate with the expenditure involved, they venture to make the following suggestions for sympathetic and kind consideration of Government.

20.  That in placing these suggestions your memorialists beg to submit that in carrying out the remedial measures the heavily taxed landholders and the poor agriculturists of this area who have been paying the rates and taxes under the Embankment and Irrigation Acts and who have now to pay further levies under the Bengal Development Act, and are not in a position to contribute any amount towards its costs be

spared from any fresh or additional imposition or contribution on this account under the Embankment or any other Act, and the cost of the schemes be entirely met out of the public revenue of this province.

## A. Control works—right bank

(a) That suitable bunds and control works be erected at the right flank of the Anderson Weir to prevent the spilling of hoarded water across the right bank through the Bodai Nullah.

(b) That strong cross bunds be thrown across the breaches or channels furrowed in the right bank between Bhasnan and Srikristopur,—such bunds being made up with clayed carth after removing deposited sand from the bed—and the crest of these bunds be placed at 2′ above the natural bank level.

(c) That the crest and slopes of the said bunds be revetted with bricks of laterite stone and few other earthen cross bunds be thrown across the eroded channels at distances 500′ to 1000′ up to natural country level.

(d) That any further breaches in the right bank may be treated in the above manner.

(e) That the crest level of the future right bank in the above-mentioned length be fixed parallel to the flood slope of August last.

(f) That the remnants of old ring bunds in front of villages be repaired at Government expense and maintained at a height of 3′ above the inundation level of last flood.

(g) That Government may direct the Civil officers to carry on extensive propaganda work among the villagers in the affected area to encourage the people to build their houses on artificially raised mounds like what is done in the area annually spillen by the rivers Dhaleswari and Padma in the district of Dacca.

(h) That a few big tanks with refuge mounds above flood level be constructed in the affected area.

(i) That the system of flood warnings now in practice be substantially improved to warn the people in the trans-Damodar area of the approach of a big flood.

(j) That the Sagrai Khal shown as J.K.L. in the map

annexed may be improved by the removal of obstructions and widening and deepening where necessary.

(k) That a new channel shown as E.O.J. in the map annexed be excavated along the comparatively higher grounds connecting the low-lying lands near Khandaghose, fed by the Kumirkola Breach, with the Sagrai Khal, so that the congestion of the Mulkati Khal may be reduced and the amount of absorption by the tanks may be increased, while affording facility of additional flushing.

(l) That a drainage channel shown as P. F. A. in the map annexed may be excavated along the low lands with a sluice gate at P. in order to drain out the waterlogged portion near Khandaghose after the flood season.

(m) That the lower reaches of the Mulkati Channel may be improved by cutting the channel M. N. near Boro shown as in the map annexed to help the discharge.

(n) That the lower and the Mohanpur channel shown as U. V. L. in the map annexed may be deepened to drain out the waterlogged portion.

### B. Control works – left bank

(o) That several paved escapes of weirs be constructed at Sonda, Raghabpur and Jujuty at places where there were bad breaches in the left embankment during the floods of 1913 and 1935 to allow escape of flood water at top of floods across country.

(p) That the openings in the E. I. R. main line between Burdwan and Talit stations be extensively increased to carry the spill water entering through the proposed escapes or weirs.

(q) That suitable and calculated openings be provided in the B. K. Railway near the crossing of Sabjola Khal with the railway at the spot where the line breached during the last flood.

(r) That all obstructions in the Banka Nullah be removed and the Nullah widened and deepned and flank bunds 500′ apart be thrown on either bank of the Nullah from Burdwan to Mirzapur the outfall of the Nullah into the river Hooghly.

(s) That suitable masonry regulators be constructed across

the Banka all along its length and a system of distributing channels be constructed to flush the areas along the Banka valley for improvement of sanitation and agriculture.

## C. Control works—left bank below Chanchal

(t) That in the scheme now under consideration of Government for flushing the area of Hooghly, Howrah and Burdwan districts between the Damodar and Hooghly the works may be designed in such a way as to leave room for future gradual widening of inlet sluices and the widening of distribution and drainage channels into the Hooghly.

And your Excellency's humble memorialists shall, as in duty bound ever pray.

We have the honour to be,<br>Sir,<br>Your most obedient memorialists,

APPENDIX III

*MEMORANDUM*

To

The Hon'ble Minister-in-Charge of
Communications and Works,
Government of Bengal.

Sir,

We the members of the Damodar Canal Deputation offer you our sincere thanks for the sympathy you have shown with the sufferings of the people of the canal area by accepting a non-official deputation representing the grievances of the of the aggrieved people and do hereby make the following submissions hoping that they will receive just and proper consideration from you, Sir, who has the honour to hold a high office as a constitutional representative of the people of Bengal.

1. The Damodar Canal complaints are genuine, they do

not proceed from self-interest and nor do they come from persons who want to have the benefit of the canal without paying for it. From the reports, personal observation and from our experience as actual cultivators we realize that there has been no perceptible increase in the yield of crops ; the assessees on account of cost of cultivation, no perceptible increase in the yield, and low price of paddy do not find themselves in a position to pay the tax charged.

2. "No large canal system works perfectly when it is first opened. In the Punjab it is accepted as an axiom that it takes five years to get a canal system into efficient working order." It is therefore highly unjust and unreasonable to realize regular tax during these five years of irregularity, imperfection and inefficiency. Owing to imperfections during the experimental stage numerous difficulties are felt some of which are :

(a) water cannot be supplied throughout the whole year.

(b) Cultivators are to depend on rain for growing of seedlings.

(c) Low lands become waterlogged and become full of *ganz* which affects the growth and produce.

(d) Manures are washed away by continual flow of water.

(e) Silt is received by negligible percentage of lands and some lands in some areas are injured by deposit of sands.

(f) Supply of water to the lands at the tail and makes the cultivation of the lands over which the water flows belated and sometimes necessitates retransplantation.

(g) Water cannot be supplied in such a way as to make simultaneous cultivation in all areas possible.

3. Insurance against drought will be the only benefit the canal will give when it will be in a position to supply adequate quantity of water whenever it will be needed. The Damodar Canal therefore is a protective and not a productive project.

4. The conclusion as to the estimated increase of out-turn, arrived at by the comparison of yields of pre-canal and post-canal period, is wrong and the data on which the calculation has been made are wholly inadequate, imaginary and unacceptable. Crop-cutting experiments were not fair and do not represent facts.

5. Classification of land is thoroughly inaccurate and mercilessly misleading.

6. From long before the British Government took charge of the administration of the area covered by and proposed to be covered by the extension of the Damodar Canal, it was satisfactorily provided with irrigation and drainage facilities and this was taken into consideration while fixing high rate of rent and revenue of this part of the province. These facilities justified the comparatively high and exorbitant rent and revenue. The Damodar Canal therefore begins merely to compensate the heavy burden and injustice which the district has so long shouldered.

7. That Rs. 3/8 in place of Rs. 5/8 is fixed for lands in Eden Canal area as maximum per acre if the Development Act is made applicable. Instead of applying the Development Act the Government realizes Rs. 4/8 per acre by agreement. In Damodar Canal area by agreement the Government used to realize Rs. 3/8 per acre for long leases and by applying the Development Act Rs. 5/8 per acre is being realized. The Government is applying the Development Act in Damodar Canal area and is going for agreement in the Eden Canal area —this is for securing maximum revenue.

8. Assessment of development levy to recoup the capital expenditure and to meet the cost of maintenance and establishment charges is not just and equitable and more so after the happy adjustment of assets and liabilities of the Province with the Central Government.

> In these circumstances your deputationists on behalf of the people affected by and likely to be affected by the extension of the Damodar Canal most respectfully demand :

1. That further extension of the canal be stopped till the canal gets into efficient working order and actual utility of the canal is ascertained.

2. Measures be taken to exempt the area proposed to be covered by the Damodar Canal from development levy on the ground of exorbitant rent and revenue fixed, from the beginning of the British regime.

3. That there be fresh classification of lands in the canal area by responsible revenue and canal officers and representatives of the people in the presence of the general public.

4. That there be fresh crop-cutting experiment by responsible revenue and canal officers and representatives of the people in the presence of the general public.

5. The realization of regular development tax be stopped till the Government be in a position to make all necessary improvments and to declare that the canal is in perfect working order.

6. That after enquiry made in the presence of the tax-payers a fair and equitable rate be fixed.

      In conclusion the members of the deputation once again offer their thanks to you, Sir, for your sympathetic attitude towards the sufferings of the people of the canal area.

We have the honour to be,

Sir,

## Appendix IV

(*Extracts from the Note of Dissent submitted by Maulavi Abul Hashem B.L., M.L.A., a member of the Damodar Canal Tax Enquiry Committee*)

Damodar Canal Tax is governed by the Bengal Development Act, 1935 (Bengal Act XVI of 1935).

In order to impose any tax under the said Act it is necessary that there should be an increased out-turn to the canal area as compared with the pre-canal outturn. The Government claim that there is a considerable increase while the people of the affected area and responsible persons entrusted in the welfare of the Burdwan and Bengal peasants contend that there should be no improvement levy. Their reasons are two fold :

(a) That there has been no increase in out-turn ;

(b) That there can be no taxation even if there is increase in out-turn as any taxation will be double taxation and against the principle of public finance.

The evidence brought before us during our enquiry regarding the Damodar Canal Tax may be summed up in the following four categories : (i) Evidence submitted by the Revenue Department ; (ii) Evidence adduced by the Memorial read by the Burdwan District Congress President at Khana ; (iii) some statements before the Committee by some individuals ; (vi) And lastly the Memorandum submitted by Kiron Chandra Dutt of Burdwan on the 29th of January at Bolgona. Let me record what they contain.

(i) The Revenue Department by their figures prepared from a large number of documents and result of their crop-cutting experience has tried to show that by the Damodar Canal there has been some increased out-turn and only on that basis they want to levy improvement tax under the Development Act.

(ii) The Memorial read by the Burdwan District Congress President wants to say that there should be reduction of improvement tax and in certain cases total remission.

(iii) Statements of individuals only show that the people of the affected area want reduction on the ground of hardship.

(iv) At the last stage of our enquiry we are faced with a Memorandum submitted by Sj. Kiron Chandra Dutt of Burdwan, which has laid an almost new and surprising case before us. In a work he has tried to establish two grounds for no taxation at all ; first that the Damodar Canal area people already pay tax for irrigation facilities for a few centuries and it was the obligation of the Government to maintain them and though the Government far from maintaining them worked in the opposite direction and by the overt act of the Government the irrigation facilities were tampered with and the Government was bound to compensate the people and by the new Damodar Canal the Government has fulfilled a part of that obligation which it owed to the people of Burdwan, Hooghly and Howrah and so any new taxation to the extent of a pie even would be double taxation and against the principles of public finance. All these Kiron Babu has shown by Government Records, Regulations, etc.. Secondly, to show that there has been no increased out-turn he has inserted in his Memorandum data of out-turn for the years 1788-89, 1869 and those for the years 1917-18 to 1926-27, and these he has shown from accepted Government records only.  From those data he has tried to show that there has not been any increased out-turn at all whereby there can be justification for any tax whatsoever under the Bengal Development Act.  Besides these, Kiron Babu has given the shrinkage of cropped area in Burdwan and Hooghly districts and also the economic condition of the people of Burdwan to show that the area of cropped areas decreased in Burdwan district from 1,248,300 acres in the last century to 463,500 acres in the year 1935-36 and an average cultivator family of Burdwan had to borrow Rs. 4/- to maintain his family in 1928 and in the year 1933 the same family had to borrow Rs. 41/- to maintain itself.  Kiron Babu has also stated that there is no equal in the whole province which decreased its cropped area in such a proportion and has stated that within the year 1931-32 the cropped area *increased* in Noakhali by 152 p.c., in Dacca 57 p.c., in Bakergunge 21 p.c., Mymensingh 19 p.c., Faridpur 13 p.c. and Trippera by 11 p.c. and *decreased* in Nadia by 7 p.c., Murshidabad 14 p.c., Jessore 13 p.c., Burdwan 40 p.c. and 45 p.c. in Hooghly.

He has also stated that no district throughout the whole province lost its surplus in such a huge proportion as Burdwan. He has stated also the abnormally highest revenue of Burdwan in comparison with the whole province.

In conclusion whatever he has said he has quoted from Government documents save and except one which he has quoted from the Report of the Indian Institute of Economics for the year 1932-33 of which the Hon'ble Finance Minister, one of the members of this Committee, was the President. I think Kiron Babu has quoted it with a motive.  Besides he has raised other points which will be taken into serious consideration when the Permanent Settlement Commission sits.

2.   Those are the evidences placed before us.  During our discussion in the Committee the issue raised by Sj. Kiron Babu regarding double taxation and compensation was seriously considered or disputed.

So I take it that the Government is not in a position to challenge the accuracy of the points raised in the memorandum,

3. Regarding increased out-turn there is a difference between figures presented by the Revenue Department and those recorded in the memorial of the Burdwan Congress President and the figures that we get from these areas and documentary evidence of the individuals. There is no evidence before us whereby we can accept or reject any one of them.

4. The question of Burdwan's claim for being compensated on the ground of shrinkage of cropped area, increase of deficit in surplus of cultivators and highest revenue of Burdwan though requires the greatest consideration by the Bengal Government is not within the scope of this Enquiry Committee.

5. I have carefully considered the financial problem of the Government. The Hon'ble Finance Minister, a member of this Committee, with his surplus budget, aware of the greatest necessity for consideration regarding Burdwan, greater portion of Hooghly and certain parts of Howrah, would be able to make provision for maintenance of the Damodar Canal and I believe Honourable Members of both the Houses will not stand in our way.

6. Further I record that I cannot take advantage of the ignorance of the illiterate poor cultivators of the canal area who in their anxiety to get immediate relief demand reduction instead of complete remission.

7. In consideration of all the facts and circumstances and also the equity of the case I record this dissentient note that there should not be any tax at all for the Damodar Canal area under the Bengal Development Act of 1935. And I am not aware of any other provision of the existing laws under which any tax can be imposed.

CHAPTER XI

## CHARMANAIR SATYAGRAHA

### I

A DACOITY COMMITTED in 1923 at Charmanair—a small village
in the district of Faridpur—created a tremendous sensation all
over Bengal. It was not only the horrible nature of the event
itself but the sequel thereto that extremely embarrassed the
British Government and administration, from the district level
to the provincial.

### II

Charmanair is a small village about 20 miles from the headquarters of the district of Faridpur. This village was at that
time inhabited mainly by Muslims and *Namasudras*. There was
hardly any educated man in the village and the economic condition of the villagers was distressing.

The story of the dacoity and events subsequent to it runs
like this : On the night of 16 May 1923 a dacoity was commi-
ted in the house of one Abu Mollah of Charmanair which was
within the jurisdiction of Sadarpur P.S. in Faridpur. Sub-
Inspector Badaruddin of the neighbouring police station at Sibchar had received previous information of an impending dacoity
and, accompanied by a Sub-Inspector and some constables
armed with guns, proceeded to Charmanair and arrived there
when the dacoity was actually being committed. He succeeded
in arresting some of the dacoits. It was reported that at first
the villagers did not care to come to the place of occurrence.
Subsequently, when the police asked their help a large number
of them came there and mistaking the police constables to be
dacoits assaulted one of them and kept some other constables
confined in the house where the dacoity was committed. Next
morning (i.e. on 17 May) Sub-Inspector Rasiuddin of Sadarpur
P.S. got information of the assault and confinement of the
police and also of the dacoity. He sent Sub-Inspector Kalipada

Chatterjee to the place of occurrence and himself started a few hours later. Mr Chatterjee got Sub-Inspector Badaruddin and his constables released. Sub-Inspector Rasiuddin reached there at about 3 p.m. and made some inquiries that day and also on the following day which was the Id day. He searched about twenty houses and at night on the same day Manilal Ghose, Deputy Magistrate, and Maulavi A. Quadery, Deputy Superintendent of Police, reached the place. The police investigation went on till 27 May, when Mr Stein, Superintendent of Police, arrived at Charmanair. He withdrew the entire police force leaving Rasiuddin and one constable there. On June 5 the SP visited Charmanair again with a strong posse of policemen A large number of houses were searched simultaneously by eleven batches of search parties. The police arrested thirty-one persons and attached some properties of absconders.[1]

After this incident allegations were made by several persons against the police to the effect that they had subjected the villagers to terrible harassment during the house-to-house search. Even murder of one villager and violation of a number of women were alleged against them. So widespread was the panic caused by the police atrocity that the village became emptied of menfolk who went into hiding or appeared before court and were remanded to *hajat*.[2]

The news of the horrible event shocked the people and the whole of Faridpur seethed with anger.[3] The savage police atrocity was condemned in several public meetings at Sibchar, Madaripur and Boalmari. In all the meetings Dr P.C. Guha Roy and other speakers narrated in detail what actually happened at Charmanair during the police searches. They alleged that : (1) sixty-three women had been raped ; (2) one pregnant woman had been so seriously injured that she was unable to move ; (3) the nipple of the breast of a woman had been bitten off ; (4) one Gaizuddin had been severely beaten and had died as a result ; (5) the wife and brother of Gaizuddin who left for Faridpur to make a complaint had been turned back by the police of Sadarpur P.S. ; (6) the wife and another relative of Gaizuddin had been forced to take his dead body to Guatala and bury it there.[4]

At the instance of Dr P.C. Guha Roy the Faridpur District Congress Committee took up the issue in right earnest. Dr Guha Roy and Subhendra Mohan Basu Majumdar were authorized by the DCC to inquire into the matter.[5] In course of their on-the-spot investigation they took photographs of the tortured women and the damaged and looted houses of the village.[6] However, the DCC enquiry committee withheld the publication of its report lest it should prejudice the impartial findings of the BPCC committee of enquiry on Charmanair affairs.[7] On being approached by Dr Guha Roy, C. R. Das asked him to arrange a meeting of the BPCC, and in that meeting it was decided to form a committee of enquiry to probe the case. The committee consisted of Sris Chandra Chattopadhyay (Dacca), Nagendra Nath Sen (Khulna), Basanta Majumdar (Comilla), Mrs Hemaprava Majumdar (Comilla), Satyen Mitra (Noakhali), Pir Badsha Mia (Faridpur) and some others with J.M. Sen Gupta and Dr Guha Roy as President and Secretary respectively.[8] However, Dr P.C. Guha Roy felt that his evidence might be called for by the provincial enquiry committee and resigned the office.[9] Nagendra Nath Sen replaced him as Secretary and Sarat Chandra Roy Chaudhuri and Jadunath Pal, President and Assistant Secretary of Faridpur DCC respectively, were included in the committee vice Dr Guha Roy resigned and Sris Chandra Chatterjee ill.[10] The PCC enquiry team consisting of J.M. Sen Gupta, Mrs Majumdar, Maulavi Samsuddin Ahmed and Nripendra Chandra Banerjee reached Faridpur on 14 June. After consultation with the local leaders and members of the bar and accompanied by many members of Faridpur DCC they reached Charmanair on the 15th.[11]

Before holding its inquiry the BPCC Enquiry Committee requested 'any person connected with the Government or the Police or the public to give information or evidence or examine or cross-examine the witnesses.'[12] In its report the committee classified all the allegations against the police under five heads : (i) murder, (ii) ravishment of women, (iii) molestation of women, (iv) beating, and finally, (v) looting of and damage to property. The committee found that one Gaizuddin was beaten to death and eleven women—eight Hindu and three Muslim—

were ravished and thirteen other women molested by the police.[13]

On behalf of the District Anjuman Islamia a deputation consisting of Maulavi Akchharuddin Ahmed, Maulavi Ibrahim and Maulavi Habibur Rahaman went to Charmanair to inquire into the matter.[14]

The following specific allegations were made to the Government : (1)  About one hundred fifty women had been molested or raped (the outrages were said to have taken place mainly on 18 May and 5 June) ; (2)  one woman had been raped eight times ; (3)  a girl had the nipple of her breast bitten off ; (4) a pregnant woman had her cheeks bitten ; (5) a man had been so tortured that he died.[15]

In the first instance two Deputy Magistrates were sent to Charmanair to inquire into the matter.  They began their work on 18 June 1923 and on the following day the District Magistrate reached Charmanair.  Over a period of three days the District Magistrate visited every house of the village to interrogate the villagers in regard to the matter.  Apart from the specific cases (stated above) the District Magistrate received a number of complaints of the following nature :

On being questioned if they had any complaints to make of oppression by the police, the women alleged that they had been abused and in some cases they had been held by the head or the arm when the police were inquiring the whereabouts of the male members of the house.[16]

But as regards the procedure of the District Magistrate's inquiry it was found that he did not know the Bengali language in which all of the villagers gave their evidence ; as a result he could not have understood their deposition.[17]  During his inquiry he advised the two Congress workers who were attending it to go to law.  However the Congress workers replied that as they had no faith in the British courts, they would not seek redress from them and that they would not even ask the villagers to have recourse to law. It was also alleged that the assurance given before inquiry by the District Magistrate that no police would be seen within four miles of the place of inquiry (presumably to enable the villagers to depose fearlessly) and that he would conduct investigation with the help of Congress workers, was not honoured. Moreover, during the inquiry the Government officials used scurrilous language while interrogating the villagers.[18]

### III

However, after the inquiry was over, the Government of Bengal issued a communique' on 2 July 1923 commenting a great deal on the affair. In the communique' the results of the investigations made by the District Magistrate and other two Deputy Magistrates were narrated. They were :

(1) *The grand-daughter-in-law of Rahimuddin.* The charge of rape on her by a constable who visited the house alone was dismissed as false.

(2) *The widow of Maniruddin.* The woman who lived by begging alleged that a constable came alone to her house on the morning of 18 May and raped her and her story was supported by her widowed sister-in-law, an elderly beggar woman who lived in the same house. She said that see would be unable to identify the man. It was held that no further investigation was possible and the evidence taken by itself was inconclusive.

(3) *An elderly beggar woman.* This woman stated that she was dragged into a jute field and raped by a constable. The Magistrate disbelieved the story on the ground that an examination of jute fields showed no trace of broken plants and that there were three houses on three sides of the spot about 60 yards from it and no evidence was forthcoming from them in support of the story.

(4) *The wife of Wahed Chaprasi.* Her husband was absconding and his house was searched on 5 June and his property was attached and taken to the zamindar's *cutchery*. She said that seven or eight constables came to the house and one took her into a hut and raped her. Her father's statements were contradictory. The villagers who signed the list of property attached as witnesses were examined by the Magistrate. They stated that they had gone there with the police and had left the place with them. They knew the wife of Wahed Chaprasi and denied that she had been in the house at the time of the search.

No previous complaints had been made and the woman said that she would not be able to recognize the man who raped her. The Magistrate disbelieved the story.

(5) *The wife of Pratap Chandra Sil.* This woman was referred to by Subhendra Mohan Basu[19] and Jatin Bhattacharyya[20] as having had the nipple of her breast bitten off. She stated that the police had come to her house on 5 June looking for her husband and asked where he was, that a constable caught her hand and she pulled it away and retired into her hut, that she was not otherwise touched and that no attempt was made to follow her or insult her. She denied having suffered any injury. Her husband corroborated her and an elderly woman who was a neighbour on examining her stated that her breasts were uninjured. The woman denied having made the charge before anyone, and stated that the volunteers had come to her house about 12 days before.

(6) *The daughter of Akram Mandal.* This girl was alleged by Subhendra Mohan Basu to be the girl whose cheeks had been bitten. At the time of the Magistrate's visit the girl was said to be at her house 15 miles away, and she did not appear. Her two brothers and sister who were of mature age informed the Magistrate that the police came to search for the men of the household who were arrested, and entered the house to search for others. The two sisters were held by the hand and interrogated but were not insulted. They denied that the girl had been manhandled or bitten on the cheek or that she had any mark on her cheek. The Magistrate rejected the story as unworthy of belief.

(7) *The daughters-in-law of Ramkanta Mal.* Subhendra Mohan Basu alleged that these were the women of whom photographs had been taken, but no reason was given why their photographs were taken. The Magistrate examined them and their mother-in-law. They denied the allegations of rape, but stated that the police came to their house to look for the absconding male members of their family and that while they were being questioned about the absent men the police had prodded them with the butts of their rifles. They denied having any marks of injury. Ramkanta Mal was present. He wept and showed

20

varicose vein on his leg which he alleged was a swelling due to a blow from the police. On being told that it was a varicose vein, he ceased weeping.

(8) *Alleged damage to the house of Afazuddin.* Subhendra Mohan Basu said that this house had been photographed to show the wanton damage done by the police. The Magistrate reported that when the house was searched false coins and implements for coining were discovered and a case had been instituted regarding that matter. The mat walls on the front of the houses had been removed and the interior of the hut was exposed at the time of the Magistrate's visit. The formal witnesses to the search and another man who was present denied that the police had removed the mat walls. They said that a portion of the matting at one end had been missing even before the date of search by the police. The mat walls were attached to the framework by strings and to remove or replace them was a simple operation.

(9) *Alleged damage to the house of Panchu Ram.* The Magistrate was informed that a photograph had been taken of this house. He found the two walls of a large corrugated iron hut detached and leaning against the plinth and framework of the building. They consisted of wooden frames fitted with panels of corrugated iron. Panchu Ram was absent when the police visited his house. He stated that when he had returned home he had found the walls intact and had removed them himself to make some repairs. He said that the volunteers had visited his mother. She and the formal witness to the search who were examined stated that the police had removed the walls.

(10) *The case of Gaijuddin.* Deceased Gaijuddin's home was at Guatala, 15 miles from Charmanair. The previous year he had come to live with his sister in a house in Charmanair about 100 yards from that of Abu Molla where the dacoity took place. He died on 20 May in that house in Charmanair and his relatives took his body to Guatala and buried it there. On 18 May he was seen by the Deputy Superintendent who spoke to him and noticed that he was suffering from a disease which was believed to be epilepsy. The Deputy Magistrate who was at Charmanair on 18 May also heard that he was lying ill

near the house of Abu Molla. But no complaint was made to either of them. This man's name was the only name mentioned to the District Magistrate before he left Faridpur. On 19 June the Magistrate met Subhendra Mohan Basu and Jatin Bhattacharyya coming away from the house where Gaijuddin had lived at Charmanair. The District Magistrate began his inquiry by examining Ayesha Bibi, sister of the deceased. She stated that on the morning of 18 May some constables met her brother and assaulted him and left him lying on the site of an old grave whence he was carried by his friends to the house of Abu Molla where he was seen by several police officers. He was then taken to the house at Charmanair where he died on 20 May. She stated that the police compelled the relatives to take the body to Guatala and bury it there. Sometime later it was decided that a complaint should be lodged at Faridpur and she, her brother Daliluddin and others went to get the assistance of zamindari manager at Baisheashi and from there they set out for Faridpur. On the way the police intercepted them and forced them to return home and consequently no complaint could be made in due course. She also stated that the Sibchar police entered into negotiation with Daliluddin through the village *matabbars* and offered him Rs 600 for keeping silent about these matters. On receipt of this statement the Magistrate had all available witnesses examined. It was found that the deceased had previously suffered from epilepsy and was seriously ill on 18 May. A Deputy Magistrate was despatched to Guatala to examine the deceased's widow and make further inquiries. The widow stated that Gaijuddin had been suffering for a year and had been under treatment for epilepsy, that he had died of natural causes and that she had been with him throughout. Four village *matabbars* of Guatala gave similar evidence and one of them stated that he had seen the body before burial and asseverated that he had not seen any marks of injury on it. They deposed that they had heard nothing about the deceased being beaten or about negotiation for the price of silence. With regard to the visit to Baisheashi a police officer of the Baisheashi patrol camp stated that he had met a party travelling by night and had questioned them.

One man was a *sardar* of the Baisheashi Estate and when asked
where he was going with two women, he had given unsatisfactory replies. He then took them to the *cutchery* of the zamindar
and being satisfied of their *bona fides* let them go and took
no further action. This officer was unaware of the allegation
of assault. The manager of the Baisheashi Estate said that
the relatives of Gaijuddin went to his officers and told them
that their brother had died as a result of beating, and he
told them to go to Faridpur to lodge a complaint in the
court. At that stage of inquiry one Guatala witness who
happened to be uncle to Daliluddin informed the Magistrate
that Daliluddin had admitted to him that the whole story was
a concoction and that he and his sister had been tutored to
make a false charge against the police and that Daliluddin
would make a statement to that effect. Daliluddin was sent
for, and on being warned by the Magistrate that he would not
be allowed to retract any statement that he might make, he
withdrew all his charges, and his sister also did the same thing.
They admitted that Gaijuddin had died of natural causes after
a year's illness and that the story of the police beating him was
false, and that the non-co-operators had tutored them to make
false charges and had promised to pay Daliluddin Rs 200. He
said that they had been called to Baisheashi by the manager
and asked to institute a case in court and had refused to do so
and returned home. He also stated that the volunteers had
visited him on several occasions and that Subhendra Mohan
Basu and Jatin Bhattacharyya had been tutoring him and his
sister to make false statements just before the Magistrate saw
them leaving his house on 19 June.[21]

It was claimed that all the cases were investigated by the
District Magistrate himself except the one in which it was
alleged that a woman had been raped eight times. It was con-
tended by the Government that the identity of the woman in
question could not be traced.[22]

Finally, in the communique' all concerned were warned
against any comments regarding the issue in view of the
possibility of judical proceedings.[23]

## IV

The communique' was, in fact, nothing but an official rejoinder to the findings of non-official inquiries. But it did not satisfy the people. Consequently in the Bengal Legislative Council the members of the Opposition voiced indignant feelings of the people.[24] Different members raised the issue and condemned the Government for handling the matter in a flagrantly light-hearted manner. Indu Bhusan Datta charged the Government with paying scant attention to such serious allegations made in the Charmanair case. "The deepest feelings of the people have been stirred, the most sacred sentiments of the whole nation have been wounded. Justice demands that the real truth must be known and the guilty suitably punished." And this could be done, according to Mr Datta, only by 'a mixed committee of officials and non-officials' and the 'sacred name of India's womanhood' demanded that.[25]

Dr J.N. Maitra said that the district of Faridpur had been convulsed by the Charmanair incident. "We are all familiar with the usual methods of police oppression in this country but they seldom attract notice unless the honour of women are trampled or the sanctity of the harem violated," asserted Dr Maitra. He also warned, "Seldom have the people of Bengal been stirred up to such depths of resentment and indignation and seldom have Government been faced with a similar situation which, like fire, if not properly and adequately handled at the earliest possible opportunity, will, I am afraid, roll in volumes from one corner of Bengal to another." Finally, Dr Maitra appealed to the members of the Council to stand by the people of Faridpur in their hour of distress.[26]

Dr P.N. Banerjee, another prominent Congress member of the Council, made a trenchant criticism of the Government communique' stating that its object was 'evidently to remove from the public mind all suspicion about the conduct of the police' in Charmanair. But "instead of achieving this object, the communique' has produced the very opposite effect on all fair-minded persons." Dr Banerjee said that the people had lost all confidence in Government officers and that it was no

wonder that they were being avoided instead of being approached.  He also insisted that the honour of beggar women was
as much valuable as that of rich women.  It was high time, he
said, that the entire system of police administration should be
thoroughly overhauled.  However, Dr Banerjee concluded, that
in the meantime they should not remain satisfied with a 'white-
washing' communique' and should demand a full inquiry into
the matter.[27]

The last important speaker was H. Suhrawardy. He said that
the Government perhaps regretted that the matter was not *sub
judice* precluding its discussion altogether. The tale unfolded was
a horrible one and the Government, if it was anxious to establish its credit with the people, should take early steps to avenge
in the name of humanity the cruelties to which the people
consigned to its care had been subjected by its agent.  The
Government should not extend official protection to the police
if they were guilty.  He requested the Government not to treat
the ferocious tiger like a pet lamb.  The people were watching
with anxiety the action that the Government proposed to take
in this connexion.[28]  Nityadhan Mukherjee, Ananda Charan
Datta, Maulavi Rahamatjan, Shah Syed Emdadul Haq, Ajay
Datta, Maulavi Emaduddin Ahmed, Hemendra Nath Chaudhuri and Kishori Mohan Chaudhuri while participating in the
debate severely criticised the Government.[29]

In reply Mr Birley, Chief Secretary to the Government of
Bengal, observed that all the allegations were merely the fabri-
cation of some interested persons.  He said that it was quite
clear that rumours had been started which nobody was willing
to support and he could not understand how they could question the action of the Magistrate.  He further said, "There is
one point that hardly any speaker has failed to mention, and
that is, why was it that when these events took place on the
18th May, the Magistrate did not inquire into the matter until
the 18th June, and the answer to this question is a very simple
one ; that he received no information until the 15th June and
that fact has been clearly stated in the Government *communique'*
and it is only begging the question to say that the Magistrate
wasted a month before going to inquire into these stories when

he himself has reported that the first information that he got of them was on the 15th June, and it is also clearly stated in the *communique'*, what he did on the 15th June when he heard the stories."[30]

Finally, Mr Stephenson, an official member, concluded that the Government was fully justified in saying that a full inquiry had been made and that no case had been made out for a further inquiry.[31]

Now it is clear, as a contemporary daily observed, that the speeches of the official members including the Chief Secretary to the Government of Bengal disclosed nothing beyond what had appeared in the communique' issued by the Government. The Government members could not convince the House ( as well as the people through it ) why the inhabitants of Charmanair deserted the village nor could they meet the serious allegations made against the police by several women.[32] The Indian Association also considered the official communique' as well as the Government defence of it in the Bengal Legislative Council on the alleged police outrages at Charmanair unsatisfactory and in view of the gravity of the allegations against the police the Association urged the appointment of an impartial committee having a majority of non-official members enjoying the confidence of the public to make a sifting inquiry into the matter.[33]

## V

Several public meetings were held in protest against the Government attitude among which two were particularly worthy of mention—one at Harish Park and the other at Mirzapur (now Shraddhananda) Park on 1 December 1923. The former was presided over by Hemaprava Majumdar and several distinguished persons like J.M. Sen Gupta, Basanta Kumar Majumdar, S.N. Haldar, Hemendranath Das Gupta and Dr P.C. Guha Roy were present in the meeting. The meeting at Mirzapur Park was presided over by Tulsidas Sen and was attended by Subhas Chandra Bose and others. In both the meetings the report of the BPCC Enquiry Committee was read.[34]

But the Government paid no heed to the public opinion, and with its customary cussedness it resorted to coercive measures

to suppress it.   And so, to start with, it accused Dr P.C. Guha
Roy, whom it considered a most dangerous person for having
publicized police terrorism in Charmanair all over Bengal, under
section 500 I.P.C. and arrested him on 13 July 1923.   He was
released on the same day on bail.[35]   It was decided that J.M.
Sen Gupta would defend his case.[36]   In this case, known as the
Charmanair Defamation case, Dr Guha Roy was sentenced to
simple imprisonment for one year.[37]

VI

In fact, the Charmanair Defamation case was instituted
against Dr P.C. Guha Roy by Rasiuddin Khan, Sub-Inspector
of Sadarpur P.S., under the instruction of Mr Stein, Superintendent of Police, Faridpur,[38] and three charges were brought
against him. These were : (1) that on 13 June at Sibchar Dr Guha
Roy said that not only the police, but also all officers ranging
from *daroga* and *chaukidar* to the District Magistrate and even
the British Government were like dogs and pigs ; (2) that on 12
June at Faridpur Dr Guha Roy had said that the Bengali constables who were like thieves had perpetrated this oppression ;
and (3) that on 19 June in his speech at Boalmari Dr Guha Roy
had complained that the constables had torn off the nipple of a
thirty-year old woman and also had bitten the cheek of an
eighteen-year old pregnant girl.[39]

Dr P.C. Guha Roy made a public statement refuting all the
charges and also justifying his going to law in spite of his being
a non-co-operator.   It is to be noted in this connexion that it
is a principle with a non-co-operator not to have recourse to
governmental machinery for redress of any grievance.   As it
was an important statement both in relation to the contemporary political situation and in relation to our study,
we are quoting, in an abridged from, the text of the said
statement.

"This defamation case ( Charmanair Defamation case ) has
been instituted against me for having disclosed the account of
oppression in Charmanair.   It is true I have spoken in detail
about the occurrence of Charmanair at Sibchar, Faridpur and
Boalmari and other places but the Government reporters, being

unable to follow my speeches, have filed a meaningless, incon-
gruous and strange report, after making omissions and filling
up with their own imaginary words in many places, by which
my speeches have not been faithfully reported.

"In my Sibchar speech I did not say 'not to speak of the
police only but the British Government themselves and the superior officers including from the Magistrate down to the Daroga
and Chowkidar were all beasts and pigs in their conduct.' The
reporter failing to understand my speech has falsely recorded it
in his own imaginary language. I have only justly criticised
the acts of Government in severe language and expressed my
remark about the beastly oppression done by the constables as
beastly acts.

"I have not made ( any ) general allegation about the police
force employed on duty at Charmanair ; I only said that the
Bengali constables oppressed in various ways.

"At the time of describing the oppression in my speeches at
Faridpur and Boalmari I said that among the constables some
tore off the breast of a woman and bit the cheek of a woman.
After careful investigation with due care from proper witnesses I
believed in good faith the same to be true and expressed the
same for the good of the public."

After narrating the activities of the different enquiry committees including the one led by him he criticised the findings of the
official enquiry. He continued, "For the purpose of an official
enquiry, making women naked, prodding them with gun ends,
dragging them by the hand, &c may be considered trivial ;[40]
but an illiterate and unlearned poor Indian as I am, I could not
pass over to ( sic ) such dishonour to the *kulabadhus* of my poor
country. It is the religious mission of my life to loudly protest
against oppression and injustice, and I have therefore severely
criticised this inhuman oppression.

"What I have said, grievously hurt in mind, being overpowered with unbearable pain caused by the dishonour and oppression, against the tyrannical police, was not to defame them,
but with a view to make my countrymen be on their guard, by
proclaiming to the world the facts of our own dishonour with
our faces besmeared with black, so that such unjust acts may

not be repeated by these public servants so devoid of any sense of public duty, and have given publicity to this story in order that the Government may be careful to take steps against such oppression."

Dr Guha Roy clarified his position regarding the legal defence resorted to by him, a non-co-operator that he was : "I am a non-co-operator—it is not my principle to defend myself in a case in court. But the only reason of my conducting this case is to preach the truth before the whole world. I have never said anything to defame anybody. I am averse to defame anybody or any community. I only seek redress for the pain of the insults inflicted on my mothers and sisters."[41]  In his interview the veteran leader told us that Deshabandhu Chitta Ranjan Das asked him to have recourse to legal defence, since his going to law would help in exposing the atrocious police action and from that point of view it would be justified.[42]

## VII

The case was first tried at the District Court, Faridpur. In this case evidence was given by the women (mentioned below) who were alleged to have been ravished or molested by the police ; they narrated their harrowing tales before the court.

[ (a) Saju Bibi (19), wife of Wachhel Sheikh (b) Ashtami Dasi (18), widowed daughter of Akrur Mandal (c) Fuljan Bibi (30), wife of Kalu Salaji (d) Baru Bibi (30) (e) Saju Bibi (30), wife of Faizuddi.]

In regard to the death of Gaijuddin his wife in course of her evidence narrated how the constables had beaten her husband to death and wanted to give her Rs 600 requesting her not to publicize the incident. All the witnesses also told the court that all of them narrated the same story before the District Magistrate and the Deputy Magistrate, Mr M. M. Ghosh, but both of them disbelieved their complaints and did not record them.[43]

The court found Dr P. C. Guha Roy guilty and sentenced him to one year's simple imprisonment.[44]  However, he was released on bail of Rs 500. An appeal was made to the District Judge's court against the order of imprisonment.[45]  The appeal

was partly allowed and the sentence was reduced to simple imprisonment for six months.[46]

An appeal was again made to the High Court. Deshabandhu
C. R. Das called upon his countrymen to donate generously to
meet the legal expenses.[47]  The appeal was admitted and the
case started on 20 January 1925.[48]  Meanwhile Dr P. C. Guha
Roy was again arrested under section 124A Cr. P. C. on 25
January 1925.[49]  However he was released on bail of Rs 2,000,
though in the first instance it was refused.[50]

The High Court delivered its judgment but the two Justices
—Mr Newbould and Mr B. B. Ghosh—were divided in their
opinion.[51]  Mr Justice Newbould opined that the first charge
had been established as it was clear from the evidence that the
imputation in the speech was made against the police force as a
whole and not against Bengali constables only.  In his opinion,
the conviction on the second charge could not be upheld.  On
the contrary, Mr Justice B. B. Ghosh remarked that the charges
failed on the ground that they referred to the personal conduct
only of a collection of persons as such.[52]  Consequently, the
case was sent up to the Chief Justice for reference to a third
Judge.[53]  Accordingly Mr Justice Buckland was selected to
hear the reference.[54]  In his judgment Mr Buckland opined
that the charges as framed against the accused (i.e., Dr P. C.
Guha Roy) did not conform to the requirements of Explanation 2 of section 500 I.P.C. under which the accused was
implicated. The defect seemed to have originated in the failure to
appreciate Explanation 2 of the above section and the principle
applicable when the words making the imputation appeared to
be general expressions.[55]  It might be that, observed Mr Buckland, the general nature of the imputations had led to the confusion in the charges.  The confusion of ideas which the charges
disclosed made it impossible for a proper trial to be held.  He
added that to give but one instance, the question of the rele-
vance of the evidence would be approached from a different
standpoint if the charges had been drawn up in accordance
with the principle applicable to the case.  Mr Buckland even
commented that there had been no trial at all of the petitioner
for having defamed the complainant and opined that there

should be a new trial upon charges properly drawn up and in that view of the case he expressed no opinion on the merits of the case even though it had been fully argued. In short, he set aside the conviction and sentence passed on the petitioner (i.e., Dr Guha Roy) and ordered retrial by the District Magistrate of Faridpur or by any Magistrate subordinate to him—but not by the SDO who tried the case previously.[56]

Ultimately when the retrial began on 16 May 1925, the Government withdrew the case as much time and money had been spent on this case[57] and it was not willing to go on with it any further. As a result Dr P. C. Guha Roy was acquitted.[58] But meanwhile between his conviction and his subsequent discharge on account of Mr Buckland's finding Dr Guha Roy had suffered imprisonment for a short time.[59]

Apart from the Defamation case, there were still two other cases over the dacoity committed at Charmanair, namely, (1) the Dacoity case and (2) the Police Assault case. In the former the defence was that the police force of Sibchar planned the dacoity with the help of a spy named Julmat Khan, a man belonging to a place bordering the district of Barisal. The defence of two out of a dozen prisoners under trial was that Sub-Inspector Badaruddin took them up in his boat on his way to Adiluddi Mollah's house on the pretext that he and his party were going somewhere to arrest some absconders, and that they were arrested when the dacoity was being committed. After a protracted trial the jury returned a verdict of not guilty in respect of all except the two mentioned above. They were sentenced to 10 years' rigorous imprisonment.[60]

In the second case, i.e., the Police Assault case, the defence was that on the day of dacoity the villagers pleaded that they mistook the police for dacoits as the latter had no uniforms on and their prompt appearance at the scene of action in the nick of time could hardly be expected at all when the dacoity was going on in full swing, and that they entered the house of Abu Mollah in large numbers and indiscriminately captured the persons engaged in the confused struggle, not excluding the police and kept them all under confinement. They further stated that Adiluddi then sent a wire to the District Magistrate and the

Superintendent of Police to the effect that the dacoits had been arrested and in the party there were police officers, and that an information to the same effect was sent to the Sadarpur P.S. The trying Magistrate, however, disbelieved this story. In a judgment which consisted of sixty-nine closely written pages he convicted one Rasik Lal Bhowmik and one Abdul Dafadar under sections 147, 323 and 350 I.P.C. and sentenced them to six months' rigorous imprisonment and a fine of Rs 200. Twenty-three others were sentenced to fines ranging between Rs 45 and Rs 75. Six men were acquitted.[61]

However, with the dismissal of the so-called Defamation case, the Charmanair affair came to an end.

## VIII

The story as outlined above shows Dr P. C. Guha Roy as the pre-eminent leader of the agitation. It was at his instance that the Congress (at the provincial as well as the district level) took up the issue. It was again due to his untiring zeal and indefatigable labour that the police atrocity at Charmanair became a live issue in Bengal politics, both inside and outside the Legislature. It was from a deep sense of urgency and individual commitment that he led, so to say, a crusade to expose the violation of the honour of Bengal's womanhood. It was because of his key role in the agitation that the Government considered him to be its chief opponent, arrested him and instituted the defamation case against him. To be brief : he pitted himself against the mighty Raj to assert the truth. From that point of view the conflict-situation at Charmanair falls under the first category of classification as mentioned above.[62]

Questions may be raised whether the Charmanair agitation can be regarded as a satyagraha. One may argue that the agitation did not follow the conventional forms of non-violent direct action, such as non-co-operation, civil disobedience, etc. Moreover, Dr Guha Roy's going to law in self-defence may be considered a gross violation of one of the fundamental rules to be observed by a satyagrahi, since he is supposed not to defend himself in any case nor to resort to the courts for resolving any conflict with the Government or any of its organs. This literalist interpretation, we are afraid, fails to take into account the special circumstances under which he, being advised by Deshabandhu, preferred to defend himself in a court of law. Dr Guha Roy's statement clarifying his position on this point may be recalled here.[63]

Despite all these so-called departures from the copy-book maxims of satyagraha, the movement remarkably succeeded in exposing the police atrocities in all their gruesomeness. Apart from that, Dr Guha Roy plunged himself into the movement from a deep sense of individual commitment. And who does not know that satyagraha is essentially 'an individual commitment'?[64] From that point of view also the agitation led by him rightly deserves the honour of being called a satyagraha.

## NOTES AND REFERENCES

1. *Amrita Bazar Patrika*, 21.1.25, 5(4). According to Dr Pratap Chandra Guha Roy, a gang of dacoits being instigated by the police raided the house of one Parbati Basu of Dattapara under Sibchar P.S. on the day of Charmanair incident. The police had two aims : first, if the dacoits could return without harm, they would have the share of the spoils, and secondly. if there was any trouble they would arrest the dacoits and thus would deserve the thanks of the people. But realizing that it was inconvenient to raid the house of Mr Basu, they directed the dacoits to raid the house of Abu Mollah of Charmanair under Sadarpur P.S. . They themselves followed the dacoits.—Interview with Dr P.C. Guha Roy, 3.9.71.

2. *Amrita Bazar Patrika*, 20.6.23, 4(2).

3. Interview with Dr P.C. Guha Roy. See also note no. 2.

4. Cited in the Government communique' issued on 2.7.23 : *Amrita Bazar Patrika*, 3.7.23, 4(6), 5(1-2) & 6(3).

5. *Amrita Bazar Patrika*, 9.6.23, 4(6) and 10.6.23, 4(4) ; *Ananda Bazar Patrika*, 9.6.23, 5(3).

6. *Ananda Bazar Patrika*, 15.6.23, 2(7) ; *Amrita Bazar Patrika*, 20.6.23, 4(2).

7. *Ananda Bazar Patrika*, 8.7.23, 3(4) ; *Amrita Bazar Patrika*, 8.7.23, 8(1).

8. Interview with Dr P.C. Guha Roy.

9. *Ananda Bazar Patrika*, 8.7.23, 3(4).

10-12. *Amrita Bazar Patrika*, 17.7.23, 5(4)

13. *Ananda Bazar Patrika*, 2.12.23.

14. ibid., 28.6.23., 2(7).

15 & 16. See note no. 4.

17. Report of the Secretary, Bhanga Congress Committee : *Ananda Bazar Patrika*, 28.6.23, 2(7).

18. Report of the Secretary, Madaripur Rashtriya Samiti : *Ananda Bazar Patrika*, 29.6.23, 3(2) ; *The Bengalee*, 1.7.23, 6(3).

19. Subhendra Mohan Basu ( Majumdar ) was Secretary, Madaripur Rashtriya Samiti.

20. Jatindra Nath Bhattacharyya was Secretary, Bhanga Congress Committee.

21-23. See note no. 4.

24. For a full account of the debate over the Charmanair case, see *Bengal Legislative Council Proceedings*, 1923, 2nd to 5th July, XII, especially the debate dated 4 July 1923, 133 and 152-176. For newspaper reports, see *Amrita Bazar Patrika*, 5.7.23, 4(5) & 5(3-6) ; 8.7.23, 5(5-6) ; 11.7.23, 4(4) & 5(3-4) ; *The Bengalee*, 5.7.23, 5(1) and *Ananda Bazar Patrika*, 5.7.23, 3(6) ; 6.7.23, 2(2).

25. *Bengal Legislative Council Proceedings*, 1923, XII, 156.

26. ibid., 156 and 158.

27. ibid., 163-5.

28. ibid., 170.

29. See note no. 24.

30. *Bengal Legislative Council Proceedings*, 1923, XII, 171-2.

31. ibid., 175.

32. *Amrita Bazar Patrika*, 5.7.23, 4 (5).

33. The *Bengalee*, 21.7.23, 4 (5).

34. See note no. 13.

35. *Amrita Bazar Patrika*, 15.7.23, 5(1).

36. *Ananda Bazar Patrika*, 15.7.23, 3(3).

37. *The Bengalee*, 23.7.24, 6(6).

38. *Amrita Bazar Patrika*, 31.1.24, 8 (6).

39. *Ananda Bazar Patrika*, 22.11.23 and 20.1.24.
Faridpur is the district town and Sibchar and Boalmari are the two neighbouring villages of Charmanair.

40. All these cases were characterized by Mr M.M. Ghosh, Deputy Magistrate, as trivial during his cross-examination in the court.

41. *Amrita Bazar Patrika*, 22.1.25, 6(1-2). For an almost similar statement made by Dr. Guha Roy before the lower court, see *Amrita Bazar Patrika*, 31.2.24, 8(1).

42. See note no. 8.

43. *Ananda Bazar Patrika*, Editorial, 24.7.24.

44. ibid., 22.7.24, 2(5).

45. ibid., 23.7.24, 2(6).

46. ibid., 1.10.24; *Amrita Bazar Patrika*, 26.9.24, 5(6).

47. *Atmasakti*, 6.8.24, 14(1).

48. *Amrita Bazar Patrika*, 21.1.25, 5(4).

49. *Ananda Bazar Patrika*, 27.1.25.

50. ibid., 28.1.25, 3(2).

51. *The Bengalee*, 13.2.25, 6(2) ; *Amrita Bazar Patrika*, 13.2.25.

52. *The Bengalee*, 20.3.25.

53. See note no. 51.

54. *Amrita Bazar Patrika*, 22.2.25, 6(6) ; *Ananda Bazar Patrika*, 22.2.25, 5(4).

55 & 56. *The Bengalee*, 24.3.25 ; *Ananda Bazar Patrika*, 25.3.25, 3(3) and *Amrita Bazar Patrika*, 24.3.25.

57. According to Dr P. C. Guha Roy, about Rs 75,000 were spent to preserve the prestige of an ordinary Sub-Inspector. See note no. 8.

58. *Ananda Bazar Patrika*, 19.5.25, 2(4).

59. See note no. 8.

60. *Amrita Bazar Patrika*, 26.2.24, 7(7).

61. ibid., 27.3.24, 4(3) and 6(7).

62. See p.1 above.

63. See note nos. 8 and 41.

64. D.K. Bedekar, *Towards Understanding Gandhi*, 120.

## CHAPTER XII

## CONCLUSION

A CLOSE ANALYSIS of the case studies made above enables us to arrive at certain broad conclusions :

Since issues differed from one case to another, the action-process of the movements varied.

Whatever be the variation or unevenness of development, a common thread runs through all these campaigns. The masses did not submit passively when faced with social and economic injustice, erosion of accepted norm and practice in religious shrines, and governmental repression. These satyagrahas, waged for the realization of local and specific demands, in most cases seemingly non-political, formed an integral part, directly or indirectly, of the anti-imperialist movement conducted on national scale.

These satyagrahas could operate in a regime which allowed some scope for expression of popular feeling. It is farthest from our intention to make out that the people of our country enjoyed democratic freedom under the British Raj. But however despotic it was, because of its constitutional commitment, it allowed a semblance of civil liberty in specious imitation of its democratic practice at home. The satyagrahis at least found it possible to reach the masses and could organize them for non-violent direct action.

These movements, because of the compulsion of objective social development, assumed multi-class character. Even when a satyagraha was launched against a zamindar (as in the case of Brikutsa), it was not organized on a class basis. The issue of class-polarization in a very rudimentary form came to the surface only during the last stage of the movement of the culti-vators of the Damodar Canal area. And this forging of class-consciousness was made possible, though to a limited extent, only by the persistent propaganda and organizational activities of the Communists and other left leaders and workers who were ideologically committed to intensifying class struggle.

21

The satyagrahis did not in all cases adhere to the basic tenets of satyagraha as enunciated by Gandhi. To put it precisely, they did not follow the rules of the game towards the opponents as Gandhi recommended (particularly in the case of Patuakhali). Nor even the leadership of these movements could educate the masses in the true satyagraha-spirit. But there are two distinct exceptions to this general pattern. (We refer to Arambagh and Mahishbathan.) At best it may be said that the satyagrahis in other places tried to keep within the bounds of non-violence and control every manifestation of violence. Satyagraha was not accepted as a matter of principle or a basic article of faith by many (perhaps most) of the satyagrahis ; the method of non-violence was adopted more as a matter of policy. The Communists' acceptance of satyagraha in the Damodar Canal movement confirms this. Satyagraha, in the words of John Lewis, a leading British Marxist theoretician, "becomes a politically realistic policy in a country like India, and wherever a mass of helpless people confront overwhelming power, or where a political minority has just grievances that the Government refuses to redress. It is a technique with immense advantages, and will be used by all sensible tacticians in those cases where violence is futile or likely to be too costly."[1]

The ideal integral relationship between satyagraha and constructive programme was found to be absent in most of the cases excepting the running of national schools here and there. It was only in Arambagh and Mahishbathan and to some extent in Brikutsa and Bandabila that the participants in the movement carried on their struggle simultaneously on two fronts – agitational campaign and constructive programme.

These local satyagrahas, from the point of view of people, were, so to say, rehearsals for bigger national movements. As has been seen above, Bandabila Satyagraha and Arambagh Settlement Boycott movement merged in the Civil Disobedience movement in 1930 and 1932 respectively. It may further be pointed out that these local campaigns provided opportunity to the Congress—even when the all-India or the provincial leadership of that body did not adequately respond to the needs of the struggle (one may here recall BPCC's role in Bandabila satyagraha) or were reluctant to support local actions (Congress leadership's attitude towards the Contai Union Board Boycott movement is a case in point)—to organize and rally the masses under its banner. Not only that. The hitherto inarticulate and disorganized masses on their part also could train themselves in the art of organization through these local struggles.

Finally, satyagraha as a method of conflict-resolution and a form of organized resistance served some positive function in all cases in the general context of our freedom movement. Ostensibly pacific, it was in essence a revolt against weakness. In all cases satyagraha was a fight against the age-old weaknesses of the people. It roused the masses from their torpor and made them conscious ; stirred them and steeled their will, made them fearless and threw them into unarmed but heroic battles. [2]

## REFERENCES

1. John Lewis, *The Case against Pacifism*, 112.

2. Buddhadeva Bhattacharyya, *Evolution of the Political Philosophy of Gandhi*, 346.

# GLOSSARY

| | |
|---|---|
| *abwab* | illegal exactions by landlords from tenants. |
| *amin* | land surveyor. |
| *anjali* | present held in cupped palms and offered to deities. |
| *Bande Mataram* | 'Hail to the Mother'; the first line of a song in Bankim Chandra Chatterjee's novel *Anandamath*, which was adopted in Bengal as the slogan of nationalism during the anti-partition agitation. |
| *bhadralok* | 'respectable people' in Bengal, generally belonging to the three highest Hindu castes. |
| *bhog* | food offered to a deity. |
| *brahmachari* | one practising abstinence from sexual or other-worldly pleasures and preparing to join order of hermits. |
| *brahmacharya* | mode of life marked by celibacy, self-discipline and abstinence and devotion to the study of Vedas and other scriptures. |
| *caranamrita* | water with which the feet of a deity has been washed. |
| *charkha* | spinning wheel. |
| *chatuspathi* | school for teaching Sanskrit, especially the four Vedas and grammar, poetry, laws and philosophy. |
| *chaukidar* | village watchman appointed under the Village Chaukidari Act of 1880, later under the Village Self-government Act, 1919. |
| *chaukidari* | tax levied on villagers for the *chaukidars* or village watchmen. |
| *chela* | disciple. |
| Cr.P.C. | Criminal Procedure Code. |

| | |
|---|---|
| *dafadar* | head of a batch of *chaukidars* or village watchmen under the Village Self-government Act, 1919. |
| *daftar* | official files or registers. |
| *dao* | heavy knife or chopper with a haft. |
| *darsan* | act of seeing or visiting (a deity) in order to pay adoration. |
| *dharmasala* | guest-house where pilgrims and travellers are accommodated temporarily free of cost. |
| *ejahar* | first information about a crime given to the police. |
| *fatwah* | ruling on a disputed point of Islamic law given by a *mufti* (jurisconsult). |
| *gaddi* | seat of a religious chief or an abbot of a monastery. |
| *garwan* | cartman. |
| *hajat* | police lock-up. |
| *harem* | women's part of Mohammedan dwelling-house ; (loosely used here to mean) the women's part of any dwelling-house. |
| *haridhvani* | loud utterance of the name of Lord Hari. |
| *hartal* | suspension of work or business to indicate mourning or protest, traditional form of strike in India. |
| *hat* | market, especially one held on fixed day or days of week. |
| *ijaradar* | lessee in respect of land, house, fishery or other property. |
| IPC | Indian Penal Code. |
| *istaphanama* | relinquishment or surrender ; writing by which surrender of tenancy is intimated to the landlord's office. |
| *jatha* | procession. |
| *jatra* | open-air opera or dramatic performance. |
| *khaddar, khadi* | cloth hand-woven from hand-spun thread. |
| *kanungo* | public surveyor ; settlement officer higher in rank than *amin* (q.v.). |

| | |
|---|---|
| *kapalik* | ascetic worshipping goddess Kali in accordance with the manner of worship laid down in the *Tantras,* i.e., religious books elaborating the system of worship of *Sakti,* the female principle taking part in the work of creation. |
| *kirtan* | singing the names of God, especially that by the different *Vaisnava* sects, i.e., worshippers of *Visnu.* |
| *khariz dakhal* | mutation of names in landlord's registers on transfer of tenancy. |
| *kisan (krishak)* | peasant. |
| *kukri* | short dagger or dirk, especially one used by the Nepalis. |
| *kulabadhu* | a married woman in a family. |
| *kutchery (cutchery)* | a zamindar's office. |
| *langarkhana* | place where cooked food is doled out in charity to needy persons during famine or scarcity. |
| *mahut* | driver of an elephant. |
| *matabbar* | headman. |
| *maulavi* | Muslim priest ; man learned in Muslim law and literature. |
| *mofussil* | localities away from great towns or cities ; rural localities as opposed to urban areas. |
| *mohunt* | head of a temple or monastery. |
| *mohuntship* | office of the *mohunt.* |
| *mukhia* | headman. |
| *muktear* | criminal lawyer of a junior order, not being a qualified Bachelor of Laws. |
| *Namasudra* | a community in Hindu society placed low in the social order. |
| *nazar* | present or extra-payment made to a dignitary or a superior at an interview, especially that offered to a landlord or a superior officer of his estate. |
| *paik* | guard or messenger armed with a staff or other weapons. |

| | |
|---|---|
| *pan (pon)* | a measure of counting (usually 80 pieces). |
| *panchayat* | originally a committee or council of five members, now a small local council ; a committee of three to five members in a village administering *chaukidari* affairs under the Chaukidari Act, 1880. Under the W.B. Panchayat Act of 1973, the Panchayat may consist of more than five members. |
| *pir* | Muslim saint or religious guide. |
| *praja* | tenant. |
| *pranami* | present or money given at the time of making obeisance to deity or religious preceptor. |
| *puja* | worship. |
| *Ras Mela* | fair to celebrate the festival of dancing of Krishna and Radha on the eve of full moon night of the month of Kartika (B.S.). |
| *ryot (raiyat, raiyot)* | peasant. |
| *sabha* | association. |
| *samiti* | association ; organization. |
| *sangathan* | a movement organized for promoting physical culture and removing social abuses during the early 1920s. |
| *sannyasi* | an ascetic mendicant. |
| *sardar* | chief or leader. |
| *sastras* | Hindu scriptures. |
| *seva* | worship. |
| *shariat* | the divinely revealed law of Islam. |
| *Sivaratri* | the night of *Sivachaturdasi*, the fourteenth lunar day in the month of Phalgoon (B.S.), a specially auspicious day for the worship of god Siva. |
| *suddhi* | 'purification' ; reconversion to Hinduism of those Hindus who have embraced other faiths. Swami Dayananda of Arya Samaj was the founder of this movement. |
| *swaraj* | self-rule;  independence. |

| *tahsildar* | officer in charge of a *tahsil,* or revenue subdivision of a district or a zamindary estate. |
| *tantric* | one who worships in accordance with the *tantras* or scriptures of the *Saktas* or worshippers of *Sakti* (q.v.). |
| *vaklatnama* | power of attorney. |
| zamindar | landholder, paying revenue direct to Government. |
| *zulum* | unlawful application of force. |

# ABOUT THE INTERVIEWEES

Short biographical notes given here are based on statements made by the interviewees excepting where sources have been indicated. In such cases they have been made up-to-date.

## CONTAI UNION BOARD BOYCOTT MOVEMENT

DAS, SUDHIR CHANDRA. Born in the subdivision of Contai; in his early youth joined Congress and participated in Quit India movement (1942); joined Praja Socialist Party and was elected to West Bengal Legislative Assembly; minister of the first United Front Government of West Bengal.

DAS, SURENDRA NATH. Born in Midnapore district; joined Contai movement; participated in all the Congress movements till 1942; a legal practitioner and one of the respected Congress veterans; author of *Gandhi Charitamrita*; now lives at Bhabani Chawk Bazar, P.O. Basudebpur, Dist. Midnapore.

GIRI, KANGAL CHANDRA. Born on 11 July 1895 in a village under Contai P.S.; passed Matriculation examination in 1916 and attended City College; gave up college education and returned to Contai; took active part in Union Board Boycott movement.

MAITY, NARENDRA NATH. Born 1902 in village Naskarpara in Midnapore district; one of the leading participants in Contai movement; suffered imprisonment on several occasions during the freedom movement; presently engaged in constructive work.

SASMAL, BIMALANANDA (Dr). Born 1926 in Midnapore district; son of Birendranath Sasmal; took active part in student organization and Congress movement; obtained the degree of D.Lit. (Paris); presently a Barrister in Calcutta High Court; also teaches at Calcutta University Law College; author of many books including *Swadhinatar Phanki* (in Bengali); edited *La Verite* for many years.

## BANDABILA UNION BOARD BOYCOTT MOVEMENT

BHATTACHARYYA, JIBANANDA. Born in January 1910 in village Ilna in Jessore district (now in Bangladesh); joined the district Congress volunteer organization in 1929; during Salt

Satyagraha of 1930 and Civil Disobedience movement of 1932 organized, as a close associate of Bijoy Chandra Roy, a powerful student movement in the district ; in 1942 organized and led a Congress Medical Mission to Indo-Burma front and also in 1946 to Malaya ; instrumental in deciding settlement of displaced persons in Andaman ; after independence worked as an adviser to rehabilitation department of Government of West Bengal for three years ; later absorbed in Government service and retired in 1969 ; now lives in Calcutta.

BHATTACHARYYA, MANOMOHAN. Born in January 1905 at Bandabila ; from his early youth engaged in village reconstruction activities ; became secretary of the local Congress Committee and also a prominent organizer of Bandabila movement ; later became president of the Union Board and retained the office even after the partition till the liberation movement in 1971 ; died in January 1974.

BISWAS, AMULYA KUMAR. Born 1301 B.S. into a zamindar family in village Kulberia in Jessore district ; passed I.A. examination ; at an early age became interested in freedom movement and joined Banadabila satyagraha ; was arrested on several occasions.

MUKHOPADHYAY, SUDHIR KUMAR. Born in Jessore ; one of the leading participants in Bandabila movement ; suffered six months' imprisonment ; joined second Civil Disobedience movement and courted arrest ; was detained again without trial in connexion with an attempt to assassinate a British police officer, Mr Tegart ; now lives in Calcutta.

ROY, BIJOY CHANDRA. Born in October 1897 at Bandabila ; as a good footballer joined Railway service but gave it up to look after his family property and lived permanently in his village after his father's death in 1923 at the instance of late Bijay Krishna Roy, a veteran revolutionary and the then secretary of Jessore District Congress Committee ; organized Bandabila movement and led the same in all its successive stages ; participated in all movements for the liberation of the country till 1942 movement ; now lives in Bangladesh.

ROY KRISHNA BENODE. Born 1903 in Jessore ; participated in Bandabila movement ; later became an important leader of

All-India Kisan Sabha and of Communist Party of India in undivided Bengal ; a leading Advocate of Calcutta High Court.

## TARAKESWAR SATYAGRAHA

CHAKRAVARTY, PANCHANAN.    Born  1900  at  Madaripur (Dist. Faridpur) ; in his early age drawn towards Congress movement ; joined C.R. Das and participated in Tarakeswar Satyagraha ;  a  prominent  organizer  of  Faridpur  Jugantar Group and  a  close collaborator of Purna Das, the well-known revolutionary leader; sided with Subhas Chandra Bose when the latter was expelled from  Congress ; joined Forward  Bloc ; spent more than ten years in jail ; now lives in Calcutta.
GUHA ROY, PRATAP CHANDRA (Dr). see p. 336 below.

## PATUAKHALI SATYAGRAHA

DE, MANMATHA NATH.    Born in Barisal (Bangladesh) ; a close associate of late Satindra Nath Sen and a  prominent Congress worker  in the district of  Barisal ; participated  in Patuakhali Satyagraha ;  presently a senior Advocate of Calcutta High Court.

## MUNSHIGANJ KALI TEMPLE SATYAGRAHA

BOSE, DAKSHINA RANJAN.    Born on 26 December 1912 in Bajrajogini (Dist.  Dacca) ; formerly news-editor of *Jugantar* and  Lecturer  in  the  Department  of  Journalism,  Calcutta University ; a litterateur of repute, author of about sixty books.
CHATTERJEE, BADAL.    Born 1906 in  village Panchan under Munshiganj subdivision (Dist.  Dacca) ;  a veteran freedom fighter ; suffered imprisonment on several occasions ;  was an active member of Jugantar party ; now lives in Calcutta.

## MAHISHBATHAN SALT SATYAGRAHA

DAS GUPTA, SATISH CHANDRA.    Born on 14 June 1880 in Kurigram (Dist. Rangpur, now in Bangladesh); one of the most renowned  leading  Gandhian  veterans  devoted  to constructive work ;   passed Entrance examination from Kurigram ;   college education in Calcutta ; joined Swadesi movement during college days ; later passed M.A. examination in Chemistry and then joined Bengal Chemical founded by Acharya P.C Ray as its superintendent ; inspired by Gandhian ideal left Bengal Chemical in 1923 and founded Khadi Pratisthan which was inaugurated by Gandhi at Sodepur in 1926 ; during Salt Satyagragha in 1930 was appointed first Dictator in Bengal and led Mahisbathan Salt Satyagraha and other satyagraha movements in different parts of Bengal ; sentenced to 2 years' r.i. for writing against the police firing on Hijli prisoners ; during Quit India movement in 1942 was detained for 2 years ; one of the leading members of the All-India Spinners' Association since its inception in 1924 ; Gandhi wanted some of his closest associates like Das Gupta to remain confined to constructive work ; after independence Das Gupta became one of the members of Khadi Board ; has been living for last few years at Gogra, 36 km. away from Bankura town, where he has been engaged in developing the perennial fallow land for intensive agricultural production ; translated many of Gandhi's writings into Bengali, namely, *An Autobiography*, *Hind Swaraj*, etc. ; author of many books relating to Gandhi, khadi and village industries ; 'one of the truest of men it has been my good fortune to meet' (Gandhi).

## BRIKUTSA TENANTS' SATYAGRAHA

BANDYOPADHYAY, PRABHAT MOHAN. Born 1904 at Chinsurah in Hooghly district ; educated at Visva-Bharati ; a student of Acharya Nanda Lal Bose ; first secretary of Karu Sangha, Santiniketan ; joined Civil Disobedience movement ( April 1930 ) ; participated in Mahishbathan Salt Satyagraha and led Brikutsa Tenants' Satyagraha in its last stage ; printer of *Satyagraha Sambad*, the illegal mimeogrophed organ of the Council of Civil Disobedience, Bengal ; poet and sculptor ; now lives at Sriniketan in Birbhum district.

LAHIRY, PRAVAS CHANDRA. Born on 2 November 1893 into a middle class Brahmin family in village Atkali in Rajsahi district (now in Bangladesh) ; had his early education at the middle English school of Arani, and then at Natore High School ;

matriculated in 1913, passed I.A. examination 1915 from Rajsahi College and took Honours in Philosophy at Metropolitan College, Calcutta ; joined Anusilan Samiti ; during the next four years organized party circles, distributed secret literature and plotted murder of police officials. This phase came to an end with his participation in Dharail Dacoity ; went underground ; in 1916-17 came to Calcutta and took charge of the North Bengal section of Anusilan Samiti ; travelled extensively in Bihar and finally made for Assam ; in 1918 in Gauhati caught in a fight with the police and sent to prison for three years ; on release joined Non-Co-operation movement in 1921 ; started working in Rajsahi but again was arrested and jailed for a year ; in 1922 became Secretary, Rajsahi District Congress Committee ; within the next two years again sentenced to four years' imprisonment ; on release in 1928 attended Calcutta session of Congress ; as a result of Chittagong Armoury Raid sentenced to six years' imprisonment but released within a year on account of the Gandhi-Irwin Pact ; again arrested in 1932 in connexion with Brikutsa tenants' movement, let out after a year but re-arrested at the jail gate and held as a security prisoner for five long years ; back again to work ; joined the Individual Civil Disobedience movement (1940) ; after release was put back into jail once again as a security prisoner to be released finally in 1946 ; in that year was elected to Bengal Legislative Assembly ; after partition remained in East Bengal and was elected to Pakistan Parliament ; in 1956 migrated to India ; publications include *Biplabi Jiban* ( an autobiography ) and *India Partitioned and Minorities in Pakistan* ; died on 2 January 1974.

(*Dictionary of National Biography*, vol. II)

SEN, MANAS GOBINDA. Born 1906 in village Kalia in Rajsahi district ; Secretary, Rajshahi District Congress Commitee ; leader of the second stage of Brikutsa Tenants' Satyagraha ; came over to West Bengal after partition ; Principal, Gram Sevak Training Centre (1953-66) ; Resident Secretary, Gandhi Smarak Samgrahalaya, Barrackpore (1968-74) ; now lives a a retired life in Calcutta.

## ARAMBAGH SETTLEMENT BOYCOTT MOVEMENT

SEN, PRAFULLA CHANDRA. Born 1897 ; started his education in Bihar and passed Entrance examination from Deoghar School ; had his college education in Scottish Church College, Calcutta and obtained B.Sc. degree of Calcutta University ; during student life was attracted by the nationalist movement and later drawn towards Gandhi and his principle of non-violence ; actively participated in nationalist movement since Non-Co-operation days ; was arrested in 1921, 1930, 1932, 1934 and 1942 and spent a total period of eleven years in jail ; in 1948 was appointed Food Minister in B.C. Roy's cabinet in West Bengal ; after Roy's death in July 1962 became Chief Minister of West Bengal and remained in office till the Congress debacle in the general election of 1967 ; returned to State Legislative Assembly in 1969 and re-elected to that body in 1971 and 1972 ; elected to Lok Sabha in 1977 ; Chairman, Janata Party, West Bengal.

*(Dictionary of National Biography,* vol. IV)

## DAMODAR CANAL TAX SATYAGRAHA

CHATTOPADHYAY, HELARAM. Originally an inhabitant of village Sonai in Burdwan district ; later settled at Ramnagar ; passed G.T. in 1928 ; a founder of Krishak Samiti in Burdwan ; joined Canal Tax movement and took active part ; died on 1 January 1974.

CHAUDHURI, DURGAPADA. Born 1895 at Giridi in Hazaribagh district (Bihar) ; passed B.A. examination in 1915 from Berhampore (District. Murshidabad) and B.L. examination in 1920 from Calcutta University ; joined Burdwan Bar in 1922 ; became President of Burdwan District Raiyats' Association which organized and led Damodar Canal Tax agitation in its early phase ; now lives a retired life at Burdwan.

DATTA, HEMANTA. Born in August 1899 into a peasant family in a village under Burdwan P.S. ; educated at Ripon College, Calcutta and obtained B.A. and law degrees ; joined Burdwan Bar in 1928 ; worked as assistant secretary of the Damodar Canal Levy Enquiry Committee appointed by the

District Congress Committee and organized the movement in its early stage.

DATTA, SIVA PRASAD. Born in June 1917 ; studied up to primary school standard ; was drawn to Krishak Samiti in 1930 by Helaram Chattopadhyay ; participated actively in Canal Tax movement ; now lives at Burdwan.

DATTA MAJUMDAR NIHARENDU, Born 1905 in village Paljanga in Mymensingh district (now in Bangaladsh) ; entered nationalist movement in Bengal during Non-Co-operation movement ; at 15 or 16 joined a small revolutionary group in Mymensingh ; was drawn towards Marxism when he went to London as a law student ; in 1927 or 1928 organized a small revolutionary group among Indian students in London and began a more serious study of Marxist literature, 'a full and active member of the Communist Party of Great Britain' (British Intelligence report) ; returned to India in August 1932 and "at once busied himself with 'rescue' work amongst those of his recruits who had fallen away since their return to India" ; worked not only in Bengal, but also toured the United Provinces, Delhi, the Punjab, and Bombay and sent an agent to Madras ; as general secretary of the Labour Party actively connected with many Trade Union organizations and also associated with Kisan Sabha ; elected a member of Bengal Legislative Assembly in 1937 ; a close associate of Subhas Chandra Bose and helped him in the work of consolidation of leftist groups ; detained for several years as a detenu ; on his release from jail joined Congress and became a minister ; presently connected with many social service organizations ; now a Barrister at Calcutta High Court.

(David M. Laushey, *Bengal Terrorism and Marxist Left*)

MANDAL, SANTOSH KUMAR. Born 1916 in Calcutta ; came to Burdwan in 1926 and attended Burdwan Municipal School and settled in 1935 in village Ramnagar ; later came into contact with Bankim Mukhopadhyay ; participated in Canal Tax Satyagraha and sentenced to 7 months' imprisonment in that connexion.

SHAHEDULLAH, SYED. Born on 24 March 1913 in Burdwan in a family connected with national movement from 1890s ; a member of the Congress from 1930 to 1935 and a member of

CPI from 1935 to 1964 ; the first Burdwan District Committee Secretary of CPI ; after the party split a member of CPI(M) and presently a member of its State Committee ; editor of *Nandan* (a Bengali cultural-political monthly organ of CPI(M) ) ; author of *Leninbadir Chokhe Gandhibad and Siksha o Sreni Samparka.*

## *CHARMANAIR SATYAGRAHA*

GUHA ROY, PRATAP CHANDRA (Dr). Born 1887 in Rajnagar ( Faridpur, Bangladesh); had his early education at Palong and then at Madaripur ; passed Entrance examination in 1905 and also Medical Faculty examination from National Medical College ; while student in Calcutta joined Jugantar group ; took an active part in Non-Co-operation movement and became an ardent supporter and follower of Deshabandhu Chitta Ranjan Das ; was one of the important leaders of Tarakeswar Satya- graha ; convicted in the Charmanair ( Madaripur ) defamation case, and acquitted in the re-trial ; participated in all political movements from 1921 to 1946 and convicted on several occasi- ons ; detained for about 12 years ; edited three dailies for some time : *The Nayak, The Marmabani* and *The Matribhoomi* ; elected to Bengal Legislative Assembly in 1946 as a Congress candidate and to Bengal Legislative Council in 1952 and conti- nued to be a member of the latter up to 1964 ; later became Chairman of the Council and held the same position till 1968 when it was abolished ; a very fluent and powerful speaker ; author of several books, namely, *Praja Sakti, Suruchir Bhagya, Pragati, Dashanan,* etc.

( Dictionary of National Biography, vol. II)

# BIBLIOGRAPHY

Only those works cited in the notes to the text are listed below.

## I  GOVERNMENT PUBLICATIONS

*Bengal Legislative Assembly Proceedings,* vols. LI, LIV.

*Bengal Legislative Council Proceedings,* vols. V, XII, XXVII, XXXIII.

*The Calcutta Gazette,* Government of Bengal, Legislative Department, 1935.

*Census 1961, West Bengal, District Census Handbook, Hooghly.*

Williams, Rushbrook L.F., *India in 1921-22,* Government Printing, India, Calcutta, 1922.

*India in 1924-25,* Government of India, Central Publication Branch, Calcutta, 1926.

*India in 1929-30,* Government of India, Central Publication Branch, Calcutta, 1931.

*India in 1930-31,* Government of India, Central Publication Branch, Calcutta, 1932.

*Report on the Administration of Bengal 1920-21,* The Bengal Secretariat Book Depot, Calcutta, 1922.

*Report on the Administration of Bengal 1924-25,* The Bengal Secretariat Book Depot, Calcutta, 1926.

*West Bengal Code,* vol. III (Bengal Acts 1890 to 1919), West Bengal Press, Alipore, 1964.

## II  NEWSPAPERS AND PERIODICALS

(A)  Dailies

*Advance,* Calcutta.

*Amrita Bazar Patrika,* Calcutta.

*Ananda Bazar Patrika* (in Bengali), Calcutta.

*The Bengalee,* Calcutta.

*Forward,* Calcutta.

*Hindusthan Standard,* Calcutta.

*Jugantar* (in Bengali), Calcutta.

*Liberty,* Calcutta.

*The Statesman,* Calcutta.

22

(*B*)   Periodicals

*Atmasakti* (in Bengali), Calcutta.
*Compass* (in Bengali), Calcutta.
*Congress Socialist* (organ of the Congress Socialist Party), Bombay.
*Desh* (in Bengali), Calcutta.
*Harijan*, Ahmedabad.
*Hijli Hitaishi* (in Bengali), Midnapore.
*La Verite'*, Calcutta.
*Medinipur Hitaishi* (in Bengali), Midnapore.
*Nabasakti* (in Bengali), Calcutta.
*Nihar* (in Bengali), Contai.
*Point of View*, New Delhi.
*Seminar*, New Delhi.
*Vardhaman Varta* (in Bengali), Burdwan.
*Young India*, Ahmedabad.

### III   MIMEOGRAPHED BULLETIN

*Satyagraha Sambad* (in Bengali), Calcutta.

### IV   UNPUBLISHED PAPER

Sarkar, Sumit : 'The Logic of Gandhian Nationalism : A Study of the Gandhi-Irwin Pact (March 1931)'. Paper read at Nehru Memorial Museum & Library, New Delhi, April 14, 1976.

### V   BOOKS & PAMPHLETS

Azad, Maulana Abul Kalam : *India Wins Freedom*, Orient Longman, Calcutta, 1959.

Balabushevich, V.V. & Dyakov, A.M. (ed.) : *A Contemporary History of India*, People's Publishing House, New Delhi, 1964.

Bamford, P.C. : *Histories of the Non-Co-operation and Khilafat Movements*, Deep Publications, Delhi, 1974.

Bandyopadhyay, Narendranath : *Tarakeswar Satyagraha Samgram* (in Bengali), Samar Lahiri, Calcutta, 1355 B.S..

Banerjea, Surendranath : *A Nation in Making*, Oxford University Press, Calcutta, 1963.

Banerjea, Surendranath : *Speeches of Surendranath Banerjea*, vol. I, Indian Association, Calcutta, 1970.

Banerjee, Pramathanath : *A Study of Indian Economics*, University of Calcutta, Calcutta, 1951.

Banerji, Nripendra Chandra : *At the Crossroads (1885-1946)*, Jijnasa, Calcutta, 1974.

Basu, Jogesh Chandra : *Medinipurer Pradhan Janhara* (in Bengali), Universal Publishers, Calcutta, n.d..

Basu, Sourendra Kumar : *Gandhipanthay Gramgathan* (in Bengali), I.A.P. Co., Ltd., Calcutta, 1948.

Bedekar, D.K. : *Towards Understanding Gandhi* (ed., Rajabhau Gawande), Popular Prakashan, Bombay, 1975.

Bhattacharyya, Buddhadeva : *Evolution of the Political Philosophy of Gandhi*, Calcutta Book House, Calcutta, 1969.

Bondurant, Joan V. : *Conquest of Violence : The Gandhian Philosophy of Conflict*, Oxford University Press, Bombay, Calcutta, etc., 1959.

Bose, Nirmal Kumar : *Lectures on Gandhism*, Navajivan Publishing House, Ahmedabad, 1971.

  — : *Studies in Gandhism*, Indian Associated Publishing Co. Ltd., Calcutta, 1947.

  — : *Studies in Gandhism*, Navajivan Publishing House, Ahmedabad, 1972.

Bose, Subhas Chandra : *The Indian Struggle 1920-1934*, Netaji Publishing Society, Thacker, Spink & Co. (1933) Ltd., Calcutta, 1948.

Broomfield, J.H. : *Elite Conflict in a Plural Society : Twentieth-Century Bengal*, Oxford University Press, Bombay, 1968.

Brown, Judith M. : *Gandhi's Rise to Power : Indian Politics 1915-1922*, Cambridge University Press, 1972.

Chatterji, Bhola : *Aspects of Bengal Politics in the Early Nineteen-Thirties*, The World Press Pvt. Ltd., Calcutta, 1969.

Choudhary, Sukhbir : *Indian People Fight for National Liberation (Non-Co-operation, Khilafat and Revivalist Movements) 1920-22*, Srijanee Prakashan, New Delhi, 1972.

Das, Narendranath : *History of Midnapur*, vol. II, Midnapur Samaskrita Parishad, Calcutta, 1961.

Das Gupta, Satish Chandra : *Khadi O Charkhar Katha* (in

Bengali), Gandhi Centenary Committee, West Bengal, Calcutta, 1969.

Datta, K.K. (ed.) : *Writings and Speeches of Mahatma Gandhi Relating to Bihar 1917-1947*, Government of Bihar, 1960.

Desai, A.R. : *Social Background of Indian Nationalism*, Popular Book Depot, Bombay, 1954.

Desai, Mahadev : *The Story of Bardoli*, Part I, Navajivan Press, Ahmedabad, 1929.

Dhanagre, D.N. : *Agrarian Movements and Gandhian Politics*, Agra University, 1975.

Diwakar, R.R. : *Saga of Satyagraha*, Gandhi Peace Foundation, New Delhi, Bharatiya Vidya Bhavan, Bombay, 1969.

   — : *Satyagraha : Its Technique and History*, Hind Kitabs, Bombay, 1946.

   — : *Satyagraha in Action : A Brief Outline of Gandhiji's Satyagraha Campaigns*, Signet Press, Calcutta, 1949.

Dutt, Rajani Palme : *India Today*, People's Publishing House, Bombay, 1949.

Gallagher, J.A., Johnson, G. & Seal, Anil (ed.) : *Locality, Province and Nation : Essays in Indian Politics : 1870 to 1940*, Cambridge University Press, 1973.

Gandhi, M.K. : *The Collected Works of Mahatma Gandhi*, vols. XIX (1966), XX (1966), XXII (1966), XXIII (1967), XXIV (1967), XXVII (1968), XXX (1968), XXXVI (1970), XLII (1970), XLIII (1971), LIII (1972), The Publications Division, Government of India.

   — : *Constructive Programme*, Navajivan Publishing House, Ahmedabad, 1946.

   — : *Satyagraha*, Navajivan Publishing House, Ahmedabad, 1958.

   — : *Young India 1919-1922*, S. Ganesan, Madras, 1922.

Ghoshal, Swarnakumar : *Tarakeswar Satyagraher Itihas* (in Bengali), Author, Calcutta, 1340 B.S..

Gordon, Leonard A. : *Bengal : The Nationalist Movement 1876-1940*, Manohar Book Service, Delhi, 1974.

Gregg, Richard : *The Power of Non-violence*, Navajivan Publishing House, Ahmedabad, 1960.

Gupta, M. N. Rai Bahadur : *Analytical Survey of Bengal Regulations*, University of Calcutta, Calcutta, 1943.

Jayakar, M.R. : *The Story of My Life*, vol. I, Asia Publishing House, Bombay, 1958.

Karim, Maulavi Abdul : *Letters On Hindu-Muslim Pact*, The Oriental Printers & Publishers Ltd., Calcutta, 1924.

Kripalani, J.B. : *Gandhi : His Life and Thought*, Publications Division, Government of India, New Delhi, 1970.

Kulkarni, V.V. : *The Indian Triumvirate : a political biography of Gandhi-Patel-Nehru*, Bharatiya Vidya Bhavan, Bombay, 1969.

Kumar, R. (ed.) : *Essays on Gandhian Politics : The Rowlatt Satyagraha of 1919*, Oxford University Press, London, 1971.

Laushey, David M. : *Bengal Terrorism and Marxist Left*, Firma K.L. Mukhopadhyay, Calcutta, 1975.

Lewis, John : *The Case Against Pacifism*, George Allen & Unwin Ltd., London, 1939 (?).

Majumdar R. C. : *History of the Freedom Movement in India*, vol. III, Firma K.L. Mukhopadhyay, Calcutta, 1963.

Masani, M.R. : *The Communist Party of India : A Short History*, Derek Verschoyle, London, 1954.

Mehta, Asoka & Patwardhan, Achyut : *The Communal Triangle in India*, Kitabistan, Allahabad, 1942.

Misra, B.B. (ed.) : *Select Documents on Mahatma Gandhi's Movement in Champaran 1917-18*, Government of Bihar, 1963.

Mukhopadhyay, Jadu Gopal : *Biplabi Jibaner Smriti* (in Bengali), Indian Associated Publishing Co., Calcutta, 1963.

Nagarkar, V.V. : *Genesis of Pakistan*, Allied Publishers (Pvt.) Ltd., Delhi, 1975.

Nanda, B.R. (ed.) : *Socialism in India*, Vikas Publications, Delhi, 1972.

Nehru, Jawaharlal : *An Autobiography*, Allied Publishers Private Limited, Bombay, New Delhi, etc., 1962.

Overstreet, Gene D. & Windmiller, Marshal : *Communism in India*, The Perennial Press, Bombay, 1960.

Pal, Pramathanath : *Desapran Sasmal* (in Bengali), Calcutta Publishers, Calcutta, 1368 B.S..

Pramanik, Prahlad Kumar : *Desapran Birendranath* (in Bengali), Orient Book Company, Calcutta, 1369 B.S..

Prasad, Rajendra : *Satyagraha in Champaran*, Navajivan Publishing House, Ahmedabad, 1949.

Ranga, N.G. (ed.) : *Kisan Handbook*, Kisan Publications, Madras, n.d..

Rasul, M.A. : *A History of the All-India Kisan Sabha*, National Book Agency Private Ltd., Calcutta, 1974.

—— : *Krishak Sabhar Itihas* (in Bengali), Nabajatak Prakashan, Calcutta, 1376 B.S..

Ray Chaudhury, P.C. : *Gandhiji's First Struggle in India*, Navajivan Publishing House, Ahmedabad, 1955.

*Report of the Damodar Canal Levy Enquiry Committee*, Burdwan District Congress Committee, Burdwan, 1939.

*Report of the Guruka-Bagh Congress Enquiry Committee*, Secretary, Guruka-Bagh Congress Enquiry Committee, 1924.

Roy, Amarendranath : *Students Fight For Freedom*, Ananda Bazar Patrika Office, Calcutta, 1967.

Sanyal Sastri, Pramathanth : *Tarakeswar* (in Bengali), Author, Dacca, 1342 B.S..

Sasmal, Birendranath : *Sroter Trina* (in Bengali), Gopinath Bharati (Publisher), 1329 B.S. (1922).

Sharp, Gene : *Gandhi Wields the Weapon of Moral Power*, Navajivan Publishing House, Ahmedabad, 1960.

Sheean, Vincent : *Lead, Kindly Light*, Random House, New York, 1949.

Shelvankar, K.S. : *The Problem of India*, Penguin Books Ltd., 1940.

Sinha, L.P. : *The Left Wing in India (1919-47)*, New Publishers, Muzaffarpur, 1965.

Sitaramayya, B. Pattabhi : *The History of the Indian National Congress*, vol. I, Padma Publications Ltd., Bombay, 1946.

Smith, Wilfred Cantwell : *Modern Islam in India : A Social Analysis*, Minerva Book Shop, Lahore, 1943.

Shridharani, Krishanlal : *War Without Violence*, Bharatiya Vidya Bhavan, Bombay, 1962.

Sundaram, G.A. : *Guruka Bagh Satyagrah*, Swadesamitran Office, Madras, 1923.

Tendulkar, D.G. : *Gandhi in Champaran*, Publications Division, Government of India, 1957.

— : *Mahatma* : *Life of Mohandas Karamchand Gandhi*, vol. II. The Publications Division, Government of India, 1961.

Tinker, Hugh : *The Foundations of Local Self-Governments in India, Pakistan and Burma*, University of London, The Athlone Press, 1954.

Willcocks, William : *Lectures on the Ancient System of Irrigation in Bengal and Its Application to Modern Problem*, University of Calcutta, Calcutta, 1930.

## VI  REFERENCE WORK

Mitra, H.N. (ed.) : *Indian Annual Register*, 1921-22, I.

— : *Indian Quarterly Register*, 1924, I.

Mitra, Nripendra Nath (ed.) : *Indian Annual Register*, 1929, II ; 1930, I ; 1935, I ; 1937, II, Calcutta.

Phatak, N.R. (ed.) : *Source Material for a History of the Freedom Movement in India* : *Mahatma Gandhi*, pt. III, vol. III, 1929-1931, Government of Maharashtra, Bombay, 1969.

Sen. S.P. (ed.) : *Dictionary of National Biography*, vols. II (1973) & IV (1974), Institute of Historical Studies. Calcutta.

# INDEX

Sil, Pratap Chandra 305
Simla 147, 196
Simon Commission 55
  Boycott movement 217
Simpra 237
Sinha Roy, Bijay Prasad 227, 238-40, 242, 244
Sinha Roy, Dharanidhar 101
Sinha Roy, Ranjanlal 91
Sivaratri festival 83
Sodepur 190-1, 193
Sodya 228, 237, 245
Som, Gour Hari 111-2, 218
Soviet Union 55
*The Statsman* 97
Stein 301, 312
Stephenson 311
*suddhi* 140, 161
Suhrawardy, Dr A. 14-5
Suhrawardy, H. 310
Sukur 237
Sutachipa 136
Swaraj 159
  Purna 185, 189-90
Swarajist movement 19-20
Swarajya (Swarajist) Party 20, 98, 100, 113
Syampur Workers' Conference 219

Tah, Dasarathi 232, 247
Tajpur 237
Taki 193
*takli* 196
Talgharia 211-2
Talkupi Union 71
Tamilnad 187
Tamluk 15
Tantubai, Phani Bhusan 69
Tantubai, Pulin Behari 61
Tantubai, Satish Chandra 61
Tarakeswar 81, 85-7, 90-1, 94-7, 168
  Arbitration Committee 106
  Deva Seva Samiti 106-7
  Managing Committee 106

*Mohunt* 81-3, 86-93, 95-8, 100, 102, 106, 113-4
*Mohunt*'s Conference 103
Satyagraha 2, 81-127
Temple 81-2, 91-4, 97
Taraknath 81
Tarkabhusan, Pramatha Nath 167
Tarkaratna, Panchanan 111, 173
Tarkasastri, Panchanan 106
Temple-entry 159-63, 171-7, 179-81
Tenancy Act 208
Tinker, Hugh 19
Townend 236
  Report 235, 240
Tripura 111
Turkey 128
24 Parganas 189, 193

United Provinces 187
Untouchability 159, 160-1, 167-8, 170, 175
  Removal Committee 179
  removal of 148, 161-2, 177, 219
Uragram 247
Urmila Devi 194-5
Utkal 187
Uttarpara 106

Vaikom (Vykom) 2, 160
Vedantasastri, Sitanath 106
Vidyabinode, Satindranath 161
Viswananda, Swami 83, 86-9, 91, 93, 101, 103, 109, 111, 140, 168, 178

Wachhel Sheikh 314
Willcocks, William 222
Wood 15
World War, First 6
Writers' Building 238

Younie 14

Zainuddin Muhammad 219